A COMPELLING TRIBUTARY

Above: The still eminently floatable James several miles above Galena.

Right: Shoreline at Aunts Creek Park maintained by the Army Corps of Engineers on the James River arm of Table Rock Lake.

The 1,455 square mile region of southwest Missouri that the James River drains is about sixteen percent larger than the state of Rhode Island. Only a quarter of the million people who reside in our smallest state live in the James basin, but even so it's a more densely inhabited Ozark watershed than most. Forty-five inches of yearly precipitation mean a goodly amount of water is collected in a basin that is 8 percent urban, 3 percent cropland, 52 percent grassland, 36 percent forest and shrubland, and 1 percent water. Before the Army Corps of Engineers built a 252-foot high dam in the late 1950s on the White River near Branson, the James emptied into the White. Table Rock Dam now backs water fifty miles up into the lower James.

River-to-reservoir is a dramatic and traumatic transformation. Hydrologically, ecologically, and culturally there is an abrupt change. There are trade-offs and winners and losers. Table Rock eliminated one of the most celebrated float trips in America, but it augmented an established tourist attraction. It is a deep, clear body of water that, unlike Truman Reservoir, even river lovers like ourselves cannot scorn. We will not dismiss problematic aspects of Corps reservoirs, but we will be equitable. Predictions by both advocates and opponents on the effects of a dam project are often wrong.

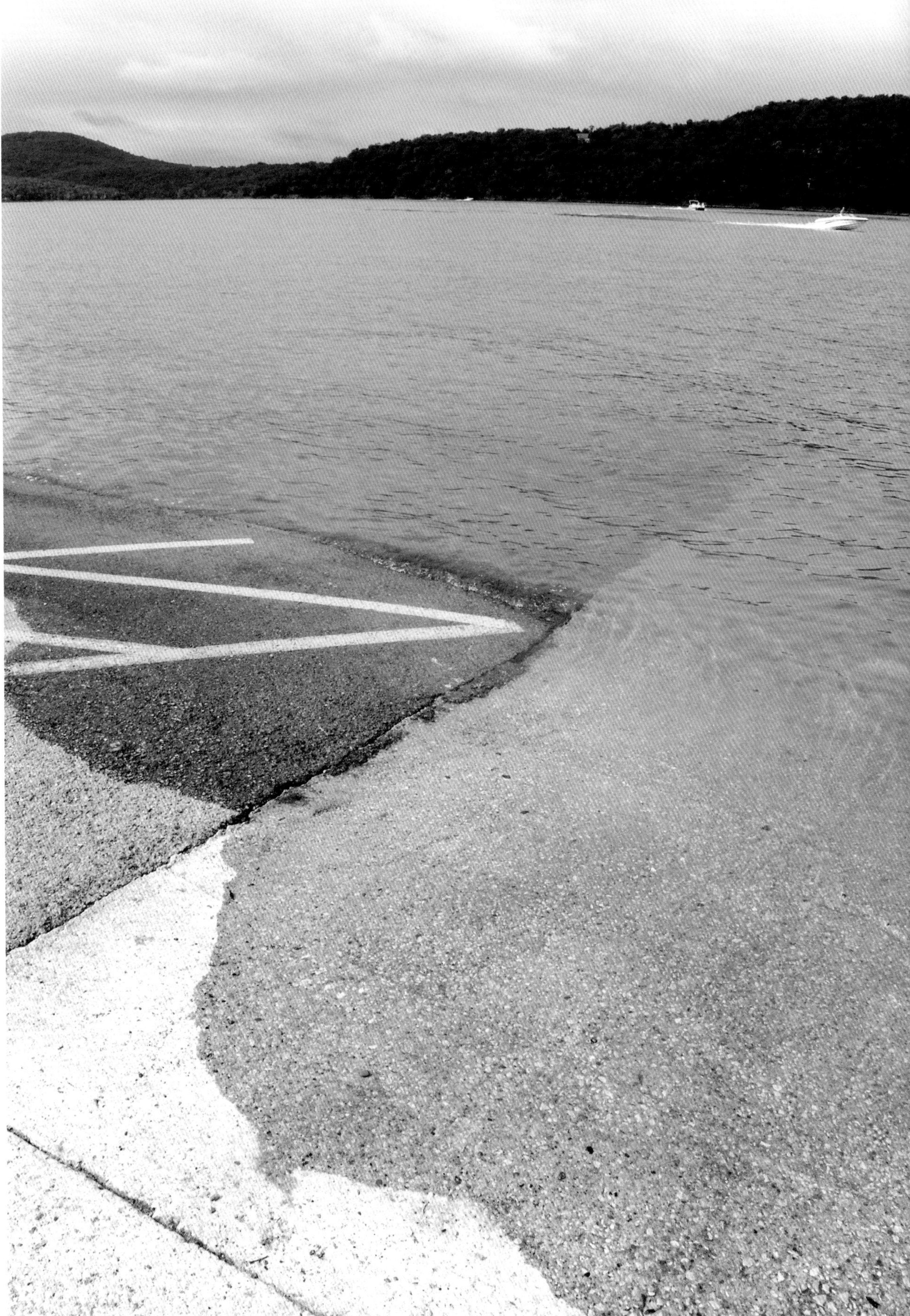

Shortly after the Delaware tribe vacated their reservation, Americans began tampering with the flow of the James. Utilization of rivers has taken many forms. After building log cabins by springs and clearing bottomland forest to open fields for corn, someone in each community of Ozark settlers would construct a water mill. Using streams to carry off sewage is obviously bad. Other employments of streams and underground water (the two are connected) have debatable aspects. Controversies arise over the public's access and blocking rivers to create lakes. Stream crossings have long been problematic. Impatient men on horseback were once swept away trying to cross flooded fords. Today, cars are washed off flooded low-water bridges with tragic results. There were arguments over costs when wagon bridges replaced fords. Recently there has been dissent over replacing historic iron bridges with new, stronger but undistinguished concrete structures.

There is a fragmentary written record of many of our hydrologic changes, and often scant physical evidence. The consequences become blended into the present landscape and it can be difficult to separate natural from human-induced features. Transformations of the James are sometimes subtle, but in the case of Table Rock Lake, obvious.

Opposite: Hootentown, nineteen miles south of Springfield, has a Missouri Department of Conservation access, a private canoe and camping business and a small restaurant.

Below: Swimming beach next to Aunts Creek Park campgrounds, James River arm of Table Rock Lake.

After rounding many bends of the James floaters will find themselves staring at a wall of limestone or dolomite. When they beach their canoes for lunch they will encounter vast bars of chert gravel. Many small streams are so choked with this durable rock that water sinks through the interstices to emerge elsewhere.

This is high karst, a wrecked, layered landscape of water's relentless assault on carbonate rock. Sinkholes as well as losing streambeds funnel the runoff of rains into vast underground waterways. The floors of caves are often wet or from their mouths flow considerable springs.

Right: The stream in Powder Mill Hollow, once called Medicine Creek, disappears under many feet of chert gravel, left behind when dolomite bedrock dissolves.

Opposite: Cave with wet-weather spring high in a bluff along Flat Creek several miles southeast of McDowell.

Following spread, left: In late winter, the James River becomes transparent.

Following spread, right: A twenty-one-foot rise on the James floats a parade of driftwood under the Y bridge at Galena.

Above: String of smallmouth bass and channel catfish from the James. The man in the center is likely a guide.

Opposite top, left: Statue of Johnny Morris's Uncle Buck with an outsize largemouth bass in front of a modern bass boat.

Opposite top, right: Fisherman with a nice smallmouth caught at Delaware Access.

Opposite, bottom: George P. Hall took hundreds of excellent images of the burgeoning recreation industry on the James in the early 1900s.

Long before Table Rock Lake, there were successful float trip enterprises on the James River. When the White River Line connected Galena with Branson, it facilitated a thirty-mile return of clients and boats after a 125-mile float. Charlie Barnes built twenty-foot-long pine boats specifically designed for Ozark stream fishing.

Later, Branson mayor and businessman Jim Owen aggressively promoted his Ozark float service nationally. Barnes supplied his boats, and most Galena guides eventually worked for Owen. Movie stars, affluent sportsmen, and writers for national publications flocked to these scenic river expeditions, shepherded by tall-tale-telling Ozark natives.

Johnny Morris, founder of mega-sporting goods chain Bass Pro Shops, grew up immersed in Ozark outdoor sporting culture. Like Jim Owen, Morris has an uncanny ability to market modern products to customers seeking a primitive outdoor experience. A Bass Pro success is the Ranger boat line. Equipped with powerful outdoor motors, electronic fish finders, and live wells, they are specifically designed to fish reservoirs, much as Barnes's johnboats were crafted for the free-flowing rivers the Corps dammed.

Insinuating old-time values into contemporary sensibilities characterizes Ozark tourism. The James River float saga played a significant, if forgotten, role in the evolution of this enterprise.

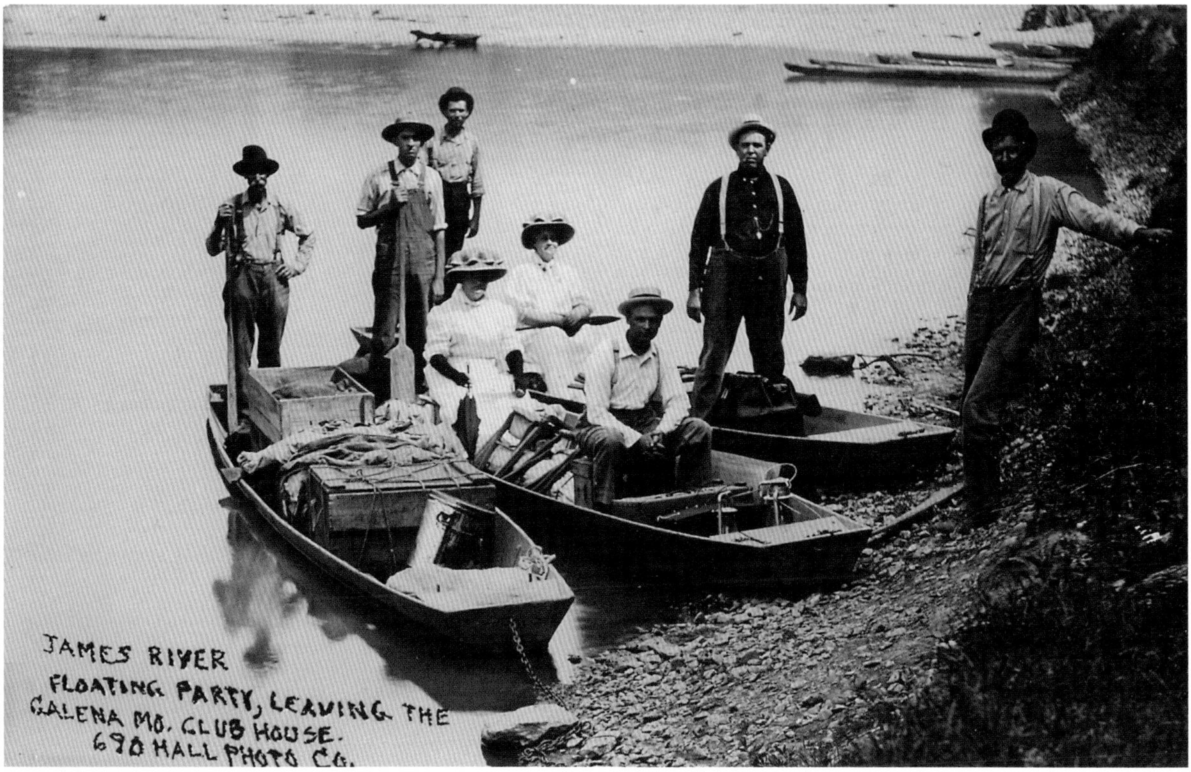

JAMES RIVER
FLOATING PARTY, LEAVING THE
GALENA MO. CLUB HOUSE.
690 HALL PHOTO CO.

River systems relentlessly carve the land without our intervention. Development can affect that process, sometimes dramatically. Scientists admit it can be challenging to separate natural from human influences on a stream's morphology.

Artifactual and architectural evidence of differing eras of technology that have modified the land are scattered throughout the James River basin. Old bridges, fallen-down barns, obsolete farm equipment and abandoned houses and businesses are evidence of past utilizations of natural resources. Connecting these relics with a specific previous cycle of economics is challenging. Understanding their impact on waterways is even harder.

Right: Remnants from the time when general farming was practiced throughout the entire watershed are fewer every year as collectors cart off old tractors and as barns continue to decay.

Opposite, above: A collection of early automotive and farm technology at Hurley, on Spring Creek.

Opposite, below: Freight train crossing the James just east of Springfield seen from the 1925 Turner Station bridge, now closed to vehicular traffic.

Top: Finley Falls, near Seymour.

Right: Amish colony along the upper Finley.

Opposite: Jordan Valley Park.

Rivers, as well as being sculptors of land, provide recreation and furnish themes for decorative public water features. The James drains a significant and varied region, and its economic, political, esthetic, and recreational significance has not gone unnoticed by its diverse inhabitants. These streams interact with Amish farmers and Springfieldians alike, but rural and urban interpretations may radically differ.

Above: Moon over abandoned mill on the Finley at Ozark.

Opposite: The James River near Springfield.

The chemistry and temperature of rivers, their water, their aquatic life, and even the conformation of their beds are shaped in part by the character of the forest through which they flow. Tree-lined banks and forested hills prevent erosion, and the wood of dead trees serves a multitude of biologic and hydrologic functions.

A few notes about our methodology. Often before sunrise, we would back our 1997 Jeep out of the driveway with a Thermos of coffee, digital cameras, and a bunch of USGS topographic maps. Many miles of the rivers and creeks of the James basin are accessible by road. We photographed what seemed to reveal the history of land use. Then we looked to geologic and ecological texts, local histories, and old newspaper accounts for insight. Sometimes we took pictures that did not illustrate these writings but seemed intrinsically expressive. Carl O. Sauer in *The Geography of the Ozark Highland of Missouri* also believed there are moments when our esthetic senses take precedence over our search for geographic explanation:

> A good deal of the meaning of an area lies beyond scientific regimentation. The best geography has never disregarded the esthetic qualities of landscape to which we know of no approach other than the subjective. Humbolt's "Physiognomy," Banse's "Soul," Volt's "Rhythm," Grandmann's "Harmony," of landscape all lie beyond science. They seem to have discovered a symphonic quality in the contemplation of the areal scene proceeding from a full novitiate in scientific studies and yet apart therefrom. To some, whatever is mystical is an abomination. Yet it is significant that there are others, and among them some of the best, who believe that having observed widely and charted diligently, there yet remains a quality of understanding at a higher plane which may not be reduced to formal processes.

Above: Palomino, or golden, rainbow trout at Mountain Spring Trout Park. Non-native trout do not become pests, as they will only survive in spring branches and rarely reproduce naturally in the Ozarks.

Right: Some undesirables that exploit altered environments are native species like broom sedge and Eastern red cedar.

Opposite: A Monet-inspired photograph of wintergreen carpeting the ground and covering trees along Flat Creek in Barry County. The Conservation Department considers this alien plant aggressive and degrading. They advocate its eradication.

Esthetic and ecological values can overlap, but not always. The photograph of a heavy infestation of wintergreen along Flat Creek near Jenkins (opposite) may resemble an Impressionist painting, but conservationists loathe this native plant-choking vine. It was brought into the U.S. more than a century ago from Asia because it is evergreen and hardy. Many plants and animals have been imported because of their decorative qualities then escaped to become obnoxious pests.

Invading flora and fauna thrive in disturbed spaces, and are generally less useful to humans or wildlife than the original biota. All of the James River basin has been affected by our occupation and is ripe for invasive foreign and domestic weed species of varying attractiveness.

GRAVELLY GEOGRAPHY

Above: James River above Galena. Extensive gravel bars are found along most Ozark rivers. Before settlement, scientists believed these streams were narrower and deeper, and expanses of chert and limestone gravel were more limited.

Ozark streams are floored with chert. This is a hard geologic fact. It is everywhere, gleaming, orangish-brown pebbles under the riffles, crunching underfoot as we walk across gravel bars, embedded in the concrete of old low-water bridges. The gravel road that crosses the crude bridge might be surfaced with chert, although crushed limestone is preferred these days, as it does not necessitate excavating streambeds.

Ozark-born Carl Ortwin Sauer traveled many backwoods cherty roads in 1914 and 1915 researching the region for his doctoral dissertation. In 1920 the University of Chicago Press published it as *The Geography of the Ozark Highland of Missouri.* Early in his classic, under the subheading "Physiographic Significance of the Chert," he describes its omnipotence and its formative effect on Ozark rivers:

> The Ozarks contain probably more chert, or flint, as it is called, than any other similar area. Over nine-tenths of the surface chert is so abundant that it covers the roads, chokes the stream beds, and in many places all but obliterates the soil.
>
> The chert ranges from small nodules to massive beds. In most places it has weathered into flattened fragments of conchoidal fracture. Because of this form it is moved with difficulty by the agencies of erosion.

Above: Real photo postcard by Hall Photo Co., circa 1910. These James River fishermen are standing on what appears to be an extensive gravel bar. This would be consistent with hydrologists' theories that by this time agriculture and timbering had resulted in the creation of such features.

Photographs of Ozark rivers rarely go back beyond 1900. This hampers scientific investigation of the morphology of these streams.

> Typically the chert consists almost entirely of silica, and is therefore little subject to chemical disintegration. Because of its hardness, fine texture, and compactness it suffers little from mechanical weathering or from corrosion. With the possible exception of the porphyry it is the most durable material in the Ozarks. Consequently, the longer the weathering and erosion of a surface the greater is the quantity of chert found on it, if the underlying formation is chert-bearing.
>
> The characteristic stream bed of the Ozarks is floored with a thick bed of chert fragments, which extend the width of the channel. These fragments are little smaller and little less angular than the chert on the hillsides. Except in the large streams there is little rounded gravel and less sand. The floor of such a stream is therefore much more resistant than are the margins of its bed. Consequently even swiftly flowing streams show a strong tendency to accomplish much lateral erosion. The first result is that the bed develops prodigious widths in many instances twenty times the width of the stream at ordinary water stages. A diagrammatic cross-section of such a bed would show a strikingly convex surface, with the stream flowing at one side of its bed, and at low water an irregular staggard line of pools along the margins. Adjacent to the water is a wide strip or "bar" of chert. In places the stream crosses this bar to the opposite margin of its gravelly bed. At such crossings wide shoals or "riffles" are developed. It is characteristic of Ozark drainage to find a rapid succession of riffles and pools, with the pools flanked by wide, white "gravel bars." This tendency to cut laterally, which is imposed by the chert, may also help to account for (1) the relatively great width of Ozark valley floors and (2) the extraordinary degree to which Ozark streams have developed meandering habits, although of rapid flow.
>
> One of the early Missouri geologists pointed out that the Ozark region is largely lacking in the brooks so familiar to every Eastern landscape. Perennial surface streams are usually large enough to be called rivers. Valleys a quarter of a mile wide may hold in dry seasons only a few detached pools. This is not due to any dryness of climate, but is rather the result of the large quantity of chert fragments in the valleys. These provide underdrainage, and through the spaces between them the water moves freely. A valley bed, therefore, which appears dry may have a moderate amount of water beneath its surface. Shallow pits dug in the bed of a creek usually fill with water in a short time. The absence of water in the smaller valleys is also partly a result of cavernous drainage.

Sauer discusses the parent carbonate strata in which chert fragments are embedded. Their properties affect the rivers as well:

> Because the Ozarks are made up largely of limestone, solution has been an important factor in the removal of rock materials. It is impossible to evaluate the relative importance of corrosion and of solution in developing the present surface. The fact, however, that limestone pebbles are rare on many Ozark streams, although limestone is the most common rock of the region, indicates the great importance of solution in the erosive process. The extreme clearness of Ozark streams is due in part to the fact that much of their water has come from underground sources, and has not had the opportunity to gather debris.

He notes the well-developed karst typography of the region through which the upper James runs. Springs, caves, sinkholes, and leaking gravelly streambeds are common topographic features:

> The large undissected areas of the central Ozarks and of the western flank furnish the best conditions for the collection of underground water and for solution. The ground water dissolves passageways for itself through the limestone, forming numerous caves. In this way an underground drainage net is formed, which may be nearly as complicated and extensive as the drainage aboveground. Some of the underground passages collect water from a wide area.

A 1993 study, *Historical Land-Use Changes and Potential Effects on Stream Disturbance in the Ozark Plateaus, Missouri*, by USGS scientist Robert B. Jacobson and oral historian Alexander T. Primm, questions why Sauer did not observe the degradation of streams they believe happened due to excessive deposits of chert caused by timbering and agriculture:

> Sauer noted the presence of thin, erodible soils in the Ozarks but made no mention of accelerated erosion because of land use: Although he observed the abundance of chert gravel in streams and included illustrative photographs, he did not interpret the gravel to be the result of detrimental land use. In fact, in a discussion of valley-bottom roads, he explicitly states that the gravel was highly stable.

Opposite, top: Across Ozarkland are numerous examples of concrete vernacular structures that contain chert like this abandoned building at Browns Spring. The usual crumbling condition of these walls, foundations, or bridges certify that, although abundant and cheap, it's an inferior building material. The almost pure silica of chert adversely reacts with the alkaline character of cement, causing cracking, spalling, and failure.

Opposite, below: Gravel-filled-in dam across Powder Mill Hollow. There has been considerable speculation by Ozark natives and by scientists about the effect of timbering, farming, and forest fires on the movement of chert from hillsides into streams. The completely filled-in small dam built to create a summer camp's swimming hole indicates chert migration can be dramatic whatever the cause.

These researchers acknowledge that "Systematic, detailed databases for direct evaluation of land-use changes from pre-settlement period to the present (1993) do not exist." Lacking hard evidence the authors resorted to interviews with longtime residents: "To gain a more detailed understanding of land use and erosional processes that existed from the turn of the century to the present (1993), oral-historical accounts were collected from elderly inhabitants of the Jacks Fork and Little Piney Creek Basins." In spite of these difficulties the paper concludes as follows:

> The variance between present (1993) conditions of Ozarks streams and pre-settlement period historical descriptions, stratigraphic observations, and accounts of oral-history respondents of river changes during the last 90 years establish that Ozarks streams are disturbed from their natural conditions. Disturbance has been characterized by accelerated aggradation of gravel, especially in formerly deep pools, accelerated channel migration and avulsion, and growth of gravel point bars. ... Oral-historical accounts, however, are consistent in their observations that natural channels of Ozarks streams have been severely affected by aggradation by coarse sediment, and that aggradation and instability continue to the present.
>
> The primary hypothesis to explain aggradation and instability is that land-use changes have disturbed parts of the hydrologic or sediment budgets, or both. Land use and land cover have changed markedly in the Ozarks since European settlement. ... Uplands have been subjected to suppression of a natural regime of wildfire, followed by logging, annual burning to support open range, patchy and transient attempts at cropping, a second wave of timber cutting, and most recently, increased grazing intensity.

Above: Two miles downstream from the crossing, a 250,000-gallon-a-day spring creates a permanent flow within the Hay's Springs Conservation Area. Presumably there is some flow under the gravel above the spring that emerges here.

Above, right: Just south of the Conservation Area is a low-water bridge and a private residence.

Opposite: Crossing on dry Crane Creek, Stone County. Throughout the James River basin there are "losing streams," i.e. chert-filled creeks which have no year-round flow.

Right: Vegetation crowds the banks of the no-longer-dry tributary of Crane Creek.

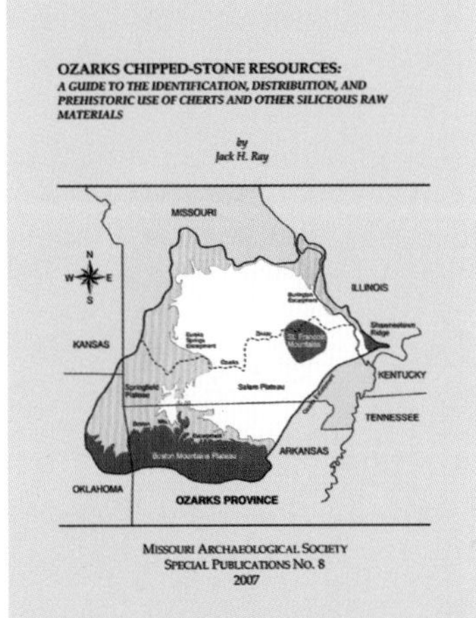

Above: *Ozarks Chipped Stone Resources* by Jack H. Ray (2007). Indians were not geologists but their utilization of cherts proves they were knowledgeable about the differing qualities of minerals and rocks.

Top: Creek gravel operation near Galena. Use of chert gravel in concrete and road building has been largely replaced by crushed limestone. Stream worn chert is extensively used today in landscaping because of its attractive colors.

Right: James River. Ozark streambeds provided Indians with an inexhaustible supply of chert from which to knap projectile points and tools.

In the preface to *Ozarks Chipped Stone Resources* archaeologist Jack H. Ray states: "Except for the Boston Mountain sub-region, you cannot walk far in upland areas of the Ozarks without treading across a pavement of chert... it is undoubtedly one of the chertist regions in the world." Not all areas of the earth are so blessed with so much of that siliceous geologic material that primitive peoples depended on. Some implements can be fashioned from other rocks, but the conchoidal fracture properties of chert, or flint as it is sometimes referred to is ideal for the manufacture of cutting tools and projectile points. From its earliest use by Paleoindians for fluted atlatl spear points ca.13,000 years ago to historic tribes augmenting European gun flints, chert was invaluable. Ozark chert was sometimes traded to tribes who lived in regions devoid of the mineral.

Within the Ozarks distinctive forms of chert are found in different strata of Paleozoic rocks. Not all of these cherts have the same knapping desirability. As the James River dissects both the Salem and Springfield plateaus, it contains a variety of cherts, several of which were favored at various times by Indians. There seems to have been preferences for specific cherts by different cultures during this long occupation. Early and Middle Paleoindian points were often made from Jefferson City chert which is found in Ordovician rocks that outcrop at the interface of the Salem and Springfield plateaus. Burlington chert from a later Mississippian era limestone was another preferred material which knapped well. Around 8,000 years ago, Indians discovered that inferior cherts could be improved by heat-treating them.

Most so-called "arrowheads" picked up by relic hunters did not tip arrows. Bows were not introduced into the Ozarks until only about 1,300 years ago. Most chipped-stone artifacts tipped atlatl spears.

All of the chipped chert artifacts on this page were collected within the James River basin except #8, which is an abundant type along the James, although this example came from the nearby White River. These artifacts tipped atlatl darts, or spears, except #7, which is a true arrowhead. Bows were not introduced until about 1,300 years ago; chipped chert spear points were used for more than ten thousand years before that.

1. Clovis dart point, Jefferson City chert. A Paleoindian fluted artifact, ca. 9350-8850 B.C. The black areas are manganese stains.
2. Dickson dart point, Burlington chert (heat treated), ca. 550 B. C.-250 A.D.
3. Graham Cave dart point, Burlington chert, ca. 6750-6150 B. C.
4. Etley dart point, Burlington chert, ca. 2350-1650 B. C.
5. Packard dart point, Burlington chert, ca. 8050-7650. An 8000 B.C. radiocarbon date was obtained from a site along the James River in Christian County where this type of spear point was found.
6. Kings dart point, Reeds Spring chert, ca. 1850-1050 B. C.
7. Scallorn arrow point, Burlington chert (heat treated), ca. 650-1350 A. D.
8. White River dart point, Pierson chert, ca. 4350-3550 B. C.

Points are shown life size.

Artifacts courtesy of the Center for Archaeological Research, Missouri State University.

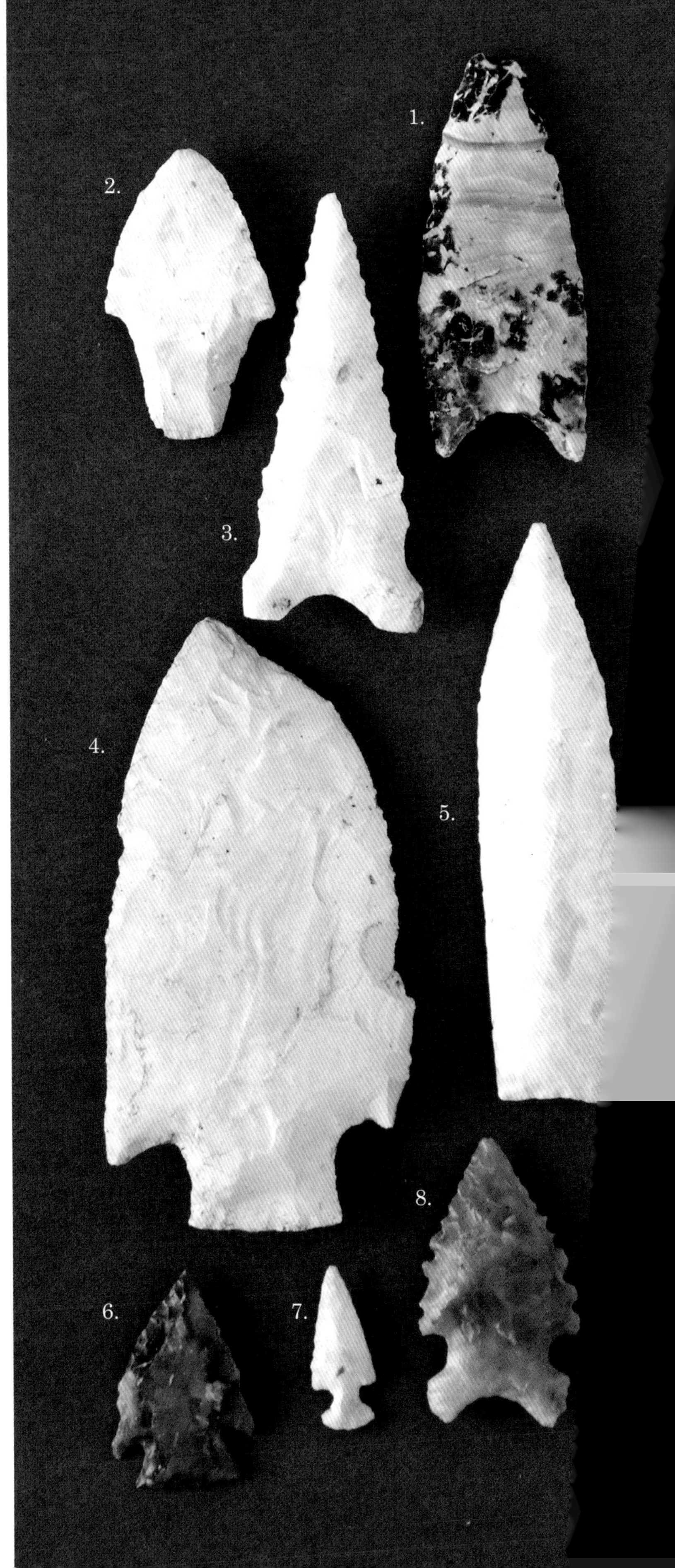

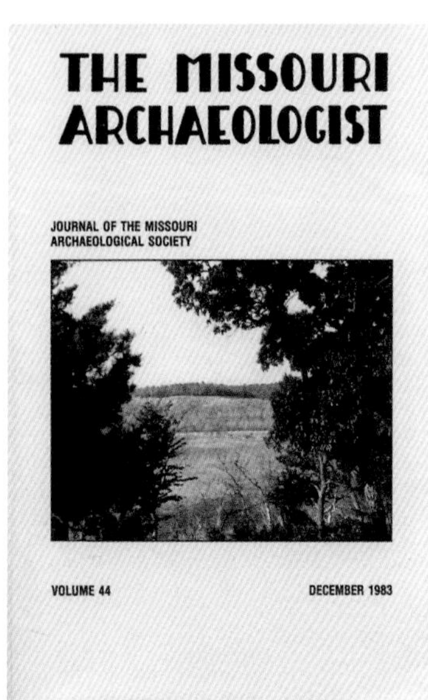

Above: *The Missouri Archaeologist*, December 1983. The cover is a photograph of the Loftin bottom from Philbert Bluff.

Top: *The Missouri Archaeologist*, October 1951. "The cover was drawn by Eleanor F. Chapman. The rock overhang shown in the cover plate was used as a shelter by Indians that lived in the White River valley and will be entirely submerged upon the completion of the Table Rock Dam. The shelter is typical of the locations in need of investigation before the dam is built."

University of Missouri professor Jesse Wrench was not an archaeologist, but he had a little experience digging in the Holy Lands before World War I. Believing in the "scientific study of the past" he co-founded in 1934 the State Archaeological Society of Missouri (changed in 1946 to the Missouri Archaeological Society). When he learned of the construction of a high dam at Table Rock, Wrench wrote in the October 1951 issue of *The Missouri Archaeologist*:

> The impending construction of another dam, this one entirely within the confines of the state, points up again the tragic loss of archaeological material which seems inevitably to attend such events. While agricultural operations, road building, railroad construction and the laying of pipelines furnish a continuous whittling away of archaeological remains, it is the dam that blots out a whole area which conceivably might contain the answer to an otherwise insoluable problem. It is in the river valleys that the story of the past is most completely told.

He closes with a plea for "half of one percent of the amount" of the cost of Table Rock Dam for archaeological salvage. Wrench incidentally questioned the "accepted aims" of the flood control and hydropower project. Nothing close to that figure would be raised to study the ancient record of human occupation of the White and lower James River valleys that would soon be covered by the deep waters of Table Rock Reservoir. Dr. Carl Chapman, Jesse's protégé and a trained archaeologist would obtain enough money from the National Park Service to conduct a survey and excavate several of the most important sites. Crews floated the river in john boats locating artifactual evidence of Indian occupation.

No archaeological recovery had been done on the Osage River before Bagnell Dam closed. Professor Chapman was determined that this would not be repeated on the White and James Rivers that would be covered by Table Rock Reservoir. Beginning in 1951, summer field sessions began work in the Table Rock basin. A large collection of chipped stone artifacts were obtained from camp sites along the waterways. A bluff shelter (the Rice site in Stone County) was excavated which yielded a chronology.

Joseph Philibert's 1822 trading post to serve the recently arrived Delaware tribe was thought to have been established a mile up the James from its confluence with the White River. It could not be found. Fragments of glass and glazed pottery were unearthed near the junction of the two rivers indicating a Delaware camp. Near there was an Indian mound and village, a rare outpost of Caddoan culture in the Ozarks highlands. This site was named Loftin after the family who owned the farm it was on. An article in the December 1983 issue of *The Missouri Archaeologist* by W. Raymond Wood summarized this important discovery:

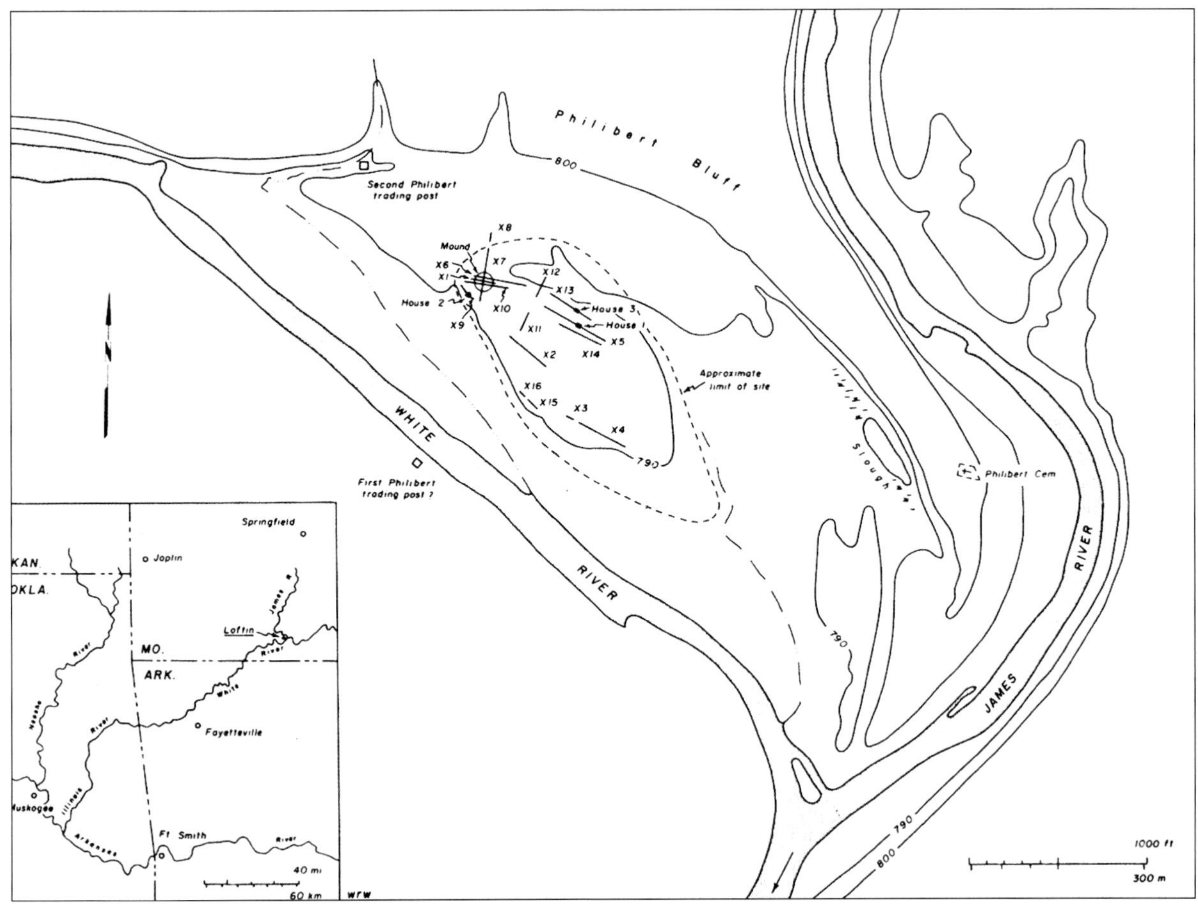

Above: Map of the Loftin site. That there are relatively few ceremonial centers with mounds in the Ozarks like this contributed to a once-held belief that Indian culture here was like later American settlement, somewhat primitive – i.e., hillbilly. Recently that notion has been challenged by archaeologists, but they acknowledge the relatively low-density Indian populations had a less complex material existence.

Map used with permission of the Missouri Archaeological Society.

The Loftin site is a late prehistoric village and ceremonial center at the confluence of the James and White rivers in southern Stone County, southwestern Missouri, within but near the western margin of the Ozark Highland. The site consisted of a large, artificial earthen mound and an indeterminable number of dwellings set on a high level terrace on the north side of the White River.

The earthen mound and five probable dwellings were excavated by the University of Missouri in the late 1950s before the area was inundated by the Table Rock Reservoir. Before the final report on the work was prepared, however, some of the artifacts from the site were damaged, and some were destroyed in a laboratory fire; the present study reports data remaining from that calamity.

Even though the rising water of Table Rock Lake cut short the dig, and fire later consumed much of what was found, the Loftin site was significant. No statues, elaborate chipped stone maces, figural pipes, or embossed copper eagles or snakes were exhumed, but there were sherds of shell-tempered pottery and carbonized corn cobs, which indicated a form of Mississippian culture had an outpost in a region archaeologists had formally characterized as a refugium outside of larger and more advanced technologies and developments.

Above: Bedrock is exposed along the James at Blunk's Access below Galena when Table Rock Lake is low.

Opposite top right: The Finley River below 160 Highway. Bridge piers can also alter flow similar to bluffs and create instabilities.

Opposite below: Finley River below Lindenlure. Trees can help stabilize a riverbank but they can also in some situations contribute to bank failure. Our hydrologic interventions are complicated even when our interests are to preserve and protect.

Massive amounts of chert line the bottom of Ozark streams. Carbonate rocks are exposed in beds and bluffs that armor the stream and resist erosion, but also can promote bank failure by creating gravel bars. These point bars decrease streambed capacity causing channel migration. The most distressing aspect of a destabilized waterway is eroding banks.

Collapsing banks not only dispirit conservationists; farmers are also dismayed by the loss of land. Both fine sediments and coarse gravel are stored in these bottomland deposits. Ozark streams are not naturally murky. Additional sediment threatens water quality, aquatic life, and can cause a loss of storage in downstream reservoirs like Table Rock.

There is already a tremendous amount of chert and limestone cobbles in Ozark waterways. Additional gravel forms large vegetation-free bars that encourage channel wandering. Earlier row cropping and timbering washed chert into the streams and some became entombed in the valley floors. Frequent bank-full rises and major floods erode banks and remobilize both fine and coarse sediments.

Controlling rivers is never simple. Natural streams constantly

Above: Bluff along Finley River between Lindenlure and Ozark. When streams encounter bluffs, gravel bars are often created below, decreasing channel capacity and contributing to river instability.

In *A Report on Greene County* (1898) Edward M. Shepard wrote: "Along the Finley, the mural bluffs of Burlington limestone break the monotony of the cherty slopes." The phrase "mural bluffs," was often preceded by the word "picturesque" in nineteenth century geologic literature. Obviously, it was more aesthetic than scientific. These mineral stained carbonate bluffs along the Finley are deserving of a description that references art.

move. Our ever-changing land use adds to the fluvial readjustment process. What was done to the watershed long ago still influences today's channel movements.

Conservationists advise planting trees along eroded banks. There are often benefits of riparian (streamside) forests, but in some cases woody vegetation can accelerate bank failure. Trees without sufficiently deep roots can fall into the river, pulling out chunks of the bank. A deeper line of forest can be an allover benefit, especially if the bank is not sheer. The promotion of a riparian buffer as an answer to all stream instability may not be scientifically valid.

In a 2011 paper, Robert T. Pavlowsky, Director, Ozarks Environmental and Water Resources Institute at Missouri State University, and Derek J. Martin compared aerial photographs of the Finley River in 1954 with its present form. In "Spatial Patterns of Channel Instability along an Ozark River, Southwest Missouri" they found only twenty-one percent of the length of the main stem studied exhibited instability. This contradicted popular expectations that the Finley's course has become erratic. Moreover, even though there was excess gravel that contributed to erosional activity, the source was supplied by the "reworking of historical floodplain deposits." Present-day land use was less of a contributing factor:

Above: Towering above Ozark streams are bluffs of limestone or dolomite, sometimes with layers of sandstone or shale. The vast beds of chert gravel below have been left from the dissolution of the carbonate sedimentary rocks.

Gravel bars are favored by contemporary campers. Because Schoolcraft mentions few gravel bars in 1818 some hydrologists theorize that deforestation and pioneer agricultural practices accelerated the erosion of residual chert from hillsides into Ozark streams.

> Ozark rivers are believed to have recovered from these previous sediment-related disturbances to some degree since 1950. However, increases in flood frequency and suburban development expansion in the Finley River watershed over the past 30 years may be contributing to recent problems with gravel inputs and channel instability in the tributaries. Currently, these unstable reaches are topics of great concern to watershed stakeholders and government managers are currently planning sediment control measures for the Finley River.
>
> While it has been determined that channel instability has been intensified by excess gravel inputs, our understanding of the watersheds response versus the natural erosion regime is quite poor. Understanding individual types of active reaches and how they relate to watershed characteristics and disturbance factors would greatly benefit watershed stakeholders by providing the knowledge needed to manage local instabilities in a manner that recognizes both the natural erosion regime as well as human impacts. For example, the stakeholder's interest in local bank stabilization practices may not be cost effective as a result of natural erosional tendencies or because they do not address the actual cause of the problem such as sediment supply.

Water quality and stability of the James River system is of special interest to Dr. Pavlowsky's department. Understanding this requires separating natural from human effects on the hydrology. Unfortunately little reference data on the watershed before our transformations is available.

Henry Rowe Schoolcraft's journal of a ninety-day trek through the Ozarks in the winter of 1818-1819 is a rare description of the natural environment before settlement. His motivation was to publish an account of the potential of the Missouri lead industry, and be then appointed a government mining superintendant.

Upon returning to the East Coast, he quickly published *A View of the Lead Mines of Missouri* (1819). It was a matter-of-fact treatise, but gained enough recognition for him to be appointed as a mineralogist on the Cass expedition to the upper Mississippi River. His skill negotiating with Indians on the government survey led to being chosen Indian agent for the upper Great Lakes tribes. Soon after, he married Jane, who was one quarter Chippewa. Aided by her fluency in Indian languages, he became an internationally known ethnologist.

Schoolcraft was a prolific author and revised his Ozark adventures twice more. Several years after his *View of the Lead Mines* he wrote *Journal of a Tour into the Interior of Missouri and Arkansas* (1821). This vividly written first-person travelogue was revised in 1853 as *Scenes and Adventures in the Semi-Alpine Regions of the Ozark Mountains of Missouri and Arkansas*. There are some subtle but intriguing differences in these different versions. He did not apply the word 'Ozarks' to the region in either the 1819 or 1821 accounts.

Above: Decal, 1960s. A developer named Louis Bolger operated Smallin Cave as Civil War Cave, claiming a significant role for it in the Battle of Wilson's Creek. His advertising inappropriately featured a clip-art Sioux Indian.

Top: Henry Rowe Schoolcraft. The twenty-five-year-old New Yorker's journal of an 1818-1819 tour established the Ozarks had commercial deposits of lead and its settlers were rough but colorful. His descriptions of the wilderness foreshadowed tourism based on the region's natural beauty.

'Ozark Mountains' appears in the title of the 1853 book.

In his first book, he mentions "a very large cave on Finley's fork" and suggests it "affords stalagmites sufficiently large, compact, and beautiful, for the sculptors." In the 1821 journal, his description of this impressive cave, now called Smallin's Civil War Cave just off the Finley River near Ozark, reveals a romantic literary sensibility that was suppressed in his *View of the Lead Mines*. Gone is the suggestion the formations of this "stupendous cavern" that "struck us with astonishment" should be ripped out to be material for "the sculptor's chisel." He devotes a paragraph describing the natural dams and lakes that "stalactitic incrustations have formed." He notes the interior "is well worthy of a day's attention," but "a boat would be necessary." Their two hunter guides were "satisfied after gazing a few minutes." In the 1853 account he reaches the great cavern on "the last day of the year 1818," a day earlier than in the 1821 book, and the cave now has a name. In the early accounts it is merely a very large cave. The name "Winoca," which he uses in the 1853 version, he identifies as "from the Osage word for underground spirit." Suspiciously it is applied after a thirty-year career studying Native American cultures:

> I observed a small stream of pure water coming in on the northside, which issued through an opening in the hills; and as this ran in the general direction we were pursuing, the guides led up it. We were soon enclosed in a lateral valley, with high corresponding hills, as if, in remote ages, they had been united. Very soon it became evident that this defile was closed across and in front of us. As we came near this barrier, it was found that it blocked up the whole valley, with the exception of the mouth of a gigantic cave. The great width and height of this cave, and its precipitous face, gave it very much the appearance of some ruinous arch, out of proportion. It stretched from hill to hill. The limpid brook we had been following ran from its mouth. On entering it, the first feeling was that of being in "a large place." There was no measure for the eye to compute height or width. We seemed suddenly to be beholding some secret of the great works of nature, which had been hid from the foundation of the world. The impulse, on these occasions, is to shout. I called it Winoca.

In the 1850s a Tennessee pioneer named Smallin settled the land and it became known as Smallin Cave. Names carved into formations document generations of picnickers who were attracted by its spectacular entrance, cool spring, and sylvan setting.

Unaware of Schoolcraft's writings, the December 13, 1867, *Troy* (Missouri) *Herald* noted, "There has never been a thorough description of this grand structure given to the public":

> On approaching the cave from the south its huge mouth is visible for several hundred yards, and every one when viewing for the first time is sure to give utterance to his admiration and wonder, and those who

Above: Looking toward the entrance of Smallin Civil War Cave, now open to visitors.

The carbonate rocks of the James River drainage are extensively penetrated by caves. Only a few are both accessible and attractive enough to become commercially operated tourist attractions. Schoolcraft's 1818 elegant description of the great cave off the Finley still makes suitable promotional copy for the operators of Smallin Civil War Cave today.

> have viewed both this and the Mammoth Cave in Kentucky say that this, though not as extensive, far exceeds that in size and grandeur at the entrance, it being upwards of sixty feet in height. ... Through this cave flows a pure stream of water, clear as a crystal, in which is found cray-fish white as snow, and eyeless.

A breezy *Springfield Daily News* reporter visited Smallin Cave with his glib friend "shepherd of the hills Ozark Oscar." In this February 23, 1927, account he described the cave's entrance with Roaring Twenties hyperbole: "This cave, Ozark Oscar announced in approved rubber-neck-wagon enunciation, has the finest and largest entrance in the world. A given number of airplanes could fly abreast into it."

After the Civil War Cave attraction closed, the property changed hands several times until a couple donated it to the Central Assembly of God. They operated Sonrise Camp here until Kevin and Wanetta Bright bought it from the religious organization in 2009. They gave away the bogus Lincoln funeral car and now operate it as a show cave called Smallin's Civil War Cave. Their tours stress the authentic natural and cultural history. Unlike Bolger, the Brights cooperate with scientific research of the cave and its archaeological, geological, and biological resources.

Right: Gentry Cave.

In *Caves of Missouri* (1956), J. Harlan Bretz discusses Gentry Cave's geology: "A rock shelter at Camp Ramona, 85 feet below cliff top and 50 feet above James River contains four of the five entrances to this joint-controlled cave system. Words are useless in describing the detailed interaction of passages; the cave pattern is too complicated. ... One place in the cave showed cherty gravel, but there is no other evidence for vadose occupation of this splendid phreatic cave system. No red clay remnants and very little dripstone were seen anywhere in the cave."

Louella Agnes Owen in *Cave Regions of the Ozarks and Black Hills* (1898) tells of her visit to Gentry Cave three miles below Galena. Hiking through the woods after the mail coach's wheel broke, the intrepid lady cave explorer found the "broken" landscape captivating:

> The topography was ... very beautiful with the dense forest lighted by the slanting yellow rays of the afternoon sun. The way leads up to the "ridge road" which is at length abandoned for no road at all and descending through the forest, more than half the distance down to the James River flowing at the base of the hill, we come suddenly in view of the cave entrance, which is probably one of the most magnificent pieces of natural architecture ever seen.

She found the cave interior worth the walk but does not mention the abundance of bat guano that would later provide the basis for an unusual industry and material for writer Vance Randolph. During the lean Depression years, one C. L. Weekly and two hires shoveled tons of dried bat manure into hundred-pound bags and shipped it off to be used for greenhouse fertilizer. He got $35 a ton. Randolph, in *We Always Lie to Strangers*, relates a tall tale about this venture:

> Not far from Cape Fair, Missouri, a man told me that Bud Spurlock went up to Gentry Cave, where some "furriners"were digging bat-manure out of the cavern and selling it by the carload to florists in St. Louis. Bud carried a pocketful of this magic fertilizer home. His woman had a sweet potater growing in a bottle of water, hung up in the kitchen. Just to see how the bat-manure worked, Bud put a little into the water with the sweet potater. That was just before bedtime. The 'tater growed so fast it busted the bottle in less than thirty minutes, and by morning the whole cabin was packed with a solid mass of vines. It was impossible for the Spurlocks to reach either door, but Bud kicked off a couple of boards at the back of the house and dragged his wife and kids to safety. He said later that it was only by God's own luck they were able to get the children out alive.

Above: Ash Cave.

Bretz wrote, Ash Cave "is a completely ruined phreatic cave; not a solution feature is left. Collapse has occurred into chambers that must lie below the valley bottom of Flat Creek. ... There are two entrances in the base of a 50-foot cliff. The larger one is 20 feet high and 30 feet wide at the base and is recessed under the concave front for 50 feet. But they are entrances to nothing. "

Ash Cave and the natural arch are along Flat Creek in Barry County about three miles north of Cassville. Unlike Gentry Cave, it is not named for a pioneer. Once there was a deep bed of burnt wood on the floor of the cave's singular light-filled room.

The place has archaeological and historical as well as geological significance. It's along V highway, parts of which follow the old Wire Road that the Cherokees traveled on one Trail of Tears route. Local legend has it that Sterling Price's retreating rebels ditched a cannon in the blue hole in Flat Creek. In 1971 three Cassville businessmen dug a 100-foot ditch, 50 feet wide, and 20 feet deep in the old channel. The *Moberly Monitor-Index* of October 21 reported, "The only thing found were some pumps and other old equipment which had been used long ago by others seeking the cannon." The digging crew drew hundreds of onlookers all summer.

In the summer of 1915, Harvard archeologist Dr. Charles Peabody, assisted by his daughter Christina, Mr. E. H. Jacobs of Bentonville, Arkansas, and seven workers excavated the deposits of Ash Cave. A paper published in the *Proceedings of the Second Pan American Scientific Congress* (1917) explained the dust-like deposits contained as well as burnt wood from Indian hearths, decayed leaves, and the bones of bison, beaver, wild turkey, raccoon, woodchuck, and deer. No human remains were found:

> The absence of burials has led to the suggestion that the caves were the summer resorts of the flood-plain Indians – a theory discredited by the total absence of whole pottery vessels and an almost equal absence of the ornaments and implements of stone and shell which the holiday-making Indians would be sure to have with them. About all we can say then is that tribes of a very simple, homogeneous culture lived, worked and ate in the rock shelters.

Above and opposite: Devil's Den.

Near the head of an intermittent branch of Panther Creek about 30 miles west of Springfield is Devil's Den. Thomas R. Beveridge in *Geologic Wonders and Curiosities of Missouri* describes it as an "elongated chasm trends N 30° E, is 20 yards wide, nearly 100 yards long, and extends downward to the surface of the water. It is in the dolomites of the Jefferson City formation and is rimmed by a more resistant sandstone .... The den is a classic example of an elongated sink formed by the enlargement of a fracture (joint) in dolomite by the dissolving action of percolating water."

Dr. Beveridge does not address a 1920s local belief that changing water levels of the lake at the bottom of the sink "correlated with the rise and fall of the upper Missouri river in Montana."

When the earth suddenly gives way and swallows houses, or recently a collection of vintage Corvettes, the tragedy makes the nightly news. Even a sinkhole collapse on a golf course is newsworthy if it is big enough. The depression in Farmer Sitze's meadow near Fordland was only one hundred yards wide and thirty feet deep, but *The Springfield Democrat* of May 28, 1895, excitedly reported it was "indeed a singular product of some giant force. Mr. Sitze had finished his dinner when he heard" a heavy underground explosion, like a powerful blast. I looked at once toward the meadow, and saw a cloud of yellowish smoke shoot toward the sky to the height of 100 or more feet." He could not see the newly formed hole in his pasture for the dust and rock that rained down.

H. Clay Neville, a journalist, visited the site "but could discover no unmistakable evidence of subterranean fires. "I was denied the coveted opportunity of announcing that a rival of Vesuvius had uncapped the Ozarks." He did acknowledge that this is a neighborhood of unsettling geology:

> The region around the Sitze farm is rugged and weird enough to suggest any freak of subterranean energy. Sinks, gorges, gulches, and caves abound and the dominion of Pluto seems to dispute here the reign of the gods of the upper world. The "Devil's Den," the famous Webster county wonder, is only two miles west of the Sitze phenomenon down Panther creek, and this hideous chasm, cut into the rocky roof of the Ozarks in some unknown geological age, would be regarded as marvel of nature's giant handiwork anywhere in the world. This huge, coffin-shaped pit with its mysterious fathomless lake, fed from some unknown water supply in the heart of the mountains, has puzzled the brain of the scientist as well as the head of the unlettered mountaineer and all who gaze into the yawning mouth of the den realize anew the awfulness of that vast world of darkness and terror upon which the creatures of daylight walk. The Sitze cave-in and den are both drawing wonders for that section of country now, and the volcano-hunters always go to see the latter when they gratify their curiosity in gazing into the new crater.

Men of science were then, as now, enthusiastic debunkers of creative explanations of natural phenomenon. Upon reading of the wondrous eruption on Mr. Sitze's farm, Dr. Edward Martin Shepard immediately took his geology class to Webster County. *The Springfield Leader* of June 4, 1895, printed his dry, scientific conclusion:

> Prof. Shepard's Drury college class in economic geology returned last night from Webster county where they went to investigate the recent drop of earth on the Sitze farm. ... They also visited Devil's Den in Panther valley. ... It is the opinion of Prof. Shepard that the cave-in on the Sitze farm was due to the eating away of earth by subsoil streams. There were no evidences of anything of a volcanic nature. Measurements were made at the now famous Devil's Den. They found the distance to the water to be 80 feet and the water to be 70 feet deep.

Above and below: Camp Cora cave and spring.

Springfield Republican (June 18, 1908): "A survey across the James River on the F. S. Hefferman farm has been completed preparatory to building a dam 200 feet north of Camp Cora. The dam will be 700 feet long and it is estimated that it will generate 1,000 horsepower. How this will be utilized has not yet been determined."

Fifty years later a dam was built not far upstream to supply cooling water for the power plant.

That a sinkhole was once an attraction speaks to the scarcity of entertainment a century ago. Other karst expressions were more naturally attractive than Devil's Den and more popular. The July 3, 1910, *Springfield Republican* lists a few of these "picnic resorts": "Numerous parties are being arranged for Percy's Cave, Camp Cora, and other beautiful picnic resorts for which Springfield is famous. James River Club will be very popular as usual, and Winoka Lodge is not slighted, for Mr. Roscoe Stewart is giving week-end party there in honor of his Harvard friend, Mr. McCreery."

The cave/spring complex that gave Camp Cora its identity is located along a railroad spur that delivers coal to the James River power plant. No picnickers come these days – only spelunkers who have penetrated 1,500 feet into the low-ceilinged cavern. A 640,000-gallon a day spring issues from its mouth and flows directly into the James. Those who attended Sunday school in Springfield between 1870 and 1920 very likely visited this picturesque place. "Hurrah for Camp Cora" headlines a September 8, 1886 *Springfield Leader* article: "Christ Church parish and Sunday school picnic to-morrow. For Camp Cora, train leaves Phelps avenue depot at 9 a.m. and coaches will be left at Camp Cora until the return in the evening."

More than a hundred short articles in the *Springfield Leader* between 1887 and 1917 document "merry parties" who took the Chadwick branch of the Frisco to make "the rocky bluffs resound with echoes of ringing laughter" and to enjoy "the musical rhythm of the flow of water." Narrow escapes from drowning and severe cases of contact with poison oak were reported but in a general, "joyousness prevailed there and the young folks knew nothing but pleasure for hours." Days were spent "exploring the cave and kodaking," and evenings were "filled with dance and song, many of the old camping

Above: Rader Spring is a textbook example of how leaky the Springfield Plateau is. Fluorescent dye introduced into creeks and sinks from as far away as I-44 have been detected in Rader's waters. From a dry branch of Nichols Creek six miles away dye was injected that reached the spring in six days.

Rader is only 1.3 miles from Springfield's Southwest Cleanwater Treatment Plant. Although its processing of sewage is now much improved, both the spring and Wilson Creek have amounts of nitrogen, phosphorous, chloride, and E. coli that exceed the Missouri Clean Water Commission's target levels.

airs being revived with delight."

It wasn't only kids from Baptist Sunday schools who visited Camp Cora. A *Leader* reporter filed this article (August 10, 1894) on flirtatious young ladies "on the classic James":

> All the ladies were dressed in beautiful summer costumes and appeared to be cool and comfortable. Miss Anita Campbell was especially delicious to look upon, arrayed in some airy material, as she disported herself in a hammock surrounded by a delegation of admiring young gentlemen with fans. It was a sight long to be remembered, and the disciple of the press was as helpless as the rest of the army of insects that hovered around, though he managed to capture a boatload of turtles and other good things to eat.

Not all springs were "picnic resorts." Rader Spring is the largest in the James River basin, but the only "kodaking" done here has been by scientists. During the years when Springfieldians flocked to relax at Camp Cora, Wilson Creek, into which Rader Spring flows, was an open sewer. Unlike the sylvan setting of Camp Cora, it boils from a hole in an old field.

The spring only a hydrologist could love pumps around six or eight million gallons a day into the now-cleaned-up Wilson Creek – a third as much as Missouri's twentieth biggest spring. Still, it's a lot of water, but size is not what endears it to geologists. The Association of Missouri Geologists took a field trip here and Kenneth C. Thompson wrote, "Perhaps the most unusual characteristic of Rader Spring and its supply system are the reversible sinkholes or estavellas that occur in the Wilson Creek valley. These curious karst features accept water in drier seasons and discharge water as springs during rainy seasons."

Above: Artificially propagated rainbow trout are a world food fish. The US produces 7 percent of this $3 billion industry.

Below: Montague Spring, now Mountain Spring Trout Park.

Montague Spring contributes around two million gallons a day to Tory Creek, which runs into the James River a few miles downstream from Hootentown. Of the ephemeral hamlet located here, local historian Wayne Glenn wrote, "Tory and Montague were both named for English elements of history. You have heard of the Tory political party. Well, one John Montague was an important figure in the Tory party in the late 1700s in England. And some of us thought so-called hillbillies were not up on foreign affairs!" It is indeed in a hilly part of Christian County.

Like many Ozark springs it issues from a bluff. Unlike Camp Cora spring it's not right on the edge of a stream. The spring has no air-filled chamber. When the valley floor deepens in the distant future, Montague Spring will become a cave, too, with a spring branch flowing from it. Its location some distance from the creek allowed the construction of a grist mill that wouldn't be flooded by every freshet. That use of the spring is long gone, and it's left no discernible architectural trace and little historical record. There are some concrete-and-creek-gravel foundations here, but no one seems to know if they supported a one-room school, blacksmith shop, or general store – all of which were said to be components of a community variously called Montague or Tory. There is yet the well-attended Pleasant Grove Baptist church and up-and-running Mountain Spring Trout Park, "You catch 'em, we clean 'em." This

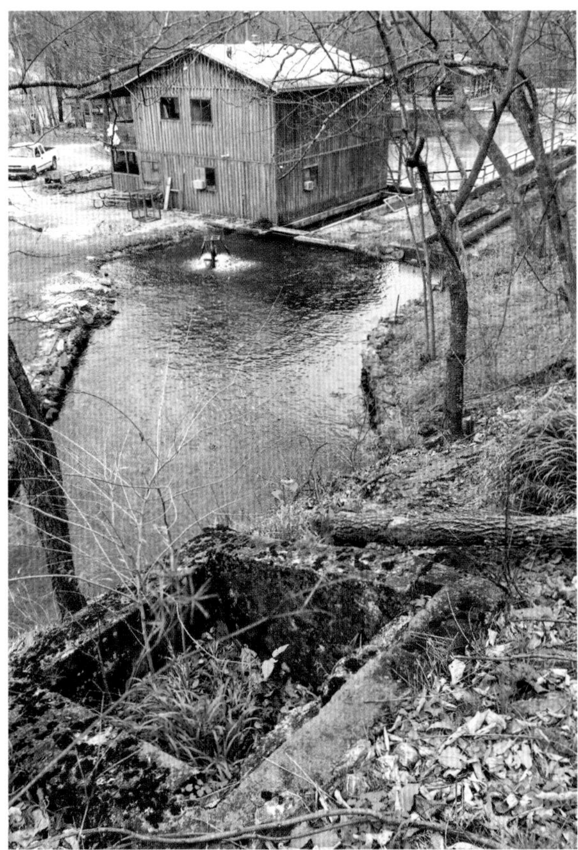

Above left: The grounds of Mountain Spring Trout Park have remnants of previous utilizations. The purpose of some, like this stone and concrete box on the hill above the spring, is unknown.

Above right: Golden Rainbow trout school at the mouth of Montague Spring. It is a transformed environment but has a natural ambience.

last utilization of the spring also has enigmatic architectural relics and a not-readily-accessible history. When and who began raising trout at Montague Spring we haven't learned. Wayne Glenn noted Henry LeComte operated a "new and improved" fish hatchery here beginning in 1939-40. The history of trout farming in Ozark springs, on the other hand, is better known. Native game fish find the year-round 58-degree water of Ozark springs a bit chilly. Trout love cold water, are good to eat, and are status-y creatures. State and federal agencies and even the railroads started introducing various salmonid species in Missouri waterways in 1878. Only a few creeks, however, have the right conditions for natural reproduction. Since 1888 rainbow trout from the McCloud River in California have been artificially raised in Missouri, first by the federal government, then by state agencies and private hatcheries.

These enterprises, like Mountain Spring Trout Park, which depends on the waters of Montague Spring, sell fresh and smoked trout and offer catch-guaranteed fishing. No license is required and one's catch is billed by the pound. Fly fishermen can catch-and-release for an hourly rate. The trout average nearly three pounds. A pavilion is available to rent for parties or weddings or special occasions in a peaceful, rustic setting.

After sixty years Crystal Springs Trout Farm recently closed. A complex of springs near Cassville that in 1940 totalled seven million gallons a day supplied the hatchery with water which was then discharged into Flat Creek.

In a 2007 letter to the editor of the *Cassville Democrat* the owners said the spring dried up completely the previous summer. They attributed the shrinking water table to population growth, drought, and the demands of the poultry industry.

Above: Domino Danzero photograph, circa 1922, of his family picnicking at Sequiota Park. Photo courtesy Missouri State University Archives, Danzero Collection.

Following two pages: In spite of changes in name, ownership, and utilization, the cave and spring at Sequiota Park still retain a natural ambience that visitors find picturesque.

In 2011 the Springfield-Greene County Park Board held a ribbon-cutting ceremony for the completion of a $1.8 million "facelift to the much needed natural water environment of Sequiota Park." Considering the variety and intensity of utilizations of the place over the last century, that expenditure seems justified.

The "daring pioneers who tamed the Ozarks" loved to explore the large cave here to kill fat hibernating bears "with a big knife," reported a *News-Democrat* piece of July 5, 1897. "A gun," the article stated, "could not be safely used on a bear." We found no record the spring here was ever harnessed to power a mill. A small dry cave provided storage and was once a mushroom farm.

Fisher Cave, as the larger cave became known, was bought in 1913 for $10,000 by H. E. Peterson, who renamed it Sequiota, which he claimed was an Indian word. The Frisco line ran a motor car service to what they called Se-qui-o-ta Park. Springfieldians flocked to picnic, fish, and take boat rides in the cave whose water level was raised by a four-foot dam. More than a thousand feet can be viewed by boat. Cave explorers have mapped another 1,600 feet of passages.

The Missouri State Fish Commission bought the property in 1920 for $23,000 and used the strong spring that flowed from the cave to create a fish hatchery. Both smallmouth bass and rainbow trout were raised. When Table Rock Dam was completed and its discharges proved too cold for native fish, the Shepherd of the Hills Trout Hatchery was built below the dam. Sequiota's hatchery equipment and manager went south in 1959 to the new facility at Branson. Springfield was deeded the property. It has continued to attract crowds, although boat tours of the main cave are limited and seasonal to protect hibernating endangered gray bats.

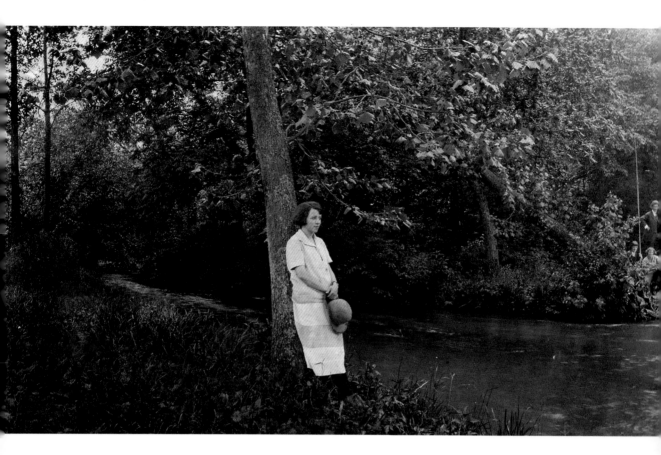

Right: Ruins of a dam on Spring Creek built by Springfield businessmen to create a resort lake after a 1908 spur of the Missouri Pacific Railroad came through Browns Spring. In 1927 the inadequate dam washed out.

Springfield picnickers could once catch a train to Browns Spring, where they could rent a rowboat, feed the ducks, or fish. When a flood took out the dam, the recreational venture ended. The Browns Spring Post Office, general store, canning factory, and church one by one gave up the ghost after the tracks were later taken up.

The Large Springs of Missouri (1944) states the flow of Browns

Spring was 7,110,000 gallons per day on May 8, 1931: "It flows from an opening at the base of a small cliff of cavernous Osage (Mississippian) cherty limestone on the west bank of Spring Creek, flows over a weir, and empties into Spring Creek."

Trout were commercially raised here, but flash floods are as much a hardship on fish farms as they are on amateurish impoundments.

Above: Hand-tinted panoramic photograph by Domino Danzero, 1923-1925. His family is posed below the soon-to-be-washed-out dam. Before marrying a girl from Monett, the Italian immigrant had been a traveling, picture-taking Harvey House restaurant supervisor. They settled in Springfield and were successful with several businesses. Photo courtesy of Special Collections, Missouri State University.

Right: Browns Spring creates a permanent flow for Spring Creek, a tributary of Crane Creek.

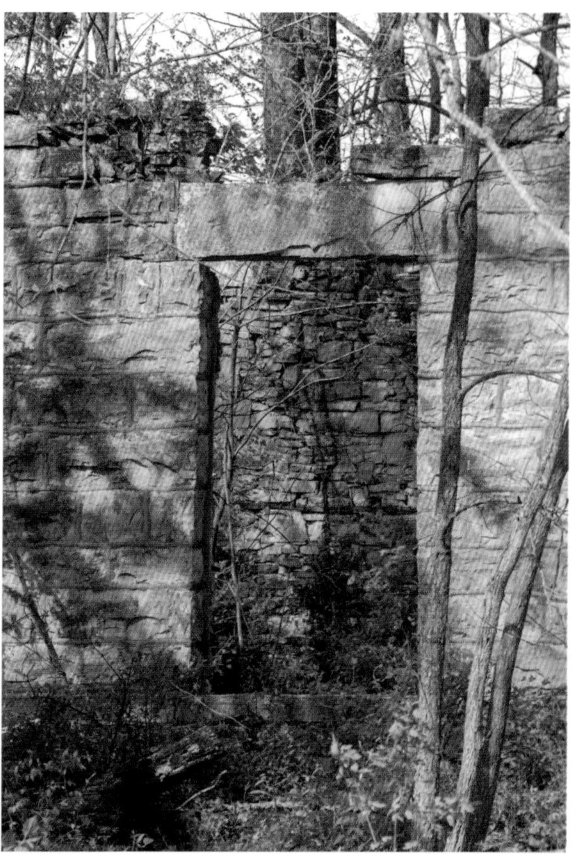

Above left: Metal detecting for lost coins at the Fountain of Youth, Ponce de Leon's medical spring. Belief in the benefits of drinking the water of several small springs resulted in a boomtown of 1,719 uncritical souls according to the 1880 census. Perhaps half a hundred now inhabit the steep valley. The ephemeral hamlet of Ponce de Leon is on the east fork of Goff Creek. Four miles west of Poncy Goff Creek joins the James.

Above, right: A ruined stone church is the grandest architectural evidence of this "Town of Departed Glory," as Lucille A. Brown aptly called it in the *White River Valley Historical Quarterly* (Winter, 1981).

In the late 1870s, Fountain T. Welsh was hunting rabbits in the forested hills of Stone County when he severely scratched his hand. He washed it off in a spring and by the next morning the wound had healed. With several associates the Springfield streetcar operator purchased land around the site of the miraculous cure and subdivided it. He named it Ponce de Leon. Lots were snapped up even though the seeps dripped typical cold, clear, limestone-filtered Ozark spring water. Most springs for which healing benefits were claimed were so heavily mineralized that a few gulps could produce gastric distress.

At the height of the boom, Poncy (as it was called) boasted two tomato-canning plants, a sawmill, four doctors, and a drugstore, two hotels, a dry goods seller, several groceries, a hardware store, an often-robbed bank, several churches, two saloons, a dance hall, and several distilleries. Springs of the Ozark highland have no medicinal benefits (nor do the odoriferous waters of curative springs) but they are highly suitable for making moonshine. Distiller Ed Kelner dispensed his whiskey a few feet inside Stone County in 1895 to thirsty citizens of surrounding dry counties. Kelner noted, "Republic has gone dry. Nothing left in the town but soda water and buttermilk."

"The News from Ponce de Leon," in the December 7, 1899, *Springfield Republican*, mournfully reported only token quantities of lead had been found, no railroad was coming through, and crops had failed for three years: "But with a good crop of corn, oats, wheat and Republican votes next year, I think the country will boil over with prosperity."

By 1910, the village began a long slide downward. A March 7, 1935, *Moberly Monitor-Index* indicated there were still true believers in Fountain R. Welsh's claim: "'We never get old in Poncy,' declared Lewis Rhea, village carpenter and barber who has lived here fifty-six years. 'Some of the old-timers still call me the dancing kid.'"

Above: One can mail a letter or attend Sunday School in Poncy – that's it. The general store is the only business that even left a ruin.

Right: The well-kept Ponce de Leon cemetery is a mile east of the hamlet.

Above: Flat Creek seen through the picture window of an abandoned house. Aesthetics, as well as economics, plays a role in development. Our utilization of natural resources shapes the earth, but our interpretation of landscape is framed by our cultural perceptions.

Chert gravel is only a small aspect of the Ozarks geologic past that affects today's riverscapes. Climate and plant and animal life are also interactive natural influences. As attentive as Carl O. Sauer was to the subtle way chert and moving water could influence stream forms, he was not a geographic determinist.

"The works of man express themselves in the cultural landscape," Sauer wrote in a 1925 paper, *The Morphology of Landscape*:

> They are derived in each case from the natural landscape, man expressing his place in nature as distinct agent of modification. ... The natural landscape is being subjected to transformation at the hands of man, the last and for us the most important morphological factor. By his culture he makes use of the natural forms, in many cases alters them, and in some destroys them. ...
>
> Culture is the agent, the natural area is the medium, the cultural landscape the result. Under the influence of a given culture, itself changing through time, the landscape undergoes development, passing through phases, and probably reaching ultimately the end of its cycle of development. With the introduction of a different, that is alien culture, a rejuvenation of the cultural landscape sets in, or a new landscape is superimposed on remnants of an older one. The natural landscape is of course of fundamental importance, for it supplies the materials out of which the cultural landscape is formed. The shaping force, however, lies in the culture itself. Within the wide limits of the physical equipment of area lie many possible choices for man. This is the meaning of adaptation, through which, aided by those suggestion

> which man has derived from nature, perhaps by an imitative process, largely subconscious, we get the feeling of harmony between the human habitation and the landscape into which it so fittingly blends. But these, too, are derived from the mind of man, not imposed by nature, and hence are cultural expressions.

It is true that moving water creates topography, but there are few places on earth where man has not affected that flow. In the case of the James River basin, these influences are considerable. Fifty miles of the lower James no longer exist in riverine form due to Table Rock Dam on the White River. Pioneer mills were constructed across tributaries, some of which continue to exert hydrologic influence. Agriculture and urbanization have altered the character of the runoff and chemistry of the streams. These utilizations of the river and its watershed confusingly merge with natural processes.

Sixty years after Carl Sauer's study, Milton Rafferty's *The Ozarks: Land and Life* was published. Rafferty concurs with Sauer that this is a place where the rural population is deeply connected to the geography:

> Generations of the same family often lived in the same community so that family history is intermingled with the landscape in an uncommon way. Life is integrated with the landscape in a natural way that is understood by everyone. Thus the Ozarker is a kind of homespun Lockian who thinks of the landscape as an object that penetrates the mind and alters the man.

Below: Unidentified cabinet photograph, circa 1890. This is likely an Ozark family.

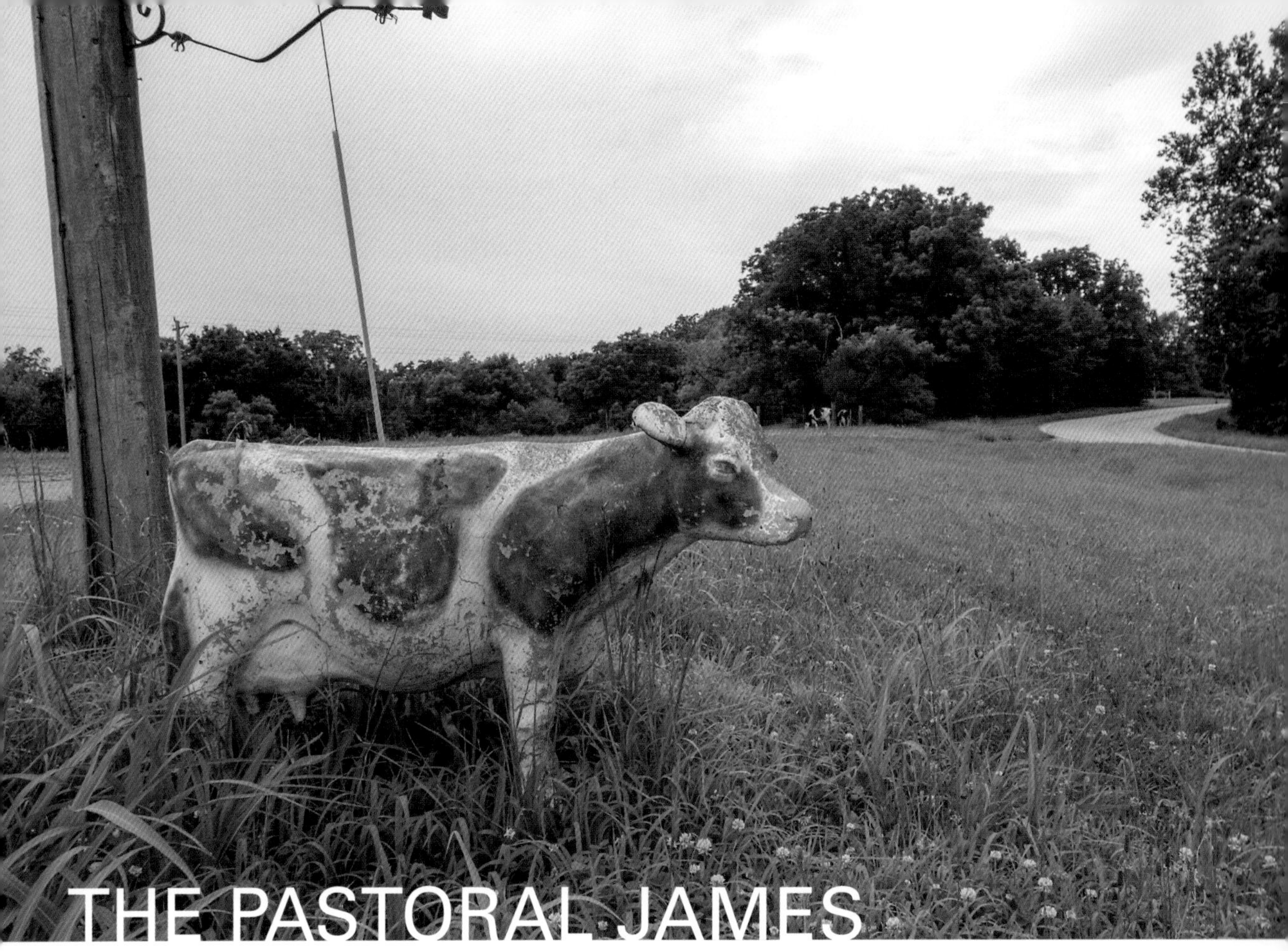

THE PASTORAL JAMES

Above: Dairy farm west of Galena. Dairy farming, which developed principally around Springfield, peaked in the 1950s.

Agriculture, as well as urbanization and dam building, profoundly affects rivers.

The eminent limnologist H. B. N. Hynes believed we should "look at streams not as purely aquatic phenomena, as one can with lakes, but rather to view them as parts of the valley that they drain. I shall probably fail in my endeavor as my eyes are always drawn to the water, and I like to paddle anyway. ... It is also clear that changes in the valley wrought by man may have large effects."

Grazed or mowed permanent pastures have replaced annually plowed cornfields throughout the lands drained by the James Fork of the White River. The effects of these differing agricultural uses on hydrology are subtle and complicated. We discussed this briefly in the previous chapter. Changing local and even international economic forces affect development, as does the inherent fertility of the soil, and other geographic realities.

Tradition also influences how natural resources are utilized. Immigrants, like the Americans who crossed the Mississippi from Tennessee, Kentucky, and other southern highland states to settle the Ozarks, brought attitudes and practices with them that would in time be molded by the possibilities of their new home. We affect our environment and it affects us. A clear, rushing, cliff-lined river, like the James, becomes a cultural as well as a geographic marker.

Earlier inhabitants as well as present-day farmers were interested in improving the grasslands. That the Osage tribe annually set fire to the prairies to repress the growth of trees is well documented. They also burned woods to open them up for hunting. Numerous accounts of early settlers confirmed that Ozark forests on decent soils consisted of large oaks with a bluestem grass understory.

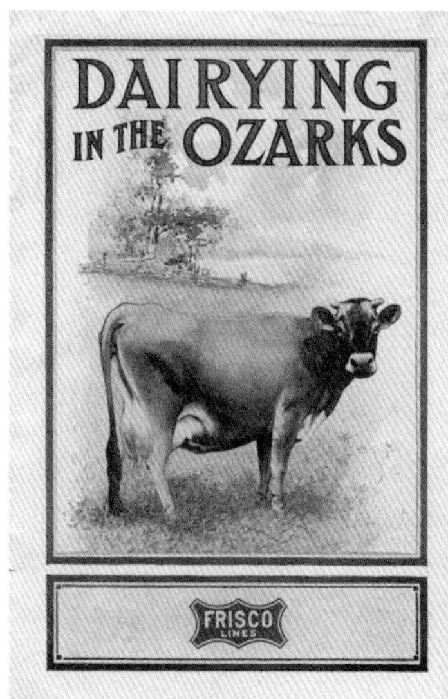

Above: Frisco Lines pamphlet, late 1920s. The less dissected lands of the upper James watershed closer to population centers permitted dairying to thrive shortly after 1900. Later, labor shortages during World War II and the boom afterward were problematic. Railroad companies' invitations to farm the Ozarks were seductive:

"The Ozarks are in many respects better suited to the man of moderate means than any other territory. The man with small capital, willingness to earnestly and conscientiously work, can here build for himself and his family, a home and a fortune.

"Nature shaped the hills, guided the streams and planted the vegetation of the Ozarks just as the dairy cow wanted them."

Today the river bottoms and the rolling hilltops have been deforested. After a century of being planted in corn and other row crops, they are now in tame grasses, principally fescue. Once the alluvial ground along streams grew monstrous hardwoods. Schoolcraft encountered the James on January 1, 1819:

> On travelling two miles this morning we entered a rich and extensive valley, and found ourselves unexpectedly on the banks of James' River, the stream we were in search of. It is the principal north western fork of White River, and a large, clear, and beautiful stream. It originates in high-lands, a little south of the Gasconade river ... and running in an opposite direction for two hundred and fifty miles, forms a junction with the south fork of White River, one hundred miles below. Along its banks are found extensive bodies of the choicest land, covered by a large growth of forest-trees and cane, and interspersed with prairies. Oak, maple, white and black walnut, elm, mulberry, hackberry, and sycamore, are the common trees, and attain a very large size. On the west commences a prairie of unexplored extent, stretching off towards the Osage river, and covered with tall rank grass. Towards its mouth, it is said to be bordered with high rocky bluffs.

Early settlers girdled these bottomland giants, and planted corn beneath their leafless branches. Schoolcraft noted their dependence on this crop. "They raised corn for bread, and for feeding their horses previous to the commencement of long journeys in the woods, but none for exportation." In 1920, the year Carl O. Sauer's PhD thesis was published, he wrote a critical article, "The Economic Problem of the Ozark Highland," in the September issue of *The Scientific Monthly*. At the beginning of the Roaring Twenties Sauer wrote, "The great prosperity that is continuing through the country has only a weak echo in the hills of the Ozarks":

> The economic system has been altered only in minor ways from that which was in force at the time of early settlement. The pursuits which he follows give little opportunity for the accumulation of a surplus. The aim of labor is hardly commercial, the labor being expended directly toward the sustenance of the family. The condition is characteristic of primitive groups. The economy is based primarily on agriculture, but agriculture is typically only a partial means of subsistence.
>
> Corn is the dominant crop. It is grown on thin uplands and on stony hillsides as predominantly as it is in rich bottoms. It is produced not only with almost total disregard of the character of farming land but of the size of yield as well, simply because it has a larger direct utility to the individual farmer than any other crop. It feeds the family, and the horses, cattle, and hogs. It will keep without means of storage. It will grow in the most poorly prepared ground. It yields the largest returns of food per acre cultivated. Also it was grown by the first settlers as the main crop and their descendants are following the old traditions. From the standpoint of commercial development, from every standpoint in fact, except that of a farm functioning as a self-sufficing unit, corn is grown very much in excess of the best interests of the region.
>
> In addition to being a corn-farmer, the resident of the interior Ozarks is normally a live-stock producer. He could not be designated, how-

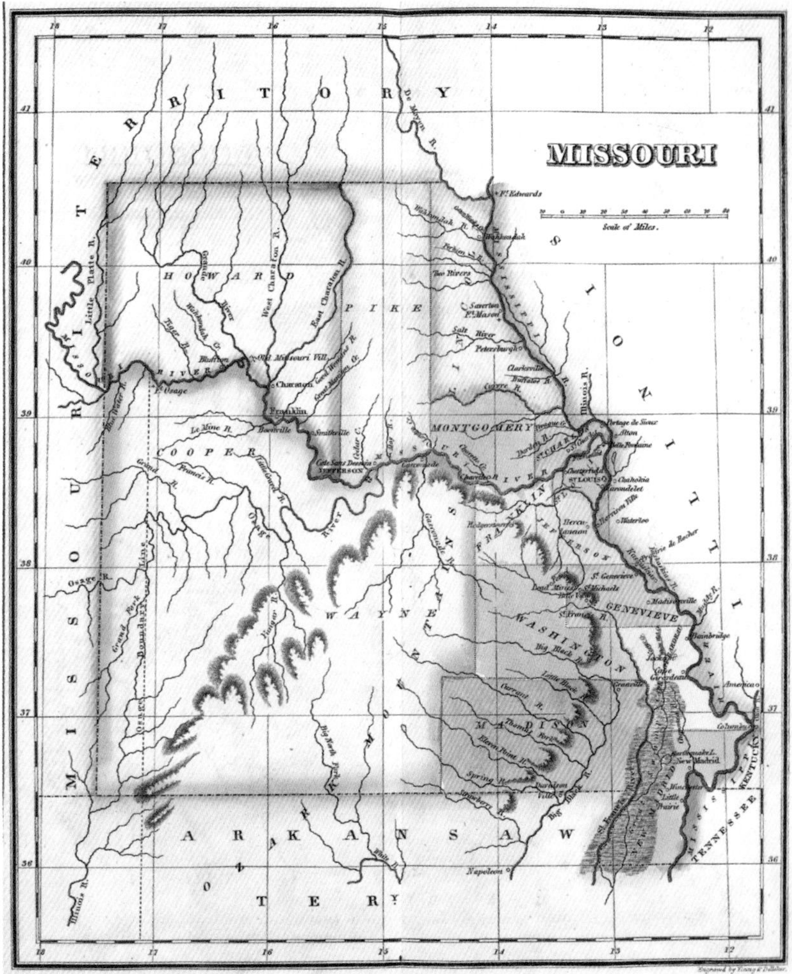

Right: Missouri map (detail), 1822. Lands along major rivers were settled first. Relocated Indian tribes, prairies, and rocky forested hills retarded development of southwest Missouri.

Opposite top: Missouri map (detail), 1841. Surveyors had begun mapping the Ozarks. The huge counties would soon be subdivided as settlers poured in.

Opposite bottom: Missouri map (detail), 1855. Christian and Webster Counties are not shown, but most of the present features are accurately depicted. Clearly Springfield is the transportation hub of the region.

> ever, a rancher, breeder, or feeder. The form of the industry also goes back to first frontier, and was responsible in large measure for pioneer immigration into the Ozarks. Fires were set habitually by the pioneers to replenish and extend the grazing lands. These fires extended the grass lands at the expense of the forests. Grazing itself extended into the forests as the population increased. Fires and long-continued grazing in the forests have interfered in many districts with the growth of seedlings, sprouts, and other undergrowth, and have resulted in a forest floor covered with grass and weeds. The ridge-tops are now converted almost entirely to plow land, and grazing has therefore suffered a restriction to the forested areas, which are nearly equivalent to the hillsides. This poor, volunteer pasturage among the trees is incapable of improvement and by reason of long-continued grazing at all seasons has been steadily deteriorating. With the elimination of the natural grass lands the cattle industry has largely passed into the condition of a relict industry.

To urban sportsmen in the early 1900s, the lower James looked wild, but decades of timber cutting, overgrazing, and cultivation had transformed it. Sauer thought a livestock industry with better management "is indicated as the dominant ideal occupation of the future." That would happen ultimately, but not before other inappropriate agricultural efforts were attempted and abandoned.

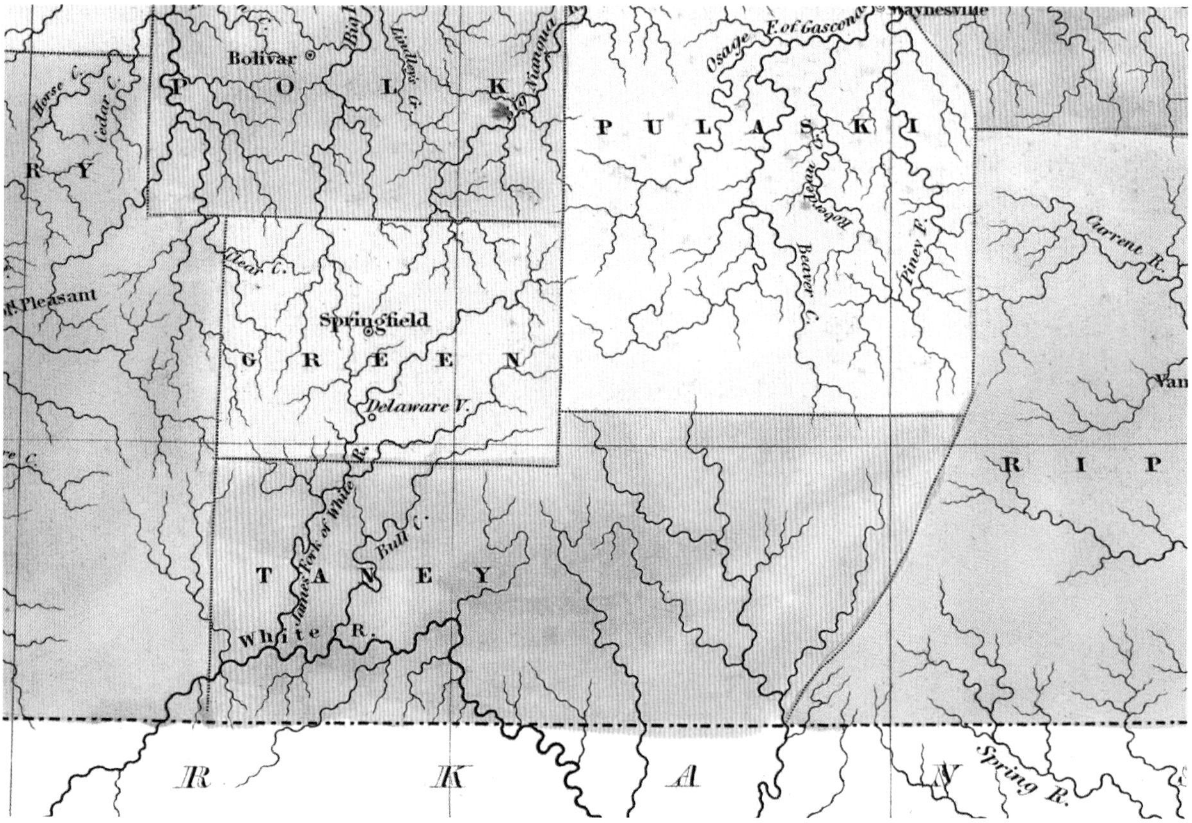

Bolivar
P O L K
Lindley's C.
Big Niangua
Waynesville
Osage F. of Gasconade
P U L A S K I
Roubidoux
Beaver C.
Piney F.
Current R.
Horse C.
Cedar C.
R Y
Mt. Pleasant
Clear C.
Springfield
G R E E N
Delaware V.
Van
R I P
James Fork of White R.
Bull C.
T A N E Y
White R.
R K A N
Spring R.

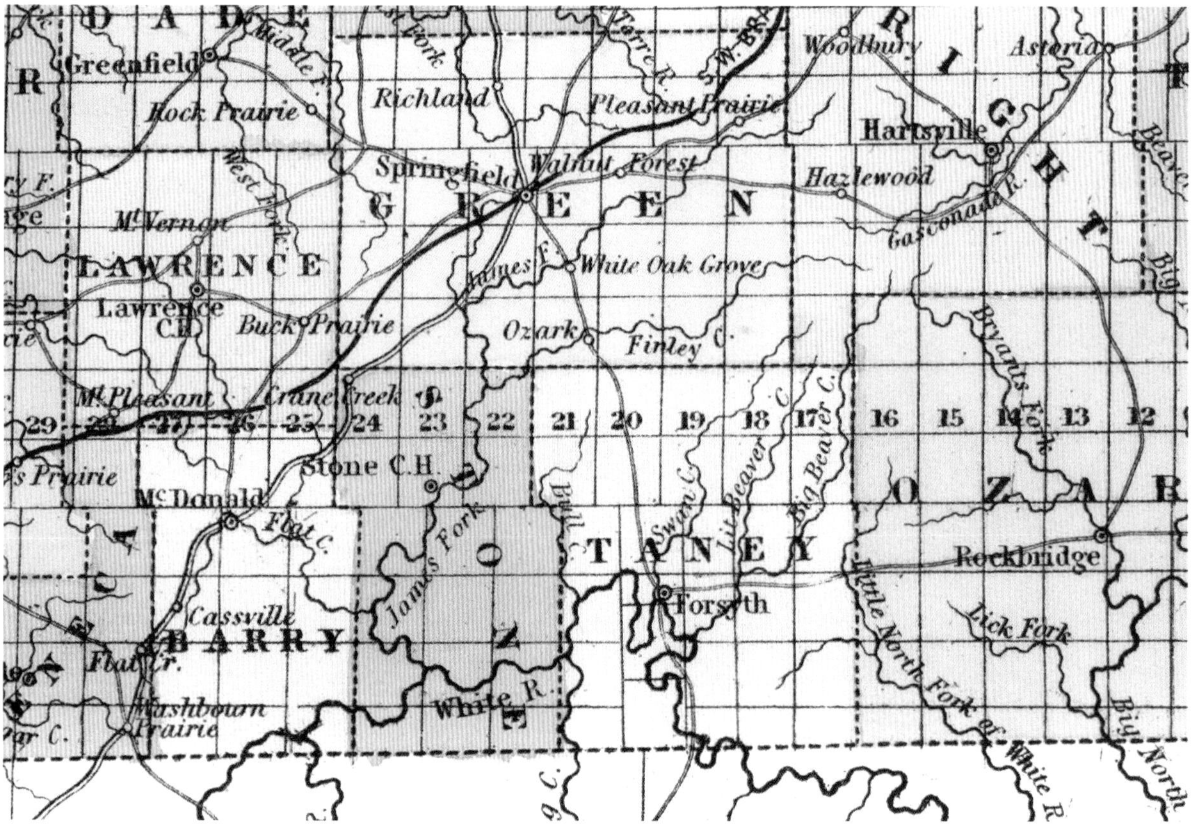

D A D E
Greenfield
Middle F.
Rock Prairie
Richland
Sac R.
S. W. Br.
Pleasant Prairie
Woodbury
Asteria
R I G H T
Hartsville
Springfield
Walnut Forest
Hazlewood
Gasconade R.
G R E E N
Mt. Vernon
West Fork
LAWRENCE
James F.
White Oak Grove
Lawrence C.H.
Buck Prairie
Ozark
Finley C.
Bryants Fork
Mt. Pleasant
Crane Creek
29 28 27 26 25 24 23 22 21 20 19 18 17 16 15 14 13 12
Stone C.H.
Lit. Beaver C.
Big Beaver C.
O Z A R
McDonald
Flat C.
James Fork
Bull C.
Swan C.
T A N E Y
Rockbridge
Forsyth
Cassville
BARRY
Little North Fork of White R.
Lick Fork
Flat Cr.
Washbourn Prairie
White R.
Big North

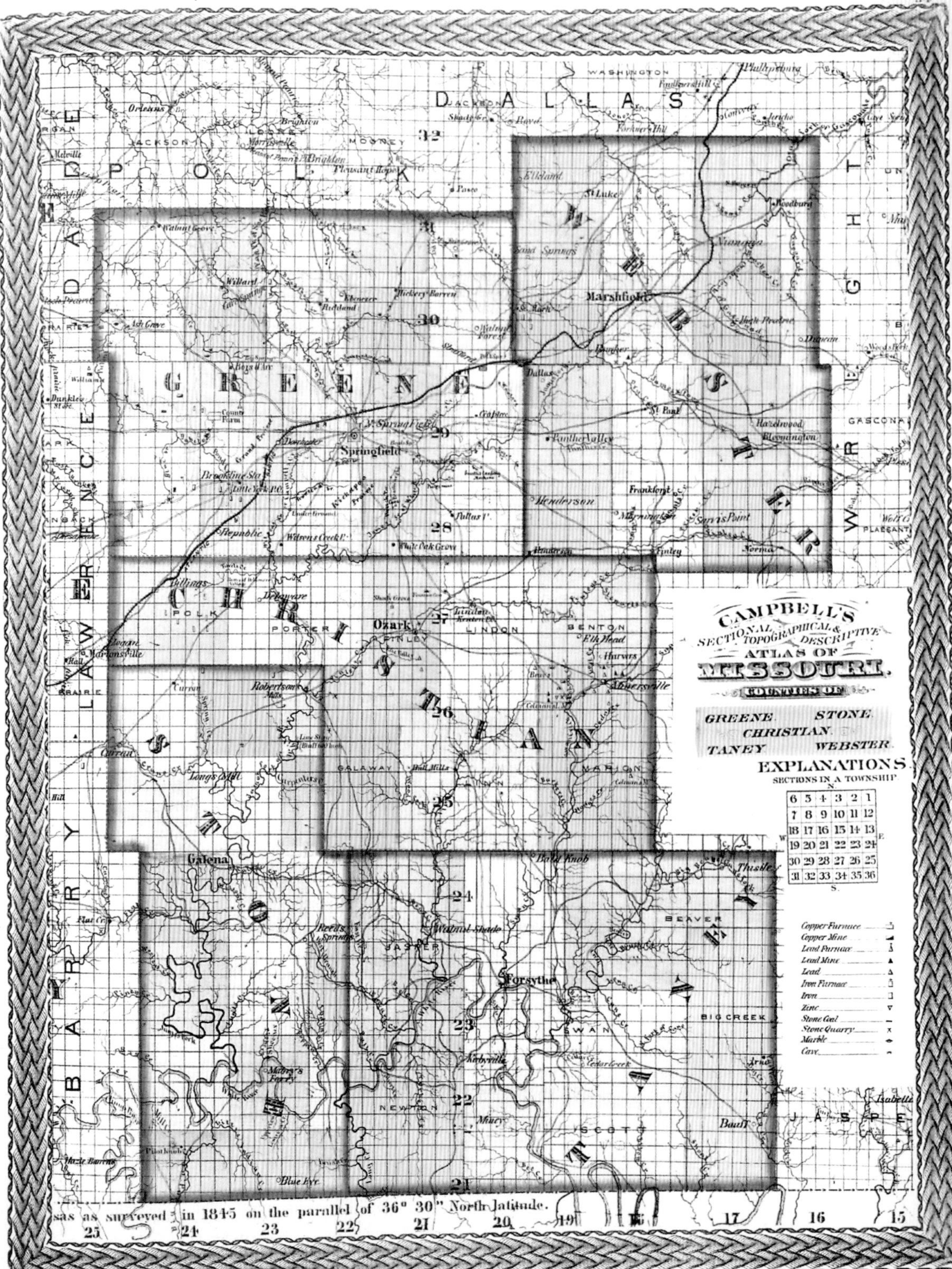
CAMPBELL'S
SECTIONAL TOPOGRAPHICAL & DESCRIPTIVE
ATLAS OF
MISSOURI.
COUNTIES OF
GREENE. STONE.
CHRISTIAN.
TANEY. WEBSTER.
EXPLANATIONS.
SECTIONS IN A TOWNSHIP
N.
6 5 4 3 2 1
7 8 9 10 11 12
18 17 16 15 14 13
W 19 20 21 22 23 24 E.
30 29 28 27 26 25
31 32 33 34 35 36
S.
Copper Furnace
Copper Mine
Lead Furnace
Lead Mine
Lead
Iron Furnace
Iron
Zinc
Stone Coal
Stone Quarry
Marble
Cave
DALLAS
POLK
GREENE
WEBSTER
CHRISTIAN
STONE
TANEY
Springfield
Marshfield
Ozark
Galena
Forsythe
Republic
Billings
Ash Grove
Walnut Grove
Willard
Niangua
Seymour
Rogersville
Henderson
Bald Knob
Thistle
Kirbyville
BEAVER
BIG CREEK
SWAN
SCOTT
NEWTON
JASPER
GALAWAY
PORTER
LINDON
BENTON
MARION
PLEASANT
GASCONADE
sas as surveyed in 1845 on the parallel of 36° 30' North Latitude.
25 24 23 22 21 20 19 18 17 16 15

Shortly after the Civil War, railroads penetrated the Ozarks to haul out lead, logs, and farm products. Immigrants from the upper Midwest as well as the southern highlands now had easy access to a large, underdeveloped region. In 1905, the Missouri Pacific White River Railway crossed the James River at Galena. It brought tourists and homesteaders who, compared to the original settlers, were progressive. The leveler land near Springfield attracted even more aspiring rural landowners.

Owning a small farm appealed to many Americans. Government policy had facilitated Jefferson's dream of a country of yeoman farmers. Cheap land and labor provided by large families, and transportation for crops to growing cities, was a formula for success, for a time. Beginning about 1870, a system called general farming was based on a mixture of subsistence and market agriculture.

Opposite: This plate from *Campbell's Missouri Atlas* (1873) contains four of the six Missouri counties the James River flows through. A bit of Finley Creek heads in Douglas County.

Barry County to the west is not shown. By this time, even the roughest sections of the Ozarks had been surveyed and land offices were open to sell federal holdings. Unfortunately these accurate new maps, based on the rational cartography of the Public Land Survey System advocated by Thomas Jefferson to facilitate settlement, do not distinguish between good and poor farmland.

Corn was the principal crop. It and oats, barley, and tall sorghum were used to feed livestock. Wheat was a cash crop. Horses and mules were bred, and of course hogs. Both beef and milk cows were raised. Chickens produced egg money, and every farm had a vegetable garden. Around 1900 some planted apple or peach orchards. Before competition and a shortage of labor around World War II tomatoes and strawberries could be profitable.

Dairy farms proliferated around Springfield, but have since diminished. Competition from better capitalized producers on better soils and locations and rising labor costs have made family operations an anachronism. In *The Ozarks in Missouri History* (2013), geographer Milton B. Rafferty's essay, "Agricultural Change in the Western Ozarks," eloquently summarizes the wild pasture to tame pasture cycle:

> Ozark agriculture appears to have come full circle. The original Ozark farmer was a part-time agriculturalist, a keeper of livestock, and a hunter. The land he plowed was safe and secure in stream bottoms. His economy was more in tune with the existing natural resources than some of the subsequent types of farming. Development of commercial agriculture in the Ozarks has been a long and sometimes destructive process replete with experimentation and constant adjustments in man-land relations. Large-scale contemporary agriculture in the Ozarks leans heavily on livestock with cultivation ancillary to livestock production. The general farm has all but disappeared, dairy farming continues under heavy pressure while only vestiges of fruit farms and truck farms remain.
>
> Like his forebear, the less progressive contemporary Ozark farmer often finds greater reward in alternate pursuits than in attempting to wrest his total livelihood from reluctant soils. One can speculate that mutual benefits may accrue to man and land.

Above: Real photo postcard by Hall. Probably taken in Stone County, Missouri, but Arkansas sounded more primitive. The hog's board collar is to keep it out of fenced gardens. Cattle and hogs were released in the woods to feed themselves. The destructive rooting of feral pigs was, and still is, an environmental problem.

Opposite: Sheet-iron roadside hillbilly. Doubtlessly the folks who have this rifle-toting rustic guarding their mailbox do not live in a house bereft of electricity or indoor plumbing. That the original pioneers of the region were behind their times two hundred years ago is an observation that has been periodically renewed.

The backwards mountaineer stereotype has some historical basis, but it is a trope that has long been objected to by some - especially advocates of progress.

Schoolcraft relied on a handful of recently arrived southern Highlanders to guide, feed, and shelter him. Nevertheless he said of these pioneers "without the pale of civil law, or the restraints upon manners and actions imposed by refined society, this population are an extraordinary instance of the regression of society."

Nearly two hundred years ago, and 116 years before *Lil' Abner* appeared in the funny papers, hillbillies were discovered in the White River hills. Like the public's mixture of attraction and repulsion to pop culture mountaineers, the young explorer had mixed feelings about the poor, buckskin-clad subsistence folk he encountered:

> In manners, morals, customs, dress, contempt of labour and hospitality, the state of society is not essentially different from that which exists among the savages. Schools, religion, and learning are alike unknown. Hunting is the principal, the most honourable, and the most profitable employment. To excel in the chace procures fame, and a man's reputation is measured by his skill as a marksman, his agility and strength, his boldness and dexterity in killing game, and his patient endurance and contempt of the hardships of the hunter's life. They are a hardy, brave, independent people, rude in appearance, frank and generous, travel without baggage, and can subsist anywhere in the woods, and would form the most efficient military corps in frontier warfare which can possibly exist. Ready trained, they require no discipline, inured to danger, and perfect in the use of the rifle.

Carl Sauer in "The Economic Problem of the Ozark Highland" links the rugged Ozark environment with its rugged inhabitants:

> The most common conception current regarding the economic character of the Ozark region is its inferiority to the regions that lie about it. The idea is substantially correct and may be demonstrated statistically in many ways by the values and amounts of crops and of other products which the area yields. ... The Ozark Highland has fallen behind seriously in the progress that may be expected of it, making all due allowances for thin soils, steep slopes and other handicaps.
>
> The true pioneersman, however, not intent on producing a surplus of crops for sale, was able to occupy step by step the whole of the Ozarks, conscious of no deterioration of his environment as he penetrated into areas of longer and steeper hills. For was there not everywhere good hunting and fishing, excellent water, grazing for his horses and cattle, mast for the hogs, and patches of bottom land for corn, beans and pumpkins? Here he could meet his own needs of lead and gunpowder, dig his iron ore and smelt it, and have ample power for his grist and carding mills. Frontiersmen, rather than agriculturists, became the permanent occupants of the area. With the filling up of adjacent regions, the Ozarks became a sort of refuge to the men who clung to frontier life. After a fashion the frontier still lingers in the Ozarks, but the unconstructive character of frontier living and the increase of population have gradually caused the disappearance of some of the more agreeable features of this life. For an understanding of the area it is essential to keep in mind its antecedents, and also that the blood of the frontiersman is still dominant among the population.

JENSEN
7930

Is the little hillbilly in the country graveyard (below) pondering eternity, or is he puzzled at his continuing, convoluted, and controversial role as symbol of the Ozark frontiersman? Yocum Pond Cemetery takes its name from a nearby plugged sinkhole that barely holds water. The Yocum or Joachim family was among the first to settle the environs of the James River. Some believe the James Fork of the White is named for a James Yocum who traded with Indians at its junction with the White. Some of that clan aided Henry Schoolcraft on his 1818-1819 safari into the wilderness. So successful was their illegal trade with the Delaware for liquor they distilled, they recast the United States silver dollars that the Indians had been allotted into their own coins to hide their crime. Lynn Morrowe, a reliable historian, thinks that's a better explanation than the tale that the source of the silver was an ancient Spanish mine. No example of a "Yocum dollar" has survived, but the legend of a lost silver mine on the James persists.

Li'l Abner Yocum and family were the stars of Al Capp's hillbilly comic strip. He claimed he derived the name from *yokel* and *hokum*.

Below: Several miles from Yocum Pond Cemetery is Reeds Spring, where hundreds of thousands of railroad ties were shipped in the early 1900s. The huge cemetery oak was spared the tie-hacker's axe. Mature trees are rarely found today in the Ozarks outside of graveyards or old house sites.

George E. Hall and wife Vallie are buried here, as is William H. Standish, whose permit to dam the James River was vetoed by President Theodore Roosevelt.

Above: A fenced section of the Short Cemetery on Spring Creek a mile south of Hurley encloses seventeen graves of that family. Other families are buried within the cemetery as well.

Though it is not very big, there are nine war dead here from the Civil War to World War II. A great many of the early markers with obliterated names represent children.

Republican United States Congressman Dewey Jackson Short's resolutely Republican pioneer ancestors are buried in the Short Cemetery near Hurley on Spring Creek. During the Civil War Short's Unionist grandfather, John, was shot by guerrillas and left for dead. When two Confederate soldiers came to his house to finish the job, John's wife killed one with an axe, sending the other fleeing.

As well as attending several American colleges, including Harvard, Dewey studied at Oxford and the University of Berlin. In Washington his "bold Chaucerian language" won him the title of "boy orator" and "the Barrymore of the Ozarks." The Galena native rarely failed to identify himself as a hillbilly at public appearances.

In looking at the following photographs of the James River watershed, be mindful that the culture of its inhabitants is, according to Carl O. Sauer, as determinant of its development as its geographic realities, many of which are understudied. The image of primitive Ozark natives is a mix of history, folklore, and fiction, which is uncommonly complicated. Lost silver mines, Yocum dollars, Congressman Dewey Short and his bank-robbing brother Leonard are only a few of the paradoxes connected with these intriguing people who transformed this landscape.

Hailey School (above) was inaccessible because of a rise in Fortune Creek, a branch of Flat Creek. Later we returned and photographed this decaying one-room school in Barry County. Poverty and isolation limited schooling in the early Ozarks. Before the state of Missouri subsidized public education there were subscription schools, but teachers were poorly paid, textbooks were few, and terms were short because children were needed to work the land.

Vine Hills School near Wheelersville, Barry County (opposite, top) was built in 1939 by the WPA. This native-stone one-room school is now a community building and interdenominational church on Sundays. The outhouses are rock.

Much better preserved are small Protestant church buildings throughout the rural Ozarks. As well as serving religious needs, they provided some education and socialization for the community during pioneer days.

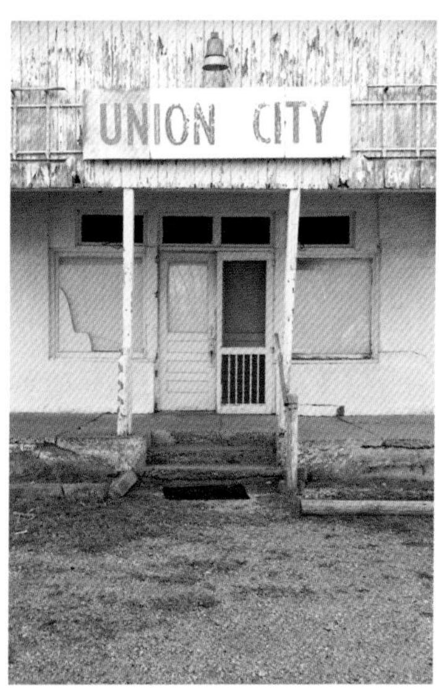

Above: Vacant crossroads store, Union City, Stone County.

Top: Deteriorating rock store at Cato, Barry County.

One-room schools persisted in the hilly Ozarks longer than elsewhere in the state, but consolidation finally brought that tradition to a close. In the first issue of Series 2 of *Ozarks Watch*, Brooks Blevins, endowed professor of Ozark Studies at Missouri State University, reflected on the fate of another component of bygone rurality – country stores:

> In the not-too-distant past the country store was a common sight in the Ozarks. They were invaluable to life in the countryside, and had been for generations. As westward-rushing waves of humanity and livestock laid claim to arable, and sometimes not so arable, land across the continent and recreated familiar farmsteads on new terrain, the country store took its place on the American and eventually Ozarks landscape. A traveler exploring in the farthest reaches of the region in the final quarter of the nineteenth century could scarcely have trundled more than five miles without encountering a tiny hamlet or crossroads with its blacksmith shop, grist mill, church house or two – perhaps doubling as schoolhouse – and false-front-sporting, frame-constructed mercantile. The great reign of the country store had begun by the late nineteenth century. As the twentieth century wore on, a series of developments emerged to challenge the vitality of the country store. Mail-order houses, rural free delivery, automobiles and improved roads, supermarkets and small-town dime stores, and finally the Ozarks' own contribution to the modern retail industry, Walmart.

Blevins rejoices that there are still some open country stores:

That's the story of the Ozarks country store. Change, evolution, adaptation. The world keeps spinning. Life doesn't slow down - even in the Ozarks. Most modern-day country stores in the region may not inspire calendars and coffee table books, but they continue to do what country stores have always done–serve a rural clientele by catering to the changing demands and needs of that clientele. They may not be your grandpa's country store, but to your grandkids and great grandkids they will be. Just give them time—and a little bit of business now and then.

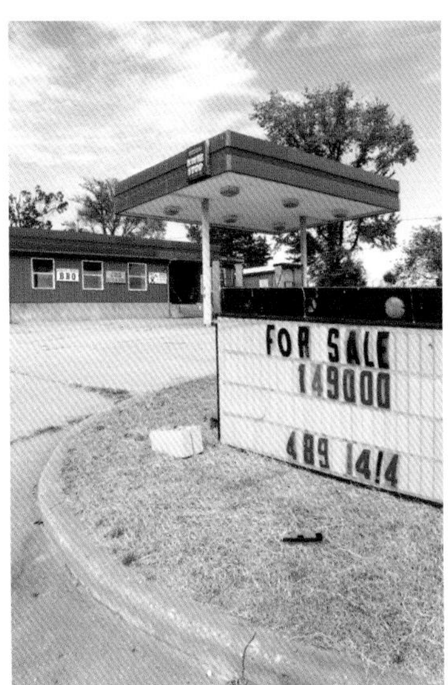

Above: Recently closed convenience store east of Jenkins.

Top: Kindall's Store, still open.

Right: Crossroads store, open but for sale.

Right: Milldam of the McDowell water mill on Flat Creek. This stream has an average fall of seven feet per mile and with good water can be floated as high up as McDowell – noting obstacles like this milldam.

Right: Vintage photograph of another McDowell mill. This one utilized rollers designed to process wheat. Courtesy Barry County Museum.

Country stores, one-room schools, and little churches in the wildwood are not uniquely Ozarkian. Their architecture, textbooks, fundamentalist theology, and manufactured goods were repeated throughout rural America, but they may have lasted longer here. Ozark water mills were not endemic either, but they flowered in the region due to isolation imposed by the deep river-cut terrain and the abundance of spring-fed streams. There were five water mills on Flat Creek alone.

Mills powered by running water were constructed soon after settlement. Overshot wheels drove most, but turbines were common after 1880. Some even employed steam power at the close of the local milling era. The handsome building (above) was the McDowell Roller Mills, which unlike many could produce flour from wheat. Most early mills used stone burrs to grind corn into meal.

Above: Calton Mill

Below: Ruins of a tomato canning plant across the road from the grist mill.

A weather-beaten mill and a fallen-down cannery are all that is left of a once-thriving agricultural complex called Tom Town. Long gone are the blacksmith shop, the grocery store, and boiler house. Morgan Calton came from Kentucky in the 1840s and settled the narrow valley in north central Barry County, where eldest son Tom built a watermill in the 1870s. Originally his product was whiskey, but during the following eighty years the little mill ground corn and wheat, powered a sawmill, and generated electricity.

Tom Town's nomination for the National Register of Historic Places chronicles the fate of folks who tried to wrest a living from a region with depleted timber and soils exhausted from generations of growing grain. They were able to hang on for a time by raising tomatoes and other vegetables then providing the labor to commercially can their produce. The energy they put into this refutes the idea Ozarkers were as work-averse as comic-strip hillbillies:

> The district symbolizes a rural Ozark hamlet's transition from a local bartering economy to a short-lived integration into the national market economy. The activities within these buildings reflect the continual adaptations many similar communities had to make to the Ozark environment. A hilly, rocky terrain with poor, shallow soils forced constant economic adjustments in order to find a competitive niche in America's mainstream economy. The milling and canning processes introduced this hamlet to the industrial work ethic and disciplines.

THE O T O BRAND
CONTENTS 1 LB. 3 OZ.
HIGH GRADE
HIGH GRADE
HAND PACKED
H. B. COX CANNING CO.
R. F. D. 2
CRANE, MO.
TOMATOES

Above: Salsa made from homegrown tomatoes by the Papa Verde Canning Company, Crane. It's been decades since boxcars of canned tomatoes left the Crane railroad station.

Above right: Real photo postcard, circa 1915. Every member of the family enthusiastically worked for pay at the tomato canneries.

Top: Unused tomato canning label for the H.B. Cox Canning Company of Crane, Missouri.

It was a labor- but not capital-intensive enterprise. Steep, timbered hillsides were cleared and plowed with mules. Tomato crops were alternated with strawberries, green beans, or cucumbers. As some family members picked and transported the crop, others toiled in the flimsy sawmill lumber canneries to clean, cook, and can. A colorful lithograph label designed and printed in Chicago or St. Louis was slapped on the steel cans. Off went the industrially produced agricultural product to a railhead. Tom Town's tomatoes traveled six miles by wagon to Monett. Most of the three hundred or so canneries in southwest Missouri were located in railroad towns.

Cannery season was only three months long but the employment opportunity was vital. Farmers only cleared and planted a few acres but they might, barring drought or blight caused by excessive rain, clear as much as $200 an acre. Women, for the first time, could receive wages working in the canneries. They, and often children, were paid by the bucket of peeled tomatoes. It usually added up to $2-$2.50 a day in the 1920s. On one good Saturday

Tom Town's little cannery produced 16,500 cans of tomatoes. Cash was so scarce in the Ozarks businessmen like Dewey Short's father worked seasonally in the Galena cannery.

The tomato-canning era was a godsend for small farmers in the lower James basin. The infusion of cash was invaluable, and cannery work, hot and hard as it was, was an opportunity to socialize. A great out-migration to cities and larger towns would finally scatter members of these large farm families. Cannery work was an initiation into the demands of the industrialized modern world.

Above: Operator of a tomato cannery east of Cape Fair built a long concrete housing structure for workers who came from surrounding farms during the three-month season.

Below: Canning plant ruins near Reeds Spring

Competition from California and Florida and other places with flatter land, better soil, and more sophisticated business operations proved too great for Ozark farmers. World War II created a demand for their product, but a shortage of labor was created when military and factory opportunities lured away many rural workers. The last cannery closed in Reeds Spring in 1968.

Erosion caused by cultivating steep slopes was not the only environmental problem. Waste from canneries was dumped into streams, killing fish and alarming anglers. "Deputy Game Wardens Apprehend Violators," headlined an article in the September 20, 1925, *Joplin Globe*. The offending business isn't named, but the

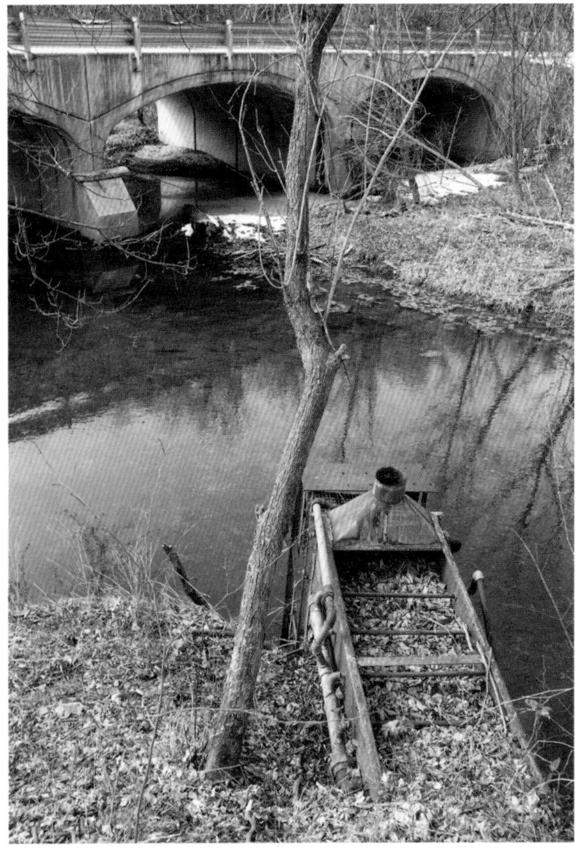

only sawmill/canning plant combo we've ever heard of was at Tom Town on Little Flat Creek:

> Deputies of the state game and fish commission have been on the job and busy during the last few weeks, according to word received by the local chapter of the Izaak Walton League. Arrests were made in Barry county, the report says, for dumping sawdust in Little Flat Creek and also for turning refuse from a canning factory into the same water.

Not only were the wastes from canning operations disposed of in streams, during bumper years when the factories were overloaded wagons of tomatoes went into the river. "When the James Ran Red" is an account by John Robert Johnson in the 1989 *History of Stone County, Missouri*:

> "When I was a boy, I saw Roy Nelson dump wagonloads of tomatoes in the river because he couldn't use 'em." So goes the recollection of Doris Johnson, a Crane resident. "Oh, he paid for 'em, but there was just too many to use in a good year."

As opportunities to earn money in hill country were limited, pollution problems were largely overlooked. Johnson states that in 1925 there were thirty-eight canneries in Stone County. About 2,500 farmers earned between $600,000 and $700,000 (an average of $240 each). Another 2,500 residents were employed by the canning plants with a total of $100,000 in payroll.

Only a few architectural remnants remain of the great tomato industry. Buried in the bank of Crane Creek is a canning factory conveyor belt (top left). Chromolithographed labels, like the Andrus & Dean's brand tomatoes at Elsey (opposite top), portray a more portentous plant than undoubtedly existed. Elsey's sole business, a small engine service, recently closed.

Tomatoes are still commercially grown in Stone County at the Quickley Farms using hydroponic methods and are sold at Springfield's Hy-Vee supermarket (left).

ANDRUS & DEAN'S
BRAND
HAND PACKED
ANDRUS & DEAN'S BRAND
TOMATOES
CONTENTS
2 LBS.
PACKED BY
ANDRUS & DEAN
ELSEY, MISSOURI

KUMHO
TIRES

ELSEY
SMALL ENGINE
SERVICE

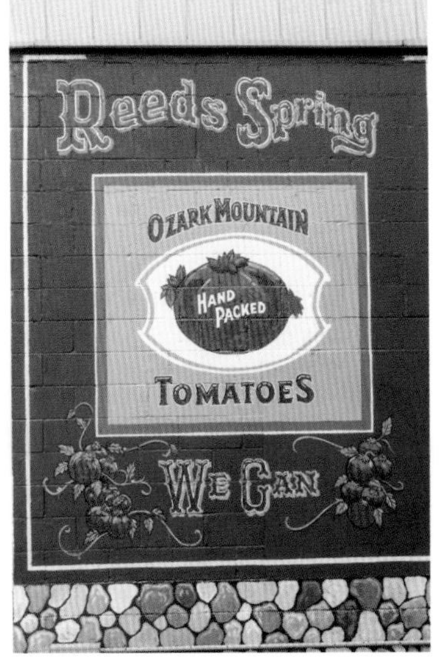

A 1927 Stone County guide located Reeds Springs "in a nook among the beautiful hills and around a mammoth spring of clear, cold water." Actually, the spring is barely a trickle but the town (current population 900) is nestled in a picturesque valley at the headwaters of Railey Creek. When the Missouri Pacific in 1906 followed the creek down from Galena, the community prospered by shipping railroad ties. It was found that the cut-over hills would grow tomatoes. By 1927, there were 22 canning factories within twelve miles. Highways put Reeds Springs on the route to the Shepherd of the Hills Country and Branson. Businesses serving tourists flourished. Locals made souvenirs sold in roadside stands. A craft tradition has survived the town being bypassed. It's a colorful village – few buildings have the same color scheme, and there is floral landscaping everywhere. *Missouri Life Magazine* selected Reeds Springs as one of the state's ten prettiest small towns.

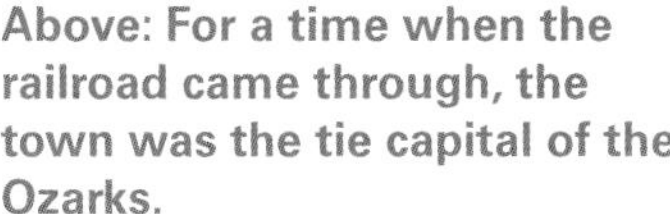

Above: For a time when the railroad came through, the town was the tie capital of the Ozarks.

Top: Two 1920s postcards when Reeds Springs thrived selling gas, pop, and Ozark drip pottery to vacationers.

Right: The eponymous spring flows under Water Street to emerge in Railey Creek, a flood-prone intermittent tributary of the James.

Top: McDowell has been a community since the 1830s. Of the three mills in the area, only one still stands. Old-time music is yet performed during winters at a former schoolhouse at the end of the road.

Right: Junction of Little Flat Creek with the main stem just below McDowell.

Opposite, top: Flat Creek is bridged by a variety of structures, but low-water crossings are still common, and still claim lives when unwisely crossed during high water.

Opposite, below: Closed filling station, McDowell.

Following spread: Much of the James River watershed consists of chert-floored creeks crisscrossed by chert backroads, although creek gravel is being replaced by crushed limestone as a road surface. It is not spectacular scenery, but the forested hills and cleared fields with their mixture of wild and domestic plants and animals create a subtle, but alluring landscape.

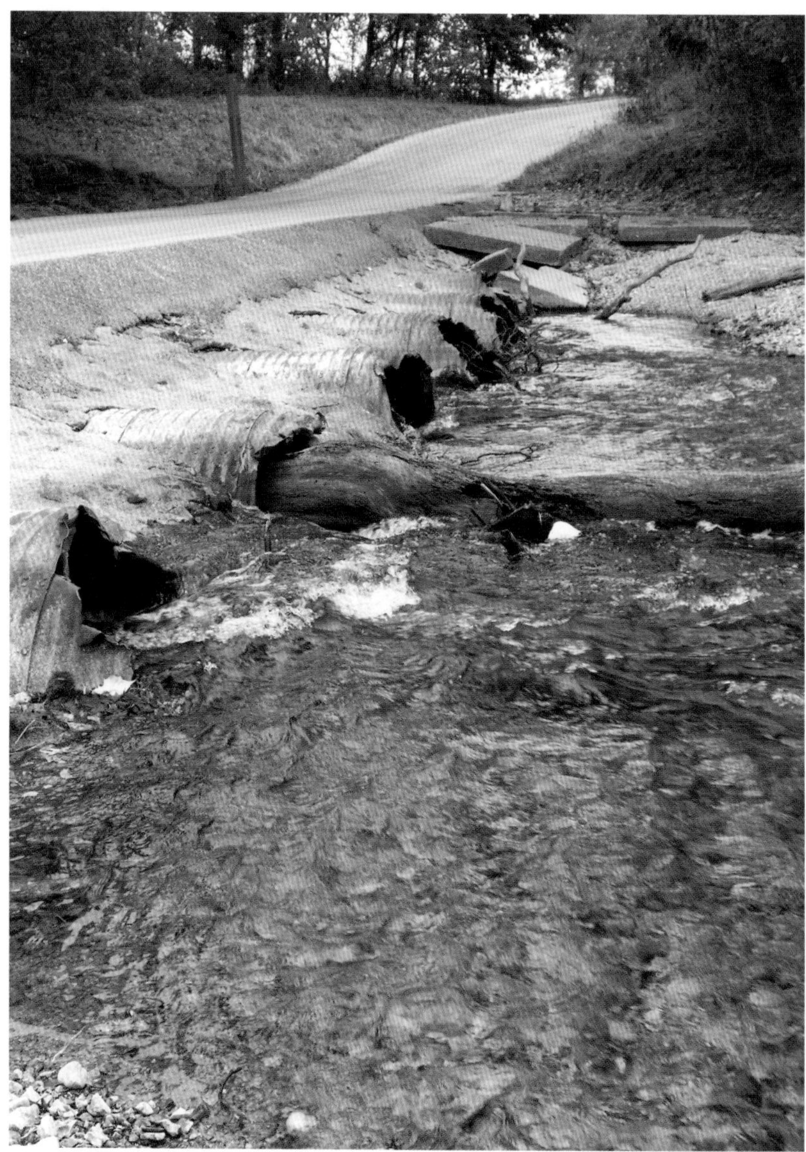

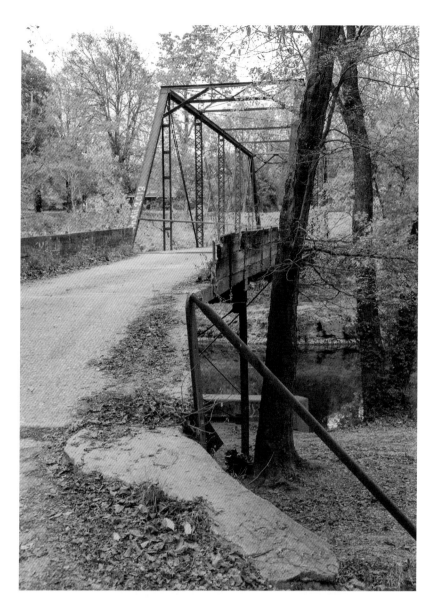

Right and below: A filigree of rust, lichens, and day-glo graffiti decorates this 1909, structurally deficient iron bridge, which is eligible for the National Register of Historic Places. It is unlikely to be nominated. Not that it's unappreciated locally - YouTube videos show young men doing scary backflips off it into Flat Creek. This is not a cohort known to fill out forms or lobby for the historic recognition of local landmarks.

Opposite page: Jenkins, which lies on the other side of the bridge, is an inhabited place, but its past has a sketchy record and its future an uncertain trajectory. There are several impressive empty structures – a commercial building and a consolidated school that was reconsolidated out of existence.

A modernized Quik Stop convenience store complex on the highway closed last year. Jenkins deserves a better elegy than our four dozen digital exposures snapped on a cloudy afternoon. However, a village with a good old, one-trick dog should not be written off.

4SV 140

10401

BIG SPRING,
ROARING RIVER STATE PARK,
NEAR CASSVILLE, MISSOURI

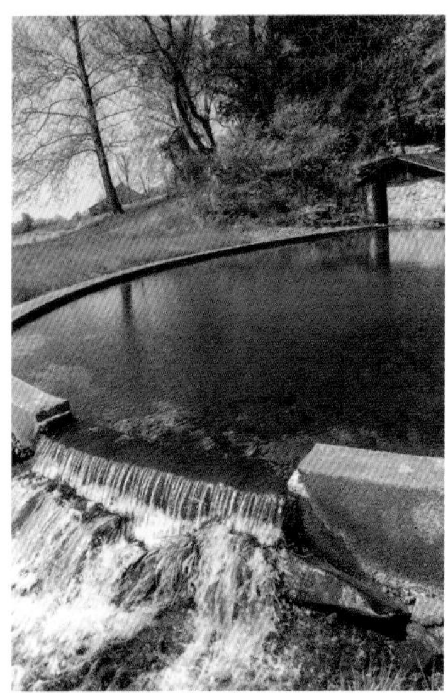

Above: McMurtry Spring, two miles south of Cassville.

Fluorescent dyes have been introduced into some dry stream beds (above, left) and sinkholes along Flat Creek a few miles from Cassville and emerged in the great spring at Roaring River (linen postcard, above, right). That twenty-six-million gallon-a-day frigid water source for a state trout park is not in the James River basin. Subsurface water movement does not always follow present-day surface stream configurations.

McMurtry Spring's flow (left) is much less than Roaring River's, and during periods of scant rainfall the circular pool doesn't overflow. It gathers its waters from nearby sinkholes. Cherokees rested here on their Trail of Tears journey, and it was a well-known camping spot for settlers coming to Cassville to trade. Missouri highway 37, which runs next to the spring, was once the Old Wire (telegraph) Road. Both sides in the Civil War traveled this road and watered their horses here.

Not all the water that falls on the upper Flat Creek basin immediately sinks into the ground to emerge in springs. Substantial rains cause these sinking creeks to run, elevating the flow of Flat Creek, which often floods low-lying developments in Cassville, the county seat of Barry County.

The valley along much of Flat Creek is broad for an Ozark stream. It's in pasture now but once was plowed for wheat and corn fields. A steam-powered roller mill (below) and power plant processed the grains grown on area farms and supplied electrical power to the town. The vintage photograph, courtesy of the Barry County Museum, shows its location in the floodplain, vulnerable to rises in Flat Creek. Even moderate rains can cover low-water bridges in Cassville (below).

Right: Real photo postcard circa 1910 of the steam powered Cassville Milling and Power Operation. Courtesy Barry County Museum.

Bottom left: Barry County Courthouse reflected in the window of a Chinese restaurant. Cassville, population 3,200, is the trade center for a large region, much of it drained by Flat Creek.

Bottom right: Flat Creek sometimes floods low-lying sections of Cassville.

CASSVILLE MILLING & POWE CO.& FOOT BRID E-PUB.BY L.C.BROW & SON-CASSVILLE.MO

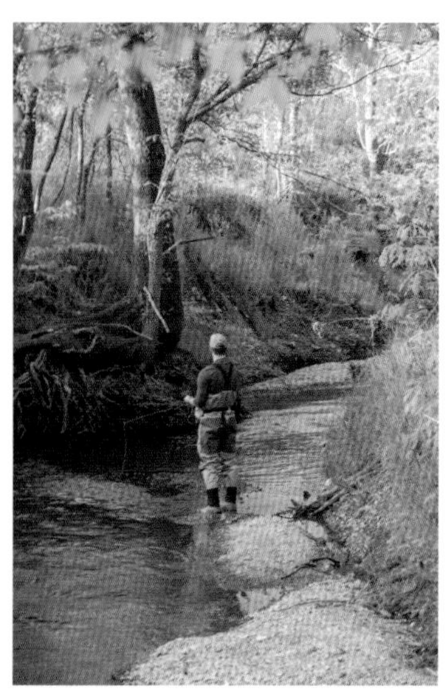

Above: Fly fishing on Crane Creek.

Millions of rainbow trout are artificially spawned by the Missouri Department of Conservation and released for fishermen to catch. Only half a dozen Ozark streams have rainbows that naturally reproduce. In the 1890s trout from a tributary of California's Sacramento River were released in Crane Creek. There is genetic evidence that the current population strongly resembles the now-threatened McCloud River redband rainbows.

Crane, the creek and the village of 1,500, are today associated with chickens and trout – not large wading birds. Those long-legged, fish-eating predators, undoubtedly great blue herons, wouldn't have been spearing trout when the creek was named in the mid-1800s. That fish is not native to the Ozarks. That said, the trout in Crane Creek are very special immigrants. "Crane Creek is perhaps the last trout water in the world to have the pure McCloud River strain of redband rainbow trout, originally found in California's McCloud River," states the website for the Missouri Trout Hunter.

Some fly fishermen assert that since the introduction of trout into Crane Creek in the late 1800s purity has been preserved by no further releases. Actually, no. Few streams have been studied as much as twenty-five-mile-long Crane Creek and its tributary Spring Creek. Missouri Department of Conservation fisheries biologist Shane Bush summarized the stocking records of Crane Creek: "Crane Creek was first stocked with rainbow trout in 1890 from the Neosho fish hatchery and they were reported reproducing in 1893. The fish raised at Neosho hatchery were McCloud River strain rainbow trout. Rainbow trout were stocked regularly in Crane Creek until 1937. Since then, stocking was only occasionally by private individuals. The stream was last stocked by MDC in 1967 when they stocked 6,000 rainbow trout from Neosho hatchery."

Spring-fed Ozark rivers will support released trout but in only a handful will they reproduce naturally. In a 2006 paper in the *Transactions of the American Fisheries Society*, researchers Dillman and Koppelman compared the genetics of Missouri's wild and hatchery trout:

> There were two important findings of the mtDNA population comparisons. First, populations from Crane Creek and its tributary, Spring Creek, were differentiable from all other rainbow trout sample collections based on the number and uniqueness of mtDNA haplotypes. The extent to which Crane Creek differed from other small, wild populations (i.e., Mill and Little Piney creeks) leads us to believe that this stream system contains descendents of the original northern California stock.

This mitochondrial DNA analysis confirms their hypothesis that "even though stocking has occurred among and within stream systems more than one hundred years, there are remnants of original stocks present today." As the streams of the California Cascades, the source of the original stockings, have been altered by dams, and the native trout often hybridized by hatchery releases, the Crane Creek population is a rare genetic pool. Purity is perhaps not an altogether useful term, as scientists suspect the late 1800s California stock had some steelhead contribution. There is no doubt the Mc-

Cloud rainbow was the primary fish from which the basic hatchery fish was created and that is now found worldwide. Generations of hatchery breeding have diminished the genetic diversity and fitness of the species. The Missouri Department of Conservation periodically collects milt from Crane Creek fish to fertilize the eggs of their hatchery strain. McCloud River redband rainbows were known for their stunning looks and ability to survive in difficult environments. It's hoped the sperm from the Crane Creek popula-

Right: Crane Creek redband rainbow caught, photographed, and released by Keith Oxby.

Below: The Missouri Department of Conservation's 818-acre Wire Road Conservation Area. More than thirty thousand trees have been planted and old fields have been converted to native grasses. Wild trout are elusive, but there are few more beautiful places where you can be skunked.

Above: Bridge over Crane Creek. Crane's city park borders the spring-fed creek.

Top: Ruins of the Missouri Pacific's roundhouse. Small towns flourished when the railroad came through.

tion can impart some of these qualities in farmed trout.

Fishermen who fell under the spell of wild trout were fearful that when Crane Creek was featured on ESPN hordes would descend on the tiny creek. Keith Oxby, an Englishman who resided in the Ozarks for several years while running a fly fishing school at Dogwood Canyon, shared that concern.

He was relieved to read a 2012 Department of Conservation report that said the population of Crane Creek rainbows, after a precipitous fall a few years earlier, "remains strong, possibly due to private ownership, low harvest rates, and adequate habitat." Oxby drolly noted, "Contributing factors were obviously the low water situation and a high level of predation from piscivores (I love that word!) like otter and heron (+ poaching?). The population improved in 2009 with 271 fish per mile possibly due to increased stream flows and reduced otter population (licensed trapping)." Presumably the herons (cranes) are allowed to eat all the trout they can catch. This small tributary of the James is a natural resource with an international reputation, Oxby discovered on a visit home:

> Crane Creek is a National Treasure and we should be proud that it is in our back yard. An anecdote I would relate about this stream involves a fly fisherman who was in a major Fly Fishing Supplier's store in London, England. On the wall was a chart giving trout species of North America and one of the smartly dressed sales associates pointed to the McCloud Rainbow trout picture and said "You know that one of the only remaining self-sustaining populations of that species are found in Crane Creek, Missouri." The fisherman replied "I know; I live there!" So even in Jolly Old England they have heard of Crane Creek, Missouri!

The small town of Crane (population 1,500) is better known regionally for tasty chickens than the hard-to-catch trout. The Crane Broiler Fest pulls in thousands from all over southwest Missouri. There are carnival rides, craft booths, and tables representing local government services. Miss Slick Chick, the queen of the Broiler Fest, rides in the lead convertible of the parade.

In the late 1940s as the tomato-canning era was winding down, farmers in northern Stone County discovered they could turn a profit raising chickens. By the 1950s, Crane was marketing millions of two-and-a-half to three-pound fowl. To celebrate the boom, the first annual Missouri Broiler Festival and Barbecue was held October 9, 1952. Since then corporations have taken over the poultry business, but the festival has grown to be four days long. Crane's Broiler Festival indicates old times and long-lost industries are not only not forgotten; they are enthusiastically celebrated.

Above and right: Crane incorporates its past into its present identity. The Crane Broiler Festival reflects this coherence.

Top left: Painting Crane Creek.

Top, right: Real photo postcard of an outing along Crane Creek circa 1910. Lest it be thought that Ozarkers are unprogressive, the gent in the center who is ignoring the ladies appears to be checking his smart phone.

Above: Machinery from the Spring Creek Mill.

Right: Spring Creek Mill at Hurley just before it burned.

Had the son of the owner of the watermill at Hurley, Missouri, been more careful with his brush fire, we could have photographed an early and conventionally nostalgic rural relic. The rambling three-story, crudely built, added-on, and deteriorating structure built in 1892 was being restored when it burned to ashes on April 3, 2005. The site today consists of a few fire-scorched and rusty pieces of machinery set among some foundation stones. Invasive weeds and sumac are already being replaced by trees. In another decade finding any evidence there was ever a historic mill here will require archaeology. In the lot next to the overgrown watermill ruins is a neat small stone filling station with a faded orange gas pump. Other machines and implements are scattered about the grounds, obsolete but not so ancient as the medieval technology of watermills.

There was a time in the 1920s and '30s when the railroad brought opportunity to this village five miles east of Crane. A 1927 Stone County booklet pronounced with only a little puffery:

> Hurley is said to be the most mutual, cooperative and moral town in Stone County. It is a small town on the Missouri Pacific between Crane and Springfield and surrounded with very fertile, productive land, and it claims proportionally, the largest trade of any town in the county. A stream of clear spring water runs through the center of the town sufficient to grind out the best flour, meal and feed; and the pretty homes and streets are all clean and the inhabitants healthy.

Mary Scott Hair, Dewey Short's cousin, wrote a column beginning in 1948 under the pen name "Samanthy" for the *Crane Chronicle*, recording the life and times of Hurleyites. Her father had once owned the Spring Creek Mill, and she and her husband and daughter worked a small farm nearby. In a 1982 interview printed in *Bittersweet* she summed up her life: "I have lived in Hurley all my life

Above: Methodist church, 1903. Down 100 from its 1920s population of 300. On an online post, Ray Gold wrote: "Even though it is not a very big place, it never was a ghost town. ...The little town of Hurley just might come back. It don't act like it's going to die."

and I probably won't live anywhere else. I am rooted and grounded in Hurley. My younger days were Hurley's best days. Sometime I wonder whether or not it was all make believe."

In the Spring 1965 issue of *White River Valley Historical Quarterly,* Mary Scott Hair described the rise and fall of milling, which was central to Hurley's economy:

> Waterpower was replaced by electricity. The great flour mills in Kansas turned out products cheap enough so that mills the size of Spring Creek Mill could not compete with them. Except for rare occasions in the 1930s, the mill did little business in making bread stuff. Mostly it ground feed of various kinds for livestock. ... The crowning blow, however, was not to the mill, but the milldam. Folks living along the Creek complained of flood hazard and petitioned the State Highway Department to blast out the dam as a safety measure. The owner, Mr. Howard, gave his consent. ... It was a sad day for us when dynamite blasts were heard. My Father turned away with tears in his eyes. I wept openly. It was no easy job, blasting out the dam, for it was put there to stay. That was 13 years ago. Nature has done her best to smooth over the rough places, but the Creek will never be the same. ...
>
> In 1918 a new concrete bridge replaced the beautiful old wooden structure. And now surveys are made every so often for the purpose, they tell us, of building a new bridge. ... Now and then in my dreams I seem to hear the rumble of wagons as they once crossed the old wooden bridge. And the distant sound of horses' hooves like muffled drums sounding the death knell of the Spring Creek Mill.

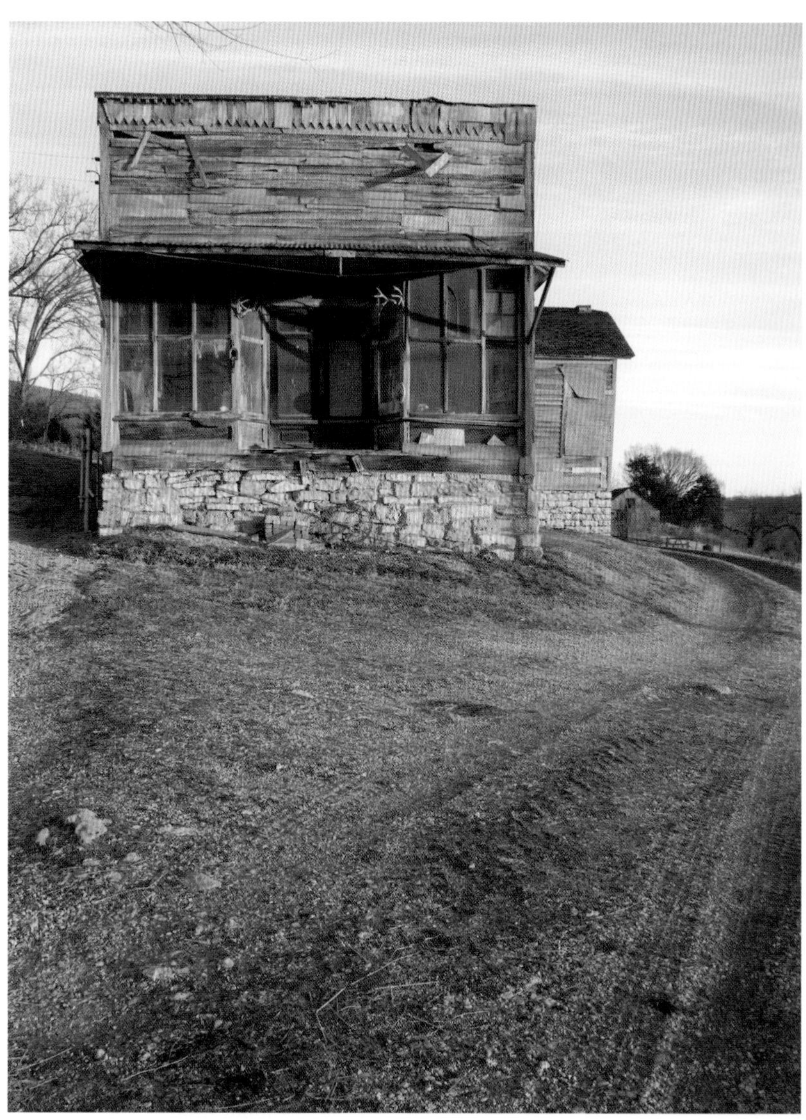

Above: Abandoned general store at Jamesville.

Charles Galloway operated the iconic Jamesville store for many years. He was referred to in the Molly Jogger book as a "pioneer merchant." A cousin, also named Charles, founded the community southeast of Springfield known as Galloway.

Jamesville is several miles north by road. Unlike Hootentown it appears on maps, and had a post office in its general store. Before 1900 the hamlet at the junction of the Finley River (or creek) was called Robertson's Mill, although the mill washed away in an 1880s flood.

Interesting as the old store/post office and its next-door resident sage, Dude White, are, a Springfield hunting and fishing club once located here is singular, even bizarre. It was a kind of *Animal House* on the James. One of its members, John Dunckel, a lumberman turned drummer, published a book, *The Molly Joggers: Tales of the Camp-fire*, in 1906 ostensibly based on the organization's outings. Most of its eighty-eight pages consist of ethnic jokes told in dialect – which is what one might expect from the pen of a traveling salesman. Irish, Swedish, Dutch, and of course African-American stereotypes fill the book, but no hillbillies. That word was just

beginning to appear in print around 1906 and had not yet replaced the hick, rube, or mountaineer as the naïve rustic of choice.

While the stories were lifted from popular books and magazines, a few pages at the beginning capture the spirit of the small club. Twice a year they pitched large tents along the James and an accomplished black cook named Shorty furnished repasts like "fried biscuits in butter, country-cured hickory-smoked ham, fried eggs, fried potatoes and onions with wild honey and sorghum on your biscuits for dessert, washed down by a cup of good coffee." Apparently copious amounts of spirits were consumed. A "neighboring mountaineer" dropped in and the boys shared their "eat and drink." As he left he acknowledged he had encountered these businessmen in town. ...

Above: Across the road from the abandoned Jamesville store, Confrey "Dude" White's barn and pasture.

Below: East of White's barn is a suburban house with a spacious driveway and a basketball court.

> "I've knowed you'uns fer many a year in your stores in Springfield, and never 'lowed they wus any fun in ye, but out here on the crick ye are just like a lot of Molly Joggers."
>
> Those who are not familiar with the different species of the finny tribe found in the James and kindred streams of Southwest Missouri, it will perhaps be interesting to know that there is a minnow inhabiting these waters – a horny-headed spotted fellow who is absolutely worthless, not even tempting the versatile appetite of gars and turtles when used as bait, and this fish is called by the natives the "Molly Jogger."

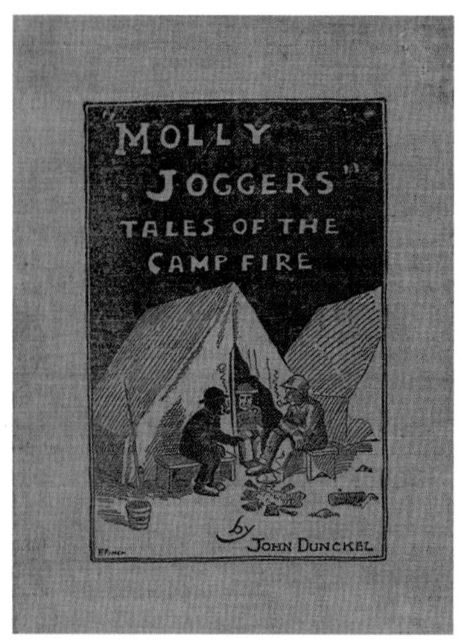

Above: Cover of the *Molly Joggers: Tales of the Campfire*, 1906. Author John Dunckel emigrated from Switzerland. He was involved in the lumber business before becoming a traveling salesman for the Springfield Grocery Company.

Below: Early 1900s photograph of the Molly Joggers, an unknown boy, and their cook Shorty. The club was organized in the late 1800s by Pennsylvania-born Cyrus H. Patterson. They became extinct in 1930 when Patterson died. Through these decades there had been a total of ten members.

> What the old mountaineer said that evening struck home, and the name was adapted at once.

Another visitor to the Molly Jogger camp did not find so much fun. "Old Phoebe" (they all used nicknames) got Pegleg Nelson, a wounded Civil War veteran, drunk, sawed off his wooden leg and floated it down the James. When the old soldier woke they tried to convince him he showed up without it.

Molly Jogger pranks continued back in Springfield. Dozens of newspaper accounts describe this group's antics. A January 26, 1897, *Leader-Democrat* reported that when member John White, "Julia," proprietor of the Springfield Candy Company, complained "the wolf was getting very close to his door," the others "at a heavy expense" purchased "a big wolf in the Indian Territory" and had it shipped to them. They muzzled the beast and tied him to the candy store's front doorknob. Unfortunately, the joke backfired as the wolf escaped before being discovered.

This amused-at-their-own-antics group did range beyond their encampment at the junction of the James and Finley. A November 6, 1899, piece in the *Leader-Democrat* gleefully related their outdoor adventures:

> The festive "Molly Joggers" of Springfield are again out on their annual hunt. Their favorite haunts are the picturesque wilds of the lower James river. They sometimes extend their savage excursions down below the mouth of the James and the fierce and reckless hunters have now and then descended the torturous White river as far as Forsyth.

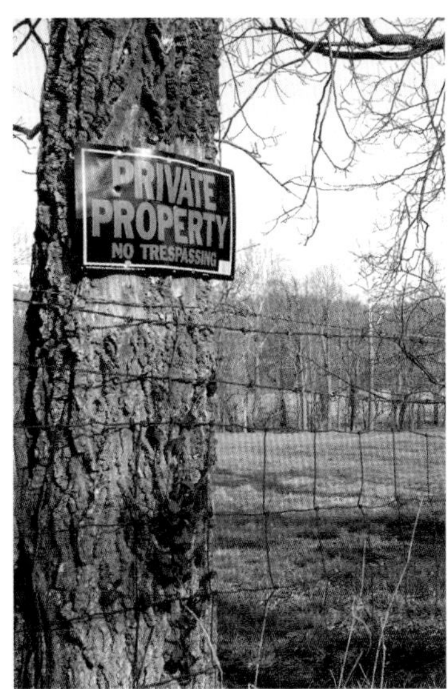

Originally Ozark natives had a very permissive attitude concerning property rights. "No Trespassing" and "Posted" signage is today common throughout the Ozarks, but universal near Springfield. Farmers take a proprietary interest in game they feed and many times hunt. Access to streams and stream banks is a more complex legal matter without universal judicial agreement or public understanding.

> The "Molly Joggers" are a strange tribe of nimrods whose real character no one ever learns till he has been initiated into this fraternity of sportsmen and taken one trip with the hunters.
>
> Woe to the squeamish-hearted tenderfoot who rashly takes the vow to obey the regulations of this fraternity, and sets out with the "Molly Joggers" on one of their autumnal expeditions. The "Molly Joggers" at home are ordinary conventional citizens. Some of them are very prominent businessmen. They are honest and industrious, make money and spend it liberally. … When required to do so by the proprieties of a social function these gentlemen wear dress coats with practiced ease and exhibit those refined manners which the best form of the times demand.
>
> But when the "Molly Joggers" cross the city limit on a hunting trip, his whole nature seems suddenly to change and the spirit of primeval savagery appears to dominate him. There are secrets among the 'Molly Joggers' that have never been revealed, but some of their wild and reckless practices are known. One inflexible law of the order is that any bird or beast or creeping thing killed on a trip must be eaten. … At night each hunter brings to camp the game he has bagged during the day. Screech owls, chicken hawks, skunks, and crows have now and then appeared on the bill of fare at the "Molly Joggers" camp.

Given the group's mean-spirited pranks and "reversion to primitive savagery," which compelled them to kill (and ceremoniously consume) anything that walked, crawled, or flew, one might guess farm folks along the James viewed the "Molly Jogger" visits with trepidation. Not so, according to Dunckel's book:

> Even to this day, in the spring or fall of the year, the "old timers" along the James river, when they meet a traveler from Springfield in the road, and after passing the usual salutations customary down there will ask "Heve you heered when the Molly Joggers is a-comin' down? Hit air about time fer them to be a-comin', and we'uns has been a-lookin' fer them fer a right smart spell."

Frontier hospitality was still practiced apparently twenty miles from bustling Springfield. City slickers hadn't yet worn out their welcome around Jamesville in the early 1900s. For all of their high jinks, the Molly Joggers shared their food and drink. Their antics gave the locals something to talk about around Galloway's potbellied stove come winter.

The old store and post office where the Molly Joggers picked up supplies has long been closed. Artfully patched up, it makes a splendid image with or without being Photoshopped. Google "Jamesville, Missouri" and several versions will come up. Dude White's barn across the highway is also no longer a required structure in the present permanent-pasture, beef cattle operation along the James. Culs-de-sac of single-family brick houses have not yet overwhelmed the rural character of Jamesville, but it's clear in the satellite photograph that the place is being suburbanized. Nixa is but ten miles;

7
6
3
2
1
4
5

Springfield is twenty. Sportsmen and sportswomen and sportskids come to this part of the James River, but not only to fish or launch canoes at the Delaware or Shelvin Rock Conservation Department Access.

Upstream, around a bend in the James, is Hidden Valley Golf Course. Would the Molly Joggers have fit in eighteen holes during their twice-yearly campouts? Just below the junction of the James and the Finley is Two Rivers Mountain Bike Park. On 380 acres Matt O'Reilly, a scion of the family that founded O'Reilly Automotive, has built eighteen miles of bike trails. The park is operated by the nonprofit Trail Spring organization. "Who's up for some major Ozark hill shredding?" was the opening sentence of a Wes Johnson *News-Leader* article (March 12, 2015). Probably not any of the Molly Joggers, we think. Golf, maybe.

Opposite: Landsat satellite image, 2014.

1. Jamesville closed country store and post office.
2. Junction of Finley Creek (River) with James River.
3. Bridge over James, no access.
4. Finley Creek.
5. Two Rivers Mountain Bike Park.
6. Highway M about 14 miles south of 14 Highway.
7. Hidden Valley Golf Course.

Right top: Finley Creek (or River) from the last bridge before its junction with the James.

Right below: Junction of the James River and the Finley.

Watermills are symbolic of the frontier's isolation and self-reliance. Iron truss bridges recall the era when the Ozarks transitioned from a subsistence, barter way of life to a market economy. Both architectural relics are endangered, particularly so the closer they are to Springfield. Route 160 crosses the Finley fifteen miles south of that hub of commerce and growth. A mile upstream (east) is Riverdale, the site of a skirmish between nostalgia and progress. This community had a succession of watermills, continually rebuilt after floods and fires, and an adjacent 1906 iron, wood-floored bridge.

Few mills are left to preserve. Even ordinary metal truss bridges are disappearing at an accelerated rate. Efforts to save these obsolete but iconic crossings usually fail. There was a spirited campaign to preserve the handsome Canton Bridge Company truss bridge at Riverdale. A 2002 www.rootsweb.com interview of Western District Christian County Commissioner, Bill Barnett, by Michelle Korgis-Fitzpatrick summarizes that conflict. Commissioner Barnett was concerned with safety and financing but sympathized with the preservationists:

Below: New concrete bridge at Riverdale across the Finley. Since 1840 a mill has been located here. A three-story structure burned in 1926, but the milldam remained a popular fishing and swimming spot. The new property owners, the Timbers at Riverdale, "a beautiful, upscale gated community," have posted heavily lawyered signage warning that trespassers will be prosecuted.

Hate to see the bridge come down because there's a lot of memories and you'd hate to destroy those memories, but its (sic) just part of the progress you might say because we're growing so fast, we are going to have to go with the flow and go with the time. ... When I was a kid, we'd go down there and jump off of the trees there with a rope on it, play in the water, and there's just not many places like that left. But now, you can't go down there and go swimming because all the landowners have got that posted that your (sic) not allowed to go on their property. ...

You'd hate to see something like that be tore down, but you've got to think of what's best for those people that travel the road and for the emergencies and things you've got to think about those things so you've got to kind of weigh them and then we couldn't afford to move the bridge and build a new one because we've got to pay for it ourselves so its (sic) just something you hate to have to do, but we just have to have a new bridge there. ... With the dam and bridge, it does make a neat and beautiful place. And I am sure a lot of people will miss it, but for safety reasons, the new bridge is going to have to be put in its place, because as the old saying goes, "Nothing last (sic) forever!"

Since Riverdale Bridge is being torn down, people have been taking a lot of pictures of the old bridge ... for the future generations yet to come that wont (sic) have the chance to see it.

Below: A near-record flood on the Finley caused the curious (like ourselves) to ignore the county's "no parking" signs and walk out on the Riverdale bridge. A small hydroelectric plant housed in the little structure uses a 115-year-old turbine from an earlier mill discovered buried in the riverbed. Plans by the Turner family to open a museum here didn't materialize and today the public is warned, "Do not enter under any circumstance."

Opposite, above: Sucker Day brings out the crowds, even attracting *Kansas City Star* feature writers.

Opposite, below: Could there be a more appropriate band booked for Sucker Day than the Finley River Boys? Eight of the eighteen species of native fish called suckers are found in that stream.

Jason Bourne is Nixa's most famous son, much better known than the ghostly bearded pioneer in the Chamber of Commerce mural. The panel explains how "Nicholas A. Inman," a mountaineer blacksmith from Tennessee, somehow morphed into Nixa. While the Chamber of Commerce has boldly proclaimed a motto, "Stability & Progress for the Future," on the wall art, six out of eight of the images are of old-time scenes including the now-replaced iron bridge and long-lost watermill at Riverdale. Nixa has progressed from a population in 1950 of five hundred to more than twenty thousand today, benefitting from Springfield's spillover.

Nixa has a celebration based on an unprogressive method of catching an Ozark bottom-dwelling fish. Sucker Day has been held in the spring since 1957 when Finis Gold, barber, one-time mayor, and American Legion commander, invented the event. Suckers are rarely caught on hook and line. When they ascend creeks to spawn they can be snagged. They are also gigged in the winter when the rivers are clear and stockpiled in freezers. Though boney, sucker are delicious when scored and deep fried. The event has grown from a novel fish fry to include talent competitions, a Little Miss Sucker Day pageant, pie-eating and bubblegum-blowing contests, numerous craft booths, and musical entertainment by bluegrass groups.

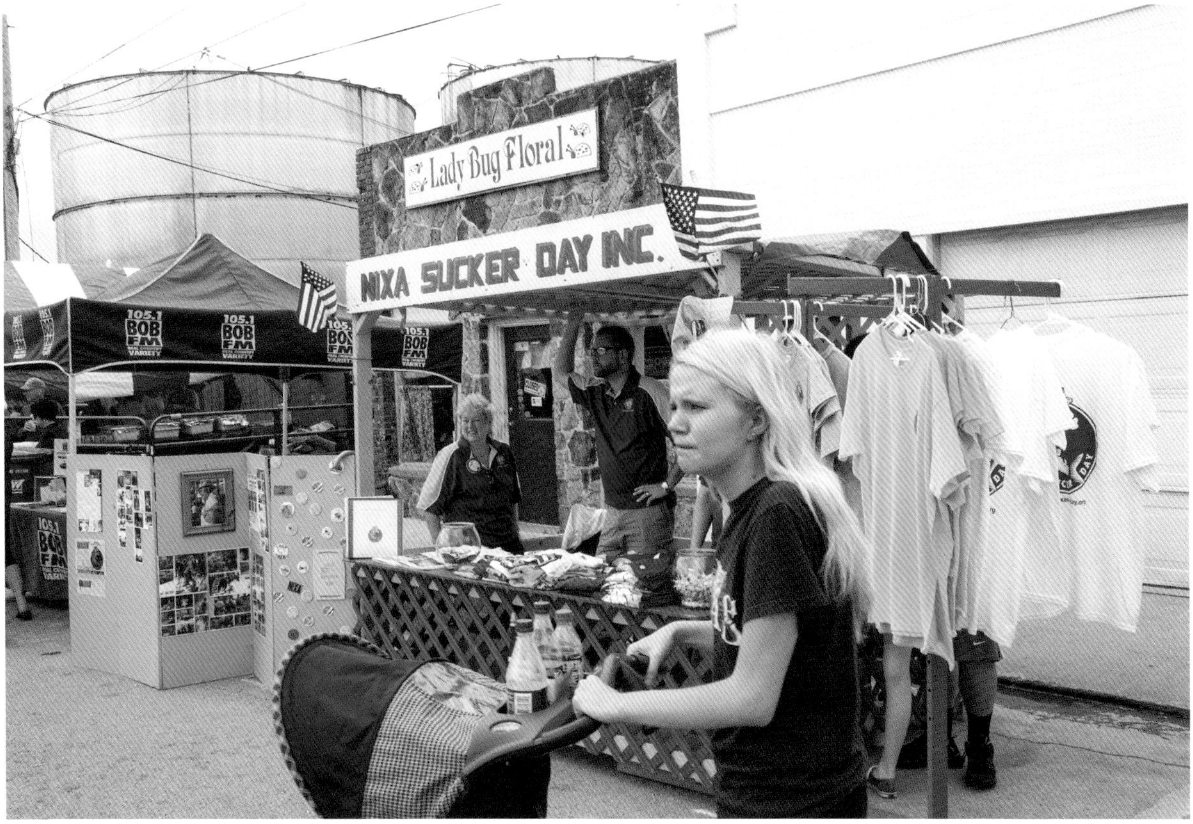
Lady Bug Floral
NIXA SUCKER DAY INC.
105.1 BOB FM

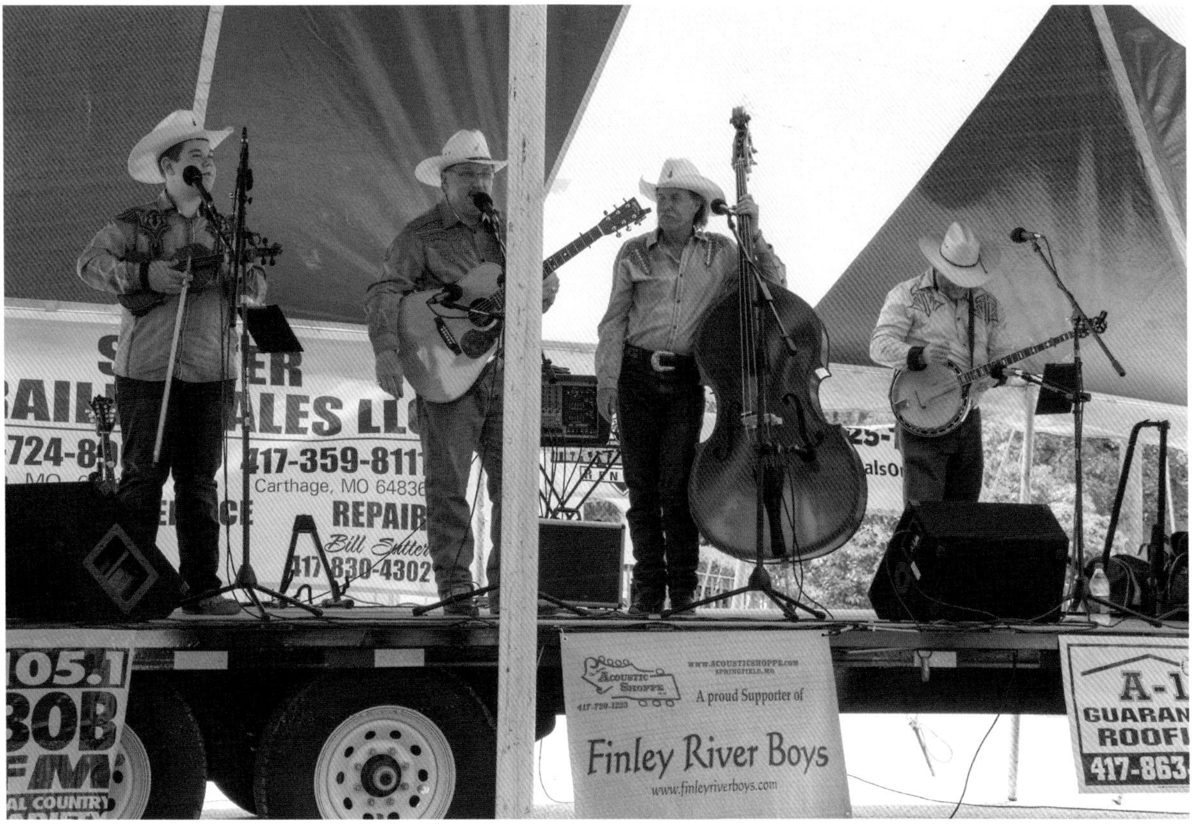
A proud Supporter of
Finley River Boys
www.finleyriverboys.com

Above: The logo of the City of Ozark features the 1922 iron bridge under which flows the Finley. The motto of the growing community is "Bridging strong tradition with bright futures."

Right: Real photo postcard, circa 1915. In 1909, the Christian County court advertised for bids for a replacement just five days after it washed away. That month they contracted with the Canton (Ohio) Bridge Company to build a metal span for $3,648.

Opposite, top: The flood of July 9, 1909 was the greatest on record. Soon after this photograph was taken the covered bridge floated off its piers and crashed into the railroad bridge visible downstream.

Opposite, bottom: Bridge at Ozark during the flood of June, 2015 when the James and Finley exceeded in places the 1909 rise. A two-lane bridge was built here in 1922. The earlier pin-connected truss bridge was taken apart and reassembled upstream at Biers Ford. Today it is known as the Riverside Bridge.

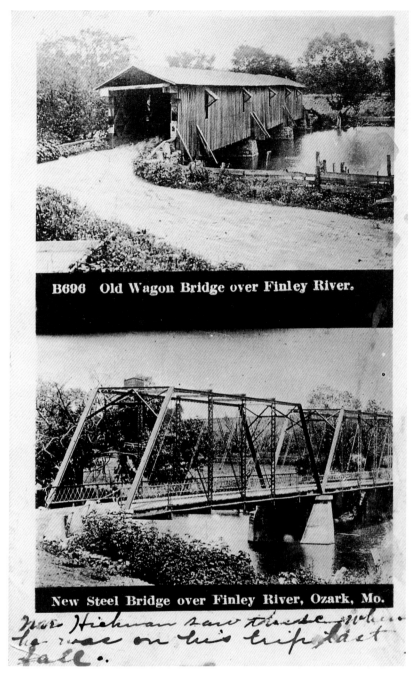

B696 Old Wagon Bridge over Finley River.

New Steel Bridge over Finley River, Ozark, Mo.

Mr. Hickman saw these when he was on his trip last fall.

Covered bridges evoke the past even more than old metal truss bridges. The popular belief that they were constructed to keep from spooking horses may have some validity, but primarily their enclosure was to protect the wood trusses from the elements. Few have survived anyway. Only four remain in Missouri.

An argument between preservationists and the forces for transportation improvement never developed in the village of Ozark. Its covered wagon bridge washed away in a 1909 flood.

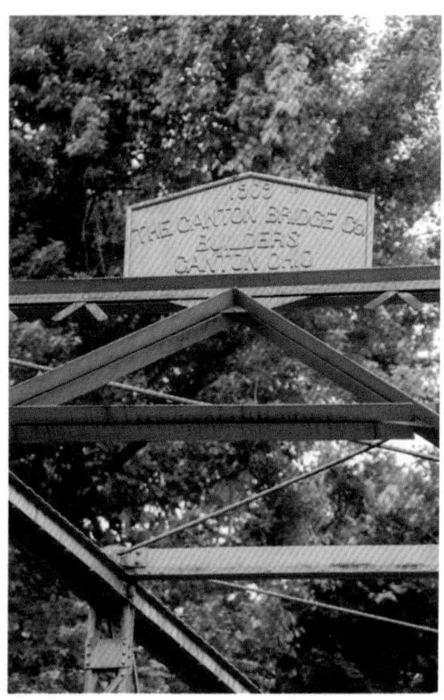

Above: Company badge, Riverside Bridge.

Christian County engaged the Canton Bridge Company of Ohio to erect half a dozen steel bridges in the early 1900s. That firm built more than six thousand bridges nationwide by 1902.

Of the popular Pratt-truss configuration, like this endangered structure, the Historic Bridge Foundation remarked:

"Pin-connected truss bridges were favored during this period because they were sturdy, reliable, and made efficient use of materials. They also could be fabricated in a factory, shipped to a site, and easily erected by local labor. ... Truss bridges themselves saw a gradual decline in popularity throughout the twentieth century as simpler structure types became feasible to construct, such as the steel stringer (beam) bridge, concrete T-beam bridge, and pre-stressed concrete bridges."

A year after the steel bridge by the mill and powerhouse at Ozark was reassembled over Biers Ford, young Howard Garrison bought five acres of a cornfield on the bank of the Finley next to the bridge and built a restaurant he named Riverside Inn. Apparently Howard believed those who were enforcing the Eighteenth Amendment would not notice that highballs were being served in such a rural setting. On the contrary, he was visited by the feds on a "rum raid" in 1929 and again in 1949 for having two slot machines. He did two years on the first charge and a year on the second. The bridge became known as the Riverside Bridge.

When Howard Garrison, restaurateur, bootlegger, artist, died in 1974, the restaurant employed thirty and could accommodate eight hundred. He had sold the legendary operation to Jack Engler four years earlier. Engler then sold the property for $945,823, primarily funded by a FEMA mitigation grant to the state for the acquisition of floodprone property. No sooner had the rambling structure been razed than new dramatics flared up along the Finley north of Ozark. This time it was the old moved metal bridge, not the speakeasy with great fried chicken and stiff old-fashioneds, that made the news.

In September 2010, a state bridge inspector declared it unsafe and closed it. By then, twelve hundred cars a day were crossing the Finley; there was pressure to replace it with a new, safe bridge. "It's a beautiful architectural piece of history and I'd like to see it here for generations to come," said Kris Dyer, who founded the Riverside Bridge Initiative. Quickly they got more than three thousand likes on Facebook and mounted a formidable public relations campaign to fix the old bridge. Miraculously, they succeeded in convincing county officials to spend $170,000 to effect a five-year fix, hoping to find federal funds for a complete overhaul, which would cost more than three million – as much as a new structure.

In 2013, the Missouri Bicycle and Pedestrian Federation website posted the good news: "Huge Victory for Save the Riverside Bridge Advocates as Historic Bridge Re-Opens." Local preservationists were elated when county officials held a ribbon cutting to re-open the newly repaired bridge. "I started crying. Crossing the bridge is emotional for me. It was lots of blood, sweat and tears," said Dyer. The group won the Ammann Award for Best Preservation Practice. Their euphoria was short-lived.

"This flood of really epic proportions certainly speeded up our timeline," said John Elkins of the Ozark Special Road District of the deleterious effect the July 10, 2015, high water had on the Riverside

Above, left: Washed-out road, Riverside Bridge.

Above, right: Riverside Inn was just around the bend on Riverside Drive. Floods periodically damaged both.

Being listed on the National Register of Historic Places (NRHP) might help preservation efforts to secure state and federal funds for restoration. Unfortunately, the Missouri Department of Transportation's (MODOT) 1988 Bridge Inventory considers the Riverside Bridge "NRHP non-eligible (typical example of common bridge type)." The Historic Bridge Foundation disagrees: "Riverside Bridge is historically and technologically significant ... (It) is further an example of a bridge that has become rare through attrition on a statewide basis."

Bridge. *The Christian County Headliner News* reported a MODOT inspector found "major damage ranging from sway bracing busting loose, to bent lower cords, to buckling steel – all from debris that crashed into the bridge." Elkins believed this will require a completely new structure. He was uncertain where that would leave preserving the historic bridge. "If a group is interested in saving the bridge for foot traffic, it's certainly a possibility." That, he said, "would require relocation of the bridge. I don't see it happening at the current location."

In 2010, the Historic Bridge Foundation listed "numerous preservation solutions for the Riverside Bridge." Recent developments may have diminished the best option of repairing it and leaving it in its present location. Because federal funds were used to buy out the Riverside Inn, restrictive covenants likely prohibit building a new road access to a new bridge.

Federal law requires that before destruction they must "first make the historic bridge available for donation to a state, locality, or responsible private entity." MODOT will even sweeten the free bridge offer by chipping in up to 80 percent of the demolition costs. Remember, it is pin-connected. It's easily disassembled. Building piers and putting it back up is another matter. But the Riverside Bridge was moved once – perhaps it can be moved again. A last resort could be taking it apart and storing it. They take up a remarkably small amount of space when in a disassembled state stacked up on the ground. Then, when our civilization realizes what a marvel of engineering and architectural perfection these solutions to stream crossings are, it can be reassembled with great fanfare.

Above: Lindenlure dam and mill. Photograph, 1920s by Domino Danzero. Courtesy Missouri State University Archives.

Dr. J. C. Young built a hotel and resort at Linden and had a contest to name his new venture. Mrs. Casper Tracey won and incorporated the winning name in a poem:

When the world looks dark and dreary; and you wouldn't give a darn Whether you go on living longer Or kick off all free from harm.

When you're traveled here and yonder, and returned dissatisfied; because all the scenes and places Failed to calm your thoughts inside.

For the scenes were artificial, All made by the hand of man; And were advertised for fishing Where there was mostly mud and sand.

If you enjoy real Ozark scenery, And water that's clear and pure; Just pack your troubles in your old kit bag, And come down to Lindenlure.

Socializing with friends by the river over a drink didn't stop after the Riverside Inn was torn down, but the new revelry was less sedate. "Riverside rowdiness creates fury on the Finley," read the headline of a May 20, 2014, *News-Leader* article: "Once the property became property of the county river-goers began taking advantage by using the land as an access point for the Finley River. Property owners who are living in a quiet neighborhood now have tourists wandering into their backyard. ... Due to a similar situation of property owners attempting to keep visitors from partying near the Linden dam north of Sparta, Kyle is familiar with the laws that govern access to Missouri rivers."

Sheriff Joey Kyle's education on riverine access law began in 2011 when his office was asked to keep recreationists out of the construction site for a new bridge on Highway 125 across the Finley at a site known as Lindenlure. Mills were gathering places in pioneer days and Linden Mill upstream from Ozark built on that tradition by becoming a commercial resort. "Spend the Week-End at Linden – Boating, Swimming, Fishing. Cabins and Tents," read an ad in a 1923 Springfield paper. By the twenty-first century it had become a gated private community. Folks still came to the river; however, not all of them were families bringing their children to wade in the Finley after Sunday school. In 2008, "Brouser" answered an online question about where to find a decent swimming hole around Springfield: "Lindenlure is a big place to go for that kind of activity, I guess. I think you are required to have at least 5 tattoos, with a minimum of one being a jailhouse tattoo. And if you bring a cooler with beer, nothing pricier than Natural Light, or you're just showing off." Not typical, perhaps, but gravel bars all over the Ozarks attest to a widespread indifference to picking up one's litter.

Members of the Lindenlure Homeowners Association apparently

believed a solution to the problem of unruly recreationists would be to hire the off-duty deputies to continue keeping people out of the river. Members of the Christian County Sheriff's Department began prohibiting parking near the now-completed bridge and restricting access to the dam, even threatening arrest over a bullhorn. When one Davy Cross was turned away he promptly organized Free Linden and set about educating the sheriff, the prosecuting attorney, and county officials on his reading of riparian law.

Reluctantly, Kyle acknowledged that recreationists had the right to use the river below the high water mark. Sheriff Joey Kyle, who the Free Linden website blamed for the harsh enforcement of trespassing laws, would later plead guilty to embezzlement and aiding fraud. He was ordered to repay $71,640 and sentenced to one year and a day in federal prison.

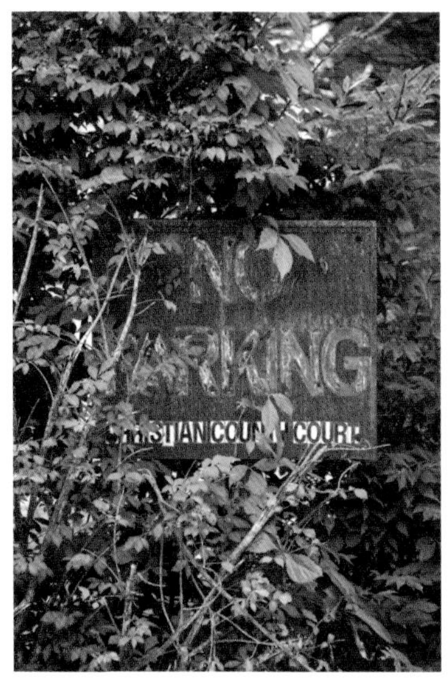

Above: Fading sign from the dispute over river access at Lindenlure.

Right top: Landowners put boulders across the Finley and spraypainted them with purple paint to deter trespassers.

Right bottom: The public has regained access to the dam at Lindenlure. Most visitors remove their trash, but not all.

The headwaters of both the James and Finley Rivers can be seen in this USGS topographic map of part of southeast Webster County. On the relatively flat divide between these two streams runs the Burlington Northern (formerly the Frisco) Railroad and US Route 60. Seymour's history is intertwined with both transportation arteries. Route 60 hasn't the cult status of Route 66 (now I-44), which slices through a corner of Webster County, just north of the James River. Route 60 follows an even older overland trail from Santa Monica, California, to Virginia Beach, Virginia.

Some gullies in Wright County are part of the James, and there are a few intermittent creeks that flow into the Finley in Douglas County, but Webster County is the primary source of both streams. Webster is overall the highest county in Missouri. Taum Sauk Mountain (elevation 1,772 feet) is only forty feet higher than the highest point in the James's watershed. Because there is not as much local relief, Webster County's landscape is not as dramatic as the granite peaks of Iron County.

When the James reaches Galena, a few miles from the backed-up waters of Table Rock Dam, it will have fallen about seven hundred feet. That's enough fall to have cut into the sedimentary rocks throughout that journey of about one hundred miles. The flow of the upper James isn't great enough to allow floating, so its recreational history is small compared to the famous float trips that put Galena on sportsmen's maps.

That vacationers haven't flocked to this pastoral scenery in the past has not deterred the Seymour Community Betterment Group from pursuing a plan to bring tourists to "our neck of the woods" to "capitalize on a quaint weekend in the country." Seymour and several small towns along Route 60 asked for help from the Missouri State University Geotourism Department. Senior instructor Linnea Iantria, assisted by her students and the Missouri Department of Tourism, MODOT, and the USDA, organized workshops to create a "Homegrown Highway" promotion of the "little known gems that highlight the uniqueness of the area's culture ... the whole idea is to protect the culture and heritage, but it's a rural area so what we're doing is enhancing that rural-ness."

White spaces on the map are cleared land. Green indicates forested areas along waterways and slopes. There are remnants of general farming days, closed-up country stores, abandoned barns, and silos, but having larger level areas and better access to markets, Webster County overall has had a more prosperous agricultural development than the White River hills.

EAST DALLAS
HIGH PRAIRIE
HAZELWOOD
FINLEY
EAST BENTON
Seymour
Diggins
SEYMOUR STATE WILDLIFE MANAGEMENT AREA

Above: Horse-drawn buggies with dark-clothed passengers are often encountered on the roads around Seymour. In 1968, a group of old order Amish found land in Webster County affordable and amenable to their farming techniques. Many Amish men find off-farm employment as carpenters or laborers. Driving automobiles is prohibited, so they contract with outsiders for transportation to work sites and rides to farmers markets in surrounding towns, where some families sell vegetables, cheeses, and honey.

Right: Mountaindale Spring essentially begins the permanent flow of the James River.

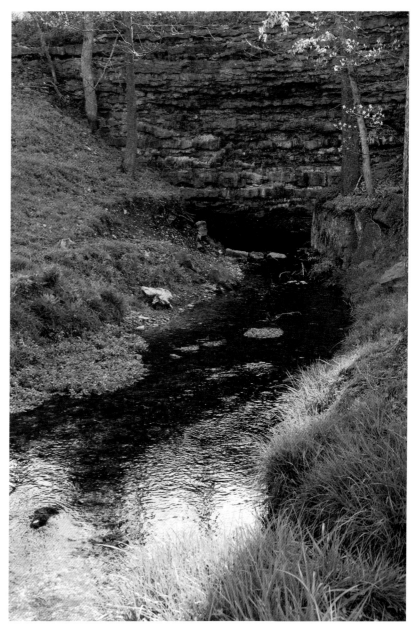

Several miles of intermittent, usually dry streams are above Mountaindale Spring (above), but this and a few smaller springs are the beginning of the permanent flow of the James. They flow from one half to more than three-and-a-half million gallons a day. *Springs of Missouri,* Vineyard and Feder (1974), describes this reliable but variable spring just north of Seymour: "Mountaindale Spring is at an altitude of 1,520 feet above sea level, one of the highest springs in Missouri to have substantial perennial flow. The spring emerges from a low bluff of limestone and flows into a small, walled-in basin. The water forms a spring branch, which is lined with water cress. ... There are numerous springs in the vicinity of Mountaindale Spring and together they serve as water supplies for cattle."

Above: Rolling uplands of Webster County have a Midwestern pastoral appearance.

Right: Not all livestock operations have a bull; many use artificial insemination.

This high plateau around Seymour contains the headwaters for both the James and the Finley. Tall fescue pastures with cow-calf ranching is the dominant land use. Amish farmers also raise cattle but grow vegetable gardens and practice a more diversified agriculture reminiscent of general farms of the past. They do not practice mechanized farming. Amish homesteads can be recognized by their windmills and the absence of power or telephone lines.

Above: Fallen trees affect the hydrology of streams.

Right: Large gravel bars on small creeks indicate instability often due to improvident clearing of stream bank trees.

Following page: The James at a low-water bridge in Webster County.

Highways follow the undissected ground between rivers. A few miles on either side of Route 60, the landscape changes. Though not as rugged as the lower James River as it nears the White, valleys cut by the upper reaches of the James and Finley are quite Ozarkian – wooded slopes through which run clear, gravel-filled streambeds.

FALLS OF FINLEY RIVER, ON THE MEMPHIS ROUTE, NEAR SEYMOUR, MO.

"By virtue of its charm, drive-in accessibility, and proximity to Highway 60, Finley Falls deserves more publicity than it gets," wrote Thomas R. Beveridge in *Geologic Wonders and Curiosities of Missouri*:

> The Falls formed where Finley Creek crosses a resistant ledge of the Swan Creek Sandstone Member of the Cotter Dolomite. Erosion of dolomite beds above and below the tougher sandstone leaves this rock locally interrupting the topography as a low escarpment which paves the bed of Finley Creek to produce a natural low-water ford with the Falls forming the downstream edge of the "slab."

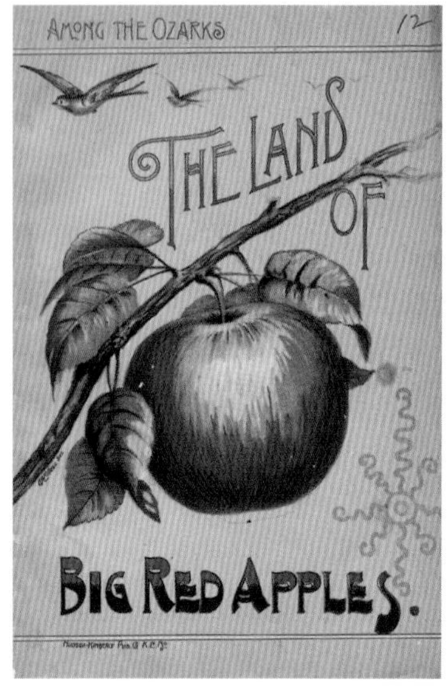

Above: Pamphlet put out in 1891 promoting the profitability of orchards along the route of the Kansas City, Ft. Scott & Memphis Railroad.

Top: Engraving from the 1891 pamphlet of Finley Falls.

Opposite: Finley Falls, the highest (possibly the only) natural waterfall in the James River basin.

In many parts of the world, the sixty-yard-wide plunge of seven feet would go unnoticed. In the context of the relatively flat Springfield Plateau in Webster County it is a curiosity. Finley Falls was wondrous enough to have a detailed steel engraving of it included in an 1891 railroad pamphlet, *The Land of Big Red Apples*. This forty-page treatise on fruit farming in the Ozarks surrendered few pages to anything that did not promote growing apples, peaches, and even raspberries in the admittedly rocky soils along the rail line's route through southern Missouri. Would D. S. Holman, treasurer of the State Horticultural Society, lie? "God must have looked on Missouri when he said: It is good, very good":

> I doubt if another section in the whole country can grow so many, and so well, the fruits which succeed in South Missouri. The adaptation to the apple and other fruits is no longer a question in Missouri, but the extent of the fruit resources of Missouri is a problem. Already millions of bushels of Missouri apples are annually grown and there are millions of acres of her best fruit lands unsubdued – in brush, woods, vines, briars, and grass to-day – cheap lands, too.
>
> I have no fruit lands to sell, sir, and no axe to grind when I call attention to the Ozark plateau of many miles in length and the timbered hills on both sides of this plateau where small money, large muscle, a good will and an active brain would achieve an annual success, when richer bottom lands, valley or prairie, better for agriculture would not, from fogs and frosts, gives (sic) crops of fruit so sweet nor so surely. Similar rough lands in other portions of the state, ignored because rough and hilly, will yet be planted to fruit and found the best.

State and federal government agencies also encouraged new agricultural specialties. The Missouri General Assembly funded a Fruit Experimental Station at Mountain Grove in 1899. Apple culture spread along Ozark railroads, but plantings were especially abundant near Koshkanong and Marionville, and around Seymour. In the early 1900s, Missouri claimed to lead the nation in apple production. Washington State today markets 64 percent of all the apples grown in the US. Missouri is number seventeen with less

Above: Mural on the wall of Seymour Auto Parts.

The old order Amish in the horse-drawn buggy will not be patronizing the Seymour Auto parts store they are passing. Depicted on the store's wall is a puffy cloud vision of the early apple industry, which began during an earlier horse-and-buggy era. These contemporary practitioners of pre-industrial farming have their treadle sewing machines repaired at Jan's Fabrics and Quilts.

All the wall art on these two pages was painted by Sharon Young. Mrs. Young, a registered nurse and CEO of a health consulting company, is knowledgeable about local history, although she is a native of Lawrence, Kansas.

than one-half a percent. What happened?

As with the tomato boom, other regions were found to be more naturally suited, had better access to markets, and their owners were more willing to invest in new technologies. Droughts, pests, periods of excess production, and the Depression adversely affected undercapitalized Ozark fruit growers. Labor shortages began during World War II and were factors for both apple and tomato producers. There are still commercial orchards, but the days when lines of boxcars full of apples rolled out of small Ozark towns are gone.

Crane celebrates its lost broiler industry with a festival. Nixa themes a street fair and fish fry on a bygone fishing technique. Seymour remembers the days when that town claimed the title of "Apple Capital of Missouri" with an annual apple festival. Sponsored by the Seymour Merchants Association the event attracts more than fifteen thousand to the town of two thousand located between the headwaters of the James and the Finley. Their promotion states, "Over the three-day event you can be entertained with 100+ craft and various vendors, FREE live entertainment, and on Saturday enjoy a 5K run, parade, Johnny Appleseed contest, decorated bike contest, several apple contests and auction, apple peel-

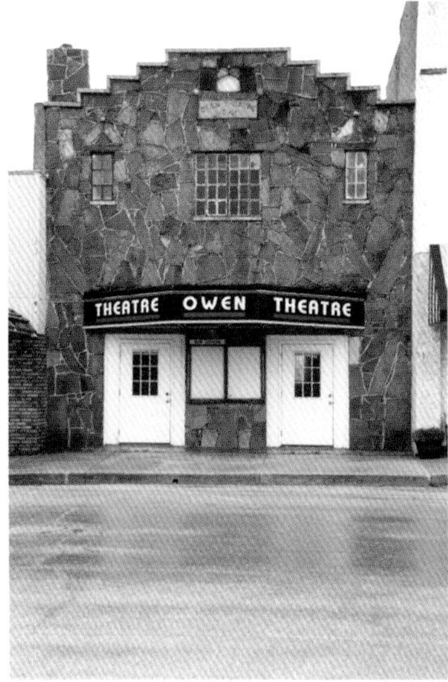

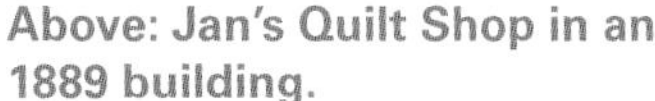

Above: Jan's Quilt Shop in an 1889 building.

Above, right: Waiting for the vanished Frisco by their vanished depot.

Top: Owen Theater. This family brought Hollywood to Seymour beginning in 1908. They also had a drive-in. Both are now closed.

ing contest, apple princess contest, and so much more."

Two murals commemorate Seymour's agricultural and transportation history respectively. The relatively flat divide between the James and the Finley is a good corridor. In the late 1800s, the Frisco railroad came through. On the side of Seymour Auto Parts building, a pastoral scene features an apple stand and fruit-laden trees. A building next to the tracks (now Burlington Northern) now depicts the long-gone Frisco Depot. US Route 60 now skirts the edge of town, north of its original route through the business district. Unlike many small bypassed towns, Seymour has open enterprises, a few with hitching posts for Amish customers. The 1941 native stone Owen movie theater on the square could not justify converting to digital projection equipment and closed in 2010. It has been purchased by the local arts council and will be refurbished.

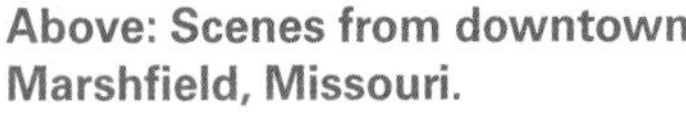

Above: Scenes from downtown Marshfield, Missouri.

Why settlers from Tennessee and Kentucky would name an Ozark county for Daniel Webster, a Whig Yankee politician, and its county seat for his hometown in Massachusetts is curious. Marshfield, population seven thousand, in Webster County, has, like Seymour, good rail and highway connections. Route 66 went through town before I-44 bypassed the square. A mural correctly states this county's superior, but imperceptible, elevation, "Top of the Ozarks." Illustrated are a horse-drawn Amish buggy and a less recognizable image of the Hubble space telescope. Astronomer Edwin Hubble was born here.

Above: There are some marshy areas in Marshfield, but that is not how it got its name. Webster County's seat got its name from Marshfield, Massachusetts in 1855. Its population is a little over seven thousand.

Below: Printed postcard. Milldam, upper James River, circa 1910.

Marshfield is at the northern edge of the James River basin. Turnbo Creek collects rains from the south part of town. Branches of the Niangua River and the Pomme de Terre drain the northern section. Dairies are mixed in with cow-calf operations in these tributaries of the Osage system, which flow through generally less hilly country than those White River tributaries.

Having interacted earlier with urban markets and having more immigration than Stone County (at least until recently when Table Rock Dam changed the demographic), the recollections of Webster countians contain less folklorish mythos. Unlike the image of life in the hills along the lower James, which has been molded by novelists, promoters of tourism, and folklorists, Webster County's local history has a more typical Midwestern rural flavor. Its landscape and land use resemble the plains of the central US, except where rivers have trenched the plateau.

There are few vintage photographs of its streams. Real photo postcards were produced to sell to visitors. Recreational development here consisted of renting cabins and selling gas to tourists on their way to the Shepherd of the Hills Country. Still, we encountered a country picker on a sidewalk off the square playing the kind of music that draws folks to Branson. There is a smattering of Ozarkian culture as the original settlers were largely southern highlanders, but its better farmland and access to markets have created subtle differences.

GUY L. WADE.
SCENE ON THE JAMES, MARSHFIELD, MO.
HAND-COLORED.

Above: Rutledge-Wilson Farm Community Park, Springfield.

Top: A country cemetery, a hay-field, and a cluster of suburban houses near Pearson Creek.

Opposite: Riverside Bridge over the Finley near Ozark is closed due to flood damage.

Deeper rivers with smaller gravel bars may never return, although grass and cattle have been reestablished as the dominant land use, which is a less erosional combination than corn and hogs. Between pioneer free ranges and today's fescue pastures, there were many now-abandoned efforts to use the region's soil to grow a profit. The public is likely unaware of these struggles, as country life is presented in movies and media as an unchanging romanticized version of the general farm at the beginning of the twentieth century. Driving the back roads of the James River basin we didn't hear any "with a cluck-cluck here, and a moo-moo there." Old MacDonald's Farm is no more. There have been leaders of Springfield's business community who strenuously objected to the unprogressive image of the Ozark hillbilly, but urban booster and suburbanite alike are attracted to a romantic vision of country life. In *Landscape and Images* (2005), John R. Stilgoe links rural nostalgia to the Jeffersonian American past:

> The single-family house on a plot of land remains a monument to the farm so fundamental to United States history. The front lawn endures as a meadow, the backyard as pasture for livestock nowadays reduced to dog and cat, while the lone fruit tree recalls the orchard and the vegetable garden recalls the arable fields. ... Hobgoblins still haunt suburbs, making clear the vitality of the ancient attachment so many Americans feel toward a piece of land and a house they shape pretty much as they please, exactly as generations of peasants, then farmers, did before them.

SPRINGFIELD

Above: Storm drain cover. The city of Springfield held a manhole cover design contest in 2007. Matt Moller's art and Tim Burrows' phrase "Upstream Starts Here" were the winners. All new storm drains hereafter will use these decorative and ecologically themed iron covers.

Trending north from its junction with the White River, the James Fork abruptly turns to the east where Wilson Creek empties in. From that point the James skirts the southern edge of Springfield and makes a big hook before reaching its headwaters in Webster County. Upstream doesn't really start in Springfield, as the manhole cover proclaims, but most of the James' environmental issues do. Along with excessive nutrients, a lot of how the James River is perceived and utilized flows from Springfield.

Springfield is not only the largest town in the James River basin; it's the only real city in the entire fifty-five thousand square mile Ozark region. The James runs along Springfield's southern edge because it encounters a plateau, a higher, less dissected part of the Ozark uplift. Plains are better construction sites than river valleys with steep hills eroded into ravines. This gently rolling landscape allowed overland access to St. Louis and the southwest. Once prairie, its farmland is more productive than the rugged, forested Ozarks.

In *The Geography of the Ozark Highland of Missouri* (1920), Carl O. Sauer notes that this juncture of forest and grasslands was an ideal town site:

Vest Pocket
Map and Epitome.
MISSOURI-ARKANSAS
OZARKS
66
65
60
160
13
123
CONVENIENT TO
SPRINGFIELD
MISSOURI

Above: Chamber of Commerce "Vest Pocket Map and Epitome," 1930s. Not only does the little giveaway depict a leaping bass bigger than a john boat, it exaggerates the town's population - 70,000 wasn't reached until the late 1950s. Paradoxically the text extols both wild river recreation and up-to-date tourist amenities. Ozark streams are "lousy" with "slim bronze beauties" (smallmouth bass). Is Springfield the gateway to primitive recreation or the hub of "excellent roads" that lead to "modern facilities with electric lighting, movies, and dance pavilions"?

> Springfield, settled in 1822-23, became the most flourishing town on the western border. It was located on the margin of Kickapoo Prairie, one of the finest and largest bodies of farmland in the Ozarks, and controlled the trade of this prairie. The site of the village was determined by an excellent spring and power site. Here also the roads from Warsaw and St. Louis crossed, the former skirting the western margin of the dissected country, the course of the latter determined by watersheds, both meeting at Springfield because of topographic conditions.

Settlers in the early 1820s needed the permission of the Delaware, who occupied the southern half of what is now Greene County from 1813 to 1829. Squatters had made their way to the upper James just before this often-displaced tribe arrived. Most squatters were sent packing. When again the Delawares were relocated to Kansas some of the Americans returned.

By 1830, the Indians signed yet more treaties, and left. Wagons began arriving bringing families from Tennessee, and other Southern border states. Before long, tradesmen, land speculators, lawyers, and sundry businessmen and professionals would arrive. Around Springfield, the tempo of life created by this class of frontiersmen sent less ambitious settlers back into the rough country to continue a less hectic lifestyle.

In 1838 the first paper was published here, *The Ozark Standard.* "So many newspapers in so sparsely settled country caused confusion, bolting and independent thinkers and parties lost to some extent the control of their members; since then Springfield has been a nursery of politicians and could trot out one or a dozen athletic intellects at any time to champion any question, home or foreign," wrote L. H. Murray in *Personal Reminiscences and Fragments of the Early History of Springfield and Greene County Missouri* (1907).

Fractured political opinions remain a Springfield specialty. Accounts of its history are less pluralistic. All seemed to accept the stock pioneer story – arrival before the Indians departed, a heroic fight to survive, poverty in a log cabin wearing homespun, and ultimate triumph over savage nature.

Local accounts acknowledge that Springfield was an excellent site for development. After proclaiming that the Kickapoo Prairie has "many intelligent and enterprising farmers," R. I. Holcombe in *The History of Greene County, Missouri* (1883) discusses the water resources of Clay Township with aesthetic appreciation:

> The James fork of White River - usually called "the James," and sometimes "the Jeems" - flows through the township from northeast to southwest and adds no little to its beauty and general advantages. There are numerous fine springs and some beautiful caves, and, in-

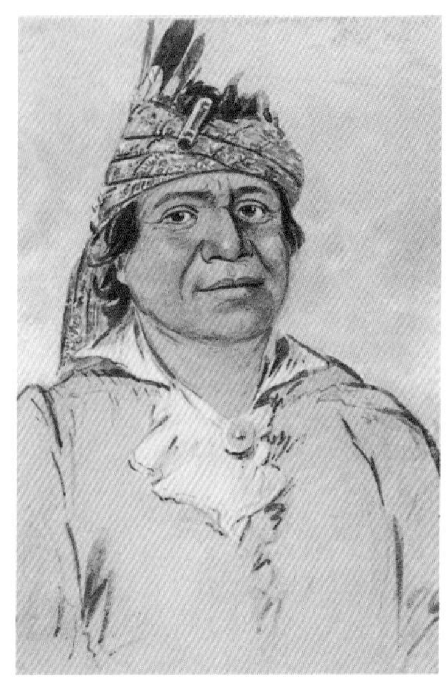

Above: Ni-co-man, a second Delaware chief. Painted in 1830 by George Catlin.

Only twelve miles from present-day Springfield along the James River was an encampment of 2,500 Delaware Indians relocated from Ohio. In the mid 1820s, there were as many as 8,000 other dislocated members of Eastern tribes in southwestern Missouri. Game became scarce. There was bitter conflict between these immigrant groups and the native Osages, who still hunted their ceded territory.

A great fortune was begun here by Indian trader William Gilliss. When the Delawares left, he accompanied them to Northeast Kansas. Gilliss became a founder of Kansas City, and one of its richest citizens.

> deed, much beautiful scenery. For not all of the land is here level and valuable for agricultural purposes, but much is broken and rough and wild, though picturesque.

Holcombe doesn't find "beautiful scenery" in Washington Township, which lies between the James and the Finley in southeast Greene County. Living a contemporary pioneer life has not imparted the virtues such a hard life gave the original settlers. Unlike later Appalachian and Ozark writers, he does not find isolated hillfolk "our contemporary ancestors in the flesh." He wishes they were dead:

> For the most part its soil is poor and unproductive, and its people are not of the most thrifty and enterprising, having little taste for books and newspapers and but a meager acquaintance with the outside world.
>
> Pioneer life, in many respects, is lived by the people of Washington. The old log cabins, with the mud-and-stick chimneys, the carpetless doors, the rough interiors and rougher exteriors; the homespun and home-made clothing, the guns, and dogs, and other adjuncts of frontier life are still to be seen here. There is no progress or desire for any improvement. The people are mostly uncommunicative, suspicious of strangers, and seemingly desire nothing but to be let alone. Their motto is "laissez faire," and while in obeying it they are singularly persistent and consistent, they are often ridiculous. Perhaps the best thing a large majority of the old fogies of this township could do would be to die and go straight to heaven, and give room on earth to others who would not become mere cumberers of the ground.

Scornful as Holcombe was of hillfolk, he thought the log cabin-dwelling founders of Springfield had the "gallantry and bravery of revolutionary soldiers."

John Polk Campbell was universally considered chief among "that army of heroes known as the old pioneers," who merited their "names emblazoned upon the pages of their country's history." He was, like most of the settlers of the Ozarks, of Scotch-Irish heritage. Campbell, and the other Tennesseans who would be instrumental in creating a town on the edge of the James and the prairie, were not like their deep Ozarks kinsmen who cleared a few acres for corn, built a cabin from the oaks, and let their hogs loose in the woods to fatten on acorns.

Before the Delaware, Kickapoo, and occasional wandering Osage vacated southwestern Missouri Territory, John and brother Madison Campbell scouted the upper James River valley. They found good land and living springs along upper Wilson Creek, now called Jordan Creek. John P. Campbell cut his initials into an ash tree near a spring accessed through a long fissure in the rock. In 1830 the Campbells returned with their families and several other Maury County, Tennessee, citizens and their slaves and began con-

Above: Marker locating the "natural well" John Polk Campbell and other settlers depended on. The marker is embedded in the wall of National Audio Company across from Founders Park. It has been moved due to development from its original 1920s location, but not far.

The town was first known as Campbell and Fulbright Springs. Within six years of its settlement, it was named the seat of the new Greene County, when Campbell donated fifty acres of land to create a grand Public Square to house the county courthouse.

As more and more settlers arrived – the majority of them from Tennessee – a general store, a school, a post office, a church, and a jail appeared. By 1838, when the town was first incorporated, its name had been changed to the shorter "Springfield." "The village was a rough-and-tumble settlement in the 1840s; municipal authority was lax and dramshop owners and temperance advocates were bitter enemies."

structing a town from the wilderness. An account of these days seen through the eyes of Campbell's daughter, Mrs. Rush C. Owen, was published in *The Daily Leader*, August 3, 1876:

> Piloted by the Kickapoos they went some distance up the James, and made arrangements with an old trapper to get out their house logs ready to be put up immediately upon their return. They had selected lands where Springfield now stands. They found four springs, whose branches united formed Wilson creek. About the center of the area between these springs was a natural well of wonderful depth, now known to be a subterranean lake, hard by, where my father "squatted" after a toilsome journey through the wilderness.
>
> Springfield soon became a habitation with a name. Cabins or round poles were hastily put up and filled with immigrants. My father vacated and built thirteen times in one year, to accommodate newcomers. Log huts filled with merchandise, groceries, soon did a thriving trade with the Indians and immigrants.

Mrs. Owen tells of an incident in which a friendly Kickapoo killed a drunken Osage, who intended to make her mother his squaw. John Campbell sadly cannot find and protect their heroic Indian friend and he fears the Osage have retaliated. She concludes with a rumination on the winning of the West:

> So ends the story of the Kickapoos, the bravest and noblest of red men. They had long loved this land, and though the last must go, he made the exit of a hero. Thus were the red faced warriors driven from the home of their ancestors, the land of crystal waters, where the sun was brightest, the air purest, and the Great Spirit watched over them and the red children with a sleepless eye.
>
> Such, however, is the law of the earth, governed by the reason of men, that is the dictates of conscience; which through the soul emanates from God. Springfield ... was destined to become a great city in a civilized and Christianized world, and though we may have robbed the savage of one of the grandest places on earth, we have done that which would have otherwise never been, and in so building a great city and developing a wonderful country, we have gained the smiling appreciation of Providence and the admiration of mankind

Founders Park, created in the 1990s, is located sixty feet south of Campbell's natural well, which was paved over in 1884. The space consists of huge concrete blocks to which are affixed enlarged historical photographs, and brass plaques with appropriate text. Said to be inspired by the Phenix Quarry in north Greene County, the architecture has a Cubist flare, the raw concrete brutal, and though the plaques are difficult to read they tell a condensed, credible, less mythological version of Springfield's genesis than Mrs. Owen:

> The men and women who settled Springfield were town-builders, not farmers. Their dreams were not of vast crops ... but of wide boulevards and grand public spaces. John Polk Campbell, one of the town's founders, modeled it after Columbus, Tennessee, a city built around a central square that was a hub for municipal office and retail trade.

Following the Civil War, the influence of the southerners who settled Springfield diminished. Immigrants poured in from the upper Midwest, the East Coast, even Europe. At last railroads arrived. The Queen City became an emergent city, with wholesaling, government services, manufacturing, churches, and schools. Springs the pioneers depended on became contaminated. The crystalline brook that drained John P. Campbell's claims, now called Jordan Creek, was an open sewer, prone to flooding.

Below: Real photo postcard, October 17, 1906. Springfield merchants organized a six-day Fall Festival, which featured a parade sponsored by a different organization every day. This postcard shows the Elks and Traveling Man's Day – "Grand Wrap Up of the Gala Week."

It was an eclectic event – an Airship Ascension, a visit by the Hon. William J. Bryan, Grand Electric Illumination, and Captain Jack, the Missouri Horse That Thinks, Figures, Plays Music and Does Everything but Talk. "Take the children to See Him!"

With a surging population and access to national distribution, the production of surrounding farms intensified. Resultant erosion altered stream flows. Progress was the catch phrase of the day, but old timers' recollections about old times were popular newspaper features. Long before Silver Dollar City, Springfieldians were fascinated with a version of the primitive past that was more than nostalgia, less than history. A 1906 Fall Festival parade expressed this developing image of the Ozarks. The carnage of the Battle of Wilson's Creek now behind them, soldiers representing the North and the South stood peacefully on a float, their hands on the staff of an American flag. The next float themed Ozark karst geology - "The Onyx Cave of the Ozarks with its Glittering Stalactites." An account of a well-attended fiddlers' contest in the October 9, 1906, *Springfield Republican* linked a survival of pioneer culture with the rugged White River hills:

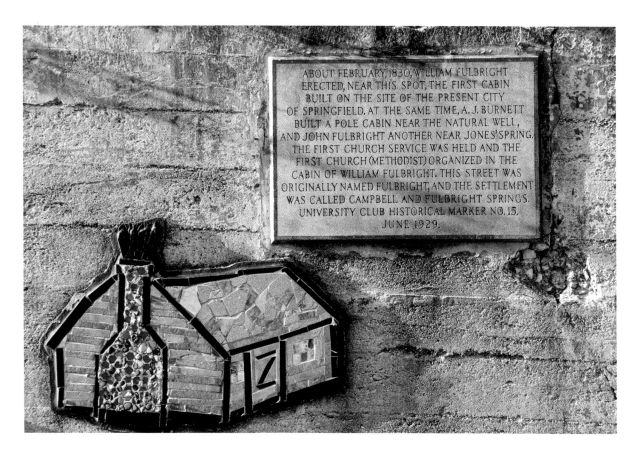

ABOUT FEBRUARY, 1830, WILLIAM FULBRIGHT
ERECTED, NEAR THIS SPOT, THE FIRST CABIN
BUILT ON THE SITE OF THE PRESENT CITY
OF SPRINGFIELD. AT THE SAME TIME, A. J. BURNETT
BUILT A POLE CABIN NEAR THE NATURAL WELL,
AND JOHN FULBRIGHT ANOTHER NEAR JONES' SPRING.
THE FIRST CHURCH SERVICE WAS HELD AND THE
FIRST CHURCH (METHODIST) ORGANIZED IN THE
CABIN OF WILLIAM FULBRIGHT. THIS STREET WAS
ORIGINALLY NAMED FULBRIGHT, AND THE SETTLEMENT
WAS CALLED CAMPBELL AND FULBRIGHT SPRINGS.
UNIVERSITY CLUB HISTORICAL MARKER NO. 15.
JUNE 1929.

URBAN
STREAM

Above: Several of the mosaics acknowledge James River tributaries that have been a part of Springfield's development.

> The fiddlers were there for the fun and those who went to hear the contest went there expecting to have a jolly time listening to those old-time tunes that are heard only "way down in the hills." There was nothing classic about it, it was a fiddlers' contest and not a violin recital. There wouldn't have been any fun about a violin recital and there was a lot of fun at the fiddlers' contest.

Like Founder's Park, the 2001 College Street Great Mosaic Wall (once Route 66) has an unpainted concrete background. Some of the mosaics have Mother Road themes. Other motifs reference hip-hop culture, skateboarding, and BMX trick bike riding. Guided by professional artist Christine Kreamer-Schilling, it was largely executed by troubled youth – outsider art constructed by outsiders. Next to a mosaic log cabin is a 1929 bronze plaque (above) marking the location of William Fulbright's 1830 homestead.

Fulbright, like John P. Campbell, did not arrive in the region that would become Springfield like most of the White River Hills settlers, many of whom were penniless squatters. An assessor's report lists his assets as "16 slaves, 14 cattle, 6 horses, some mules, and a $5 watch." He had twelve sons and one daughter. Gently rolling geography combined with ambitious pioneers made Springfield's development differ from that of the rougher country along the lower James River with its less materialistic settlers.

"BEAUTIFUL LAKE TANEYCOMO"

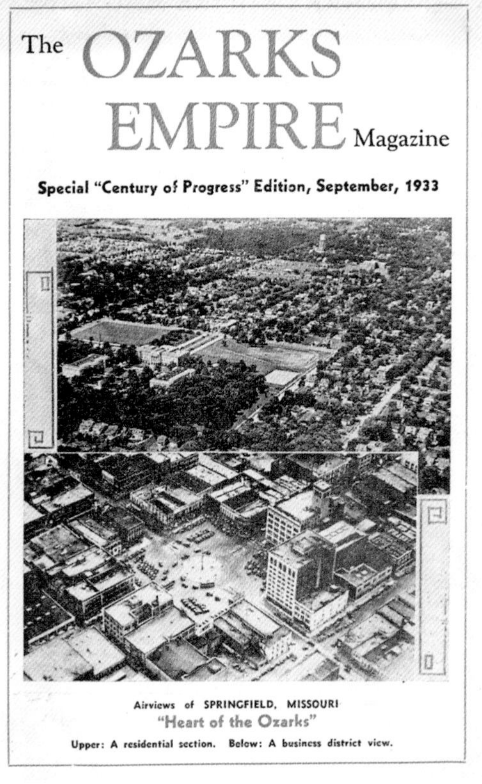

The OZARKS EMPIRE Magazine

Special "Century of Progress" Edition, September, 1933

Airviews of SPRINGFIELD, MISSOURI

"Heart of the Ozarks"

Upper: A residential section. Below: A business district view.

Eighty Thousand square miles of verdant hills and fertile valleys in Central United States, interspersed with countless springs and traversed by many beautiful rivers now being harnessed for power development, with railroads and highways forming a network of transportation to hundreds of places of scenic beauty not surpassed in the wide world, and peopled by the purest Anglo-Saxon blood on the Western Hemisphere—this is the Ozarks Empire. In the Heart of this Empire is Springfield, Missouri, the commercial, educational and social center of the region, "the best place in the world to live."

By JOHN T. WOODRUFF
President of Chamber of Commerce,
Springfield, Missouri.

Above: John Thomas Woodruff, like John Polk Campbell, Springfield's original booster, was dedicated to growing his town by improving transportation. He is considered the father of Route 66. Woodruff came to Springfield as a lawyer for the Frisco Railroad, built half a dozen important buildings, and tirelessly promoted the city. Both men sought to alter the White River to make it commercially useful. Campbell pulled snags to improve it for steamboats. Woodruff lobbied successfully for high dams that would transform the free-flowing river into reservoirs.

Right: The committee for the first Springfield Folk Festival, held in 1933. Vance Randolph is third from left, and Sarah Gertrude Knott, the woman he was attracted to, is on the far right. Bascom Lamar Lunsford, who also fancied Miss Knott, is the gent with the bow tie. May Kennedy McCord is fifth from the left.

Springfield Chamber of Commerce President John T. Woodruff authorized printing thousands of *The Ozark Empire Magazine* (opposite) to be given away at the 1933 Century of Progress Exposition in Chicago. More than forty-eight million Depression-dazed Americans sauntered through the modernistic buildings to be amazed by GM "dream cars," streamlined trains, and numerous consumer products redesigned in the Art Deco style. The sixteen-page pamphlet selling the Ozarks did not have a commensurate modern design, nor a futuristic text. On the President's Page, Woodruff mentioned the "countless springs" and "beautiful rivers, some of them harnessed for power development." A piece titled "An Enchanted Land" pitched the Ozarks as a "unlimited opportunity for the home seeker, whatever his occupation or calling." The caption for a snapshot of three guys with a string of a hundred bass reads "Fishing is good in the Ozarks." *A Nomad Speaks*, a short poem by May Kennedy McCord, ends with, *I am tired of man-made wonders; I am tired of man-made wonders; Domes so vast and towers so high; Let me pitch my tent forever 'neath a glorious Ozark sky!* Not a very urban promotion, but big-city folks were known to vacation in the Ozarks.

In the spring of 1934 the Springfield Chamber of Commerce was presented with another very different opportunity to celebrate the Ozarks Empire. May Kennedy McCord, of KWTO's radio show "Hillbilly Heartbeats," was on the advisory committee for the upcoming First National Folk Festival to be held in St. Louis, Missouri, beginning April 29. Folk-play and folk-dance enthusiast Sarah Gertrude Knott conceived of that four-day event. Banjo-playing, bowtie-wearing, ballad-singing Bascom Lamar Lunsford, "Min-

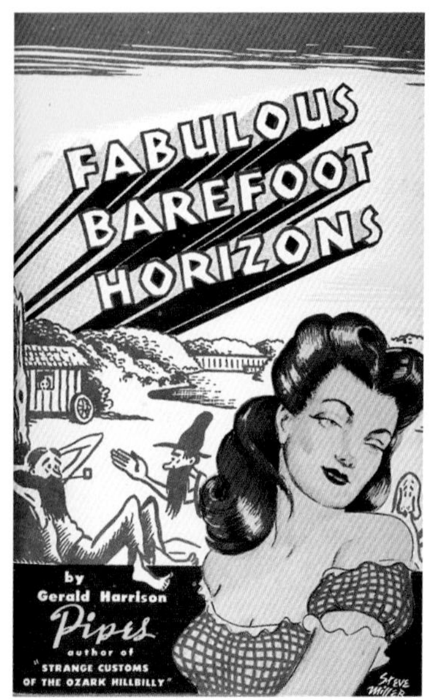

Above: Not long after Lil' Abner and Snuffy Smith appeared in newspaper comics in 1934, God-fearing Shepherd of the Hills Country bucolics began to be perceived degenerating into unsavory rustics. By 1958, when Reed Springs native Gerald Pipes published this collection of misbehaving mountaineers, Stone and Taney counties were represented by the tourist industry as the heartland of hell-raising, cousin-kissing hillbillies, to the chagrin of middle class Springfieldians.

Right: Chalk figurine. To the relief of Springfield's Chamber of Commerce, there are few souvenirs like this. Most are marked Branson. Hillbillies are a hybrid of early folk studies' version of pioneer life and pop culture's simplifications. Self-satisfied rurals with no money, credit, or prospects are anathema to the business community. In every possible way, the hillbilly is a potent symbol of anti-modernity.

strel of the Appalachians," assisted her. The St. Louis Chamber of Commerce enthusiastically backed the venture. Leading up to the main event, contests at smaller festivals would decide who would take the stage in St. Louis to fiddle, yodel, or clog. McCord's friend Vance Randolph was asked to be one of the judges. She asked if the local committee could meet in late March with the Chamber to solicit support for a Springfield venue.

That meeting did not go well. A blow-by-blow account appeared in The *Pittsburgh* (Kansas) *Headlight* of March 22, 1934. On March 27, the *Springfield Leader and Press* reprinted highlights from it entitled, "The Ozarks and Culture." "A lot of freaks should not be selected to go to the national festival," John T. Woodruff, a Chamber official told the shocked group. "Why call back the things we've been trying to forget for fifty years? Why advertise to the world that we are ignorant?"

> "We are not trying to present freaks or ignoramuses," the honorable district chairman said. "We are just trying to preserve some of the old, lovely, beautiful, wonderful things that went into the making of the country. I am not ashamed of some of the things my parents did." "Of course, it does not have to be rough, rowdy, and hoedownish," the Springfield city chairman said. "Oh, yes it does," put another leader. "It wouldn't be the Ozarks if it didn't." "You mean we're not going to have hill billies with beards?"

This rancor went on for two hours. The reporter wrote optimistically, "in the end it was decided everybody could work together and put on a big show. ... Anyway Springfield is not in good shape to get touchy about the Ozark hill billy stuff. No town can afford to be particular about the folk in its trade territory."

THE
WOODS COLT
A Novel of the Ozark Hills
THAMES WILLIAMSON

Above: Thames Williamson's 1932 turgid but well-written novel is set in the deep Ozarks. Backwoods realism became a popular genre in the 1920s and '30s. The South was a steamier location, but the Ozarks was also thought to harbor colorful, misbehaving primitives. Whether such fiction negatively influences a region's identity has long been debated. Woodruff thought it did. Randolph apparently didn't.

It isn't clear how much funding the Chamber of Commerce contributed, if any. Things had apparently gotten smoothed out enough that a gala banquet was held in the spacious Crystal Ballroom on the fifth floor of Woodruff's Kentwood Arms Hotel on April 16, the day before the festival. When it opened, the papers hardly covered the actual event. More newsworthy was the bloodbath at the banquet. Mayor Harry Durst thanked the honored guests and turned the podium over to Mr. Woodruff, who had had a few weeks to think of some more stinging objections to the way Ozarkers were being presented. The next day's headline in the *Jefferson City Post-Tribune* read,

> Mountain Music Lovers On March To Springfield; Chamber of Commerce Looks Askance at Hill Billy Antics; Old Fiddlers Will Torture Ears of Progressive Ozark City.
>
> The new broadside was fired by John T. Woodruff, president of the Chamber, who told sponsors of the Ozarks folk festival across the table last night that writers on Ozarkian subjects are "a lot of carpetbaggers" and that Harold Bell Wright, who first "touted the Ozarks hardly knew a thing about them and held up the class of citizenship at the foot of the ladder." He said that Vance Randolph, Ozark author who was present, had been "consorting with some of the undercrust and took them as typical."
>
> And he added he wondered why "the woods colt" [sic], a recent Ozarks novel by Thames Williamson had not been suppressed. "The Ozarkians," said Woodruff, "are a lovable people. Never get the idea that they are uncouth, illiterate and mean - the real Ozarkian is high-minded, patriotic and God fearing and he made here a near perfect a civilization as it is possible to make in a wilderness."

The *Springfield Leader and Press* covered the banquet as well. "The worst thing about Vance," said Woodruff, "is his association with the author of '*The Wood's Colt*.'" That novel was described in *Kirkus Review* as "a story of the Ozarks, with the seemingly unavoidable component parts: bootleggers, moonshiners, revenue officers, sheriffs, blood feuds, the hero of the piece, and the villain." Vance Randolph had gone over the dialect for authenticity, and Williamson dedicated the book to him. *Time* thought it deserved a Pulitzer. The author of the book that Woodruff thought "should be suppressed" wasn't present, but Randolph was.

McCord leapt to his defense. "Vance Randolph is the greatest authority on the Ozarks living today." Eureka Springs Chamber of Commerce president praised Woodruff for his "pioneering in the way of better roads" but said he was indebted to Randolph for his interest in things Ozarkian.

Vance refused to comment. "Mr. Ozark" had signed on to be a judge largely because he found Sarah Gertrude Knott fetching.

Roads, Rivers
Recreations
Around
Springfield
CHAMBER OF COMMERCE
SPRINGFIELD, MO

This 1930s brochure is more typical of the Queen City of the Ozarks' efforts to balance progress and primitivism than Woodruff's puzzling assault on the folk festival. There's money to be made in travel and tourism, no matter what the nature of the attraction.

These attractive maps promoting rusticated leisure near Springfield were designed by Paul Holland. He was the owner of Holland Engraving Company and a weekend painter active in the Ozarks' Artists Guild in the 1930s. Holland was a lifelong defender of the Ozarks as a fit subject for art. "Ozarks Treat Artists Better" read the title of a July 25, 1930, *Springfield Leader* article about Holland's misadventures going back east to paint that landscape. Not only was he unimpressed by the art he viewed; he found the landowners inhospitable. After a three-week survey of the situation, Paul Holland, "hillbilly artist" and leader in the Ozarks Artists Guild, has returned from a tour through New England and southeastern Canada more convinced than ever that the Ozarks offers to artists "all the advantages and none of the disadvantages of the East." "'The natives,' he said, 'seem averse to having sketchers on their land, and even the docks, and virtually all homes are posted 'no trespassing.'"

Above: Oil painting by Paul Holland titled "Ozark Village."

Top: Brochure published by the Springfield Chamber of Commerce circa 1930s.

How much John T. Woodruff had to do with the content of this advertising piece we don't know. Woodruff had lambasted Harold Bell Wright, but this promotion is hyper-Arcadian in style. If anything, it's more effusively romantic than Wright's prose, which can be credibly descriptive:

> All highways from Springfield are Roads to Romance that follow sinuous ridges or lead into lovely valleys wherein wind crystal rivers, rushing pell-mell over boulders or eddying quietly through shaded pools beneath precipitous palisades. Rivers that are born in unexplored grottos before emerging into sunlight. Rivers that still turn creaking wheels in ancient watermills, grinding for a country-side that cling to its yesterdays. Rivers that abound in trout and bass, jacks and channel cat, sunfish, goggle-eye, perch, and many other denizens.

Such leftover arts and crafts era promotions aside, most of the rhetoric of Woodruff and his crowd was aimed at improving the region's infrastructure. After the success of Lake Taneycomo as a draw, dam building became a mantra of the Chamber of Commerce and like-minded individuals. Realism may be what Woodruff really objected to in Randolph's and Williamson's writings. He, like many

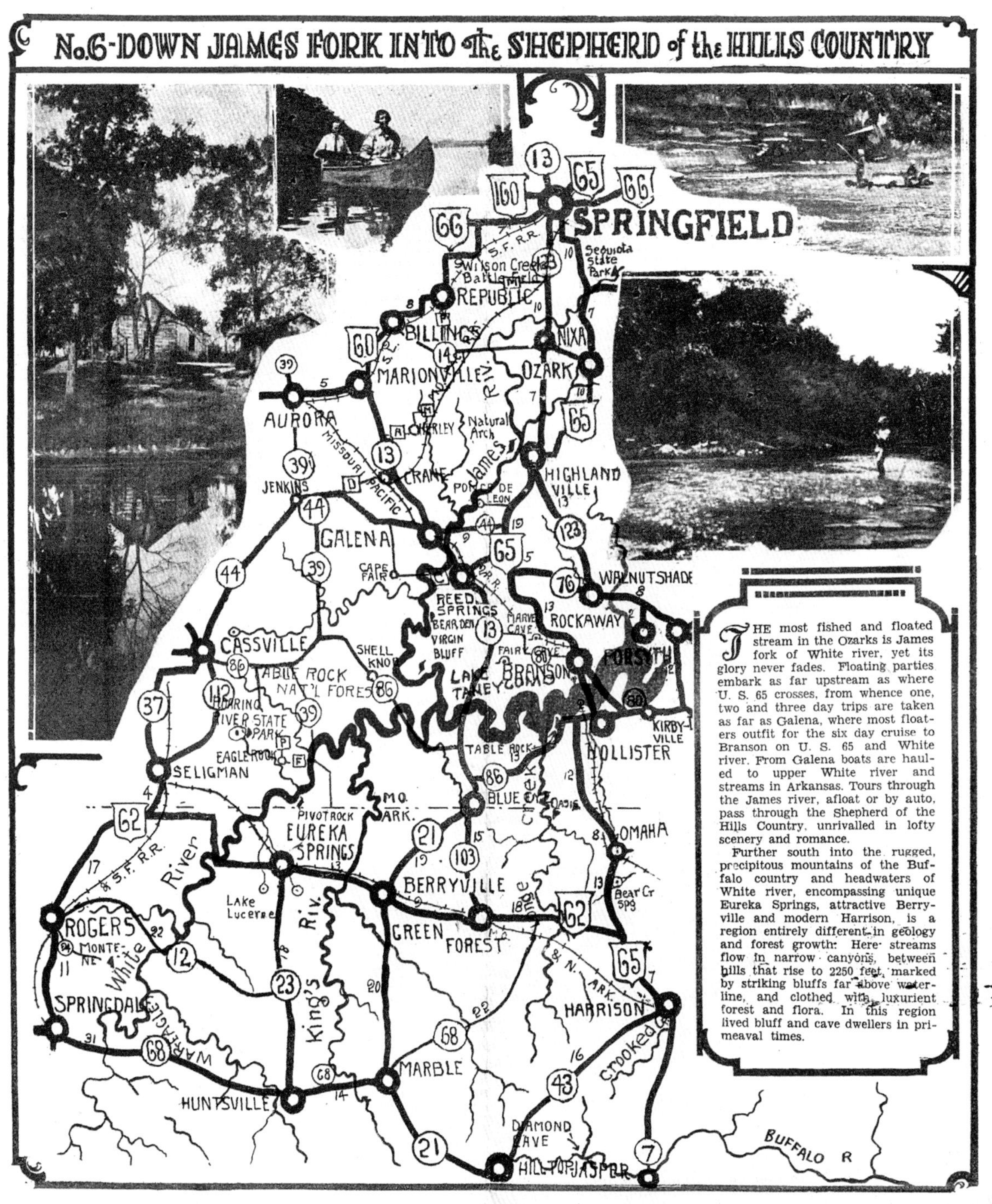

Above: Map of rivers around Springfield, Chamber of Commerce brochure, 1930s, designed by Paul Holland.

Americans of that era, was for progress, but not in the arts. Technological advancement was grand, modern art disturbing. The most wondrous of all inventions was the hydro-electric dam. Harvesting what was going to waste in nature, its electricity would power factories and illuminate homes. Tourists would fill hotel rooms on the way and rent cabins at the lake. They might put money down on a lot before returning to their good-paying city jobs.

Top: Trifold postcard of Pinebrook Inn, 1920s. On the back, the rates posted for "a room with private bath, double. $10." Also listed are the distances – to St. Louis, 214 miles; Memphis, 200 miles. Pricey and distant.

For all his antipathy for Ozarks rusticity, John T. Woodruff had a taste for country life. In 1922, he bought an unfinished health resort at Siloam Springs, Missouri, near the North Fork River, seventeen miles from West Plains. Woodruff finished the impressive four-story Pinebrook Inn, built a nine-hole golf course, constructed a dance pavilion and dug a swimming pool. Excavations to attempt to increase the flow of the place's ten medicinal springs apparently had the reverse effect. Few believed by this date that drinking mineralized spring water cured diseases anyhow. Nevertheless, the progressive businessman advertised that "Siloam Springs water is recommended by physicians and praised by thousands of people

Above: When a couple from California bought Pinebrook in 1990 it had been neglected for years. They restored it and opened a bed and breakfast. In 2013 it changed hands. The ninety-one year old hotel caught fire on a Saturday morning, April 12, 2014, and within thirty minutes after he arrived, the fire chief of Pumpkin Center said, "It was flat."

who have been benefited or cured by using it." He would spend the rest of his life waiting for guests to find the money pit in the middle of an isolated patch of cut-over mixed pine and oak forest.

Good roads and a surge in automobile ownership in the 1920s led many developers to believe the rural Ozarks could become a playground for the newly minted, moneyed middle class. "Land of a Million Smiles" promotions did succeed, but only at select locations like Lake Taneycomo, which had better touristic infrastructure and access. Former Frisco lawyer Woodruff had uncritical faith in the magic improved transportation worked. Apparently he believed

Above: Only six miles from Pinebrook is the North Fork of the White River, a famous float stream fed by large springs. Had Woodruff built a resort in this more scenic location perhaps his venture would have succeeded.

Opposite, upper left: By the time local fire districts reached Pinebrook all they could do was keep the flames from spreading.

Opposite, upper right: Two years after the fire, the lane to Pinebrook is rutted and nearly impassible.

Opposite, bottom left: The medical springs contribute little to the small creek flowing through the property. Most of its flow comes from a leak in a five-acre pond.

Opposite, bottom right: Woodruff's golf course is now a rough pasture.

that with better highways, if you build it they will come. The enigma is not that he acquired Pinebrook; it is that he held on to it after it proved unprofitable.

Astutely, Woodruff sold his ten-story office building for $750,000 in January 1929, nine months before the stock market crash that began the Great Depression. He, his wife, and children continued to spend time at Pinebrook, but paying customers dwindled. The country club tone of Woodruff's hard-to-get-to resort became out of sync with the increasing hillbilly-ization of Ozark identity during the populist, regionalist 1930s. Impoverished, truculent, alcohol-indulgent mountaineers were certainly not customers, nor were they the kind of locals his genteel guests would wish to encounter. His experiences with the reality of back country Ozarkers, which were unavoidable at his remote hotel, might have caused him to boil over at the banquet preceding the Folk Festival. The image the organizers were propagating – that the region's inhabitants were unprogressive, wildly independent, unruly but musical – may have galled Woodruff, causing him to uncharacteristically lash out. Thomas A. Peters in *John T. Woodruff of Springfield, Missouri in the Ozarks* describes him as "calm, intense, taciturn."

Hillbillies were not Woodruff's kind of people. At the formal August 8, 1923, opening of Pinebrook Inn, there were "more than fifty well-known lawyers, bankers, and businessmen," the "best people of the country," he said. He described the hotel grounds as a "large and beautiful natural park." Since the fire, this property has become a tangle of weeds, thorny brush, and aggressive young trees. Parks are manmade artifacts, like the artificial lakes Woodruff wished to see created from the rivers of the Ozarks. Parks and reservoirs require maintenance, something Pinebrook no longer receives.

In 1943, at age seventy-five, Woodruff and wife, Lydia, retired to his failed upscale resort in the sticks. Apparently he loved the place if no one else did. That, or it was, if nothing else, affordable. There are no advertisements to indicate it was still open to the public. He remained active on behalf of some of his causes. Two years later he was elected chairman of the newly organized dam-promoting White River Valley Association. On a 1949 trip to visit his daughter in Minnesota, he died of heart failure. Lydia returned to Pinebrook and six months later also died. After debts, the estate was worth $8,195. All his Springfield properties had been sold. Pierce-Arrow, the fast, luxury automobile John Woodruff loved, had gone out of business in 1938. His last car was a Chevrolet business coupe worth $400. He left a modest estate, but unlike many promoters of his era, he had not taken a bankruptcy during the Depression.

FIRE LI
INE

Above: Winoka Spring. Dr. Edward Shepard, a Drury College science professor, purchased fifty-four acres on the James in the 1890s and organized Winoka Lodge. The grounds were preserved in a natural state for outings by the faculty and students. Today Winoka Spring Branch flows into the upper reaches of Lake Springfield.

Right: Three postcards show the James River as it skirts south Springfield just before World War 1 to be an attractive, tree-lined, occasionally clifty, greenish stream. The club referred to is the James River Hunting and Fishing Club, organized around 1900. Barbecues, game suppers, card parties, and picnics held at this private club were frequent society items in local newspapers. The club disbanded in 1948.

Above: Stereo card stamped G.W. Sittler, 1880s. George Sittler had a thriving studio in Springfield. Pencilled on the back is "Dinner time on the James." Presumably this was an informal outing of family and friends, even though it was winter.

"Death From A Trivial Cause" was the heading of a notice in the *Wichita Eagle* of September 24, 1887. Visiting Perry Cave, (Percy's Cave?) which had been newly illuminated with electric lights, the photographer "collided against a stalactite, inflicting a bruise to which little attention was paid." The next day, he passed out and died from the contusion.

Sittler's widow Lizzie, also a photographer, continued to operate the studio.

In the *Springfield Republican*, June 3, 1902, the social column described a Saturday Club picnic at Winoka Lodge. After a lunch of the "club's best cookery," the students went exploring:

> After that, there was opportunity to visit the cave, go down to the river; the boys tried to fish, but did not catch anything – go to the spring, stroll about at will and sit on the rocks overlooking the deep ravines. The scenery about Winoka Lodge is very picturesque and attractive. It was a great sight to watch the black clouds as they suddenly formed late in the afternoon and rolled along in great vans and billows.

Later the property became the country home of the Schweitzer family. Their improvements burned in the 1970s. This tangled site just south of the great flyover at the US 60-65 interchange was once, according to legend, a Girl Scout camp where three young girls were murdered. On June 13, 1977, three Girl Scouts were killed at Camp Scott in northeast Oklahoma – not here.

Winoka Lodge's grounds are a place of cryptozoological intrigue. A birdwatcher photographed Paul, the Nixa hellhound, bathing in Winoka's spring. This elusive creature, also called a "booger dog," has been variously described as a mutated deer, hybrid fox/wolf man, or dog-ish lion. Sightings are regularly reported by radio station KSPJ (Power 96.5.)

Neither of the two private clubs on the James near Springfield was as architecturally rustic or devoted to outdoor recreation as most

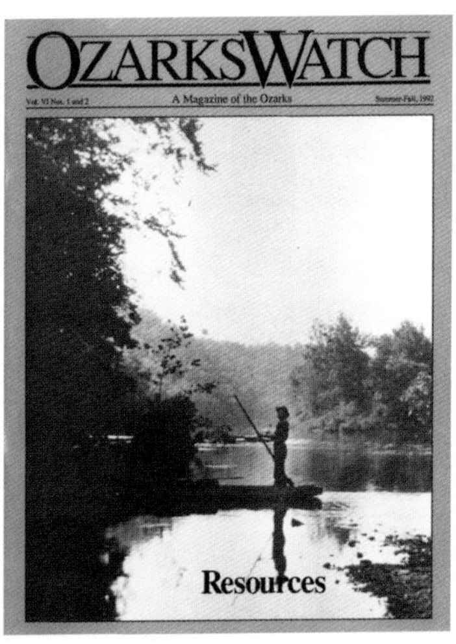

Galena resorts. Forward-looking Springfieldians viewed nature as a pleasant backdrop but not a source of inspiration. In years to come they would accept, even welcome, artificial lakes as a substitute for natural rivers. Certainly John T. Woodruff promoted dams.

Not all businessmen shared Woodruff's fear that books about uninhibited rural Ozarkers would crash civilization. Many probably didn't care for the improprieties in Randolph's and Williamson's writing, however. Other, less vulgar, versions of hill life were acceptable to the middle class. The Chamber of Commerce president wasn't wrong about the genre's anti-modern undercurrents. Even Harold Bell Wright's bucolic novels had misgivings about progress.

Otto Ernest Rayburn left Kansas to buy forty acres on the James River after reading *The Shepherd of the Hills*. *Rayburn's Arcadian Life* (top left) was only one of the magazines he would publish promoting the idea of the Ozarks as a refuge from the over-civilized world, populated by ballad-singing, self-reliant hillfolk. Rayburn, in the words of his pal Vance Randolph, "did more to arouse popular interest in Ozark folklore than all the professors put together."

Due in part to Rayburn's magazines and Randolph's books, the Ozarks gained a reputation as a sanctuary from the tribulations of modern times. Before it suffered the fate of specialized print publications, *The Ozarks Mountaineer* (middle left) was for sixty years a widely read compendium of rural nostalgia. A letter in the February 1971 issue from a reader in Buxton, Derbyshire, England, summarized its appeal: "Your magazine is giving me an understanding of Ozark people and how very different you are from the North of the U. S. Because you seem to be community minded, and you seem very easy going, something the world in general is not. I love all those stories of your country life, and the Uncle Zeke's column."

Ozarks Watch (left), published by the Ozarks Studies Institute of Missouri State University, does not present a past that is as trouble-free as *The Ozarks Mountaineer*. Earlier Ozark writers' belief that man and nature can harmoniously coexist persists, but university-educated regional writers are less mystical about the interface. Environmentalism, which has biological roots, has supplanted Arcadianism, which has literary origins. Dr. Robert Gilmore in the premier issue of *Ozarks Watch* (1987) wrote: "Our enterprise will focus on that special kind of human habitation that is distinctive in ways keenly felt but often difficult to describe and even to understand. ... This Ozarks environment includes not only the land and the people but the influence of time ... that whole matrix of interactions between land and people over many generations."

On a recent blue sky, mid-September weekend, sixty-nine white tents were set up for craftsmen, vendors, and exhibitors around the "historic quadrangle" of Missouri State University. This celebration of Ozark heritage presents none of the image problems of the 1934 Ozark Folk Festival. Rural nostalgia is no longer seen as an anti-modern challenge to progress and commerce. Sponsored by the university's Ozarks Studies Institute, the Ozark Celebration Festival had no "rough stuff" that John Woodruff had scorned. Those who wandered through on their way to an MSU football game found nothing offensive among the tables of homemade soap, pieced quilts, wood carvings, clover honey, and hooked rugs. Some paused to listen to the gently amplified local bluegrass bands. The marching band at nearby Plaster Stadium needed no amplification. The dim strains of John Phillip Sousa was curiously not dissonant blended with the melodic bluegrass tune.

Above: Issues of authenticity that once bothered folk and country music audiences have largely been laid to rest. Electronic instruments and amplification and even drum kits are accepted in country music today.

Right top: There are numerous proficient local amateur string bands whose style tends toward bluegrass. Few local festivals lack a background of old-time music.

Right bottom: Much of the repertoire of marching bands goes back a century, but this music isn't considered as traditional as the string groups. Folk is not defined by age alone.

All are cordially invited to call at our sample rooms and inspect our various lines of machines, a few of which are shown below
INTERNATIONAL HARVESTER COMPANY
BLUE BELL
International Harvester Company of America
(INCORPORATED)
301, 303, 305 West Commercial Street

Above: Ad from a 1910 Annual Convention of the Missouri Retail Merchants Association held in Springfield. Prairie farmers were better customers for machinery than hill farmers.

Above right: Agricultural trade was a larger part of Springfield's economy in the past. Corn and small grain fields of the surrounding plateau have largely been converted to pasture. Many grain elevators have been razed, or are unused. All were located next to railroads.

Springfield picked up the nickname "Queen City of the Ozarks" or just "Queen of the Ozarks" in the 1870s. As most of its early trade and wealth derived from farms and commerce from the plateau, not the less productive rough, forested Ozarks, "Queen City of the Prairies" might have been more appropriate. Sedalia, Missouri, and Fort Worth, Texas, though, went by that sobriquet.

Farmers who produce a surplus have money to invest in machinery and consumer goods. Subsistence farm hillfolk are cash poor. That folk culture – its music, humor, love of hunting and fishing, self-sufficiency, and independence bordering on rebelliousness – is alluring compared to the stereotype of the laboring-from-dawn-to-dusk agriculturalist. Given its Ozarkian geography there is familiarity with backwoods lifestyles, but Springfield's core culture is mercantile. Popular characterizations of both rurality and urbanity are primarily products of mass media.

WOODRUFF BUILDING
THE FREEHOLD INVESTMENT COMPANY
OWNERS
SPRINGFIELD, MISSOURI
CHAS. H. COLE, PRES. GEO. W. CALDWELL, V. PRES. JOHN T. WOODRUFF, SEC'Y & TREAS.
Ten Story Fireproof Modern Office Building
Ready for Occupancy, Jan. 1, 1911
FOR SPACE APPLY TO
JOHN T. WOODRUFF, 505 Baker Block, Springfield, Missouri

Above: Ad from the 1910 booklet. When John T. Woodruff started renting his ten-story building in 1911 he was justified in calling it "Springfield's first skyscraper."

Above right: John Q. Hammons' 1986 twenty-two story, 268-foot tower is twice as high as Woodruff's building, but half as tall as it needs to be today to merit that term. Springfield grew out, not up.

John T. Woodruff and John Q. Hammons were both hoteliers. Both bought land in anticipation of the completion of dam projects and created their own towns. Woodruff purchased 320 acres at the junction of two highways and laid out a new county seat he named Camdenton. Linn Creek, the previous county seat, was drowned by Lake of the Ozarks. John Q. bought several thousand acres where a bridge would cross Table Rock Lake. He named the new town Kimberling City, after a long-ago ferry crossing on the White River.

Neither of those cities' websites or Wikipedia acknowledges the origins of these privately conceived communities. Springfield was created by a similar capitalistic play, but the story is celebrated. John Polk Campbell in 1835 donated fifty acres to assure there would be a government and commercial center within his 160-acre holdings. Land speculation mixed with pioneer mythos is apparently more palatable than recent town-founding real estate schemes.

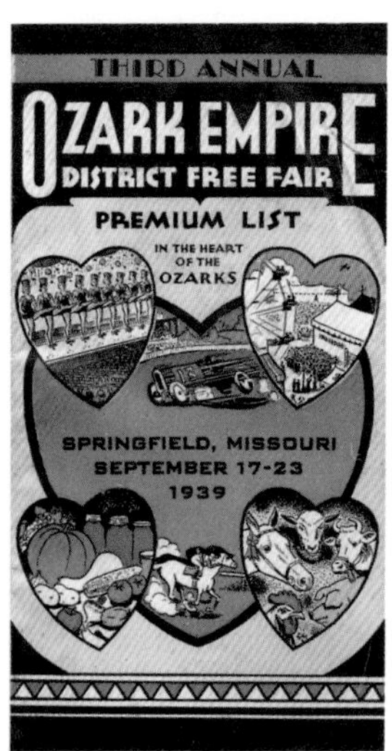

Farmers could have their Hampshire hogs judged, ride a Ferris wheel, and take in Ernie Young's Follies International featuring a "Bevy of Beautiful Girls" at the 1939 Ozark Empire District Free Fair (premium list, left). Today it costs $6, but the "Ozark Empire Fair maintains a continuing commitment to the original charter objectives of promoting manufacture, agriculture, horticulture, poultry, dairying, raising of livestock and products of domestic industry by maintaining fairs and exhibits ... for the amusement and pleasure of persons visiting fairs and exhibitions."

Another event devoted solely to agriculture is held at the same location just north of I-44. Ozark Fall Farm Fest is sponsored by the Ozark Empire Fair and *Farm Talk* newspaper of Parsons,

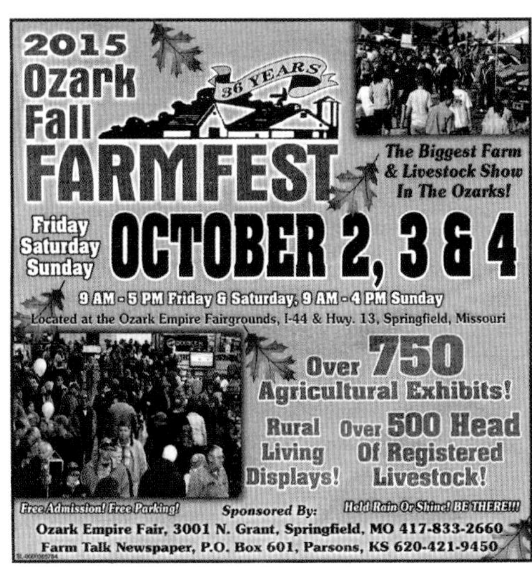

Kansas. Farmers and their families come from southwest Missouri to review several dozen breeds of beef cattle, shop for tractors big and small, gates, livestock waterers, and veterinary supplies. Antique equipment reminds fairgoers of the changing nature of agriculture – less row cropping, more pastured cattle. This is still a free event but it no longer offers a chorus line of beautiful girls. Farm Fest entertainment is a stock dog demonstration.

A teenager takes a selfie with a young bull (opposite page). Gaggles of young people indicated that, contrary to predictions, the family farm may not disappear.

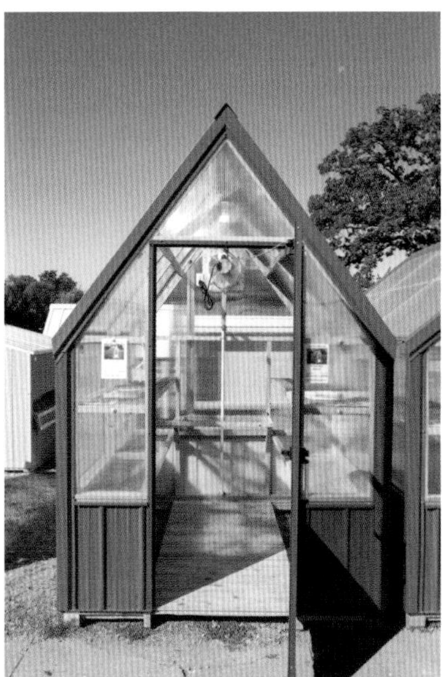

4
9
6
12
5
11
7
10

12
6
4
5
11
7
8

Turn & Lock
CWD
KNOW THE FACTS
mdc.mo.gov

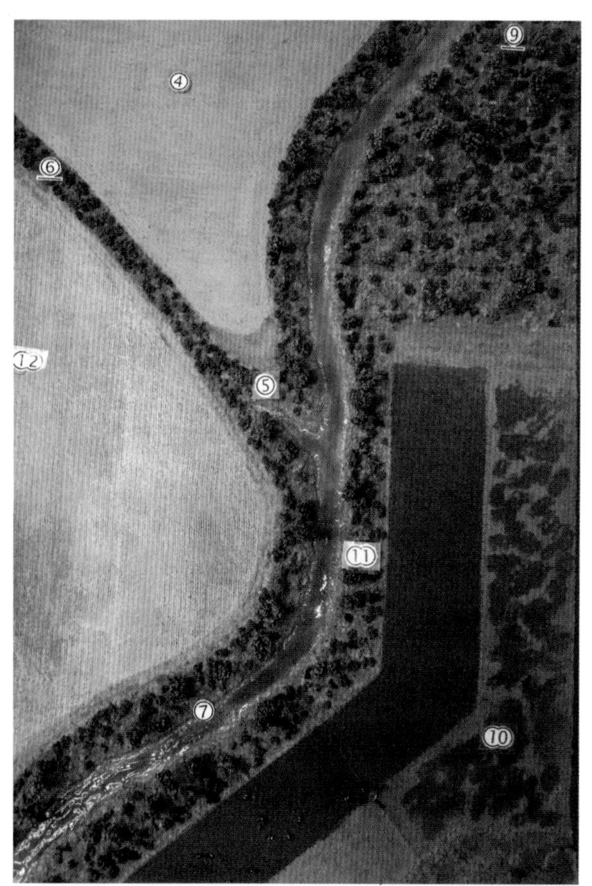

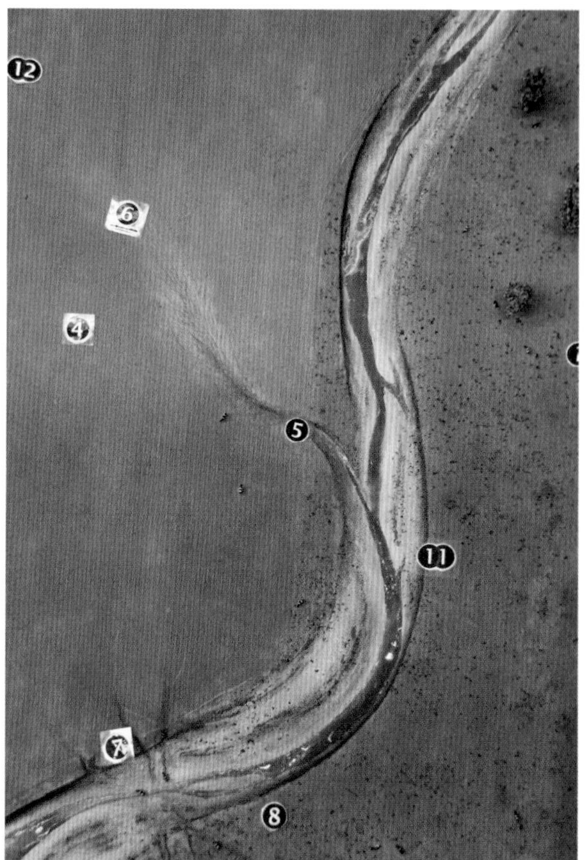

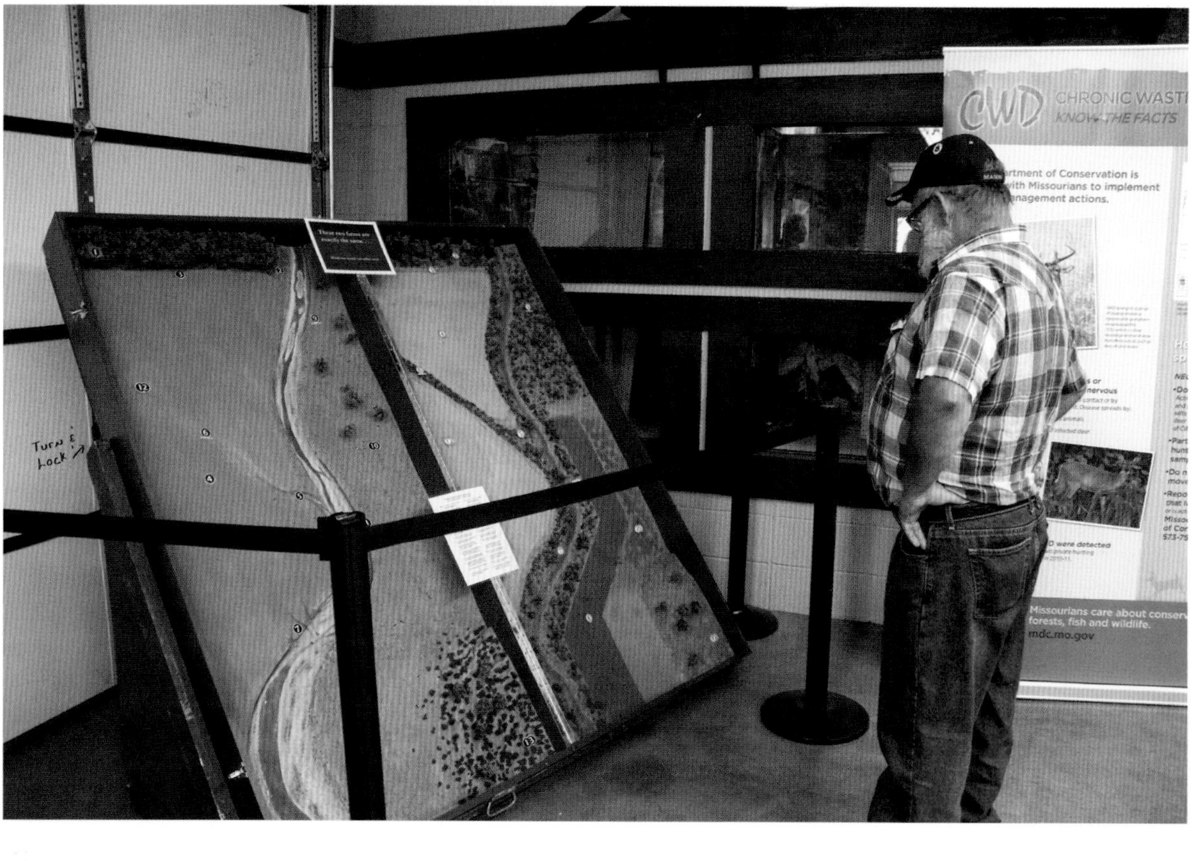

Above: *Man and Wildlife in Missouri* (1953), by Charles Callison.

As early as 1939, the Conservation Commission announced that the Department had an obligation to look into the effect on "bird, fish, game, forestry and all wildlife resources of the state" that would be impacted by the myriad huge federal water resource developments that were then being proposed. Should these dams and reservoirs be judged destructive of natural resources, they would alert the public, and seek reparations if they were built. This aroused the ire of dam supporters, but the department effectively opposed dams on the Current, Eleven Point, and Meramec rivers. Later Table Rock Dam was not opposed.

Political influence affected the department during the Truman Dam lawsuit of the early 1970s. But they did oppose the Meramec Dam project during that same era. No big dams have been advocated recently, so what their stance would be today is unknown.

As a trade center for farmers, Springfield is a locus for government outreach relating to agriculture. The Missouri Department of Conservation has its own building on the Ozark Empire Fairgrounds. During Farm Fest, it contained an installation encouraging land management techniques compatible with wildlife, sustained productivity, and profitable agriculture. A model relief (opposite) contrasts the effects of poor and good farming practices along a waterway. The text for bad practices reads, "Eroding stream bank and gravel-filled streams due to absence of riparian corridor and lack of livestock control." Good practices included "Woody draw left intact with mostly low-growing, shrub species."

Eighty years of such messaging has had its effect. Likely most of the farmers sauntering through the building subscribe to the *Missouri Conservationist* magazine and are in agreement with the agency's vision of utilizing natural resources without degrading them. Many problems with erosion in the James River watershed derive from earlier, indifferent land management. Insufficient tree lines along waterways and allowing livestock access to streams are still problems.

Relations between rural landowners and sportsmen have not always been good. When Missourians voted in 1936 to transition from a politicized Fish and Game Department to an agency of scientifically trained personnel, the amendment failed in many Ozark counties. Outside authority over the taking of game was resented in isolated, frontier-like regions. It passed, however, in the James River watershed. Fishing regulations made sense to float guides who were early advocates of catch-and-release. Though the White River hills are geographically similar to the central Ozarks, its natives had profited from tourism and had fewer suspicions of city folks and their ways.

Missouri's Conservation Department became one of the country's first apolitical agencies regulating wildlife. Because biologists like Aldo Leopold and his son Starker influenced its early policies, it differed from many state conservation departments which were based on the dated rational planning and the gospel of efficiency doctrines left over from the Teddy Roosevelt/Gifford Pinchot era. Teddy is often given credit as the founder of the conservation movement, but many of his beliefs, especially concerning water resource development, have no scientific basis. Pinchot's discredited idea that all forest fires should be eliminated did take root in the Missouri Conservation Department for a time. Recently the role of fire has been reappraised, however, and proscribed burns have been employed.

Bass Pro's architectural and decorative rusticity defies formal classification. Possibilities include post-Adirondacks; backwoods Byzantine; Ozark Gothic; Mark Trail Baroque. Whatever it is, the style evokes outdoor sporting tradition.

When it dawned on businessmen that a buck could be made selling gas, food, or lodging to city folks headed for Taneycomo, they began promoting their towns as "gateways," but few were located to benefit from tourism. Springfield, due to its transportation hub and infrastructure, was. Not all purveyors of tourist services understood their customers' motivations to travel to the primitive Ozarks.

The son of a Springfield liquor store owner, Johnny Morris grew up immersed in the fishing and hunting culture of the White River hills. Snapshots document young Morris on family excursions to the woods and waters south of Springfield. During college he began fishing in tournaments and became aware of deficiencies in tackle availability and motorized fishing boat design. Starting with a few shelves of tackle in his father's liquor stores, Morris created Bass Pro, now the nation's largest seller of outdoor merchandise.

Essential to this firm's success is their novel presentation of merchandise. The outdoor editor of the *Augusta Chronicle* (Georgia), Rob Pavey, published a typical first encounter with the original Bass Pro store. He was in Springfield in July 2015 attending an antique fishing lure show when a cab driver recommended he visit

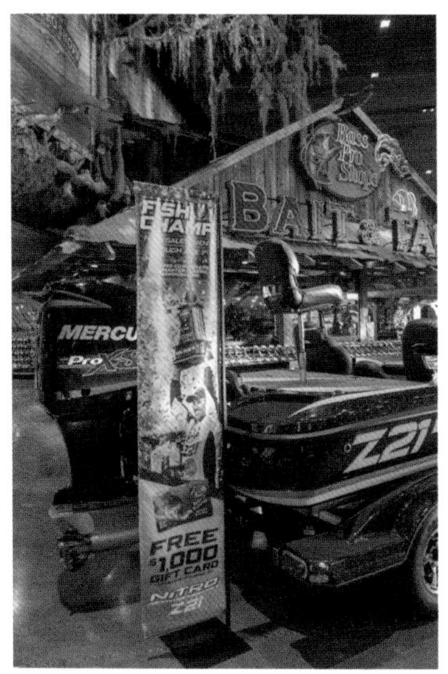

their headquarters. "They call it the granddaddy of outdoor stores," the cabby said. "We just call it the mother ship." Pavey continued, "It is part theme park, part retail store, and part museum. Everything in between, from floor to ceiling, is covered with exhibits, fish tanks, taxidermy, vintage outdoor gear and other enchanting distractions that can almost make you forget you can also shop."

Like the building of a medieval cathedral, this temple of the great outdoors is proceeding slowly. Products migrate from one area to another, sculptures and boats are added or subtracted. The Wonders of Wildlife National Museum and Aquarium will be connected to the store and features creatures from land and sea.

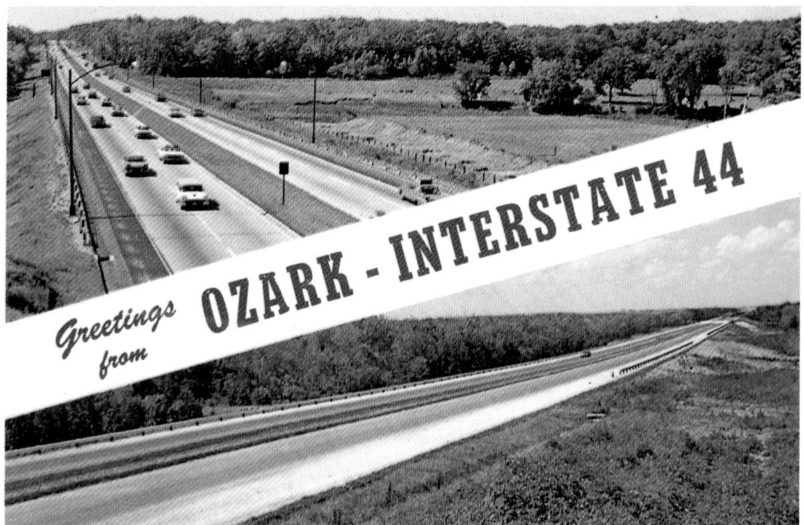

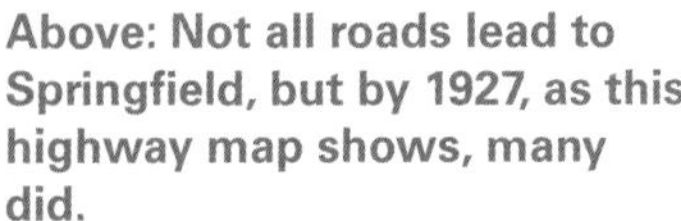

Above: Not all roads lead to Springfield, but by 1927, as this highway map shows, many did.

Above, right: John T. Woodruff was instrumental in the building of Route 66, which became I-44. Indian trails crossed where Springfield is now located. These became wagon roads. Rail lines brought growth in the late nineteenth century and highways created prosperity after World War II.

Miss Springfield Chamber of Commerce welcomes you to "a gem of a city, set in the picturesque Ozark hills ... an hour from the Lake of the Ozarks, Lake Taneycomo, Bull Shoals and famous Table Rock Lake." By the early 1960s, Springfield extolled its wealth of artificial lakes in this ad (opposite) in an Ozark Playground Association Annual.

Woodruff and the Chamber had encouraged private companies in the 1920s and '30s to harness the hydropower from Ozark streams. When they didn't and the Army Corps of Engineers embarked on their massive White River multi-purpose dam campaign, Woodruff and packs of Springfield leaders traveled to Washington, DC, to testify before Congress on behalf of these projects.

An anonymous letter to the editor in the October 31, 1925, *Springfield Leader* captures the mystical association dams, roads, and prosperity had for that era's believers in progress. Springfield, the author implies, should become the Queen City of Ozark water resource development. Transforming the free-flowing streams into reservoirs, along with "excellent highways," would make the town a "fountainhead" of wealth:

> Springfield is the nipple on the breast of the Ozarks. Within the circumference of this Ozarkian breast are more stupendous hydro-electric projects than in any same area in America. No less than six enormous projects, involving $200,000,000! ... Not dreams, but projects as sure to be developed as water runs down hill, and its running may be changed into gold. Why Florida is a piker compared to our Ozarks. And these enormous dams will empound vast inland lakes, converting the Ozarks into a wonderland for the tourists developing hotels and pleasure resorts rivaling the dreams of Florida. Now consider our excellent highways, draining like milk ducts, the wealth and patronage of these marvelous Ozarks into Springfield, its fountain's head. Will Springfield grow? We guess yes.

MISSOURI'S FASTEST GROWING CITY !

THE

Ozarks

MOST CONVENIENT VACATION CITY !

. . . a gem of a city, set in the picturesque Ozarks hills . . . a very unusual city, famed for its friendliness and its prosperity that's skyrocketed far above the national average . . . a city that puts hospitality, excellent dining facilities, family recreation, fabulous motels, gracious hotels, rolling green golf courses (one is lighted) and blue swimming pools at your comand . . .

Kel-Lake Motel
Hwy. 66 & 71 By Pass
Carthage, Mo.

Photo by DePew - Springfield

Third largest city in the state, Springfield is the Ozarks' marketbasket . . . and in the heart of the mid-west, it's only minutes away from nearby lakes, an hour from the Lake of the Ozarks, Lake Taneycomo, Bull Shoals and famous Table Rock lake . . . the best in fishing, water-skiing and boating . . . and Springfield is the center of this vacation paradise!

WRITE OR PHONE
ME FOR MORE
INFORMATION

MISS SPRINGFIELD
CHAMBER OF COMMERCE
SPRINGFIELD, MO.

Assertions by the author of the 1925 letter that "Florida is a piker compared to our Ozarks" proved to be wishful thinking. Ozark "inland lakes" developed robust tourism, but Florida has year-around sun and two oceans. To our knowledge, the Chamber of Commerce never adopted his phrase "Springfield is the nipple of the breast of the Ozarks," catchy as it is. "Will Springfield grow? We guess yes" displayed more insight. As the Landsat satellite photograph shows (opposite) Springfield today has enough sprawl to be considered a small city. Its current urban population is around 215,000 and the Springfield-Branson Metropolitan region is over 537,000. Every booster website will claim its third largest city in Missouri status, often in the first sentence.

1. **Fellows Lake 1,273 ft.**
2. **Little Sac River above Fellows Lake 1,339 ft.**
3. **McDaniel Lake 1,142 ft.**
4. **Fulbright Water Treatment Plant 1,100 ft.**
5. **I-44 1,335 ft.**
6. **Campbell's Natural Well 1,276 ft.**
7. **Jordan Creek 1,280 ft.**
8. **Southwest Cleanwater Treatment Plant 1,132 ft.**
9. **Wilson Creek 1,083 ft.**
10. **Lake Springfield 1,159 ft.**
11. **James River below dam 1,119 ft.**
12. **Blackman Intake 1,150 ft.**
13. **Schoolcraft's Camp 1,160 ft.**
14. **Pearson Creek 1,257 ft.**

At the close of the Civil War, the village founded in 1830 by John Polk Campbell had only a little more than one thousand souls. When the St. Louis & San Francisco Railroad arrived in 1870, "the city began its remarkable growth," as the 1904 *State of Missouri* stated. Explanations in that volume for its "steady and rapid development" credit transportation, public schools, fine homes, civic organizations, surrounding productive farmland, a manufacturing and wholesaling sector, and an altitude of 1,345 feet for making it "nature's sanitarium" and "noted for its healthfulness."

This elevation had a corollary: "The city is fortunate in having good natural drainage, and having added therein 32 miles of excellent sewers." Later the account mentions another important component of infrastructure: "The Springfield Waterworks Company, a private corporation, takes its supply from deep springs three miles from the city and furnishes pure and abundant water. Its present capacity aggregates 100 gallons per capita." Elevation isn't linked as an influence on the water supply like it was for wastewater, but it could have been. Fulbright Spring, the source of the water (and still a source), is just north of the city. Once pumped to the edge of Springfield, it flows downhill to customers.

Gravity facilitated the early development of both water and sewage systems. These topographic realities still mean that most of Springfield's water comes from the Sac/Osage River system and most of the wastewater drains into the James/White basin. Recently water has been taken from the James River, but even so, most still originates as an interbasin transfer in order to exploit altitudinal differences. "Upstream Starts Here" refers to these geographic realities. Whatever is contained in Springfield's wastewater, unless it is filtered out, flows into the James River and then Table Rock Lake. For much of the town's history, the removal of that pollution has been spotty. Only lately has treatment been adequate.

1
2
3
4
5
6
7
14
13
12
8
10
11

In an overgrown pasture on private land near Pearson Creek's junction with the James River is a marker inscribed, "Henry Schoolcraft, geologist, explorer and ethnologist, camped here Jan. 1, 1819. Site of first lead mine and primitive smelter in southwest Missouri. Also of Osage Camp. Marker erected 1921 by Rotary Club of Springfield, Missouri."

In Schoolcraft's 1819 *A View of the Lead Mines of Missouri*, he wrote, "On the immediate banks of James River are situated some valuable lead mines, which have been known to the Osage Indians and to some White River hunters, for many years. ... There is not one inhabitant on all this stream; my own cabin, erected for a temporary purpose at the mines January last, is the only human habitation within two hundred miles of that place."

Above: Neglected historic marker of Schoolcraft's' 1819 visit to an outcropping of lead on the James River.

The young New York explorer repeatedly expressed astonishment at the clarity of Ozark streams. At his James River camp at the lead mine he observed lumps of ore "through the water, which is very clear and transparent."

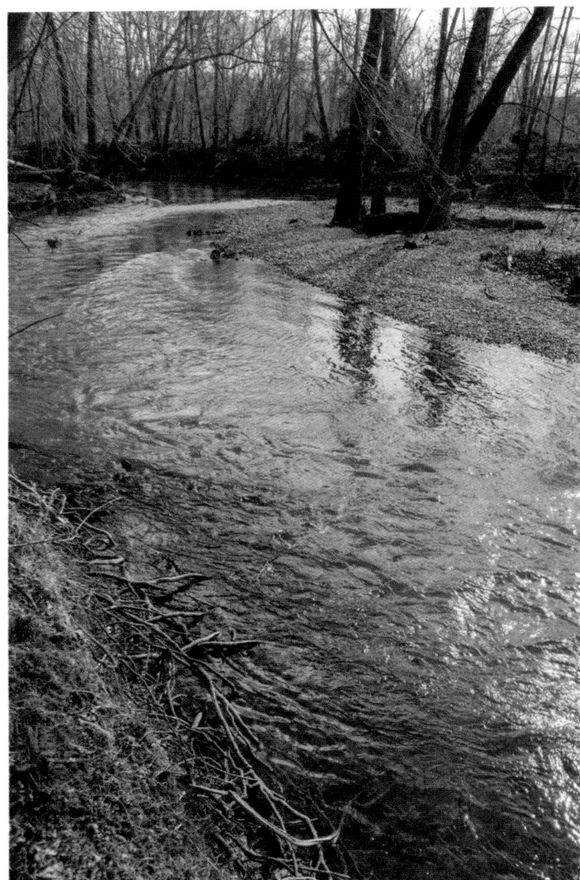

Right: Train and highway crossing of Pearson Creek, one mile north of where Schoolcraft found lead and a primitive furnace where Indians and white trappers made bullets for muzzle-loading rifles.

Right: Lead mine along Pearson Creek, circa 1900 (photo courtesy of History Museum on the Square). Commercial extraction of lead here began in the 1840s and ended around 1920.

Dr. Robert T. Pavlowsky and his associates and students at Missouri State University's Ozark Environmental and Water Resources Institute have investigated the effect of these old mines on water quality. They found lead contamination from mine waste has been stored in alluvial deposits of floodplains.

Right: Remnants of lead diggings can be seen in the hills along lower Pearson Creek.

Lead that washed into streams is now embedded in sediments in Pearson Creek and the James River. It will eventually degrade, but there is a danger if channel instability uncovers this mining-related metal contamination.

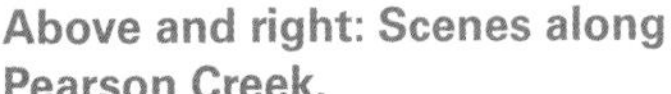

Above and right: Scenes along Pearson Creek.

American pioneers were dependent on springs. Of the hundreds of springs they found in Greene County, many have been altered, or even eliminated by development. Along the ten miles of Pearson Creek some of its springs remain in a more or less natural state.

Living along a scenic waterway is appealing, but Pearson Creek is "flashy," and periodic floods block access roads.

Pearson Creek's hilly, wooded watershed is considered a desirable location for upscale residential development. There are remnants of its pioneer past like the springhouse (left) once used to cool and store food.

Jeremiah Pearson was given permission by the Indians to settle here within the Delaware Reservation in the late 1820s. Both he and John Campbell emigrated from Tennessee, but their aspirations and selection of property differed. Campbell recognized the leveler land along what is now Jordan Creek as a perfect townsite. Pearson, like most underfinanced log-cabin types, chose rougher country along a waterway ideal for a water mill and distillery. He, his wife, and thirteen children later moved into wilder Webster County seeking frontier conditions they were adapted to. Such subsistence farmers populated the White River hills of the lower James. They would not be displaced by a growing town as "old Jerry" Pearson was. Scenic landscapes like the country through which Pearson Creek flows are often transformed from agricultural use to prime luxury-house building sites. A spring house along the headwaters, a relic log cabin downstream, and several old cemeteries are reminders of earlier, less affluent occupants.

In spite of its clarity and attractiveness, Pearson Creek has evidence of "unknown toxicity and elevated bacteria," according to biologists working for City Utilities. They found there was significant reduction in aquatic invertebrate species between 1960 and 1990. The creek, which feeds into the James and Springfield's water supply, is now monitored by several government agencies. The Missouri Department of Natural Resources awarded a grant to the Greene County Soil and Water Conservation District to implement the Agricultural Non Point Source Special Land Treatment Program for Pearson Creek watershed. A century ago there were lead mines on the lower reaches of Pearson Creek. Today, the upper reaches are farmed and suburbanization is spreading throughout.

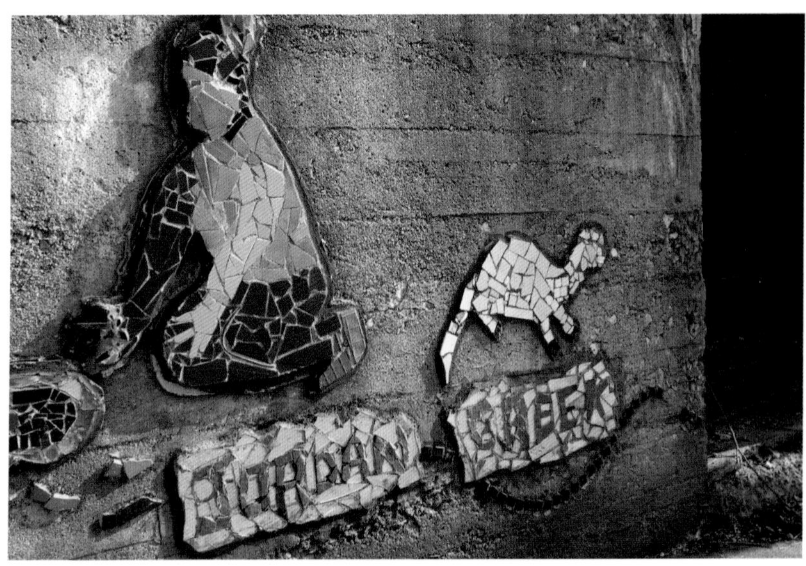

Above: College Street Great Mosaic Wall.

John Campbell found the country along the spring-fed stream currently known as Jordan Creek an ideal place to found a frontier settlement. For a short time it was called Campbell Creek. Mapmakers preferred to label it Wilson Creek – it is a headwaters reach of that stream. An African American church once baptized members in its then-clear waters, and the Biblical name became attached around the Civil War.

If hydrologically insignificant, Springfield's Jordan has a real and mythological significance some mighty rivers might envy. There is archaeological proof Indians lived along its banks, but searches for Spanish gold have uncovered no proof Cortez or any other conquistador ever watered their horses here or drank from its many springs as legends claim.

Jordan Creek drains downtown Springfield. Just a trickle and seven miles long before it joins Fassnight Creek to become Wilson Creek, poems, books, government reports, and newspaper articles too numerous to list have been written about it. Printed words on Jordan Creek may rival the lengthy literature of the Mississippi per mile. Unlike descriptions of that mighty waterway, adjectives like "majestic" or phrases like "Father of Waters" are not used. At a Young Men's Business Club meeting held on April 8, 1915 to discuss the beautification of Jordan valley, J. R. Roberts, superintendent of Greene County schools, dashed off this ode:

Dear Jordan, once the lovliest [sic] rill
Dear Jordan, once the loveliest rill
We come tonight to give thee cheer
By finding means thy banks to clear.
To lay some bold, effective plan
To rid thee of the old tin can.

That nauseating smell of gas
That greets us as thy way we pass
We hope to banish from thee quite,
As morning sun drives back the night.
We hope once more to walk thy vale
And breath or virgin flower inhale.

Again we hope the song of bird
Along thy borders will be heard;
Again we hope to see thy shore
As clean as when in days of yore
The Indian maiden stooped to see
Her happy face sent back by thee.

In the fall of 1939, the *Springfield Leader & Press* published a four-part feature, "The Jordan: A History of Springfield's Fast Disappearing Stream." Allen Oliver, the waggish lead writer, and photojournalist Jim (the light is poor) Billings, inspired by the saga of the search for the origin of the Nile, set out to discover the head of Jordan Creek. Before departing on this safari, with "an extra roll of film and plenty of cigarettes," Oliver put the project in historical perspective:

> In recent years the stream has come to be regarded as something of a nuisance to everyone but old timers, who, with many a nostalgic tear, cherish the memory of the stream as it used to be. They see it not as it is today, an ugly and somewhat odorous rivulet which winds through narrow, muddy beds (when it has enough life to wind at all), but rather as it was when Springfield was young and life was simple. They see it as a pretty stream which would cool and clear through the Jordan valley (before it became known as the levee). Its banks, they will tell you, were lined with green pastures or fragrant woods. Here and there a weeping willow tree bent gently over to brush the surface of the water with its leaves. Wild plum, hazelnut, blackberry bushes and other forms of wild life flourished along the banks. Its waters, they will tell you, were crystal clear, and if you dropped a dime on the sand pebbles which lay like polished gems on the creek bed, you could still read E. Pluribus Unum and the date, through three feet of water.
>
> It's debatable whether the Jordan was ever the asset to the landscape that memory pictures – memory does those things – but there is no doubt that the Jordan was once a more sightly stream, and doubtless a more respectable one, than it is today. However, the Jordan is approaching the twilight of its existence, so to speak.

Poking around just north of the Downtown Airport, the pair searched for a definitive origin of the Jordan. Traipsing up an overgrown ditch, they found "some very interesting specimens, in the form of whiskey bottles, tin cans and paper sacks." Mostly the creek was dry as it threaded through pastures. As they followed it, approaching downtown, "There was water in the river and, more important, minnows." Residents living along the banks provided

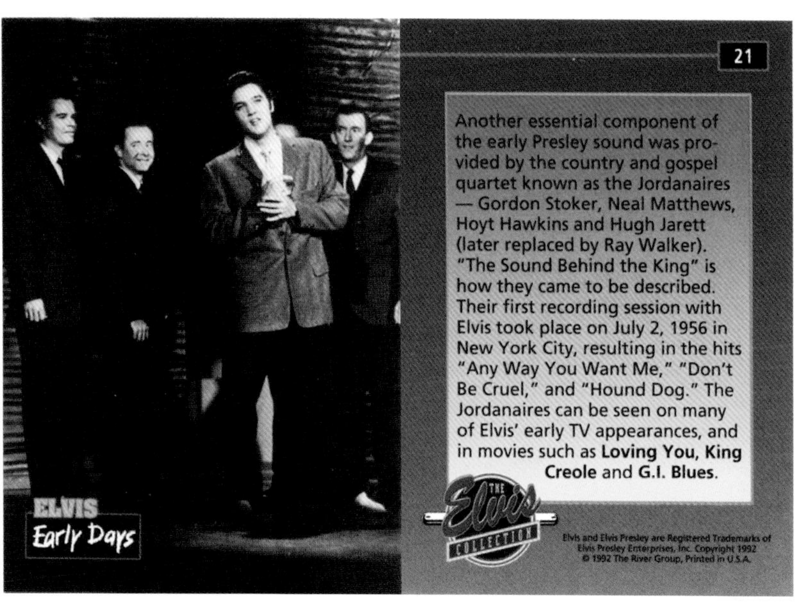

21
Another essential component of the early Presley sound was provided by the country and gospel quartet known as the Jordanaires — Gordon Stoker, Neal Matthews, Hoyt Hawkins and Hugh Jarett (later replaced by Ray Walker). "The Sound Behind the King" is how they came to be described. Their first recording session with Elvis took place on July 2, 1956 in New York City, resulting in the hits "Any Way You Want Me," "Don't Be Cruel," and "Hound Dog." The Jordanaires can be seen on many of Elvis' early TV appearances, and in movies such as Loving You, King Creole and G.I. Blues.
ELVIS
Early Days
The Elvis Collection
Elvis and Elvis Presley are Registered Trademarks of Elvis Presley Enterprises, Inc. Copyright 1992 © 1992 The River Group, Printed in U.S.A.

Right: Elvis Presley Collection Series Card #21.

From 1956 to 1972, the Jordanaires backed up the King of Rock-and-Roll (and many other top pop performers) on records, stage, and film. Originally a quartet of Gospel singing ministers with a Springfield connection, they named their group after Jordan Creek, not the famous river in the Holy Land.

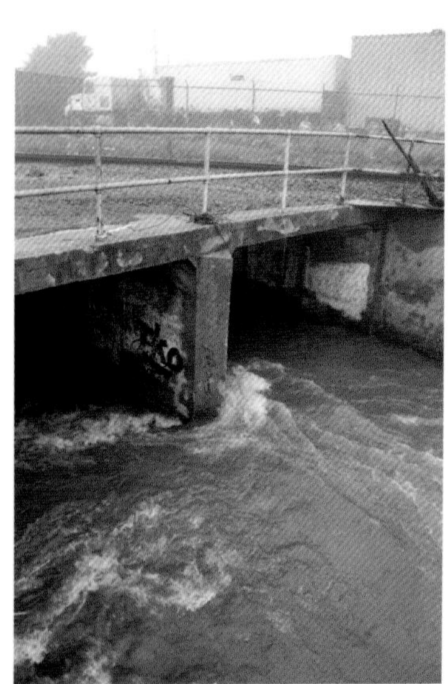

Above and opposite: After a heavy rain, Jordan Creek rises and falls quickly. Only a few hours before these photographs were taken it was over the road.

Springfield's infamous "aqueduct" or "box" begins where the north and south branches of Jordan Creek join. Though the two side-by-side concrete culverts combined are ten feet by thirty feet, it doesn't take much of a freshet to exceed their capacity. Thousands of pages of studies suggest ways to reduce flooding, but this 3,520-foot effort to bury Jordan Creek under the center of Springfield poses a nearly intractable impediment. Since they were built, extensive development covers them.

Programs to buy out floodplain homes and businesses are ongoing but underfunded. Building retention basins and enlarging bridge openings may reduce flood crests, but it's unlikely the Jordan will ever be completely tamed.

local color. Mostly they found junk: "We discovered where old automobiles go to die. They go to the Jordan river. How they got there is still a mystery, but the very last stage of their existence, after the salvage yard, is the Jordan. From its source to its mouth, the thing we found most of was rusting and rotting automobile parts. We daresay that the old automobiles from all over the country come to the Jordan for a final resting place." Writing in 1939, the journalists believed recent engineering works had made the flood-prone creek "resigned to the harness":

> In days gone by, folks might forget the Jordan for periods of time, but sooner or later the Jordan would remind them of its presence by rising out of its banks and flooding a sizeable section of the valley. At such times the little stream would assume delusions of grandeur and run pell mell over the country side, flooding streets and front yards for all the world as though its one ambition in life was to make the news reels.
>
> But it can't even do that any more. The main body of the stream, that which flows through the city proper, has been walled in beneath the surface of the ground, harnessed by an aqueduct which conducts it peacefully and quietly beneath the city. Outside the city limits, its channels have been deepened and widened to care for flood waters. The many springs which used to dot its course and contribute to its strength have long since been lugged or converted to other uses.
>
> All this seems to have had its effect upon the morale of the Jordan. Maybe it knows that it has been broken and harnessed. It no longer displays any disposition to act up. In fact, it seems to have just about lost interest in life altogether. It goes for long stretches without even showing its face above the surface of the ground. And when it does show above the surface, it isn't the Jordan river of old. Anyone can see that at a glance.

Concrete-lined boxes under the business district were built in 1928, and extended in 1934 with WPA money. Called the Jordan "aqueduct," these 3,520-foot-long underground conduits have been from their inception a mysterious, legend-spawning realm:

> The aqueduct, since it was completed, has taken on something of a personality. It winds dark and cavernous beneath factories, railroad tracks, wholesale houses and whatnot. Along its course are piles of debris which have been washed down from all along the course of the Jordan by high waters, and among the debris one finds everything from bed springs and whiskey bottles to parts of stoves and automobile fenders. Anyway by the time one has traversed about half of it, one has reached the state of mind where one wouldn't be surprised to come upon a dead body, or a skeleton with its bleached bones reflecting one of the few pin points of light which battle their way into the darkness through occasional air vents.

The series ends with a reflection on our transformed streams, but not altogether negatively:

> So on this romantic note we leave the Jordan, which, while it still isn't a river, has at least achieved the dignity of a creek, and achieved also,

Above: *Jordan Creek: Story of an Urban Stream* (2008).

Illustrated with vintage photographs, this account of Springfield's legendary stream was written by Loring Bullard and published by the Watershed Press. Bullard was the original executive director of the Watershed Committee of the Ozarks, a partnership of the city, county, City Utilities, and other government agencies and nonprofits concerned with clean water.

By connecting streams with political, economic, and social developments, Bullard makes a case that river systems, even impaired ones, are objects worthy of our attention. "Raising the Jordan," the last chapter, proclaims that although flooding problems persist, efforts to rehabilitate it have had some notable successes.

> to an extent, some of its former respectability. If Cortez hid treasure on its banks, he and his men doubtless camped on its shores. The Indians probably camped along it also. It has seen them come and go, and the settlers arrive. Perhaps it will see Springfield come and go also and live to laugh at the civilization that had it down for the count, but not out.

Americans have transformed the entire watershed of the James River, but urbanization has had a greater impact on surface waters than agriculture. Fields and pastures have better absorption of rain than roofs, streets, and parking lots. Space is at a premium in densely populated areas so floodplains are built upon. A common response to periodic overflows and resulting property damage is channelization and hardening of stream banks with rock and concrete. This worsens downstream flooding. Every growing city in America abused streams. Springfield recognized and acknowledged water management deficiencies more openly than many metropolises. Its press aired these problems, and city leaders were generally willing to address them. Some of the solutions, especially the simplistic approaches to hydrology, however, had unintended consequences.

Civic leaders like Woodruff were not only responsive to infrastructure inadequacies; some were nostalgic for a remembered Jordan Creek in its natural state. Vance Randolph's appreciation of cultural primitivism and naturalist literature may have met with disapproval, but the effort to restore the Jordan to a more primitive and natural state has a considerable history.

At a Young Men's Business Club meeting in 1914, a year before J.R. Roberts penned his satiric poem, Louis Brownlow, a Washington, DC, representative of Haskin Syndicate News Service, suggested a beautification plan for the Jordan Creek valley. He compared it to an "unsightly landscape with an almost identical natural condition existing in Edinburg, Scotland, where a similar eyesore had been transformed into one of the city's most beautiful parks."

"Local Isaac Walton League Plans Campaign to Prevent Pollution of Jordan Creek," read the headline of an article in a Feb. 3, 1925, *Springfield Missouri Republican*. Claiming "Fish are dying by the thousands and can be scooped up in baskets in the James River," the Sequoita Chapter blamed "oil, gas and other foreign substances" being dumped into Jordan Creek. Sportsmen from the club planned to visit the heads of the offending industries: "It will not take many years before fish cannot live in Lake Taneycomo if the pollution of the stream keeps pace with increase of population, it was said."

City administrators and politicians often agreed with citizen complaints, but lacked funds and technology. As advances in water and sewage treatment were made, some of Jordan Creek's ills were addressed. Ordinances were passed and enforced prohibiting using the creek as an open sewer. "That nauseating smell of gas / That greets us as thy way we pass" abated. But as the city grew and Jordan Creek's watershed became less permeable, it still flooded even after the costly engineering works of the 1920s and '30s.

Unacceptable as subterranean channelization is by current standards of good water management, the architecture of these failed projects has followers among those with a dark, romantic sensibility. When Jordan Creek is low, these tunnels can be traversed; lovers of gloom can encounter bats, catfish, crawdads, frogs, water snakes, and occasionally troglodyte transients.

Above: Entrance to a box culvert off Fremont dated 1955. Springfield's tradition of burying troublesome streams persisted until recently.

The best known and longest of Springfield's subsurface stream conduits is the Jordan Underground, but there are three other tunnels.

Right: This intrepid adventurer emerged from the 1,643-foot-long Fremont-to-National tunnel. He was looking for a place to exit the high concrete walls containing the south branch of Jordan Creek.

Above: Urban explorers find the Jordan Creek Underground irresistible, as do the homeless during dry weather.

Top: Behind this wall is the old Jordan Creek box culvert, now decorated with sanctioned graphics.

There is a long history of citizens inscribing messages on water infrastructure. Ancient Roman aqueducts were covered with scratched graffiti, much of it vulgar. Springfield's misnamed "aqueducts" have both authorized and unauthorized decorations. The roof of the last two hundred yards of Jordan Creek's boxed culvert is above ground. Reproductions of Picasso and Munch on its north wall validate the progressive city's claims of cultural sophistication (above right).The mural by Missouri State University art students fulfilled their professor's assignment to "focus on social progress." A cartoon balloon added to Munch's painting screams, "Modern technology owes ecology an apology." This commendable green message has not reached every resident of center city. Dead horses no longer befoul Jordan Creek, but as it emerges from the tunnel it's still full of trash. The walls here are covered with spray-can graffiti. None of it references high art, much of it is profane, and all of it is illegal. The Community Partnership of the Ozarks diligently tries to obliterate such antisocial expressions with rectangles of blue paint that sometimes look vaguely like Rothko knockoffs. Taggers often overwrite this censorship. Gang signings are a priority for masking.

In 2007, a 15-year-old runaway brought attention to Springfield's vampire community, who were holding meetings in "Hell's Church," within the tunnels. "They believe I'm a vampire queen," the girl said. "They just need to awaken me. It's nice to be accepted like that." The girl was found by police and in time abandoned drinking blood and her dream of becoming the vampire queen of Queen City.

end
violence
Modern technology
Owes ecology
An apology
MUNCH, THE SCREAM 1893
Jill Hetherington
Cindy Holman
NAZI

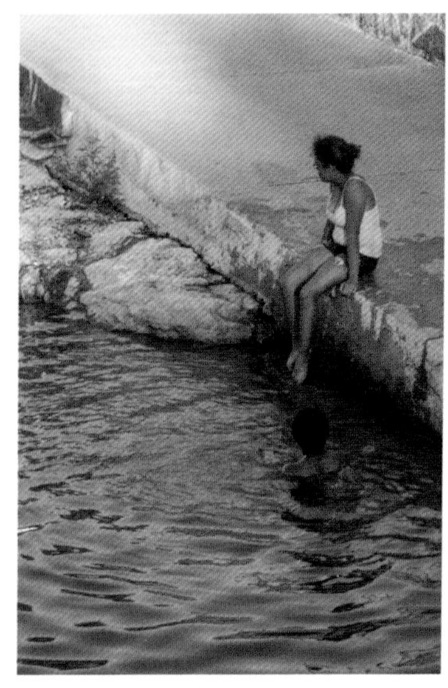

Above and below: Though its bed has been armored by WPA rock work through Smith Park, Jordan Creek has excavated a hole deep enough to cool off in.

Concurrent with the needs of practical types who wanted to keep flood waters out of downtown businesses and homes, some Springfieldians wished to preserve streams in a more natural state. The park movement took root here in the nineteenth century. While not all of their plans to beautify Jordan Creek came to fruition, there are several native rock-lined stretches. Smith Park is one.

In the 1970s, the federal Clean Water Act gave those with environmental goals a valuable tool. Improvements in the nation's water quality were not only encouraged, they were mandated. In time, efforts to undo ugly water engineering became part of federal/local programs, along with improving water and sewer systems. "Daylighting," or tearing open box culverts, is an especially favored restoration. An Ozarks Water Watch post on August 13, 2012, "Hidden Treasure Under Springfield," lauded the transformation:

> Imagine a clear, cold, spring-fed creek rippling over rocks through downtown Springfield. You take refuge from the hot August sun in the shade of a nearby grove of trees, and delight in the beauty of brightly colored minnows flashing in the sunlight. This image may soon, once again be a reality as the "hidden treasure" of Jordan Creek is brought out of its dark tomb and reborn into a sparking asset. ...
>
> The Jordan Creek Renewal is a multi-purpose project along the Jordan Creek corridor through the heart of Springfield. Multiple objectives for the project include flood damage reduction, water quality

> improvements and habitat creation through stream corridor restoration and storm water and transportation infrastructure replacement. Other benefits include potential for increases in property values, economic development and aesthetic, cultural and other quality of life improvements, particularly in the downtown area.

With a budget of $2,876,000, largely funded from a 2001 Storm Water Bond, the project ripped off the cover of the concrete box between Smith Park and Silver Springs Park. A trail now runs along a native plant-lined rocky trickle full of minnows and an occasional well-fed night heron. The Army Corps of Engineers has offered to help the city fix Jordan Creek. Having failed to prevent catastrophic flooding on big rivers with big dams, the Corps now wants to control floods on small creeks with small retention basins. The cost for the first installation of this hydrologic magic would be $21,873,000 – trails or parks not included.

Above and right: Below Smith Park at the beginning of the Jordan Creek North Branch Daylighting Project, a sign explains how the too-small tunnel once caused flooding. Some houses subject to overflow were bought, and the project has widened the flood plain, which is planted with native vegetation.

Above: "The Big Green Cage," a bridge over Kansas Expressway for users of the South Creek Greenway.

Top: Upper South Creek drains suburbia. The creek takes on a more natural appearance as it runs through the restoration, and then Nathanael Greene/ Close Memorial Park.

Back when the Springfield Wagon factory and Dingeldeins Brewery were periodically flooded by Jordan Creek, the bottoms along South Creek were cornfields. When developers converted these farms into suburbs, this small meandering tributary of Wilson Creek was channelized. Unlike Jordan Creek, its wide conduit was uncapped, making a makeover less complex than the Jordan Creek box culvert project. The June 13, 2014, *News-Leader* summarized the South Creek deal:

> The city of Springfield has received a $715,000 grant for its South Creek restoration project from the Missouri Department of Natural Resources, according to a news release. The project will remove the concrete channel and restore the creek to a more natural condition in the one-mile portion along Sunset Street between Campbell Avenue and Kansas Expressway. The purpose of the project is to improve water quality and habitat for aquatic life. Sales tax along with contributions of time from city staff and grant partner Ozark Greenways brings the project's total value to more than $1.1 million.

Both restorations have adjacent paths for bikers and hikers. These trails often link parks and most run along streams. Ozark Greenways is a nonprofit that facilitates adding on to the city's seventy-plus miles of urban trails. *Field Guide 2030 – A Strategic Path to Springfield's Future* lists the organization as a partner in achieving salutatory "Green Space Infrastructure." These efforts, the planning document insists, have a larger purpose than recreation:

> Green space can be utilized for stormwater and floodwater management; groundwater recharge; soil and water conservation; pollution filtration for the water we drink, the air we breathe, and the soil that grows our food; brownfield rehabilitation and greyfield re-use; and habitat for pollinators of food crops. ... Conservation of unique natural features and wildlife habitat is accomplished within green space systems. Community character is enhanced, and recreation opportunities and routes for non-motorized transportation within green space systems provide benefits for public health, as well as for lower-income citizens, especially in urban areas.

Perhaps a tad aspirational, but Springfield's ventures into stream restoration are modest compared to the elaborate justifications (and corresponding budgets) made by some municipalities. Returning the Los Angeles River to a more natural state would cost the city $1.35 billion – and that number is "evolving" as it involves the Army Corps of Engineers and celebrity architect Frank Gehry. An advocate promised comparable large benefits: "Freeing the river from its concrete straitjacket and restoring it to its natural beauty will transform Los Angeles." Ugly that the "giant gutter" is, it is considered an engineering masterpiece that has kept downtown LA from flooding. The Los Angeles River in its natural state was unstable, and except during the rainy season, was often dry. Streams differ in their hydrology, their restorability, and in the outcome of even extreme efforts to undo our transformations.

Right: South Creek Restoration Project under construction and finished.

There is disagreement between engineers who design these restorations and scientists. In *Rivers in the Landscape,* Ellen Wohl points out, "River restoration as currently practiced is not commonly scientific because hypotheses regarding river response to a given restoration action are not posed and tested. A large-scale survey of river restoration in the United States found that fewer than 10 percent of projects included any form of monitoring or assessment.

"Small- to medium-scale river restoration has become an industry with designs developed by those with relatively little knowledge of river process and form that are implemented by consulting firms most likely to have a background in civil engineering works rather than in river science. Under these circumstances, the scientific community has become increasingly vocal in criticizing restoration practices."

Dr. Wohl distinguishes between *restoration,* "a return to a close approximation of the river prior to disturbance," and *rehabilitation,*" improvement of a visual nature." This project is really a rehabilitation.

At the southern edge of the Euticals Chemical Plant, Jordan and Fassnight Creeks join, creating Wilson Creek. The setting is surprisingly natural (bottom). A quarter mile downstream is an Adopt-A-Stream sign on the Scenic Avenue bridge (left, middle). The headwaters of Wilson Creek are trashy, but run over its own chert gravel bed. Compared to channelized, concrete-walled conduits it would seem to be cost-effective to rehabilitate. This condition of a sullied but semi-wild environment persists for several miles. Actually there are reaches of several urban streams like this draining Springfield, but restoring them will involve more than fraternity boys, who recently adopted this stream, picking up junk along Wilson Creek. It will require naturalists with chainsaws, not Sunday afternoon volunteers. Some qualified groups do improve Springfield waterways. The Greater Ozarks Audubon Society has performed wonders on a stretch of South Creek, creating a habitat for more than a hundred bird species. If streams are involved in expanding trails, the Greenways organization supports improvements. But most of these degraded but essentially natural creeks have become inventory for future riparian rescue projects.

Twenty-five years ago, a bridge crossed Wilson Creek about a mile downstream from the busy Scenic Avenue bridge. When it washed out, it was not rebuilt due to its low traffic volume (left top, closed road sign). A relic of that failed bridge is a monster half-oval galvanized, corrugated steel pipe culvert. Divorced from its original function, the thing lies in the stream bed, an alien artifact glimpsed in the morning's early light (opposite). Have we stumbled on an unknown avant-garde art project? After several shots of the enigmatic object, the photographer found Wilson Creek (left bottom) to be a prototypical, albeit trashier, Ozarkian brook, though fringed with an uncommonly virulent growth of poison ivy.

Elfindale--St. DeChantal Akademy, Springfield, Mo.
Made in Germany. Fairbank's Book Store, Sole Agents, Springfield, Mo.

Above: Postcard of St. deChantal Academy of the Visitation, mailed July 7, 1911. The stone mansion built by John O'Day in the early 1890s near South Creek was bought by an order of Catholic nuns from St. Louis.

An October 12, 1902 headline in the *St. Louis Post-Dispatch* stated, "Offers Her Home As Public Park: Mrs. Alice O'Day Will Give Elfindale To Springfield If They Will Allow Her A Life Interest In The Place." As well as lifelong tenancy, she wanted the city to pay her interest on the value of the park annually. Springfield declined.

When the nuns put the property up for sale, a group, Save Elfindale, formed in 1974 to preserve the "last, large unspoiled natural tract within city limits." The nonprofit was unsuccessful, and the land was zoned for development.

The small dam that creates a small lake on Fassnight Creek doesn't look new (opposite bottom). We don't know if it is the dam that Mrs. Alice O'Day had constructed in 1900 to create "one of the chief attractions of Elfin-Dale," as a lengthy article in the September 8, 1901, *St. Louis Post-Dispatc*h describes that lake. The current pond doesn't fulfill the newspaper description, but then the journalistic description may be as enhanced as the hand-tinted postcard mailed in 1911 (opposite top):

> It is entirely artificial, an old stock pond having been transformed into a beautiful sheet of water, mirroring in its depths the overhanging trees and reflecting the clouds by day and the stars by night. The lake is deep and clear. At one end is a pretty boathouse, in which several canopied rowboats are kept. These boats furnish delightful recreation for Mrs. O'Day's friends when they visit "Elfin-Dale." ...
>
> The island in this lake is of particular interest. It is here that Mrs. O'Day has bestowed her greatest care, and her most artistic skill in landscaping has been given to the beautifying of the island.
>
> Mrs. O'Day has caused to blossom with beauty these 200 acres of hers by her energy and artistic ability transforming the hills and vales into a delightful expanse of woods and waters, with roads and paths and bridges and rustic nooks.

A remarkable feat considering that thirteen months before, after an argument with her Frisco Railroad magnate husband over the division of assets in an impending divorce, Alice shot herself through the left lung with a .38 caliber derringer. She survived her suicide attempt, and got the thirty-five-room turreted Victorian mansion and 200-acre farm. In 1905, the money ran out, and she sold Elfindale to the Sisters of Visitation for $30,000. The nuns established a school for girls that closed in 1964. In 1978, the property was sold to a group of Iranian investors. Today the mansion is a bed and breakfast, and the grounds have been commercially developed.

ELFINDALE LAKE, SPRINGFIELD, MO.

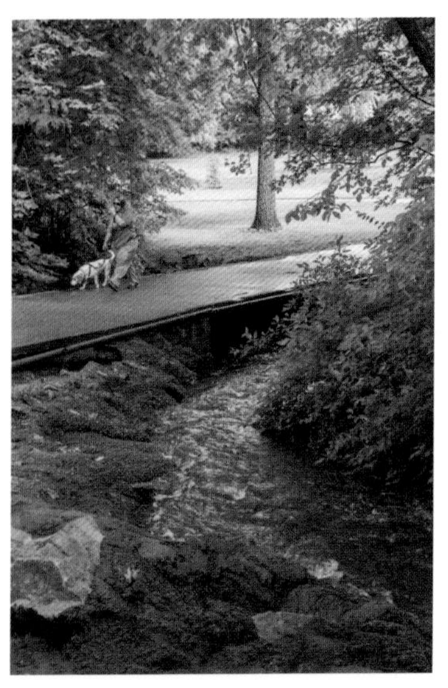

Parks are preferred by many Springfieldians to wild, or unkempt nature. Almost all the plants in the Nathanael Greene/Close Memorial Park are planted and maintained by volunteers. Many are foreign like hostas, but there is an arboretum with seventy species of native trees. An article in the April 2, 2008, *Missouri Conservationist* attributed the popularity of the verdant park to Springfield's urban tempo: "Blooming flowers and ornamental shrubs greet visitors at the parking lot of Close Memorial Park and lead them away from Springfield's urban bustle. A paved path takes them to Anne Drummond Lake, where calming views of swimming waterfowl and perhaps a great blue heron wading at the well-manicured lake's far end help visitors unwind from the day's tensions." Also included in the complex is a relocated historic log house, a Japanese Stroll Garden, a butterfly house, and a Botanical Center.

Above: Fountain in the Hostas Garden.

Top: The South Creek Greenway passes through many segments of a creek in differing states of development.

Right: The spillway of Lake Drummond has a fountain-like aesthetic.

Right: A Pokémon Go player sitting with a bronze life-sized sculpture of Annie Drummond reading a book. She was a Springfield civic leader and the mother-in-law of Major Close, who donated money to purchase land along South Creek in 1998. The overgrown acreage had a small lake that was dredged, enlarged, and named Lake Drummond.

Below: A gaggle of Pokémon Go players assembled in Close Memorial Park oblivious to the rain. Generational embrace of, and defense of, nature changes, but pleasant public spaces are universally appreciated.

Above: Middle Lake, Southern Hills subdivision.

Between the streams that drain into Wilson Creek and Pearson Creek is the 6.8 mile-long Galloway branch. Its headwaters were rural until two prominent Springfield developers bought many of the farms to create the upscale subdivision.

The little creek was dammed in three places to create small lakes. For a time they were relatively clear and considered an enhancement. Residents fished and swam in them. When the area above became urban and suburbanized, these ponds began changing as well, and not for the better.

Artificial lakes, great or small, do not age well. Three water features, four, seven, and ten acres, were created by John Q. Hammons and his partner Lee McLean, Jr., as amenities in an upscale suburban development on upper Galloway Creek assembled from nine farms in the 1950s. Steven Pokin, the *News-Leader* Answer Man, looked into an inquiry on August 5, 2016, concerning the ownership of these algae-plagued ponds in the Southern Hills subdivision. Pokin discovered no one really owns them. The liability-conscious developers set up a shell company to avoid lawsuits. Robert Smith has owned a house on the upper lake since 1977 and has become an expert on eutrophication:

> Smith says the lake has deteriorated as many small, stagnant bodies of water naturally do. As nearby Sunshine Street has been commercially developed, open fields that once absorbed rainwater have been replaced with impervious asphalt and concrete. As a result, rainwater carries more dirt and silt into the lake, along with fertilizers homeowners use on their lawns and gardens. The dirt and silt have settled at the bottom of the lake, making it shallower. Smith says the deepest point of the lake near his house was once 10 feet. Now it's 6 or 7 feet. Because it's not as deep, the lake heats up easier, which is conducive to algae growth. The addition of the nitrogen and phosphorus found

Resident swans and Canada geese contribute to the nutrients from yards that promote the hated algae bloom on the small lakes.

> in fertilizer also breeds algae. As a result, for four months every summer, he says, 85 percent of the lake is covered with algae. The other two lakes, he says, have the same problem but to a lesser degree. It's an eyesore, not a health menace, he says. As yet, there is not a major mosquito infestation. "Other factors in these lakes are goose and duck fecal matter which contribute to the nutrient load as well," he says. "Mix these with dirt that is swept into the lake during storm events, and you have the makings of lake problems. Unless there is a way for these materials to wash out of the lake, you are left with nutrient-rich sediment at the bottom of the lake which continues to cause algae problems every spring when the water warms and through fall of the year when the first frost causes the algae to die."

Residents talked the city into rehabilitating the ponds. They put in aerators, then chemicals, even carp, but nothing worked.

Further downstream, the city did renovate the lake at Sequiota Park. Unlike the three stagnant ponds in Southern Hills, this remnant of a fish hatchery is fed by a spring that flows five to eleven million gallons a day. Sediment removal and some improved circulation structures were part of a $1.8 million facelift. Even so, algae is still a problem. All the waters of the James River Basin are excessively enriched.

Above: *The Battle of Wilson's Creek* (detail), a twelve-foot half-circle mural by N. C. Wyeth in the Missouri State Capital. The artist visited Wilson Creek in 1920. While the creek with the old sycamore is accurate, the most intensive fighting took place on Bloody Hill.

Right: Civil War reenactors frequently hold demonstrations.

Confederates called it the Battle of Oak Hill. On August 10, 1861, 12,000 rebels from the Missouri State Guard and Confederate units from Louisiana, Texas, and Arkansas fought a force of 4,200 Yankee volunteers from the Midwest and some regular army soldiers. Brig. General Benjamin McCulloch led the Secessionists. The Union troops were commanded by Brig. General Nathaniel Lyon. It proved costly to both. The North suffered 1,317 casualties and the South 1,222. Confederate forces won, but they couldn't hold Missouri. Ultimately they lost everything, including the right to name the battle. Today, the rolling site is within Wilson's Creek National Battlefield, the Union's name for the bloody encounter.

Wilson Creek (cartographers have dropped the possessive apostrophe) drains more of Springfield than any other tributary of the James. Within its watershed of fifty-eight square miles live more than 100,000 people. Few Ozark creeks have a richer human past. The Delaware settlement on the James River extended up the

Above: A raceway, 1,669 feet long, was dug to transport water from an upstream dam to power a gristmill. Archaeologists in 1967 had to clear vexatious undergrowth to find it. That "uncommonly dense brush" has grown back.

Below: Wilson Creek near the site of Gibson's Mill. Improvements in Springfield's wastewater treatment and sensitive park management have created a pleasant, tree-lined stretch of Wilson Creek.

creek, which was named for Indian trader, James Wilson. One of its farthest branches is Jordan Creek, whose varied states of development embody the city's changing strategies of water management. Because Wilson Creek flows through a hallowed battlefield, now protected by the National Park Service, this section receives a high standard of care compared to the neglected upstream stretch available for adoption. Experts have studied every natural and cultural aspect of the memorial, and the management plan derives from these scientific and historical inquiries.

Efforts to establish a national monument at the battlefield were spearheaded by Springfield's civic leaders, including John T. Woodruff, as early as 1925. In 1960, the farm properties on which the battle was waged became a national park. Research was commissioned, resulting in a 2001 report, *Wilson's Creek National Battlefield Natural Resource Condition Assessment.*

While the water quality of Wilson Creek was found to be technically poor, researchers discovered that "even with stream degradation invertebrate populations have not decreased from the levels recorded in earlier surveys." Forty-two fish species were found, even though Springfield's Southwest Cleanwater Treatment Plant is upstream, and much of the watershed has expanding developments. Upgrades in water treatment have increased dissolved oxygen concentrations, the study noted. Planned improvements in phosphorous removal will continue to aid Wilson Creek's recovery.

Early investigators coped with a substantially more impaired stream. In 1967, a team from University of Missouri led by Robert T. Bray produced "An Archaeological Survey and Excavations at Wilson's Creek Battlefield National Park, Missouri." Attempting to

Above: Riders cross Shuyler Creek on a section of the equestrian trail that follows the Wire Road.

Before the Civil War parts of it were used by a contingent of the Cherokee Indians on their trek to Indian Territory, on what became known as the Trail of Tears. For a short time before the Civil War it was the route of the Butterfield Stage Line. Both armies made extensive use of the Wire Road.

document the long-gone Gibson Water Mill they noted the difficulty of photographing remnants in the streambed, "particularly if they are clouded by fluffs of detergent and other sewer effluents as they were at three sites at Wilson's Creek."

Finding relics from the battle was equally challenging, but not odiferous. Bray and his crew discovered they were following "generations of collectors who have literally picked the place clean." Farm boys began picking up brass buttons, Minié balls, and gun parts to sell shortly after the battle.

On the grounds, a Civil War museum and the Halston Library educate visitors about the battle and its military significance. There is a five-mile auto tour with eight interpretive stops at important battle locations. Walkers and runners use trails throughout the bucolic setting. Seven miles of trails are available for horseback riders. One part of that trail follows the Wire Road, named for the telegraph strung along an improved Osage path between St. Louis and Fort Smith, Arkansas. The outnumbered Union forces marched down the Wire Road to attack the Confederates.

Wilson's Creek National Battlefield's peaceful, 1,749-acre rural landscape evokes its frontier agricultural development when ten thousand Confederate troops once camped to access food and water for themselves and their horses. It was a singularly unstrategic location for the second major battle of the Civil War. Here Nathaniel Lyon became the first Union general of the war to die in combat. America in 1861 had not fully realized what horrors lay ahead. The battle, wrote a participant, Sergeant William Tunnard of the Third Louisiana Infantry, "enlightened many ignorant minds as to the seriousness and fearful certainty of the contest."

Right: Spring-fed Shuyler Creek, also known as Skagg's Branch, has better water quality and a higher Biotic Index than Wilson Creek. Its headwaters are in rapidly growing Republic, but much of it drains farmlands, principally pasture.

Terrell Creek, Wilson Creek's next tributary, drains no urban area and has correspondingly good water quality. The waterways within the battlegrounds are noted in period military accounts, but as they are small creeks, they apparently didn't play a tactical role as major rivers might have.

Above: Thermal pollution is a little known environmental liability of the James River Power Plant. Its history of air pollution from coal burning is well publicized. The deleterious effect on the biota of the James from the release of water 44°F hotter than the river has not, to our knowledge, been studied here. Elsewhere thermal pollution has been found to be ecologically damaging.

When a hunk of obsolete industrial infrastructure sits in the middle of a river, its removal can cost more than its construction. This is a reality rarely considered by dam builders. The piece of concrete that creates Lake Springfield also functions as a bridge. People get used to backed-up waters, filled in that they inevitably become. Questions of what to do with the only dam on the James River may present themselves, as the reason it was built may disappear.

Few Springfieldians have ever heard of Kissick Dam. Lake Springfield, its reservoir, is a 318-acre shallow lake just south of town, well known to local fishermen and picnickers. On its south shore is the hulking James River Power Plant built by City Utilities in the 1950s. The lake supplies water to cool its condensers.

Virgin Bluff Dam, the failed scheme to create a hydroelectric installation on the James in the early 1900s, has left an extensive paper trail. About all that can be Googled up on the James River Power Plant stems from a war waged by the Sierra Club against the utility over the many environmental issues raised by burning coal to generate electricity. The Environmental Protection Agency is also no fan of coal-operated plants, and they don't just threaten lawsuits. The EPA prevailed upon CU to switch to natural gas. Ironically, the facility was originally gas operated. After the oil em-

Above and right: Kissick Dam. There have been fish kills above and below the dam at Lake Springfield. In June 2002, conservation agents found sixty-six dead paddlefish below the spillway. The causes are not known, but may be related to the power plant's release of heated water. There are alternative methods of obtaining cooling water, but in the 1950s, this was probably the most expedient.

What effect this blockage has had on the inability of paddlefish to reproduce in the James is not certain. Apart from thermal pollution from the power plant, the dam alters the river's regime.

bargo of 1973, the feds required CU to burn coal in order to ensure an ample supply of natural gas for home heating.

There have been upgrades to the sixty-year-old technology here, but the James River plant may be abandoned. What then for the dam and silted-in lake? Would taking out the dam improve the chances that paddlefish might reproduce in the James? Who would pay?

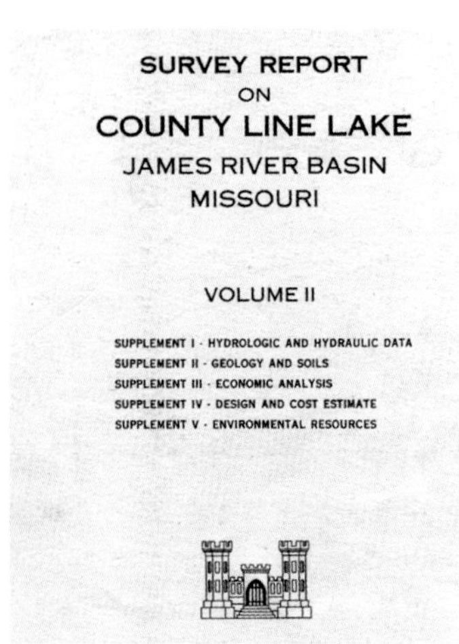

SURVEY REPORT
ON
COUNTY LINE LAKE
JAMES RIVER BASIN
MISSOURI

VOLUME II

SUPPLEMENT I - HYDROLOGIC AND HYDRAULIC DATA
SUPPLEMENT II - GEOLOGY AND SOILS
SUPPLEMENT III - ECONOMIC ANALYSIS
SUPPLEMENT IV - DESIGN AND COST ESTIMATE
SUPPLEMENT V - ENVIRONMENTAL RESOURCES

Above: *Survey Report on County Line Lake, James River Basin, Missouri*, three volumes, 1972.

Having run out of major dam projects, the Little Rock District of the Army Corps of Engineers proposed a smallish reservoir on the upper James. Lacking adequate conventional justification, the Corps desperately needed to sell its water to the City of Springfield. The passage of the National Environmental Policy Act of 1969 required the preparation of a detailed Environmental Impact Statement, which revealed many of the benefits of this project were dubious.

Table Rock backs up fifty miles of the lower James, but the only dam on the main stem is Kissick. Pioneers found the James River a bit too big to harness for watermills, while the Corps of Engineers thought it too small – until they ran out of prime dam sites. In the Corps' original 308 survey of all potential dam sites (1932), they did list a location above Galena, but they preferred to impound the larger White River. There is enough relief in places along the James for a lake, but the flow isn't dependable enough for hydroelectric development, which was an early selling point.

Through the years other schemes to dam the James have been proposed. Bizarre Virgin Bluff Dam below Galena will be discussed in the next chapter. In 1899, Col. H. N. Armstrong wanted to build a hydroelectric project on the James to supply an electric railroad that would connect Iowa with the Gulf of Mexico. These schemes were laughable, but when the Army Corps of Engineers begins unrolling blueprints and churning out reports of needed hydrologic fixes, it's no joke.

The never (but nearly) built County Line Dam was planned on the Greene-Webster county line ten miles east of Springfield. Unlike Table Rock Dam, there was no magic about this prosaically named and minuscule (by Corps' standards) effort to make running water surrender its benefits. County Line Dam (according to a three-volume 1973 *Survey Report*) would be 146 feet high with a rolled earth embankment 4,800 feet long. The proposed 7,480-acre lake extended thirteen miles upstream. Its 69,100-acre-feet of flood storage equaled .0013 percent of the flood storage capacity of the six Corps reservoirs already built on the White River system.

If County Line Lake's flood storage would add an insignificant amount to that of the giant reservoirs already in existence, what good was it? Vol. 1 of the Little Rock District's *Survey Report* lists the contributions to human betterment of this multi-purpose project. Along with the once-dominant rationale of flood control, "water supply, water quality control, general recreation, fish and wildlife enhancement, redevelopment, and intangible" were listed and quantified. County Line Dam would cost $28,490,000 (later $40 million) and return $3,867,000 in benefits per year.

A federal water project needs local and congressional support. Meetings to gauge public interest are required by law. At such an assembly, held on April 15, 1965, in Springfield, the mayor "pointed out the growing need for an additional source of water supply for the city and expressed the desire for assistance with the problem." Property owners who would be displaced opposed.

Above: Although the earthen dam of County Line Lake was less than a mile from Greene County, the entire project would have been completely in Webster County.

Alternative locations, required by the EIS process, included five other dams, all even more problematic. The US Department of Agriculture pushed a system of thirty-seven floodwater retention structures. Such glorified farm ponds have received a poor report from hydrologists as flood control methods, worse even than the Corps' mega-dam solution.

Supplying water for Springfield quickly became the Corps' strongest argument for building the mini-multipurpose reservoir. Only eight years earlier the city had purchased the privately owned water company. In 1965 they hired Burns & McDonnell Engineers to assess the long-term needs of the growing mini-metropolis. At a December 9, 1967, Corps hearing, the chairman of the City Utilities Commission reported Burns & McDonnell concluded, "The water supply requirements for Springfield will be more than twice the present-day use by the year 2000." Congressman Durward G. Hall concurred and now supported the project. Citizens to Preserve James River Valley voiced opposition.

By the time a third meeting was held on June 12, 1971, supporters and opponents were organized. About 180 people attended. Many gave statements, and several petitions were submitted. According to the *Survey Report*, "The project was endorsed by the state of Missouri, the board of City Utilities of Springfield, and the Springfield Chamber of Commerce. ... The project was opposed by landowner organizations, the Mid-America Dairyman's Association, the Webster and Greene Counties Soil and Water Conservation Districts and a few individual homeowners."

In spite of considerable official support, the dam on the upper James faced hurdles. The Corps' creativity in crafting a favorable cost-benefit ratio for dams is legendary, but this particular earth-moving endeavor lacked conventional justifications.

President Richard Nixon signed the National Environmental Policy Act (NEPA) on January 1, 1970. This law required the preparation of a detailed Environmental Impact Statement (EIS) whenever federal funds were expended. Government agencies and concerned organizations were supplied a draft EIS and allowed to comment. Hopes that revealing adverse consequences would stop water projects cold were dashed when federal courts ultimately decided they did not have authority to override congressional authorizations. Nevertheless the EIS process annoyed the Corps and alerted the press and decision-makers to defects.

A lengthy response on November 10, 1971, by the Missouri Chapter of the American Fisheries Society highlighted the preposterous claims the Corps was making. As well as supplying water to Springfield, they had assigned monetary benefits for diluting pollution from Wilson Creek. Both these issues, wrote the Society, "should be the responsibility of the City of Springfield." Although surrounded by large reservoirs, the Corps "concluded that a significant need exists in the market area for all types of rural outdoor recreational activity." Most members of the Fisheries Society were professional biologists involved in managing these resources. They called the need for more flat water recreation "ridiculous." Citizens to Preserve Upper James River Valley also used the word "ridiculous" to refute the claim that the dam would prevent flood damage to farm homes and crops amounting to $100,000 a year: "In fact, in the 106 years since records have been kept, no recorded loss of life nor destruction of major farm buildings is shown."

Opposite, top: This large cornfield along the James would have been inundated by the Corps' proposed County Line Lake.

Opposite, middle: At one time there were many dairy operations on the upper James. Atkinson Dairy is unsure if it will continue or switch to beef cattle as many have.

Opposite, below: Map of the proposed County Line Lake.

Had the Corps' 7,000-acre lake, ten miles east of Springfield, been completed, it would have been a good source of water, and because of its elevation would not have required pumping. The project, however, was costly, displaced many farm families, and would alter the natural environment of the upper James irreparably. Better solutions to Springfield's future water requirements were found.

It had not yet been discovered when the EIS was published that significant lead contaminants were stored in James River flood plain sediments. Dams promote channel instability and could release these old lead mine wastes into the James River.

The Ecological Preservation Council of the Springfield, Missouri, Chamber of Commerce, on the other hand, "felt that the (EIS) statement was very objective and thorough in its evaluation ... and leaves no doubt what-so-ever as to the urgent need for completion of the County Line Dam project." Adverse commentary damaged the reputation of the yet-unfunded dam on the James, but other developments were even more injurious. Gene Taylor, 7th District Congressman, said he received much mail on both sides, and didn't know if he would support the dam or not. Then-Governor Christopher Bond wouldn't commit $7 million in state money for the development of recreation.

The project had always depended on a commitment from Springfield to buy water from the Corps' impoundment. City Utilities made other plans. Deep wells were drilled and the Blackman Intake on the James supplied water to the new treatment plant on the east side of town. Then in 1990, City Utilities' Board voted to purchase 50,000 acre-feet of water from Stockton Lake, thirty miles away. A pipeline named for Saul Nuccitelli, one of their former engineers, began feeding Fellows Lake in 1996.

To the horror of its opponents, the dreaded County Line Lake project did not die. In 1978 the Little Rock District wrangled $100,000 from Congress for a restudy; then in 1984 it procured another $120,000. County Line Dam became one of that zombie army of undead Corps of Engineers' developments that could be resuscitated with a transfusion of federal funds.

A 2009 Tri-State Water Resource Coalition study concluded "it would not be economically feasible to construct one reservoir to serve the entire region." In the report the Corps did define fourteen potential smaller dam sites most of which were on the western side of the "tri-state waters footprint." Engineers with Springfield's Water Department do not however believe a dam on the James river system is likely to be advocated as a solution to the city's future needs for more water.

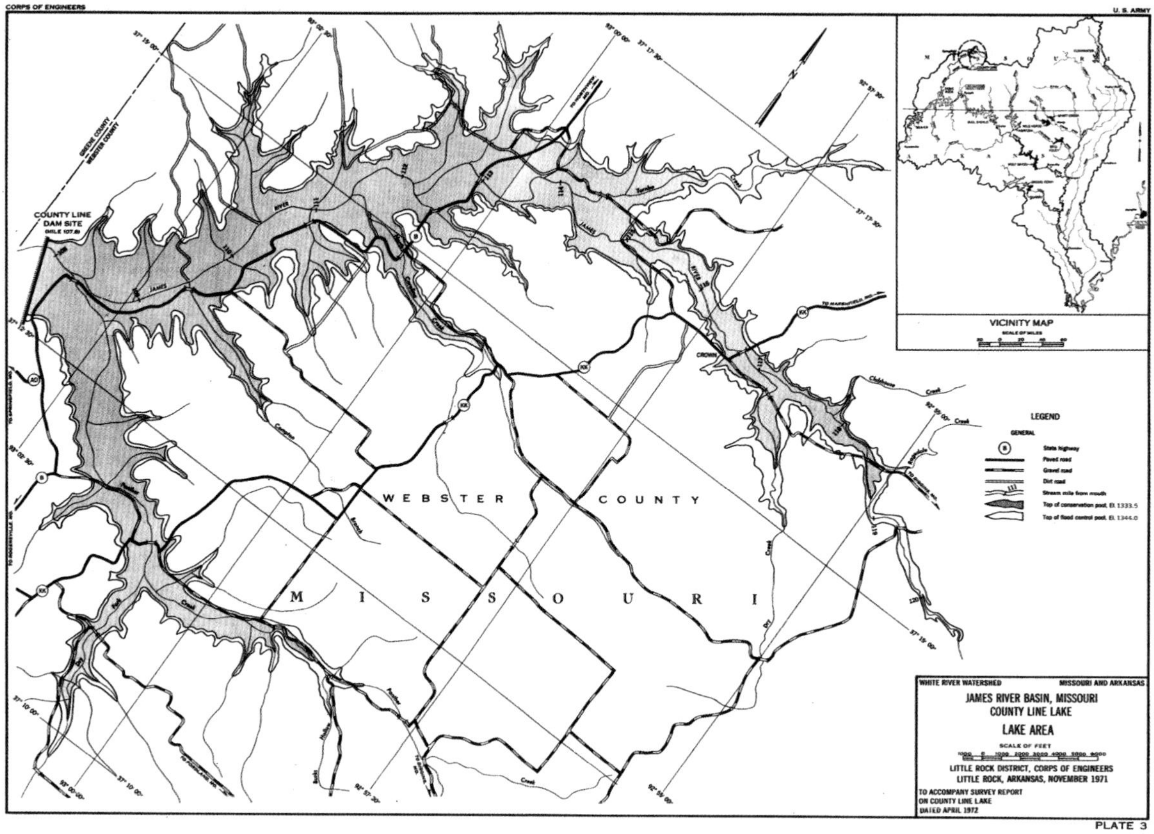

CORPS OF ENGINEERS

U. S. ARMY

COUNTY LINE DAM SITE

WEBSTER COUNTY

MISSOURI

VICINITY MAP

SCALE OF MILES

20 0 20 40 60

LEGEND

GENERAL

State highway

Paved road

Gravel road

Dirt road

Stream mile from mouth

Top of conservation pool, El. 1333.5

Top of flood control pool, El. 1344.0

WHITE RIVER WATERSHED

MISSOURI AND ARKANSAS

JAMES RIVER BASIN, MISSOURI
COUNTY LINE LAKE

LAKE AREA

SCALE OF FEET

LITTLE ROCK DISTRICT, CORPS OF ENGINEERS
LITTLE ROCK, ARKANSAS, NOVEMBER 1971

TO ACCOMPANY SURVEY REPORT
ON COUNTY LINE LAKE
DATED APRIL 1972

PLATE 3

Creeks that feed the upper James are chert-floored and crystal clear. The main river is large enough to float, but public access is limited. Its valley, seen just above the dam site (top), is still bucolic. Improvements in US 60 have allowed some suburbanization, but the overall character is still rural.

Charles R. Leick, representing two farmers groups, testified at a court hearing on June 12, 1971, that in spite of the James flooding every fifty years, "That is not a great enough threat to justify the removal of rich bottomland from production. He called it another recreation-oriented invasion of our rich Missouri Ozark heritage."

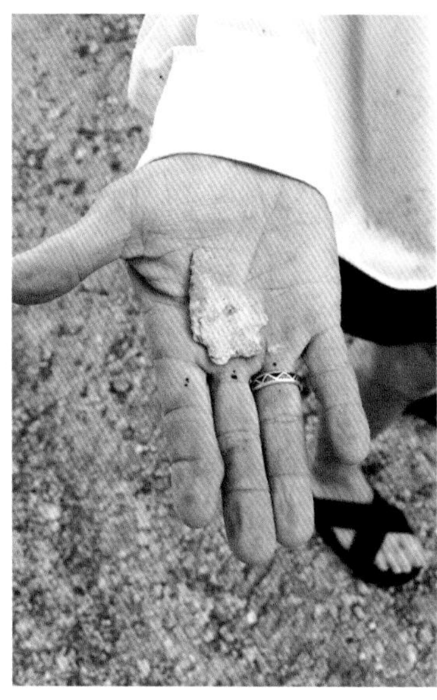

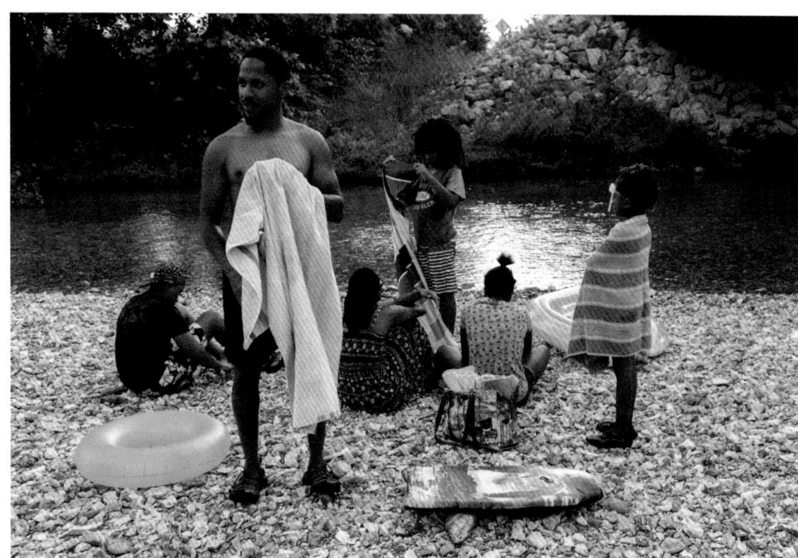

Above: Indian projectile point found in Panther Creek.

Right: Patrick Mureithi, a Kenyan born musician and filmmaker, and family recreating on Panther Creek. This would have been covered by the County Line Reservoir.

The EIS of the Missouri Chapter of the American Fisheries Society put the stream-versus-artificial-lake question into perspective:

> An impoundment can be created in any fold in the landscape by anyone with sufficient money, be it a private individual or any one of several great federal agencies. We never hear of anyone creating a stream. ... Lake-type recreation is abundant within a short radius of Springfield, but free-flowing, unpolluted streams are rare in this area. Diversity in human experience is highly valued, diversity in recreation especially so. The upper James River, no doubt, is much more valuable from the recreational and esthetic standpoint in its free-flowing state.

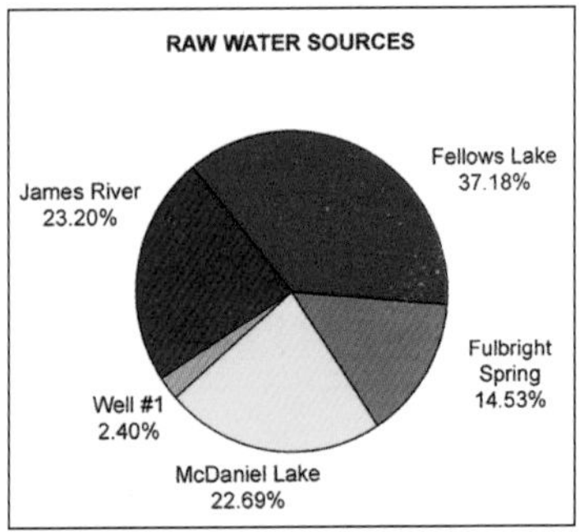

Above: Sources of Springfield's water, 2015.

Top: John Polk Campbell, Springfield's founder, built his cabin near a fissure that exposed a vein of water. Founders Park is near that location. The fountain memorializes that natural well, which has been covered over by Water Street.

That dalliance with the Army Corps of Engineers over damming the James River at the Greene-Webster county line wasn't the first time Springfield sought to expand its sources of water. With more people, and more industry, the city needed more water. Yet until 1980, it did not tap the James.

At the beginning of the Civil War, Springfield's population was a little more than one thousand. It was 5,500 by 1870 and would top 21,000 by 1890. Springs, wells, and cisterns were adequate during pioneer days, but vulnerable to pollution and unreliable as the town grew. The Queen City's first water works utilized Fulbright Spring on the Little Sac River (really a creek). Since 1883, that location, four miles north of town, has been the centerpiece of a complex of springs, wells, and reservoirs that in 2015 supplied Springfield with 77 percent of its water (pie chart, bottom left). An 1889 book, *Springfield, Missouri and Surroundings*, extols the expanding community's earliest industrialized solution to slaking the thirst of its citizens:

> The Fulbright Spring, which issues from a rocky cavern in the hills, two miles north of the city, and the Jones Spring, another splendid fountain issuing from the rocks in the very heart of the town, yield great volumes of the purest living water, from which are obtained the finest public water supply between the great lakes and mountains. From these two noble springs issue streams as pure and limpid as a mountain trout brook, with volume equal to the needs of a city of 150,000 people. The utilization of these matchless waters, by the Springfield Water Co., whose admirable works were constructed in 1883, has proven a strong factor in the health, growth and general prosperity of the city. ... The company – which is now composed of P. B. Perkins, John Francis, B. F. Hobart and W. C. Hornbeak – has a capital stock of $400,000, and is furnishing the people of Springfield with a water supply, which, for volume, purity, healthfulness and low temperature, any city in the West might envy; a water supply, to the purity and brilliancy of which the people of St. Louis, Kansas City and St. Joseph are unfortunately strangers.

Not entirely. Well before Springfield reached a population of 150,000 in the year 2000, many other sources of municipal water would need to be found. The puffery about the "perfect and complete" water company, however, did have some validity. In *Consider the Source: A History of the Springfield, Missouri, Public Water Supply*, Loring Bullard wrote, "By the time City Utilities of Springfield took over operation of the water system, adequate infrastructure for precision water treatment and efficient delivery was largely in place." From its beginnings in 1883, until its purchase by the city in 1957, the water company was privately owned. Interestingly, several of the principal stockholders were capitalists from the state of Maine. Paul B. Perkins, who engineered and built the first system, intended to convey it to the city, but they declined. Over the next seventy-four years, several offers were made to sell

THE "FULBRIGHT" CAVE SPRING AND FLUME OF THE SPRINGFIELD WATER COMPANY.

Above: Fulbright Spring is still an important source of water. It has long been encased by a masonry wall to protect it from contamination.

Top, right: Fulbright Spring, 1889, in its more natural state.

Right: Printed postcard of Fulbright Spring, 1920s. The spring by that time had been encased, but the new treatment building had not been built.

Below: Blackman Intake on James River (1980). River water is purified at a nearby plant, which also receives water from Fellows Lake. Some James River water is also transferred to that reservoir.

Above: Fellows Lake, completed in 1955. It now receives water from Stockton Lake and the James River as well as the Little Sac River. Most of Springfield's supply comes from this 815-acre reservoir.

Top: The 300-acre McDaniel Lake was added to Springfield's water system in 1929.

the operation to Springfield. Bond issues to finance purchase were turned down until May 14, 1957, when voters approved buying the operation for $20,701,779.

Expansions made before City Utilities took over included Jones Spring (1887); Ruth Spring and Owen Spring (1897); Valley Water Mills (1899); Fulbright Reservoir (1922); McDaniel Lake (1929); and Fellows Lake (1955). All but Jones Spring were located within the Sac River drainage.

Relations with customers were not always perfect, even if water quality was generally good. When McDaniel Lake came online, there were complaints about its pondy taste. Typhoid scares were blamed on city water, but most cases were traced to wells. Rate increases were resented. Through the years, the privately run system

Loring Bullard wrote of the 1940 building: "For the water company, the new Fulbright plant was a welcome addition – massive and handsome, reflecting the architectural pride of the era. Solidly built, it featured thick masonry walls and smooth limestone trim. ... The beautiful ornate filter chamber, reminiscent of a Roman bathhouse, shone with reflections in the glazed Welsh floor tiles. A marvel to this day, the Fulbright plant has been placed on the state register of historic places."

embraced new technologies, culminating in an impressive modern treatment facility completed in 1940 and still in use.

After the city acquired the water company, the search for additional sources intensified. Burns & McDonnell Consultants recommended buying into the Corps of Engineers' County Line Dam project. Instead, Springfield applied for a federal permit to draw water directly from the James River and built a larger treatment plant nearby. In 1990 City Utilities negotiated purchase of water from Stockton Lake, a Corps multi-purpose project thirty miles northwest of Springfield. A $5.75 million revenue bond was passed, and the Nuccitelli Pipeline was built to connect with Fellows Lake. Like most other Springfield water sources, this addition is from the Osage/Missouri system.

Above: Postcard from Bill Rogers Float Fishing Service mailed May 29, 1966, to a client in Larned, Kansas.

Rogers had moved his motel and float fishing operation from beside the old Kimberly City bridge to Galena when Table Rock Lake came in. He had hoped to serve both river and reservoir fishermen.

He advertised "Small Mouth – Large Mouth – Kentucky Bass taken on leisurely floats through beautiful country," even though the lake had ended the famed Galena-to-Branson float.

On the other side of the postcard of the smiling man with six big largemouth bass (left) is the typewritten message: "Bass season opens May 29, we have had wonderful water conditions and it looks favorable for excellent fishing results this year. We will be looking forward to your reservation and to seeing you. Sincerely, Bill Rogers." His optimism about "wonderful water conditions" soured in less than ninety days. On July 19th, 1966, Rogers sought a court injunction against the city of Springfield for polluting the James River and "causing loss of business." The *Kansas City Star* of July 20, 1966, reported,

> State biologists have said an excessive runoff of sewage and ground wastes from heavy rains caused 50,000 fish to die from lack of oxygen in the James River and Finley Creek last weekend. The Rogers firm asked no money damage in the action, filed in Greene County Circuit court. Springfield city officials have contended the Springfield sewer system was not responsible for the fish kill.

Dr. James Whitley, Conservation Department biologist, blamed the fish kill on "low oxygen levels resulting from decomposition of organic waste which flowed down Wilson Creek from the Springfield area." Heavy rains on July 15 were blamed.

Four decades earlier, Fred J. Foster, chief of state hatcheries, warned about the adverse effects of excess organic matter on the James River issuing from Wilson Creek. "Fish Life in Nearby Streams Made Impossible by Sewage," read the headlines in the January 31, 1927, *Springfield Leader*. In support of proposed improvements to Springfield's sewage disposal plant, Foster enumerated the many ways pollution kills fish and harms people.

Dr. K. C. Sullivan advanced a benign view of rivers enriched by wastewater discharges. In 1930, the state Game and Fish Commission engaged the entomologist to study the biota of several Ozark rivers. "From the great quantity of aquatic life encountered, it seemed evident that the material from the sewage reduction plant at Springfield entering Wilson Creek, has little or no detrimental effect upon life in the James River." Sullivan blamed "illegal fishing, including gigging" for the poor fishing.

Table Rock Dam closed in 1958. The James contributed 30 percent of its inflow. Its excessively fertile waters would have growing ecological and economic consequences. Complaints that fishing on the James wasn't as good as it used to be had not gone anywhere in the courts, or become a concern of Springfield's leaders. Table Rock Lake attracted many more recreationalists and was a key piece of a successful tourist industry that many Springfieldians were invested in. Scientists, not just a disgruntled Galena float trip outfitter,

Above: "Dirty Old James," a ballad of the inadequacies of Springfield's wastewater treatment is on the album Big Smith by the bluegrass band *Big Smith* (1998).

Below: Aerial photograph of a motorboat turning a figure-eight in the pea-soup-hued James River arm (1999). Along with numerous news releases, this image taken by the DNR contributed to the growing concern over Table Rock Lake's eutrophication. Courtesy of DNR.

were making serious charges about its deteriorating water quality.

Professor John R. Jones of the University of Missouri had been testing Table Rock's water since 1978. "Table Rock Lake Data Ominous," asserted the boldfaced headline of a story in the *St. Louis Post-Dispatch* (December 26, 1994): "Scientists don't ring alarms very often. Environmentalists do, but scientists don't. I have sounded an alarm." After a visit last summer, Jones thought, "Wait a minute. This isn't the same lake I know." He found the water "green and not transparent":

> Jones said he's particularly alarmed because Table Rock Lake's phosphorous count is double and in some places triple what it was five years ago. The highest counts were found in the James River arm of the lake, downstream from Springfield's Southwest Wastewater Treatment Plant. "At that time Table Rock was the jewel of the Ozarks: the biggest, cleanest, clearest, least fertile water body in the state," he said. "If I would do that same ranking based upon more recent data, it wouldn't come out that way."

This unhappy transformation was not only observed by scientists; everyone could see it. Phosphorous became a public enemy in numerous late 1990s page-one articles in the *Springfield News-Leader:* "Cure for Green Water Costly, City Learns," read the headline of March 6, 1996. "Everyone agrees that phosphorous-eating algae are turning Table Rock green. But fixing the problem will be expen-

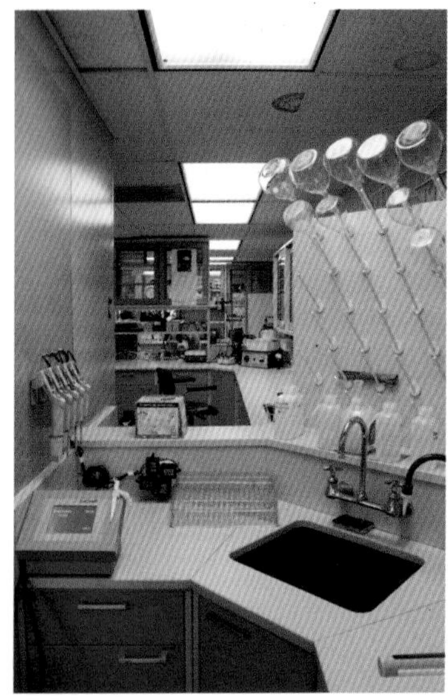

Above: Over 5,800 samples are tested per month for compliance with state and federal regulations at the Southwest Wastewater Treatment Plant (also named Southwest Cleanwater Plant).

Above right: Springfield's primary waste treatment plant employs sophisticated purification techniques to treat over 42 million gallons of wastewater a day. Phosphorus is removed by both chemical and biological methods.

For several years, Springfield's Southwest Wastewater Plant has been a recipient of the National Association of Clean Water Agencies' Platinum Award. This requires going for five years without a single permit violation.

sive." A $13 million upgrade to the Southwest Cleanwater Treatment Plant would be necessary, according to the paper. "Branson-area anglers carp about scum," was a March 6, 1996 headline. The next day's editorial stated, "Cleaner lake vital, costly." Another *News-Leader* editorial (Aug. 30, 1998) stated, "Keep clarity in lake, rates." How to pay for the plant's upgrade was problematic, but it was a "moral responsibility for the city to clean up our mess."

In 1999, state and federal government agencies became involved in the "Algae-feeding nutrient" problem, as a July 15 article put it. "State imposes phosphorous limits," was the headline. "At the apex of the greening of Table Rock Lake, help was on its way." An October 16 piece announced, "Federal cash to help stem lake pollution." Environmental activism of the 1960s had resulted in the passage of federal legislation protecting air, water, and endangered species. Requiring environmental impact statements altered, or stopped some improvident projects. Though not a cabinet-level department, the Environmental Protection Agency (EPA) had both authority and money. State agencies like the Missouri Department of Natural Resources administered EPA funds locally. A host of private organizations "partnered" with government agencies to protect and restore the environment. Some of these concerns were aesthetic or ethical, but many addressed problems like Springfield's wastewater treatment, which had significant economic consequences. "The lake is a pillar of southern Missouri's billion-dollar tourist trade," stated that October 1999 *News-Leader* piece.

An April 2, 2004, *Springfield News-Leader* headline announced, "Phosphorus removal working; sampling suggests rapid decrease in pollution of James River arm of Table Rock Lake." The paper pointed out that "millions of dollars spent on equipment was worth every dime." An editorial published two days later cautioned, "Cleaner lake many victories away; new report good news, but much to be done." Now that phosphorus discharges have been radically reduced at the Southwest Treatment Plant, further control of the algae's food would be harder. Throughout the James River watershed were numerous leaking septic tanks. Runoff of fertilizer from lawns and farms and poultry and cattle waste are pollutants. Agriculture had been politically effective securing exemption from EPA regulations, for so-called nonpoint sources.

Table Rock is an artificial lake, but reservoir tourism continued to emphasize nature as did the earlier Arcadian recreational attractions. Pete and Jack Herschend, founders of Silver Dollar City, cringed at reports of Table Rock's algae bloom. With others they organized a foundation in 2001 that would ultimately be called Ozarks Water Watch. It lobbies for the passage of laws that would improve the rivers, lakes, and subsurface water of the upper White River. Failing septic tanks have been a special concern. In cooperation with the DNR they administer grants to homeowners to prevent ground water pollution from inadequate septic systems.

Below, left: An April 2014 article in the *Ozone Wastewater Treatment News* noted, "Operators and management take pride in ozone residuals being at more than safe levels, and also to have plant effluents 'looking very much like a mountain stream, with an effervescent quality coming out, that we like to show visitors.'"

Below, right: As the wastewater plant discharges its clear, phosphorous-reduced waters into Wilson Creek, it cuts into the stream bank. Alluvial soils contain phosphorous and erosion releases these nutrients into the water. Planting riparian vegetation to control crumbling banks has been undertaken by the James River Basin Partnership with the Missouri Department of Conservation.

A mile west of the Southwest Cleanwater Treatment Plant is the John Twitty Energy Center. At dawn the coal-fired power plant is a vision of backlit colored steam flowing around the architecture of functionalism punctuated by twinkling lights. It might have caught Monet's eye. Like the suburban Paris train station he painted in 1877, it is hard industrialization softened by atmosphere. Impressionists found modern technology fit subjects for art, but don't look for coal-fired power plants in Sierra Club calendars. The Twitty Energy Center, however, conforms to EPA air quality standards.

Unlike the James River power plant, a stream was not dammed to provide cooling water for Unit 2, which went on line in 2011. A 1976 component drilled deep wells for water. This 300-megawatt addition gets its cooling water from the adjacent Southwest Cleanwater Treatment Plant. Engineers were skeptical about using processed municipal wastewater, but testing proved the water sufficiently pure. This means five million gallons per day wouldn't need to be pumped from underground aquifers. In another bit of recycling by the cleanwater treatment plant, methane gas furnishes half their energy needs. Treated bio-solids are distributed for agricultural fertilizer. Both of City Utilities' big pieces of infrastructure are improvements over earlier technologies.

Below: Unit 2 James River Power Plant. "Modern technology owes ecology an apology," the slogan painted on the chamber wall enclosing Jordan Creek, doesn't acknowledge the necessity of using modern technology to keep growing human populations alive. Industrialization has caused environmental degradation, but advances in science can mitigate some of these deleterious side effects.

This is hopeful, especially if there is political will to anticipate environmental harm and correct previous problems. Springfield's citizens, institutions, businesses, and infrastructure providers seem committed to the judicious use of technology.

Above: In 1861, soldiers and their horses and mules undoubtedly drank from Wilson's Creek. As Springfield grew, the stream, which is fed by Jordan Creek, became badly polluted. When the battlefield was acquired by the federal government in 1960, the creek smelled. Today, Wilson Creek meets EPA water quality standards, and there is interest in further improvements.

About five miles downstream from Springfield's principal source of power and largest wastewater treatment plant, Wilson Creek flows over a concrete slab on Old Limey Road. In less than a mile it joins the James Fork of the White, which is what Civil War commanders called the James. The esthetics of this place is classical Ozark country, though it's only ten miles from town. Monet would approve of this landscape, too. Bucolic views, it turned out, sold better than the raw scenes of industrialization he painted early in his career.

Manley Ford is at the southeast tip of Wilson's Creek National Battlefield. Here at 5 o'clock in the morning of August 10, 1861, Union Colonel Franz Sigel led a brigade of 1,200 men and two artillery pieces across the creek. Just before crossing, Sigel positioned four guns on a hill just upstream overlooking a Confederate camp. His plan was to flank the rebels as General Nathaniel Lyon's main force attacked from the north. Lyon would die at Bloody Hill, and Sigel's ambush was routed. The Confederates outnumbered the Yankees two to one. Some think the Union lost partly because Sigel confused the uniforms of a charging Southern regiment. Lincoln would later make Sigel a general because of his popularity with German immigrant volunteers. His military victories, however, were few.

Shooting rainwater downstream in a concrete ditch may spare local flooding, but it causes downstream overflows. Channelization, if indifferently engineered, doesn't work. It's also ugly (left).

Concurrent with such expedient water management, some Springfield streams were treated with aesthetic consideration. Through several parks like Fassnight (above) run creeks whose curvilinear forms have been respected. Wide channel walls and bridges of native rock express the Arts and Crafts movement's effort to achieve harmony with nature.

Wilderness has had few devotees. By the time that preservationists' ethos became a movement, there was virtually no pristine nature left in the James River watershed. Springfieldians' taste is for meandering, unpolluted streams (or even lakes), in a sylvan setting – i.e. parks. Citizen groups, supportive businesses, and city and state governmental departments collaborate cleaning up and refurbishing water resources. Goals as diverse as protecting the water supply, improving recreation, and encouraging native species are accommodated. Public education efforts marshal support for federal clean-water mandates. Some of these endeavors may be more symbolic than effectual, or lack scientific rigor, but they are sincere, civic, and enlightened.

Opposite top left: James River Basin Partnership's River Jam, 2015.

Opposite top right: Artist-decorated storm drain.

Opposite bottom: Cleanup of Lake Springfield by the James River Basin Partnership.

A LEGENDARY FLOAT

Above: Galena on the James has been a river resort for more than a century. There are recent and long-established players in this enterprise. The elevated rental cabins on the left were built a few years ago by the owner of an Alaskan whitewater rafting company. On the right is the Y Bridge Canoe Rental and Store owned by Kenny Short, whose family settled the area before the Civil War.

James River float trips now end at Galena, where they once began. A few miles below town, the flow melts into the slack water of the James River arm of Table Rock Lake. Canoers need to paddle harder and might have to cope with the wake of bass boats like the Skeeter FX-20 with "blistering top-end speeds in excess of 75-mph." The transformation of river to reservoir is profound.

Table Rock Dam is a manmade multipurpose federal water project that enhanced the tourist industry of Branson. A century ago, the float from Galena down the James to the undammed White River nourished a complex in Galena of boat builders, lodge operators, outfitters, and guides. A 1920s Ozark Playgrounds Association booklet stated, "Galena is the county seat of Stone County, Missouri. Here will be found a town of intelligent, up-to-date busy business people, whose very password is 'hospitality.' Once a visitor within their gates, never forgotten":

> To the old-time fisherman in the Ozarks, the word "Galena" is synonymous with "fishing," "Galena-Branson Float Trip," "Virgin Shoals," "Bee Bluff," "Table Rock" and "Horseshoe Bend." For it is from there that a dozen different float trips on the beautiful James and White rivers are equipped with provision, boats and guides, and parties started on their way rejoicing. On any summer's night the smoke may

be seen curling from a hundred different camp-fires on the James and there the river guides are telling stories of long-since vanquished foes. The long trip is one hundred twenty-five miles over the waters of the crookedest rivers in America, back to the railroad within twenty-two miles of the point of beginning. Words are inadequate to picture the beauty and grandeur of these float trips.

The actual distance of the great Galena-to-Branson float is not the often quoted 125 miles but is closer to 65 miles, as determined by using Google Earth and GPS Visualizer's sandbox feature. Nevertheless, the 125-mile-distance appears in numerous newspaper and magazine stories, period brochures, and tourism advertisements from 1910 to the present. On its website, the usually precise Missouri Department of Conservation also states the river distance of Galena to Branson during the float era was 125 miles.

Usually, these guided floats took four or five days. A 65-mile-distance would be around thirteen to sixteen miles a day, which squares with accounts that they were leisurely, relaxing affairs. There were lots of stops to fish, and long lunches and late breakfasts prepared by guides, who were not only good at retrieving fishing lures from overhanging tree branches but accomplished campfire cooks.

Today's James River float is shorter, but there are still a few Galena businesses who serve a clientele that is partial to free-flowing river recreation. Kenny and Michelle Short have owned the Y-Bridge Canoe Rental for fourteen years. Before that, Kenny played in a country band. Shorts were living in the James country when Stone was broken out of western Taney County in 1851. Kenny's ancestors include Dewey Jackson Short, US Congressman, and Dewey's brother, Leonard "Shock" Short, bank robber.

We asked Kenny why Leonard was called "Shock." "Don't have a clue. Asked my great grandpa that when I was a little bitty 'un, and he said, the only thing I know to tell you is there's not very much bothers Leonard. ... Everyone around here called him 'Shock' and they called him Robin Hood. ... My great-grandfather and granddad and dad told me – as far as the family's concerned, we don't know which one did the most good, you know? Because Dewey did his good one way, and 'Shock' did his good the other way."

"Shock" Short's equitable redistribution of the capital of lending institutions is legendary. Kenny's grandparents were the recipients of Leonard's largesse. They were crossing Cox Ford with their wagon piled with a plow, a treadle sewing machine (which Kenny still has), and a cow tied behind – all to sell to buy groceries to make it through the winter and seeds for spring planting. They met Leonard "riding a coal-black horse, stud horse, and he (Granddad) said, one of the prettiest saddles he ever seen in his life, silver all over it." Leonard sized up their situation and peeled off about $300 and told the desperate Short family not to worry about repayment. "We'll work it out sometime":

> So Granddad went on into town and tied the cow up there by the river where she could get a drink and went on into town and bought what he needed, and he said, "I thought well, I'd better put the rest of this in the bank in my account," you know. He said he opened the door and walked into the bank, and the banker looked at him and said, "You might as well turn around and leave. Your kinfolk just left here a while ago." Which I (Kenny Short) thought was funny, that Granddad's putting money back in the bank that Leonard took it out of.

In *Dewey Short, Orator of the Ozarks,* Robert S. Wiley tells of the brothers' divergent career paths: "As young Dewey was excelling in his studies at Marionville in the early months of 1916, there was much excitement back at the Short household in Galena. Leonard

Above: Opening ceremony for the Y Bridge, November 23, 1927, over the James River at Galena.

Opposite: Real photo postcard by George Hall of young Dewey Short, his donkey-powered dray, and "jolly sportsmen back from the James River," circa 1913. Dewey Short's advocacy for Ozark tourism throughout his long career in the US House of Representatives culminated in his securing funding for Table Rock Dam.

had purchased an Indian motorcycle, and brother Charlie was pursuing his career as a pugilist, travelling to Hot Springs February 3, to fight 'Mexican Benny Palmer.'" Leonard would graduate from a fight promoter to bank robber as Dewey graduated from the Boston School of Theology with the highest-yet grade average.

Galena was proud of their high-achieving son, so Dewey gave the dedication speech for the new $109,000 Art Moderne reinforced concrete Y Bridge. This "most visually impressive and physically imposing public works monument in Stone County," (as its application form for the National Register of Historic Places describes it), had been eagerly anticipated. The businessmen in the capital of float fishing believed the new bridge and better roads that would connect Galena with the Shepherd of the Hills Country, Branson, and Lake Taneycomo would benefit them. The November 23, 1927, opening was a gala event. The headline of an article in a Springfield paper read, "3000 Ozarkians at Stone County Bridge Ceremony – Dr. Short makes plea for more development – says southwest

THE FISHERMEN'S DRAY & TWO JOLLY SPORTSMEN
BACK FROM THE JAMES RIVER, GALENA MO.
732 HALL PHOTO CO.

Above: Missouri Pacific railroad bridge at Galena, real photo postcard, circa 1915.

Missourians fail to appreciate scenery and advantages of Ozark region." Dewey Short was elected to Congress the next year.

Galena boosters lobbied hard for improved transportation, but initial advantages are sometimes reversed. Earlier railroad connections gave local farmers access to urban markets, but then the trains brought in cheaper flour and foodstuffs produced and processed with the cost-saving advantages of modern technology. Little did local believers in the Good Roads movement anticipate that the Y Bridge and better highways would adversely impact their float-centered tourist businesses. In the Y Bridge's form for entry in the National Register of Historic Places (1990), Lynn Morrow and David Quick succinctly relate these changes:

> All looked promising for Galena and Stone County. Between the bridge and town local investors built a new gas station, tavern-grocery store, and fisherman's camp. These immediate results remained modest and within a short time the Depression began. Galena continued as a rural service center with five grocery stores on the square. ...
>
> The Y Bridge allowed easier access into the Shepherd of the Hills country by auto where travelers spent time in motor courts, hotels, restaurants, boating on Lake Taneycomo, and after 1932 viewing a monumental arch bridge across White River. The Lake, on the southeast edge of the Shepherd of the Hills, increased its role as the geographic center for capital investments in the tourist trade. By 1935 Jim Owen had hired Charley Barnes to build a fleet of three dozen Ozark john boats to be stationed in Branson, moved Barnes to a home in Branson, and reoriented the tourist flow of James River float trips from Branson to river entry at Galena to end of trip at Branson. Jim Owen packaged a standardized hillbilly experience on the river that made him a household word in Ozarks tourism. With the center of float fishing in Branson, Galena's notoriety in tourism declined although tourists still had their pictures taken on Y Bridge, an imposing Ozarks corridor structure, and several camps thrived until construction of Table Rock Dam during the 1950s.

Truman Powell, newspaperman and early promoter of Stone County, submitted an editorial, "About Galena," that was published in the August 27, 1914, *James River Republican.* Powell quoted a friend's comments about Galena many years ago: "Oh, Galena is not much, and never can be. It is simply a churchless hamlet on the hillside." Powell countered, "But it is very different now." There is a "great stone school" now and its houses are "tasty and all built in recent years." He concludes, "Galena is situated in the right place and surrounded by the right scenery and has all the environments to make it the best summer resort of all the towns in the Ozark region of Missouri."

Galena's population did increase as a result of improved transportation from twenty-seven in 1870 to 353 in 1910, but since has not grown above 508, reached in 1930. The 2010 census counted 440 residents.

Most of the buildings on the west side of the courthouse square were constructed in conjunction with the arrival of the White River Division of the Missouri Pacific–Iron Mountain route. Truman Powell commented, "Good and extensive mercantile establishments in good substantial buildings, mostly of brick and stone, are found here, and a good trade appears to be enjoyed by all. "

Galena was the home of often re-elected Member of the US House of Representatives, Dewey Short. Big-city newspapers often picked up his vivid characterizations of politics.

Dewey's brother Leonard's activities as a fight promoter were reported in local papers. He also made the national news when he began robbing banks in four states, including one in his hometown, owned by his relatives. That case was dropped. When "Shock," as he was called, started holding up larger, federally insured institutions, the FBI became involved and his luck ran out.

These three real photo postcards of Galena in the 1930s are by D. F. (David Frank) Fox. His work overlapped George Hall's but lasted longer.

Fox took six photos for Vance Randolph to illustrate an article in the June 19, 1937, *Life* entitled "Ozark Superstitions."

GALENA, MO. AND STATE HIGHWAY BRIDGE ACROSS JAMES RIVER. FOX STUDIO PHOTO

In *Vance Randolph: An Ozark Life,* Robert Cochran noted the folklorist's appreciation of Galena's "availability of good room and board at amazing prices." Randolph recalled renting from Fanny Mathes in 1934 "a big airy front room … with a fine view of the village and the river" that came with meals for $1 a day:

> Lunch and dinner were served in good country fashion, with two great platters of fried chicken. There was cornbread, and mashed potatoes, and gravy, and green beans, and cole slaw, and sliced tomatoes, and cottage cheese. There was a choice of coffee or tea, and a little bowl of sliced lemon and sprigs of mint with the latter. There was a big dish of hominy, and a pitcher of real Ozark molasses, and some good American cheese, and great wedges of huckleberry pie by way of dessert.

Galena, Cochran explained, was a godsend for a freelance writer weathering the Depression. No longer was Vance Randolph receiving advances from book publishers or drawing $200 a week as a Hollywood consultant on hillbillies. Most of "Mr. Ozarks'" income was from magazine articles and often-salacious titles for Haldeman-Julius' Little Blue Books. Other Little Blue Books of his were on outlaws and gunfighters. Randolph loved guns. He wrote eight articles for sporting magazines on handguns: "The American has always held the pistol in high esteem." His hobby of hunting small game (unsuccessfully) near town with an old Colt .45, however, upset some Galena residents. Dr. J. H. Young, the mayor, made Vance a deputy sheriff, which authorized him to pack a sidearm.

Highway development rearranges business opportunities, but early railroads did more than provide better access. They described the landscape along the tracks in great detail, suggesting what could or should be done to profit from its resources. "A Land of Boundless Mineral and Agricultural Wealth and Marvelous Scenic Beauty" immodestly proclaimed the subtitle of the third edition of the Missouri Pacific-Iron Mountain system booklet circa 1916 (next page).

Golden opportunities in agriculture, timbering, mining, fruit raising, and the pearl and shell industry have either come and gone, or failed to fulfill their promise. "Tourists, excursionists, and sportsmen," however, are still tempted to "linger and enjoy at leisure the refreshing breezes of the uplands and the incomparable view of winding stream and distant forest-clad hills." Many of those views are now of reservoirs, not streams, but rack cards for Table Rock Lake resorts employ similar descriptions.

Following spread: White River (now Table Rock Lake) landscape at dawn from a scenic overlook near Shell Knob. On the left, the row of three knobs (erosional remnants) rising out of the fog marks where the James entered the White River.

Geographers like Carl O. Sauer, as well as writers of railroad promotions, have found this scenery competitive with views from other celebrated places: "The relief of the area is nearly as great as in the St. Francois region. ... The topography combines, however, more varied elements ... and the scenery accordingly is more attractive. Here are forested slopes, gleaming limestone cliffs, and parklike cedar glades. ... The result is a scene which combines magnificence and charm to a rare degree."

The mystique of the White River country persists. This overlook has its own Facebook page.

Ozark rivers were floated by locals and adventurous sportsmen before the railroads came through, but getting back to one's starting point on a mule-drawn wagon was arduous. Artistic descriptions of the pleasures of float trips published by railroads created urban interest:

> The lower James and upper White Rivers are becoming, from topographic formation, a great resort for hunters and fishermen. For instance, one can take a canoe, and, entering the river at Galena, Mo. ride for 100 miles to Branson, floating downstream all the way, in about five or six days, and return to Galena in about fifty minutes by rail. ... The scenery along the James and upper White Rivers is beautiful and varied. It is not stupendous or overpowering, but a charming panorama of nature at her best. In the fall of the year when the river is as clear as crystal, and the mountainsides are covered with the many colored hues of autumn leaves, occasionally brown and bare, or of an emerald green of pine and cedar forests, the scene is beautiful beyond compare. A few miles below Galena, we paddled through a lake-like part of the river under the Virgin Bluff, which rises 700 feet of hard limestone rock, with the top of the cliff projecting at least thirty to fifty feet out over the river. ...
>
> As the boat floats along, great beauty is seen in the bottom of the river, and words to describe this wonderful, ever-changing, many-hued picture are hard to find. ... As you notice the strata of the rocks above, the trunks and foliage of the trees are reflected so plainly in this beautiful water, as to make a double picture on the face of the camera. The boat shooting down a rapid would come to a limpid pond a quarter of a mile wide, and from three to thirty feet deep, but at any point in this clear, pellucid water the bottom was plainly discernible. Sometimes the color ranged from pure white to dark green, through the most beautiful shades of green and white combined, or it would be a tessalated pavement in blocks and squares of brown, gray and black. ...
>
> As we floated along all manner of fish were seen. Bass of three kinds, rainbow trout, jack salmon, buffalo, redhorse, suckers and enormous

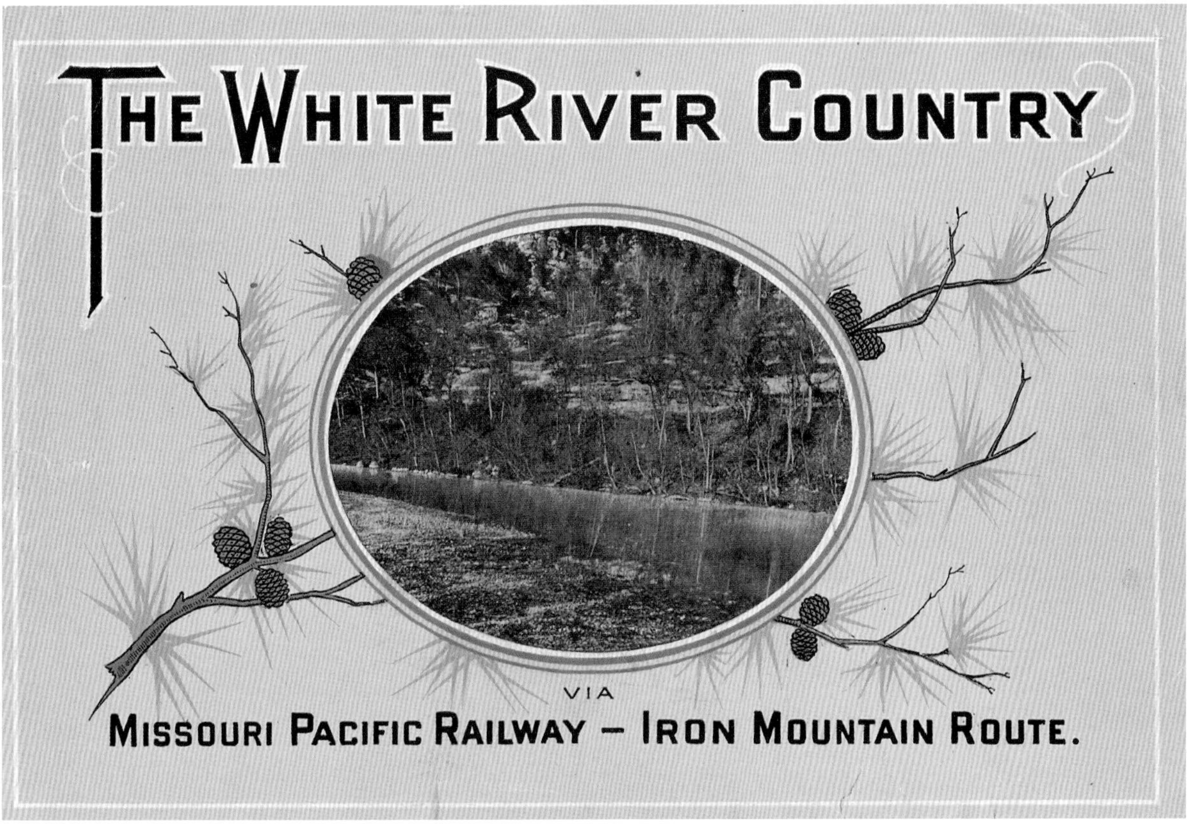

THE WHITE RIVER COUNTRY

VIA

MISSOURI PACIFIC RAILWAY – IRON MOUNTAIN ROUTE.

VIEW OF JAMES RIVER AT GALENA

A NEW HAND AT THE BUSINESS

ONE OF THE JAMES RIVER BLUFFS

> catfish. Not the flabby fish that congregate at the mouth of city sewers, but large, firm-fleshed, fighting fellows which give the fishermen all the sport they desire to handle them on rod and line.

"Flabby" city fish? Country fish that were by contrast "large, firm-fleshed, fighting fellows"? That urban life was unhealthy and modernity compromised old-fashioned values are themes that have played through American literature from the nineteenth century on. These ideas popped up in railroad pamphlets and permeated a novel by young Harold Bell Wright, who had come to the peace and quiet of the White River country to recover from respiratory problems and the stress of his ministry in Kansas City. His 1907 novel, *The Shepherd of the Hills*, told the story of a troubled urbanite who found solace among virtuous Ozark hillfolk. It sold millions of copies, was made into movies four times, and branded the region where the melodrama is set a tourist destination.

HAROLD BELL WRIGHT.
THE SHEPHERD OF THE HILLS
·NOW IN PICTURES·

Harold Bell Wright's first encounter with the Ozarks was in the late 1800s on a visit to an uncle on Flat Creek in Barry County.

In a mule-drawn wagon, they went on a fishing trip along that James River tributary. Wright attended a church service but found fault with the fundamentalist preaching. In general, the author disdained Ozark folk culture.

John Barnes said he guided Wright on two float trips around 1904. Wright hiked up to Marvel Cave and the Ross cabin from the river, as many did on floats. Barnes speculated that experience gave him the idea for *The Shepherd of the Hills*. In spite of familiarity with the region's rivers, his scenes all take place on hilltop farms.

Wright's description of the landscape of Stone and Taney Counties differs little from those in the Missouri Pacific Railroad promotion: "The stranger seated himself upon the rude steps. Below and far away he saw the low hills, rolling ridge on ridge like the waves of a great sea, until in the blue distance they were so lost in the sky that he could not say which was mountain and which was cloud." His log cabin characters spoke with what was described as Elizabethan dialect. "Preachin' Bill" who operated the ferry, said, "When God looked upon th' work of his hands an' called hit good, he war sure a-lookin' at this here Ozark country." Soon after the novel's publication curious visitors began to inquire, "Who was the real-life old shepherd? And what farm girl was the lovely Sammy Lane?"

It mattered little that the author repeatedly said that only Uncle Ike (Levi Morrill) was drawn from life. When the novel became a huge success, locals began identifying themselves as specific characters. Postcard portraits of these natives were produced for sale labeled with their book attribution. Years later, when laid to rest in Evergreen Cemetery, these fictional roles were chipped into their tombstones under their real names.

Rustication and a mild form of anti-modernism became attached to the image of the area. Visitors expected to see log cabins and hear natives speak with a twang. Many complied. This performance art had sacred and profane schools. Harold Bell Wright camped out and worked on his manuscript on a hilltop next to a cabin built by J. K. Ross not far from Branson. Inspiration Point, as it became known, is ground zero for fans of the redemptive Christian parable. An outdoor drama based on the book has often been presented here at the Shepherd of the Hills theme park.

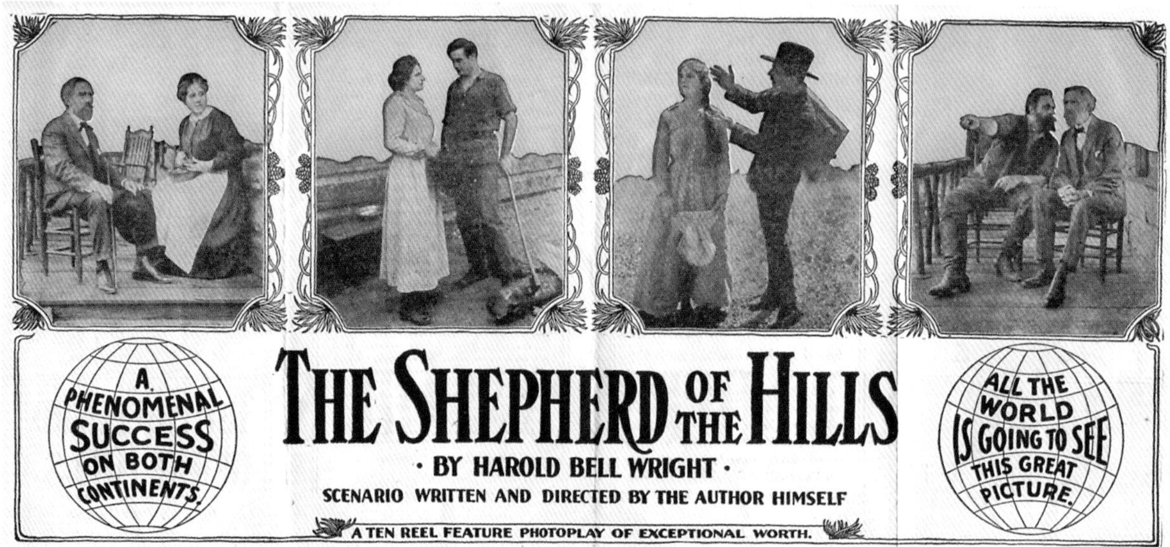

A PHENOMENAL SUCCESS ON BOTH CONTINENTS
THE SHEPHERD OF THE HILLS
· BY HAROLD BELL WRIGHT ·
SCENARIO WRITTEN AND DIRECTED BY THE AUTHOR HIMSELF
A TEN REEL FEATURE PHOTOPLAY OF EXCEPTIONAL WORTH.
ALL THE WORLD IS GOING TO SEE THIS GREAT PICTURE.

Above: The folder for the first film of *The Shepherd of the Hills,* which Wright wrote, produced and directed. The last of four film versions of his book starred John Wayne.

Right: Real photo postcard, circa 1915. J. K. and Anna Ross, who claimed to be the models for Old Matt and Aunt Molly. The couple had only been in the Ozarks for several years before Wright showed up on their doorstep. The cabin that carpenter Ross built is the centerpiece of the Shepherd of the Hills Homestead.

Below: Pre-show shenanigans at the outdoor theater at Shepherd of the Hills Homestead, 1993. Wright would likely be displeased, but the raucous hillbilly persona and laudable hillfolk characters are often indiscriminately mixed in Branson entertainment.

Above: Real photo postcard, 1920s.

The rustic building of the Care-Away Club (originally Arnold's Lodge) was three miles downstream from Galena. When J. R. Blunk acquired it, he kept its original name, as did Kansan Lon Ernest, who purchased the property in 1926. Ernest offered a membership plan – an early version of time share.

By 1932, Richard Lloyd Jones, owner and editor of the *Tulsa Tribune*, had acquired it. Called "Millionaire Jones" by Stone Countians, the civic-minded publisher added on a rifle range, archery course, baseball diamond, and volleyball court and operated it as a camp for Hi-Y Teens, a YMCA organization.

Branson's association with fundamentalist Christianity is well known. In *Holy Hills of the Ozarks: Religion and Tourism in Branson, Missouri* (2007), Aaron K. Ketchell gives credit to Harold Bell Wright's book for laying the groundwork for a Branson that draws millions of visitors who wish to combine religion and recreation on their vacations:

> *The Shepherd of the Hills* may have lamented ever encroaching modernity and a pending loss of agrarian simplicity, but it also suggested to readers that there was a place where the perceived troubles of industrialization or urbanization could be allayed—a locale populated by folks who, according to the text, "pause in the hurried rush to listen to the call of life" and "who serve as examples of "what God meant men and women to be" away from "the shame and ugliness of the world." Utilizing an Ozark vacation to assuage such pressures, a St. Louis businessman floated on the James River in 1908 for an escape from the "awfully hard" business climate of his day.

Shepherd of the Hills Country included the lower James River valley. Not all floaters were purely escapists. Fishermen, on the whole, are not as pious as pilgrims to the sites described in Wright's novels.

Before the railroad and highways connected the White River hills with the outside world fragments of pioneer traditions had survived. Most early river guides were familiar with more of these folkways than the Rome, New York, novelist. They might enhance their stories and accents, but compared to Wright's version of hillfolk, they were authentic. Vance Randolph and Otto Ernest Rayburn felt they had struck folktale gold when they interviewed with these old-time river guides.

The lodging where floaters stayed was as inauthentic to the Ozarks as Harold Bell Wright's moralistic, bucolic characters. In and around Galena, resorts sprang up to serve tourists who came to cast for smallmouth and wonder at the cliffs as they floated down the James and White to Branson. They camped out on gravel bars on the way, but while waiting to embark on a float trip or resting afterward, the city folk expected big-city amenities. Running water, electricity, bathtubs, and indoor toilets were provided by most.

Though constructed of local materials, the buildings of the accommodations were not of native design. Rustic as it appears, Adirondack style is not vernacular – it's an architectural style that began in Europe and was popularized on millionaires' woodsy estates in upstate New York. Undoubtedly the more modest James River versions similarly contained bent willow furniture and mounted bass.

Below: Dam on Powder Mill Hollow near Care-Away Camp. Filled completely with gravel, this small blockage of a smallish, usually dry draw is proof that massive amounts of chert and limestone rubble move constantly into Ozark rivers from steep hillsides.

Just upstream from this example of the inevitability of storage loss in manmade lakes is the foundation for a dining room that once spanned the hollow. R. L. Jones owned the land in the 1930s. Was he imitating Falling Waters, the famous house over a stream? Jones's cousin was Frank Lloyd Wright.

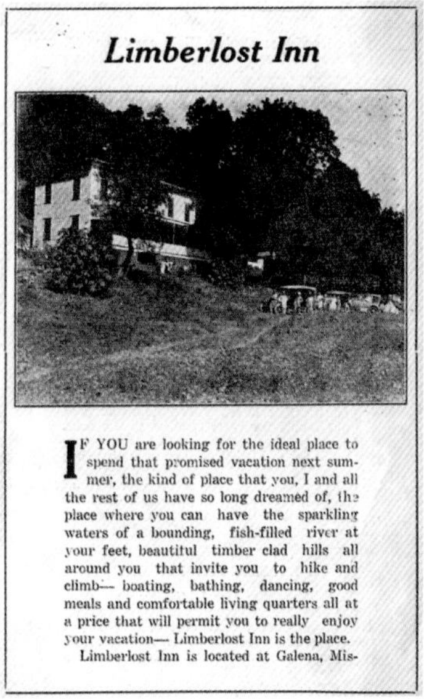

Limberlost Inn

IF YOU are looking for the ideal place to spend that promised vacation next summer, the kind of place that you, I and all the rest of us have so long dreamed of, the place where you can have the sparkling waters of a bounding, fish-filled river at your feet, beautiful timber clad hills all around you that invite you to hike and climb— boating, bathing, dancing, good meals and comfortable living quarters all at a price that will permit you to really enjoy your vacation— Limberlost Inn is the place.

Limberlost Inn is located at Galena, Mis-

Above: Folder from the 1920s.

"This is a club for the happy-go-lucky clean living people who know how to enjoy the-out-of-doors."

This real photo postcard by Hall Photo Co. was mailed to San Diego, California, postmarked Galena, June 28, 1920. Part of the message stated: "Mother Harriet & I are spending a few days here in the Ozarks – The most beautiful & neglected, because unknown, vacation spot in the country, better than anything we found in California, I think."

Hall's card was produced sometime before 1915, when the name of the resort on the banks of the James was changed from the Galena Club House to Limberlost Camp. We have no idea why; Gene Stratton-Porter's 1909 sentimental romance, *A Girl of the Limberlost*, is set in an Indiana swamp. The resort was owned by Dr. A. L. McQuary who had been a traveling evangelist who prescribed eyeglasses. He had been a farmer, sold saddles, and within a few years of moving to Galena in 1908, became the county collector. He also owned Camp Clark, a set of bungalows and tents on a hill overlooking the James a few miles north. An ad for that resort in a 1913 *Springfield Republican* stated, "Only people of good morals are admitted." McQuary ultimately sold both lodges. Limberlost exploded in the 1980s due to the owner storing dynamite in the basement.

George Hall quit the business in the 1920s, and David F. (Frank) Fox became Galena's commercial photographer. We know little about Hall and less about Fox. Both photographers were engaged

Above: "Moonshiners cabin" real photo postcard, 1920s, by Fox Studio, Galena, Mo.

in promoting tourism. Encountering the log home of a moonshiner is not exactly a standard Arcadian tourist draw. Even before the hillbilly image became an icon, there evidently was awareness that the Ozarks was the natural habitat of violators of the Volstead Act.

Springfield newspapers are full of encounters between lawmen and still operators in the hills to the south. "Quits Cornfield for Corn Spirits," reads an August 3, 1921, headline about the arrest of a Stone County farmer on moonshining charges. A grim episode occurred near Hurley on Spring Creek when a raid ended with a "Young Farmer Shot in Back by Officers." The September 27, 1921, *Springfield Republican* continued, "Fred Geren Said to have been left to Die by Stone County Deputies Who Were Seeking Moonshine Still." Geren was thirty-six years old and left a wife and six children. Geren's friends had Deputy Sheriff Hugh Henry, who had participated in the August 3 enforcement action, charged with murder. In October, a circuit court judge dismissed the case.

Some myths about mountaineers were factual. Scots-Irish pioneers did indeed make whiskey. Prohibition allowed this skill to be commercialized. Compared to the Appalachians, which were closer to big-city markets, Ozark moonshine production was minimal. Nevertheless, struggling farmers along the James found a gallon of 'shine was worth much more than a bushel of corn.

Pub. by Craig Mercantile Co.
James River, June, 24, 1907 Galena, Mo.

Above: Printed postcard, 1907: The genesis of the square-ended, flat-bottomed boats specifically adapted for commercial floating on the James and White Rivers is poorly documented. Many theories have been advanced as to how they were developed, and how they came to be called johnboats.

Boats could be rented from lodges, and self-guided trips were common throughout the float trip era. Both paddles and poles are evident. We wish this group, dressed for Sunday school, all the best as they prepare to drift down the beautiful James in these odd overloaded, probably unstable, pointed-bow skiffs, or punts, or whatever they were called.

River boats underwent evolution when rail networks allowed economic shipping of regional vernacular designs across watersheds.

The legendary johnboat was an Ozarkian adaptation of flat-bottomed, locally made wooden craft built throughout the Mississippi River system. An appreciation of its significance was expressed in "What's in a Name, Like John Boat" by Lynn Morrow in the winter, 1998, issue of *White River Valley Historical Quarterly*:

> The johnboat became, perhaps, the Ozarks' most famous folk product. The locally crafted johnboat was and is revered by fishermen and folklorists alike. Its historic role as the watercraft which introduced tourists, journalists, artists, and businessmen to pristine Ozarks streams is significant. The johnboat and associated float fishing became a fundamental part of the experience sought by the new people coming into the region – an urban clientele in search of health, pleasure, and sport in the outdoors. Many of these floaters, with the hire of skilled guides, were carried into a landscape filled with romantic legends, and spectacular scenery. ... The romantic images in the press owed their origin to floaters in flat-bottomed boats who placed their testimonials in print. As in prior generations, various types of river craft on the Western waters had been key to economic developments, so, too, the johnboat and its associated commercial float fishing became an historic foundation upon which modern Ozark tourism was built. While the floats themselves never generated great amounts of money, the float experience and the way it was advertised provided a potent theme for Ozarks tourism that all promoters embraced. Float fishing became part of a social landscape for conviviality and recreation, whether floaters were visiting sportsmen or native fishermen.

Above: Missouri Pacific brochure, 1920s: Canoes photograph well and railroad promotions frequently depicted them in advertising aimed at affluent travelers. They are less stable and carry less camping gear than the johnboats fishermen preferred.

The name "johnboat," Morrow speculates, may have originated in the Deep South and migrated up the White River into the eastern Ozarks. An account of a fishing trip to the Current River printed in the *Jackson Herald*, November 21, 1907, said, "The river men fish from a 'john' boat. It is a long, slim craft and is propelled with poles. Our boat was 26 feet long and 26 inches wide. The boatman stands in one end and, poling always from one side, sends his boat upstream swiftly." It was night and the boats were fitted with gasoline torches. Men with three-tined spears set in fourteen-foot pine handles speared many fish, including a three foot eel. Long, slender crafts like that were known on the James and White and were also used for gigging.

Charley Barnes guided Galena-to-Branson floats for forty years and built more than three hundred of the craft used in these trips. In a 1956 interview with *Springfield News-Leader* reporter Don Payton, Barnes said although he had "taken commercial floats on the Current River" and heard the term johnboat applied there, "We have never used that name here." Barnes got in to the James River float business during its earliest commercialization, but soon realized, "The boats available weren't big enough to accommodate occupants for much longer than a day." Barnes quickly came to the realization that greater cargo space was needed for tents, food, equipment, and other gear. The result was that Barnes, still working in Branson, fabricated a boat "about 20 feet long and a yard wide with a snub nose and flat bottom." The classic "float boat" created by Barnes and other Galena builders was more stable than "jack boats," as earlier long, narrow, flat-bottomed wooden boats were called. John-

Right: Robert Page Lincoln was a prominent writer on hunting and fishing in the 1930s through the 1950s. Seen here dressed like a running buddy of Ernest Hemingway, Lincoln observes Charley Barnes crafting a float boat. Lincoln wrote Barnes didn't care for the name "johnboat."

Above: The caption from Robert Page Lincoln's 1948 article reads, "This photo of Charley Barnes and his two brothers, Herbert and John, was taken in 1909 about the time that the Barnes float trip business at Galena, Mo., was at the height of its success. Barnes told Lincoln that the bass shown in this photo are the same average size as those taken now. Reading left to right are Herbert, John, and Charley Barnes."

Charley later developed a distaste for trophy photos. Fishermen would keep more fish than they could eat in order to take an impressive picture. All the early river guides were supporters of the conservation movement and fish and game laws as they viewed the protection of natural resources to be in their business interests and encouraged an early form of catch-and-release.

boats couldn't be as easily poled upstream, but return by railroad made going upriver by boat unnecessary.

Outdoor writers like Ozark Ripley (John Baptiste Thompson) and Robert Page Lincoln found the name "johnboat" colorful. They, and many other journalists, associated the guided, overnight trips down the James and White Rivers with johnboats, regardless of Barnes's indifference to the word.

Robert Page Lincoln profiled the James River guide and boat builder within a long article titled "Floating Down the River" in the March 1948 issue of *Fur-Fish-Game* magazine: "It is odd that a great deal of the interest attached to float trips in the Ozarks is connected inseparably with this boat invention of Charley's. Without the boat, something of the charm and originality of this manner of fishing would be lost."

Barnes was born near Mount Vernon in 1878. The family moved to a farm near the James three miles from Galena when he was eight. He and his brothers "spent much time fishing this historic river and their catches were such that Barnes conceived of the idea of making boats and taking out fishing parties. At the age of 26 in 1904 Barnes started taking out his first parties. ... 'We started in around the turn of the century and sport fishing in the Ozarks, from St. Louis west, was practically unknown at that time'":

> Charley Barnes was in the float trip business 29 years, from 1904 to 1933 when he came over to Branson. ... Barnes went in with Jim Owen in 1933 and has been with him ever since. Under Jim Owen's guidance the float trip business was given its great impetus and instead of being confined, in popularity, to a mid-west range only this manner of fishing is now known the length and breadth of the country. ... Possibly the charm manifest in float trips down these Ozark streams of

Above and top: Real photo postcards by George Hall, circa 1918: Tom Yocum had an early fishing camp along the James on his farm three miles above Galena. Like Charley Barnes he was a prominent guide throughout most of the float fishing era.

> Missouri lies in the youthful spirit of the thing, harking back to Tom Sawyer and Huckleberry Finn; a sort of sweeping adventure, just floatin' down the river and soaking up the glories of nature en route.

As well as perfecting and building hundreds of boats stable enough for fishermen, shallow drafted enough to clear riffles, and large enough to carry camping equipment, Barnes and his brothers operated a garage and Ford dealership in Galena. For the entertainment of their parties, river guides linked legend with landscapes as they floated downstream and spun tall tales around the campfire. But clearly, however, the Barneses and their associates weren't the simple sons of the soil memorialized in *The Shepherd of the Hills*. Robert Page Lincoln was not Harold Bell Wright, either. There's just a pinch of Arcadian reverie in his how-to-catch fish prose.

Clients of these guide services were more likely to attach transcendental meaning to a float trip than the locals who were hired to paddle the boats, clean, cook, often catch the fish they ate, and pitch their tents on a gravel bar. George H. Evans, publisher of the *Chickasha Express* in Oklahoma, editorialized a 1926 Galena-to-Branson fishing trip:

> It was in the "Heart of the Ozarks" the "Shepherd of the Hills" country. For six days, with three congenial companions and with never-to-be-forgotten "Rat and Charley" as guides, we floated lazily along wide, wandering streams of limpid water, camping at night on gravel bars amid scenes of matchless beauty. ... It was a continuous "movie" of natural beauty, a constant feast on the eyes. Gazing upward at the greenery or downward at the rippling water, who could help dreaming and feeling that it is good to slow down and drift, forgetful of all that irks and grinds in the far-away busy world?
>
> Was not the clear stream which bore us onward so safely and surely a symbol of God's love in which we live and move and have our being? ... If we stay in the cosmic current, trusting our Guide, why need we worry about time, place, or circumstance? Life is adventure and death the great adventure. Ever onward the good and gracious stream bears us.

That metaphor-laden prose editor Evans used to describe his James River fishing trip in 1926 belonged more to the past than to the future. In literature, realism would replace local color, and sentimentality was satirized. Ozark tourists may not have packed Hemingway or Faulkner in their luggage, but the public gradually became less enamored of bucolic mythologies. Some of the language of Arcadianism survived in diminished form. "These beautiful, swift crystal rivers, set around surroundings that are simply enchanting, furnish opportunities for the fisherman, the hunter and the canoeist that are scarcely surpassed anywhere and better yet, they are almost at the very door of every resident in the Mississippi Valley," read a 1940s Galena Boat Company folder. Americans after the Depression and World War II bought far fewer stories that

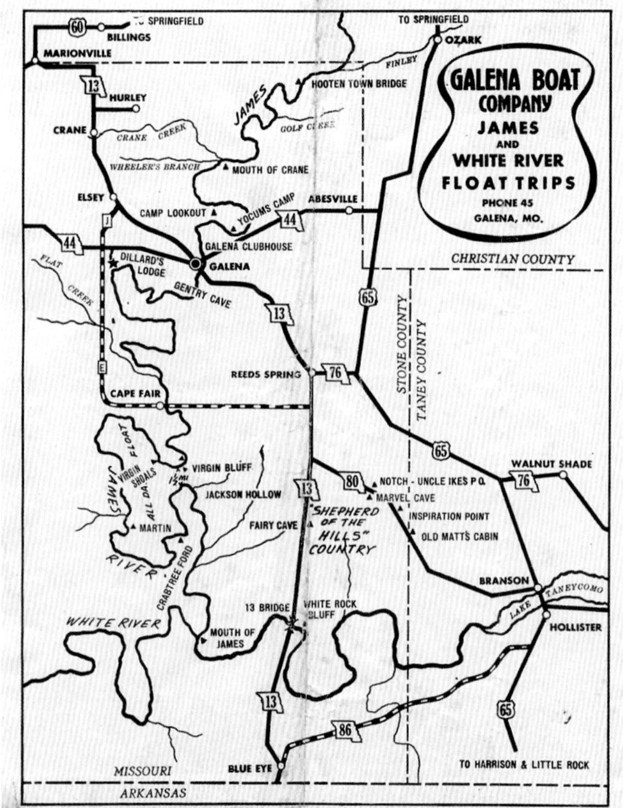

Above: Map from a folder promoting the Galena Boat Company, 1940s. Barnes started this service, but sold it when he went to work with Jim Owen in Branson. Harry Dillard was manager when this was printed.

Owen booked his business from Branson but frequently began his floats from Galena. Some guides worked for both Galena companies and Owen. All the float businesses cooperated with each other.

were "sweet and appealing in their pathos and vibrant with the local color of the mystic, enchanted Ozarks – the Shepherd of the Hills Country," as the Book Supply Company described Harold Bell Wright's novels. Floaters from the 1930s on did not often return from the river having discovered cosmic harmony between man and nature.

The Y Bridge was part of a road-improvement campaign that benefited Branson more than Galena. Hollister, Branson, and Rockaway Beach offered more modern accommodations to auto tourists. They also had access to Lake Taneycomo, which permitted motorboats and pleasure cruisers. To this day, there are businesses that cater to floaters in the little river town on the James, but in the early '30s Galena was displaced as the center of the float industry. The agent of that transformation was an ad salesman for the Jefferson City *Capital News.* He moved to Branson when his father bought a drugstore there in 1930. The caption under the photo of a fat man in the doorway of what looks like a log cabin undergoing reconstruction in Robert Page Lincoln's article says it all: "The man who made Branson, MO., 'float trip capital of the world,' Jim Owen." James Mason Owen was many things – twelve-time mayor of Branson, bank president, car dealer, restaurateur, movie theater owner, dairyman, fishing columnist, breeder of fox hounds, manufacturer of dog food, and publicity genius. Never was he accused of being an Arcadian.

Cigar-chomping capitalist and master of mass media that he was, Owen had the good sense to recruit old-time river men when he launched the Owen Boat Line. Charley Barnes "came over to Branson," wrote Lincoln. "Barnes went in with Jim Owen in 1933 and has been with him ever since. Under Jim Owen's guidance the float trip business was given its greatest impetus and instead of being confined, in popularity, to a mid-west range only this manner of fishing is now known the length and breadth of the country."

The venture started with six Barnes-built boats and six Galena guides. By this time, floaters were no longer dependent on the Missouri Pacific railroad to ship their boats back. Owen used trucks

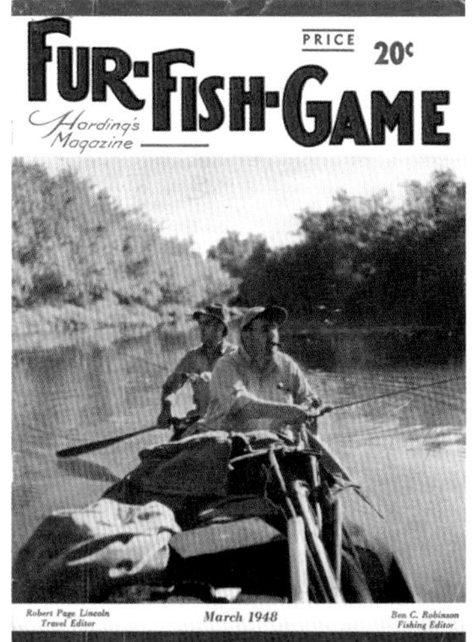

and trailers to put in and take out. Painted on the door was "The Jim Owen Fishing Service, Branson, Mo." Along the bed was "Float for fish and contentment." When Table Rock Dam closed in 1958, he had forty boats and employed thirty-five guides. With considerable fanfare he quit the business. The next year he announced he was returning to the float trip service but would only take a limited number of clients on three-day trips.

Owen's roster included many who had pioneered floating the James and White back in the days when city folks detrained at Galena. Few guides worked full time. Some continued to offer their services to Galena operators. The Branson businessman's aggressive advertising reeled in the most clients, and in the twenty-six years he packaged trips he would use almost every river man at one time or another. Jim Owen became an institution, but some of his guides had reputations for their fishing acumen, campfire cooking skills, or country wit. A jokester himself, Owen encouraged colorful rustic behavior that fulfilled visitors' expectations of being escorted downstream by a tractable variety of hillbilly. Of course, like Barnes, most could work on a V-8 engine as well as hook, filet, and fry a goggle-eye. Some of Owen's alumnae were Tom and Zeb Yocum, "Little Hoss" Jennings, Glen Henderson, Frank (Deacon) Hembree, Lefty Allman, James "Snowball" Haskett, Dave and Theodore Barnes, Delmar Gentry, Ed Stockstill, C. P. Henderson, Flip Crockett, Herb Hicks, John Hall, Ted Butler, Clint Carr, Buster Tilden, Charles Evans, "Rusty" Coiner, Dutch Barnhart, Wayne Cobb, Junior Cobb, Willie "Little Bear" Hembree, and Ted Sare.

Above: *Fur-Fish-Game*, 1948: Jim Owen cover with long Robert Page Lincoln article.

Top: *Life*, June 23, 1941. In this cover story of a Jim Owen James River float are photos of old Charley Barnes and Tom Yocum, still guiding after forty years in the business.

Right: Jim Owen, artist Steve Miller, and Owen's guides in front of his Hillbilly Theater, 1940.

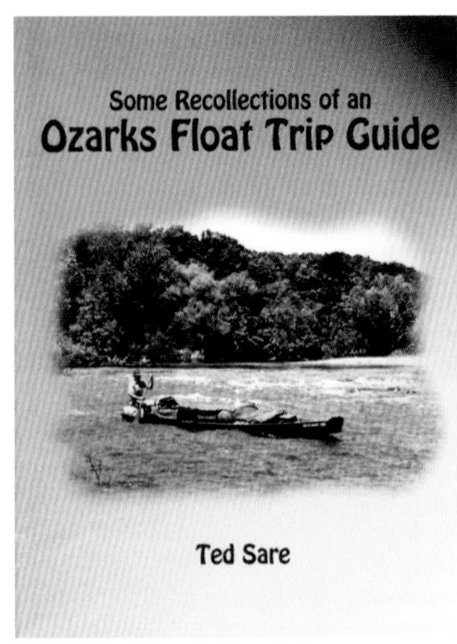

Above: Self-published book by Ted Sare, a guide for Owen in the late 1940s. River guides were a resourceful and capable lot, and apparently enjoyed floating as much as their clients. Sare later went to work for the Missouri State Highway Department. He was a breeder of Beefmaster cattle, had a pilot's license, and produced a video on training horses.

Ted Sare, born on the south shore of Lake Taneycomo, was an Owen guide in the late 1940s before he attended the University of Missouri on the G.I. Bill and became an inspector for the Missouri State Highway Department. In a 1997 self-published book, *Some Recollections of an Ozark Float Trip Guide*, Sare captures the flavor of guided floats just before Corps of Engineers dams ended the tradition:

> Float fishing is one of the very best and most enjoyable ways to fish. You just float down that river, and if you are being guided, you don't even have to be concerned with the boat, just sit and fish or sit and watch the scenery go by, and wonder, can the world really be this quiet? ... This method of float fishing, and doing it on what was probably the best bass river in the United States, was just the ultimate in fishing. There was no better promoter of that than Jim Owen. He was an ex-newspaperman and knew the value of advertising and also knew how to reach the famous and important people, and he did. He had some of the biggest names in the country and a lot of Hollywood movie stars as his clientele. Jim did more than any other one man to put White River and Branson, Missouri on the map. ...
>
> The rivers that we floated were the lower White in both Missouri and Arkansas, the upper White and James in Missouri, and the Buffalo and occasionally the Kings River in Arkansas and a little bit of Kings in Missouri. Each river had its own character. The James River, or "the James Fork" of the White as it was sometimes called back then, was floated a lot. Not just by Jim Owen's Boat Line, but mostly by Galena Boat Company of Galena, Missouri, Lyle Chamberlin of Cape Fair, Missouri, and by Bill Rogers Line of the old Kimberling Bridge on the White.

With truck transportation the Branson-based operation expanded into other White River tributaries. Owen boasted he could provide sportsmen with thirty-one days of fishing and never float the same waters twice. This required planning, logistics, and experienced personnel. It was never an inexpensive pastime, and Owen

Right: Floating was never exclusively a male sport. Commercial float operators always welcomed women in their advertising and many participated.

Above: Milk bottle label by Steve Miller. Jim Owen was responsible for the artist setting up a studio in Branson. Miller's commercial art rarely lacked hillbilly motifs.

Right: Miller drew the mailing piece from Owen about the time Table Rock Lake was filling.

expanded the comforts of overnight camping. Along with an understanding of modern media, Owen was an excellent organizer. His competition, and all of Branson tourism, benefited from the national publicity his float service got. He personally received a lot of this attention.

Dan Saults, editor of the *Missouri Conservationist*, had just become deputy director when he wrote "Jim Owen's Discontinued White River Floats," published in the March 1957 *Sports Afield*. Like many outdoor writers of that time he was distrustful of the huge multi-purpose dams that the Army Corps of Engineers was building throughout Middle America. Saults was a literate journalist, and grasped the drama of government concrete drowning a traditional way of life and killing the now-exotic primitive float business. "Dams make more fishing for more people, and I guess that's good, but for a lot of folks, nothing can ever substitute for the way of life that was an Ozark float trip," read his subtitle. The piece begins with the receipt of a piece of mail from Owen:

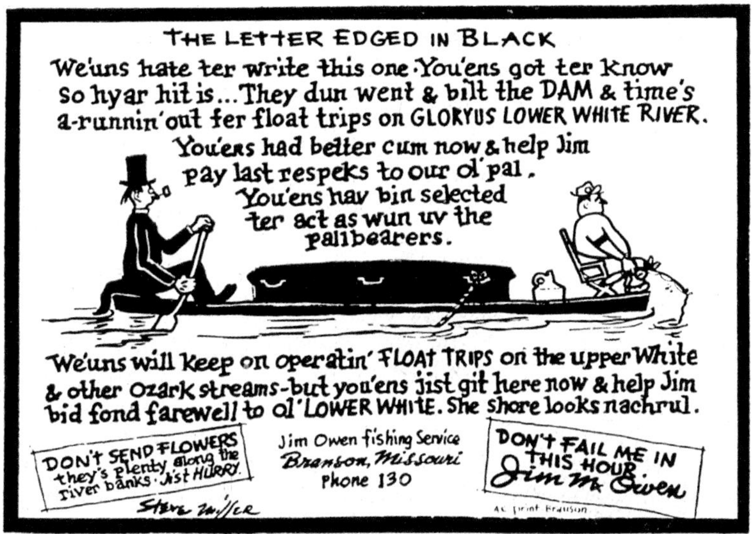

THE LETTER EDGED IN BLACK

We'uns hate ter write this one·You'ens got ter know so hyar hit is...They dun went & bilt the DAM & time's a-runnin'out fer float trips on GLORYUS LOWER WHITE RIVER. You'ens had better cum now & help Jim pay last respeks to our ol'pal. You'ens hav bin selected ter act as wun uv the pallbearers.

We'uns will keep on operatin' FLOAT TRIPS on the upper White & other Ozark streams-but you'ens jist git here now & help Jim bid fond farewell to ol' LOWER WHITE. She shore looks nachrul.

DON'T SEND FLOWERS they's plenty along the river banks· Jist HURRY.

Jim Owen fishing Service
Branson, Missouri
Phone 130

DON'T FAIL ME IN THIS HOUR.
Jim M. Owen

Steve Miller

It came in a black-bordered envelope with a heavy black line all around the page, and it started out:

Despite the tortured dialect, this elegiac epistle was signed in a neat hand by its composer, who also has a neat brain behind an exterior that sometimes looks like the letter sounds. For it was scribed by Jim M. Owen, the genius of the John boat, the most fabulous float-fishin' operator of this or any other country. And it was his way of announcing last fall that the business was closing up shop because his beloved river was about gone. As he delicately put it: "Cum spring, Table Rock Lake is buryin' old White." The letter edged in black was a typical Owen tribute.

So the White River, first of the Ozark great float streams, and the

Owen Boat Line, greatest of the float operators, yielded up the ghost together, after a 23-year partnership based upon two principles: shrewd publicity and honest affection. Jim Owen contributed both emotions, since rivers can't write letters or get fond of people. But if streams *could* like humans, then the White must have loved Jim, for it was good to him. The two made quite a team.

After Owen's death in 1972, Saults revisited the linkage between the Branson float trip impresario and the lost river. The "King of the White River" was eulogized in a May, 1974 *Sports Afield* article, "Gently Down the Stream – The legendary Ozark float rivers are gone now but memories of the man who made them famous will forever ride the waters":

> Here's the recipe for making a Jim Owen: Take a generous helping of P. T. Barnum, an equal quantity of Izaak Walton, add a generous pinch of country-cured Bernard Baruch and a strong dash of Harry Truman. Blend into this mixture a cup of Nash Buckingham, another of Rabelais and a pinch of H. L. Mencken. Sprinkle in ready Wit and add vast quantities of Ozark river water. Season with sassafras hickory smoke, persimmons and pawpaws; garnish with sallat greens. Cook for twenty-five years over a fire of white oak and ash on a gravel bar with the White River murmuring ten feet away and hounds baying foxes upon the ridge, then serve with fried smallmouth. ...
>
> He was an author too; Jim Owen's *Hillbilly Humor* was published in paperback as a Pocket Book original in 1970. While his tome doesn't touch upon the question, there are those in America who suspect Jim invented the hillbilly. But he didn't; it just seems like it. There isn't much in the book about fish or dogs, because Jim didn't think those subjects were funny. Reverence was more like it.

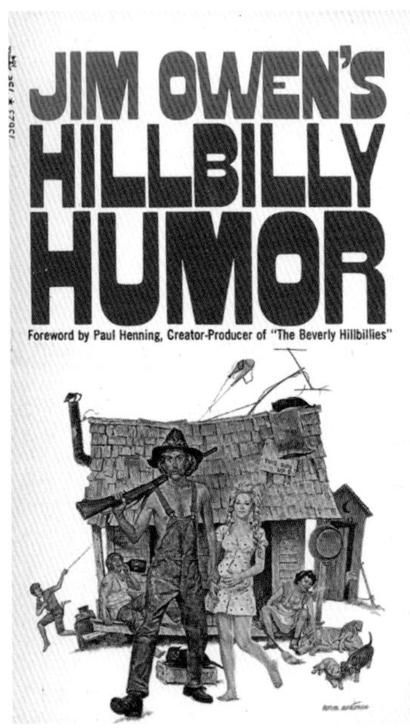

Above: Paperback joke book (1970) by Jim Owen with a foreword by Paul Henning, creator-producer of *The Beverly Hillbillies*.

Creator of the *Beverly Hillbillies*, Paul Henning, wrote the foreword to Owen's little book. Henning credits his "wonderful stories and anecdotes, originally told to amuse fishermen on Jim's famous Ozark float trips" for helping "write my programs." Hollywood celebrities brought Owen's "expressions and observations" back, and Henning said he put some of them in the mouths of Jed Clampett, Granny, and other characters in his rural television sitcoms. Perhaps. Owen's writing owed more to jokes in men's magazines than to Ozark vernacular sources. Occasionally a bit of folksy lingo would creep in, possibly picked up from his guides, who may have heard it on the Grand Ol' Opry radio broadcast. Wrote Henning, "It's hard to beat the combination of wit and sagacity in some of these hillbilly expressions ... in fact as Jim would say, 'it's harder than sneaking dawn past a rooster.'"

Printed on pulp paper, the jokes don't come off as they would if delivered by Owen in his theatrical, backwoods twang. Saults acknowledged, "Jim spoke a dialect that was sort of Owen *lingua franca*, the way hill people *ought* to talk; there were rumors he held language classes for his guides to be sure they mispronounced

Above: Real photo postcard of the interior of Owen's Hillbilly Theater. Many devotees of Harold Bell Wright's pious pioneers hated the word hillbilly. The genesis of float fishing was Arcadian, but Jim Owen, realizing the fad for things hillbilly in the 1930s and '40s, attached it to his businesses. Still he was aware that not everybody approved of the stereotyped truculent mountaineer.

When the final movie version of *The Shepherd of the Hills*, starring John Wayne in Technicolor, was released, lovers of the novel were appalled. Saintly Old Matt is a doddering fool, and kindly Aunt Molly is moonshiner. Only the title remains true to the book.

Owen picked up on the local outrage. He played the film, but posted a banner, "Neighbors we don't like it but here it is." Then he hired a man to picket his own theater, carrying the sign, "Unfair to Original Characters – Hillbilly Local 0001."

correctly." The 1974 article noted the avuncular "Lord of the Smallmouth" discussed Thoreau or Emerson "in that same dialect," and wrote "some God-awful panegyrics about the privilege of living in the Ozarks and being a hillbilly."

Li'l Abner, Snuffy Smith, and Paul Webb's Mountain Boys were launched a year after Jim Owen launched his float business. A year before Owen died, CBS purged its "rusticoms" (rustic sitcoms) of Paul Henning's shows. The *Beverly Hillbillies* and *Green Acres* were considered too unsophisticated for the young urban audience the network sought to attract.

Word didn't reach Branson that country was out, at least for another thirty years. Today there are still music shows with fiddlers and rube comedians, but that vacation destination now courts, as CBS did in 1971, a younger crowd with contemporary consumer tastes. Even after Table Rock Dam destroyed the guided float business and transformed the Shepherd of the Hills Country into a less Arcadian and more standardized family vacation spot, Branson remained stuck in time. There remained a hint of hillbillyness here as the nation's tastemakers had decided it was time to cycle out of old-timeyness.

In 1969, the same year Paul Henning filmed five episodes of *The Beverly Hillbillies* at Silver Dollar City, the theme park dedicated a ride based on Jim Owen's float trips. Somewhat sourly, Saults pondered the meaning of this conversion of actual to themed reality:

> But the myth lingers on. At Silver Dollar City, an Ozark answer to Disneyland that has grown into a huge amusement park in the Owen country, there's a popular ride, developed in 1969 and named the Jim Owen Float Trip. Here ersatz johnboats loaded with passengers are

ALL BUSY IN CAMP ON WHITE RIVER
385 HALL PHOTO CO

Above: Real photo postcard, Hall Photo Co., circa 1911. Possibly the figure on the left holding a camera is Hall.

George Edward Hall came with his family to the Ozarks from Illinois in 1906 when he was 22. His first souvenir postcards related to Wright's Shepherd of the Hills novel, but he later produced pictures of the nascent recreational activities at Galena and Branson. Before he quit the photo business and moved back to Illinois to sell insurance about 1923, Hall produced a thousand different sharp, well-composed images of early Ozark tourism.

> run through *haunted hollers* and mystic caves on a controlled flow of piped water. More people take that fun-ride in one season today than those who floated the White with the Owen Boat Co. in a quarter of a century of operation. This seems to carry a moral of some sort about what has happened to our world.

Is Saults anticipating postmodernism in this philosophical reflection? To French Marxist intellectuals, Disneyland was symbolic of Americans' inability to distinguish between reality and fiction. Before classifying rustic Silver Dollar City hyperreal, consider the confluence of players in the transformation of the White River Hills. Making a ride themed on actual float fishing gave Saults a surreal moment.

May Kennedy McCord was not bothered by such contradictions. Unlike some outsiders identified with Ozarkian rusticity, she had "kinfolk and five connections" all over the Ozarks and could strum a guitar, or play the piano, while singing "Barbara Allen."

May A. Kennedy was born in Carthage in 1880, but grew up in Galena. She married Charles McCord, the son of Dr. Thomas Jefferson McCord, who not only practiced medicine but who practically owned Galena and fifteen hundred acres of the best farmland along the James. She and her husband moved to Springfield in 1917, and there they had three children. Her short story, "Burying in the Ozarks," was published in *The Sample Case* magazine when she was forty, launching her career interpreting rural Ozarkers to presumably overly citified outsiders.

"Hillbilly Heartbeats" was her newspaper column and radio show. She dished out a hearty stew of old-time songs, folk medicine cures, superstitions and ghost stories, pioneer remembrances, and stories

Seekers of idyllic relaxation posed beside the rustic cabins at Camp Clark, Galena. Were middle class Arcadians with automobiles contradictory? This variety of primitivism was not radically anti-technological.

Locals at this hoe-down appear to be wearing store bought. Once the train arrived, Stone Countians had access to clothing just like the tourists in the Camp Clark postcard.

Some of the Arcadian resorts built dance floors, and natives joined in with visitors. Distinctions between locals and visitors were not always clear.

The idea the Ozarks is inhabited by primitives has been perpetuated in books by educated travelers like Schoolcraft, in popular songs like the "Arkansas Traveler," and in souvenir postcards, like this one by George Hall.

of her Stone County childhood. "I lived on the bank of the James River and we swam every day from May until October. When the weather got so cold it would freeze the egg on your Uncle Snazzy's whiskers you quit swimming in the river, but not until then."

By all accounts she was personable, but she could articulate well-chosen words for those she perceived to have maligned her friends or the Ozarks. She denounced John Woodruff's harsh criticism of Vance Randolph, and defended Dewey Short against a smear by the *Ozark Mountaineer*. In a January 19,1935 *Springfield Leader* front-page article titled "How to Paint Barn Scarlet in New Style," she lambasted Thomas Hart Benton for "going arty."

Above: "Old Gospel Ship," a rare 78 record of the Leverett brothers.

Top: *Thomas Hart Benton and the American Sounds* (2012). Benton sketched Homer and Wilbur Leverett and their cousins Neville Oatman in Galena in 1931. His painting, "Missouri Musicians," shows all three. The book by Leo Mazow is on the influence of Benton's passion for playing and teaching folk harmonica.

Ostensibly the "Hillbilly Queen" was upset because the mother of two young Galena musicians Benton painted so disliked the results that she wanted the artist arrested. May agreed. "Poor little Homer and Wilbur came out of the picture, after Mr. Benton had juggied the works looking like a cross between 'horse thieves' and 'The Man with the Hoe.'"

This lack of verisimilitude was a trigger to fire off a critique of the failings of modern art, and the special crime when the perpetrator claimed, like Benton, to be an "Ozarkian." Claiming not to know much about art, McCord nevertheless references Cubism, Futurism, and Gertrude Stein, concluding, "If you start to make a red barn you don't make a red red barn. You make an impression of a red barn, and it must resemble a turkey gobbler."

A lady told her Benton was doing for the Ozarks with his brush what she was doing with her pen. "If that is what I am doing for the Ozarks, then someone take me to the creek and baptize me under three times and lift me out twice!" She closes:

> You know I never had "three fits and a bad spell" over art anyway. But I do know this: Whenever you introduce anything whatsoever of a modern or futuristic or nightmarish note into anything Ozarkian, you have killed it completely. It won't work. It's like a fine saddle on a burry-tailed mule. It's like a jazz band accompanying the old-age chimes of Normandy. It's like a red dime store frame on an old ivory etching or a pair of spatz on the Pope! You'd as well back up and start all over!

The newspaper's editor forewarned Thomas Hart Benton that Mrs. McCord would be writing a critical piece on him. "Fine," he laughed. "Tell her to do her damndest."

In a defense against the negative image of her homeland picked up by the U.P. in November 1932, she named "The Ozarks a Great Refuge," adding it was becoming "the literary mecca of America":

Right: Oil painting, "The Vanished River Guide," by Jim McCord. James Allen McCord was the grandson of May Kennedy McCord. He had been a Marine, a lawyer, and a world traveler before becoming an artist. McCord explained his painting:

"A caricature of my late Pa based on a 1930s snapshot of him guiding a float-boat. ... My essay on archetypal Ozarkian art indicates how he grew up relatively wild on the James River through Galena, Mo. – and became a window for me back into the primal frontier mentality that survived in the mountains for centuries. In his youth, as here, he was among the legendary 'river rats' who guided these once pristine streams. I present his image, with an exaggerated stylization influenced notably by Tom Benton, as part of an effort to show our American roots."

Jim's sister, Patricia McDonald, said their father, Charles C. McCord, Jr., drew a detailed map of the best fishing holes in the James which he shared with good friends.

Their cousin, Charles E. McCord, owns the work and we reproduce it with his permission. May's gift of gab was passed on to Charles. He was Don Imus's sidekick on the radio for thirty years.

> It is not all together its beauty. Other countries have beauty and grandeur. But there is about this Ozark country a peculiar fascination – its intimacy, its nearness, its primitiveness, its lore, its backwoodsiness and its absence of "cultural development." The world is sick of pink teas and golf and domestic triangles and swivel chairs and elevators. People come here and are fascinated with our folklore, our songs, our superstitions, our bizarre religions, our laziness and our yarns.
>
> Any country may have dairies and pigs and chickens and cattle on a thousand hills. It may have hot dog stands and highways and "kulture" and concrete swimming holes and overstuffed divans. But any country can't have Pick-shin-Ridge, Smack Out Holler and Dewey Bald. Harold Bell Wright brought the world to our door with his book, *The Shepherd of the Hills*, and I often wonder if we realize the debt we owe him. And Vance Randolph has gone farther as far as the Ozarks are concerned. His book, *The Ozarks, A Survival of a Primitive Society*, will live as long as a history of a people endures.

If May McCord was the "Queen of Hillbillies" and Jim Owen "King of the White River," Vance Randolph was "God of Ozark Folklorists." John T. Woodruff did not think Randolph a deity, nor did he worship at the altar of Ozark primitivism. Along with hating Randolph's books, the Springfield Chamber of Commerce president sat on the boards of several lending institutions and would have disapproved of the eminent folklorist's friendship with a bank robber from Galena. Vance boarded sometimes with Uncle Jack Short and became acquainted with his sons, Dewey and Leonard. "Shock," as Leonard was called, he liked better than the Congressman. When Leonard, a leader of the "Ozark Mountain Boys" gang, was killed after an Oklahoma jail break in which a detective was shot dead,

Convicted Bank Robber Escapes

Leonard Short, Galena, Mo., wrestling promoter and a brother of Missouri's only Republican congressman, Dewey Short, was one of four convicted bank robbers who escaped jail at Muskogee, Okla., today after critically wounding the chief of detectives. Officers said Short helped pass out guns to the six men in the break, one of whom was slain.

Above: From the front page of the *Moberly Monitor-Index*, December 3, 1935. Leonard Short was one of four bank robbers and two other prisoners who, with a smuggled revolver, shot their way out of the Muskogee City-federal jail. The chief of detectives and one escapee were killed. A few days later, the brother of Congressman Dewey Short was captured, but died under unexplained circumstances.

Above, right: Vance Randolph drove a covered wagon from Pineville, Missouri, to Little Rock, Arkansas, in 1932 as a publicity stunt.

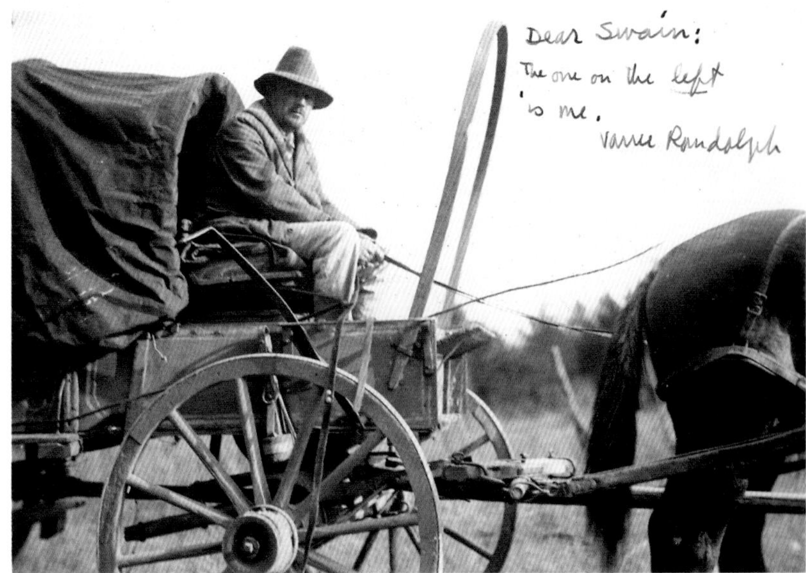

Randolph courted the dead outlaw's attractive widow. Apparently she did not wish to have another mate with irregular income and declined his proposal. Lillian Short did contribute more than seventy songs to Randolph's *Ozark Folk Songs.*

Galena had been Vance's getaway in the 1930s when he was unhappily married to a woman from Pineville. After Marie Wilbur died in 1937, he moved to the little town on the James. In 1941, he began capturing folk songs with a wire recording machine he borrowed (and kept forgetting to return) from Alan Lomax of the Library of Congress. The book business was "shot to hell," but Randolph kept writing. In his collection of Ozark yarns, *We Always Lie to Strangers: Tall Tales from the Ozarks* (1951), Randolph confirms these men were masters of the alchemy of converting the ordinary to the preposterous:

> One of the best float trip guides in Missouri is so old and feeble that he can scarcely handle a boat, but he entertains everybody with tall tales around the campfire at night. "Jeff ain't no good to work," I was told, "but when it comes to stretchin' blankets on a gravel bar, he's the best hand we've got." Jeff makes more money than boatmen half his age, and many anglers from Kansas City and St. Louis will not go fishing without him. I called at Jeff's cabin once, and his wife answered my knock. "Jeff ain't here," she said sourly. "He hangs round the boat-landin' all day, a-lyin' to them fool tourists." The woman did not realize that telling wacks is an essential part of Jeff's business, and in a large measure accounts for his popularity among sportsmen from the city.

Randolph, who had been coming down from Pittsburg, Kansas, since childhood to float and fish the clear rivers of the Ozarks, embarked on a career to preserve in print the last traces of its folk culture. In a 1943 Haldeman Julius pamphlet, *Wild Stories from*

the Ozarks, he credits a river guide for inspiring his lifelong quest:

> There is only one place in the world that really seems like home to me, and that is the Ozark region of southern Missouri and northern Arkansas. I was born in Kansas, and never saw the Ozarks until 1899 when my parents brought me down for a week's stay at the O-Joe Club near Noel, Mo. I was only seven years old at the time, but I perceived at once that a guide named Price Payne was the greatest man in the world, and that the Ozark country was the garden spot of all creation.

Dewey Short was "an avowed Hill-Billy" and Vance Randolph never disavowed the term. Unlike the transplanted Kansas folklorist, the educated congressman was an Ozark native. Like politicians from Andrew Jackson on, he exploited his backwoods credentials. The cutline of a May 9, 1938, press photo (below) of Short, Rep. Dudley White, and their wives dressed in "approved rustic styles" at a DC barn dance begins "Chicken and Fixin's YUM YUM."

Galena's famous son alternately postured as an Oxford-schooled philosophy professor and a Stone County hillbilly. His positions on water resource development were similarly contradictory. On a 1933 KMOX St. Louis radio broadcast, he lauded the great James River float and seconds later advocated Table Rock Dam, which would destroy a significant reach of that famous river. Paradoxically, he ended by voicing an Arcadian suspicion of progress:

> One has never tasted fully the joy of living who has not floated the 125 miles down the James and White rivers – from Galena to Branson. ... The proposed Table Rock Dam, when completed, will create a lake 60 miles long on James and White rivers. The project will cost $35,000,000 and generate electric power for new factories which will offer employment to thousands, increasing our prosperity. However, the Ozarks are not now, and I trust never will be, despoiled with too much civilization.

Above: An ambitious documentary on the trials of Branson entertainers.

Top: Cover of *We Always Lie to Strangers* (1951).

Middle: Sticker reflecting the penetration of a folky image of the Ozarks into tourist advertising.

Above: Oil painting by Charles Dahlgreen.

The version of the Ozarks that Congressman Dewey Short hoped would "never be despoiled with too much civilization" had been in large part created by writers. Local color novelist Harold Bell Wright and later folklorist Vance Randolph emphasized the primitive lifestyle of the region's inhabitants who lived in a semi-wild, river-cut landscape.

Fine artists from St. Louis and Chicago were attracted to the scenery of the White River, but, unlike writers, their work made little contribution to the region's image.

"Chicago Artist Highly Praises Ozark Region," read the headline in the Nov. 11, 1924, *Joplin Globe*. Charles Dahlgreen (1864-1955) said the Ozarks was a "painter's paradise" and that the "subject matter found in the region far surpassed that of Colorado." He spent eighteen days sketching the hills around Eureka Springs, Arkansas. Fragments of writing on the back of the 22 x 26 oil (above) indicate it might be a view of the upper White River. Finding patrons as well as subject matter may have incentivized big city artists to come to the Ozarks. Thirty-two painters of the Chicago Society of Artists exhibited at the Joplin Library in May 1923. Displayed along with Dahlgreen was work by Rudolph Ingerle (1879-1950) of Chicago. He was a charter member of the Society of Ozark Painters, founded around 1914 with property on the shore of Lake Taneycomo. His 18 x 20 oil painting, *Lover's Leap, Galena Missouri Ozark Mountains,* might be a less provocative title than Virgin Bluff, where, as legend goes an Indian maid leapt to her death.

These Impressionist-influenced painters were successful in capturing the rugged White River landscape in a manner that complements the region's literary Arcadianism. Unfortunately, efforts failed to capture collectors or patrons that would support an art colony. Charles Dahlgreen said in 1925, "I could paint a lifetime from the material in the Ozarks." Brown County, Indiana, was closer to home, and his depictions of its rolling country proved salable in Chicago, a more reliable art market than the Ozarks. Rudolph Ingerle also became a participant in the established Brown County art colony.

Above: *Lover's Leap* (Virgin Bluff?) by Rudolph Ingerle, courtesy of Skinner Inc.

Right: Printed postcard of a 1925 painting by Charles Dahlgreen. The November 2, 1926, *Springfield Leader* reported Dahlgreen, "Recently spent a fortnight in the Shepherd of the Hills Country, painting scenes." They noted the Chicago painter traveled in a "specially artist's automobile equipped with a skylight."

OLD
MATT'S
CABIN

SHEPHERD
OF THE
HILLS
COUNTRY

PUBLISHED BY GRANT R. DAHLGREEN 409 N. CUYLER AVE., OAK PARK, ILL.

Above: Railroad bridge over Highway 248 into Galena.

Once Galena was the launching point of multi-day floats down the James to the White River, and extending at times several hundred miles. These long trips are gone, but there are still about 106 miles of combined floatable reaches on the James, Finley, and Flat Creek.

Opposite above: The L.B. Price Mercantile Co. of Kansas City treated their traveling salesmen to a James River excursion in 1923. From the amount of gear on the johnboats, it would be a trip involving camping. One can hardly imagine the interchange of jokes between the salesmen and river guides.

Opposite below: Still fishing a pool just below Kerr Access, above Galena.

It's been a long while since the White River Line of the Missouri Pacific dropped tourists off at Galena. The line that rumbles through town without slowing down is now the Missouri and Northern Arkansas Railroad. It transports coal, grain, steel, asphalt, and frozen food – not city sportsmen. Signs in front of the railroad bridge over Main Street confirm there are still businesses here that serve floaters. Now they arrive by car and they will not be engaging a lanky, local guide who knows the name of every cliff and deep hole and could spin campfire yarns about the hickelsnoopus, the galoopus, and other terrible Stone County creatures.

The guide these suburbanites rely on is a spiral-bound book sold by the Missouri Department of Conservation titled *A Paddler's Guide to Missouri: Featuring 58 Streams to Canoe and Kayak*. These days, floaters are transported upstream ten or twenty miles and float back to Galena in a day. River recreationists, like their boats, have changed. There's not much camping out on gravel bars. Fewer visitors fish, and those who do catch and release. As the subtitle of this book of maps based on Oz Hawksley's *Missouri Ozark Waterways* indicates, they are not likely to be traveling in a johnboat.

Some think the James itself is not what it used to be. Dr. Pavlovsky and his colleagues are working to understand how our towns, farms, factories, parking lots, and other developments alter the flow. Perhaps the worst traumas this cherished river has suffered at our hands are past. Permanent pastures do not wash as much chert gravel into the streambeds as row cropping once did. Its popularity indicates there has been improvement in water quality.

Putting in at Hootentown and drifting to Galena is a modern replacement for the famous five-day Galena-to-Branson trip. A

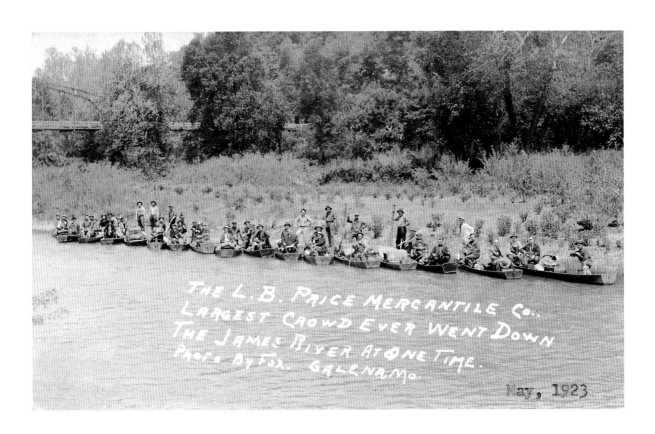

THE L. B. PRICE MERCANTILE CO.
LARGEST CROWD EVER WENT DOWN
THE JAMES RIVER AT ONE TIME.
PHOTO BY FOX. GALENA, MO.

May, 1923

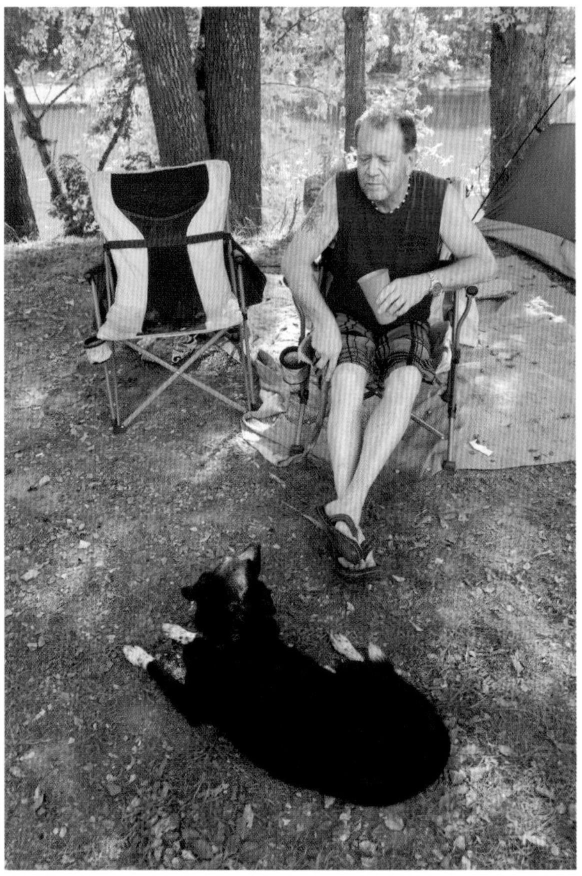

Opposite and right: Floaters today sometimes camp out along the James in privately run campgrounds at Hootentown and Galena. Few spend nights on gravel bars anymore. Canoes don't carry as much gear as johnboats, and long floats are a thing of the past due to dams.

Right: The production of aluminum canoes in the late 1940s by Grumman Aircraft opened up new possibilities for recreational floating in the Ozarks. Wood framed, canvas-covered canoes had been used in the early 1900s, but they were heavy and fragile. Fiberglass canoes were developed in the 1950s and are quieter.

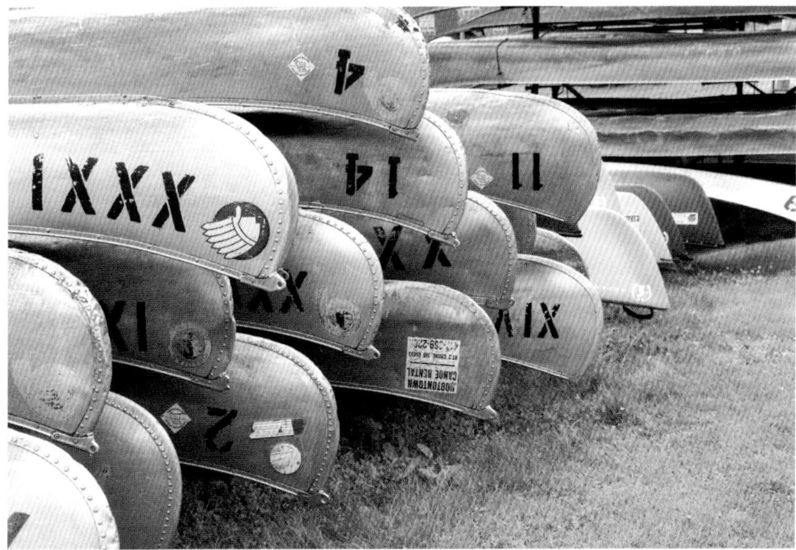

Following two pages: As the James approaches Galena, the river cuts deeper into the uplifted limestone. The banks are tree lined and the stream is surprisingly secluded though close to Springfield.

much-used Conservation Department access at Hootentown with a concrete ramp, but like the other MDC accesses, camping is prohibited. Just across the road is the Hootentown Canoe Rental and Store, which offers camping. They rent canoes, rafts, and kayaks. Their campgrounds have showers, restrooms, and RV hookups. The store sells supplies and food. A shuttle service takes floaters to put in upriver or pick them up downstream. Nearby is the Smokin' Cozy Country Café.

As the photographs on the following pages show, the remaining free-flowing lower James River is attractive in all seasons. It's not as wild as those streams that flow through blocks of public land and have been afforded legislative protection from development, but it's still an appealing, pastoral river with cliffs, chert gravel bars, fast riffles, and submerged logs that hide smallmouth bass.

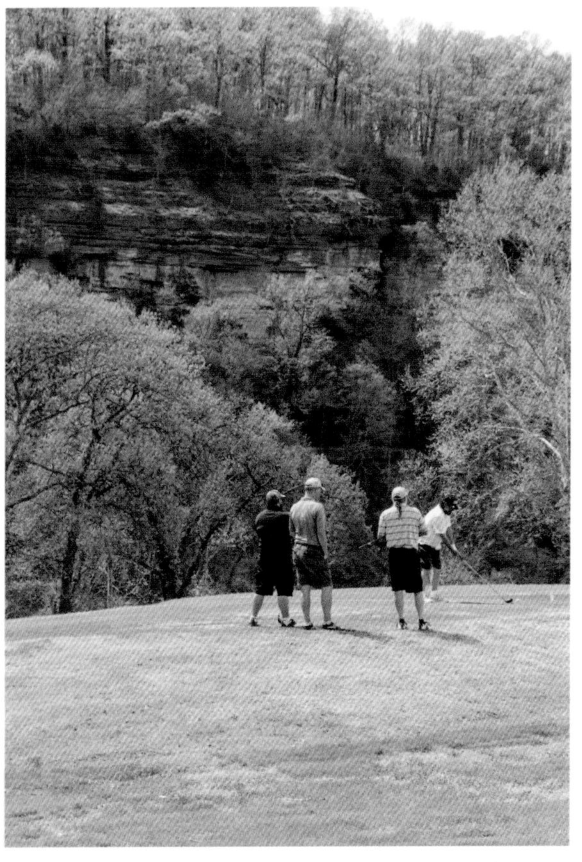

A slip-off slope opposite a limestone bluff along the James ten miles upstream from Galena has gone from pasture to fairway. Indian Tree Golf Course (both pages) has 420 house and condominium lots marked on a map, but as yet there is little construction. Players find the course interesting and the scenery attractive. Trees line the river so floaters are oblivious to the course.

Rivercut Golf Community is another course and residential combination on the banks of the James. Located where the river bends south near Springfield, it is flanked by a neighborhood that features "diverse homes designed with architectural styles such as French Country & Old English." There are no bluffs, but the rolling landscape is noted as scenic.

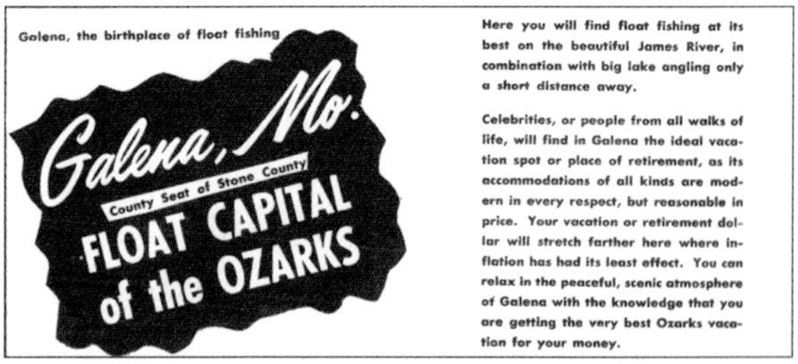

When in 1964 the promo (above) proclaimed Galena the Float Capital of the Ozarks, it hadn't been for thirty years. Jim Owen took the title to Branson in the 1930s. After the Corps' high dams were built, there wasn't really any center of floating. Canoers began exploring streams all over the Ozarks.

Galena was the place where the guided commercial float flourished, but it doesn't seem right to call it the "ex-" or "one-time" float capital. Many people still come here to rent a canoe, kayak, plastic raft, or even occasionally an aluminum johnboat. The outfitters let you take your dog along in all these except rafts.

When Table Rock Lake is low there can be a short float below Galena. Water fluctuations have caused some shoreline erosion and beavers have killed trees that would stabilize the banks, but it is more river than lake.

Opposite: The cliffs rise above the James' green hue much like they always have along these five transitional miles of riverine/reservoir landscape.

Attention Anglers
WE NEED YOUR HELP!
Paddlefish Tagging Project
REWARD FOR 1st TAG & ALL TAGS ENTERED IN RAFFLE FOR UP TO $500
Do NOT remove tags from SUBLEGAL paddlefish, rewards will not be given.
Thank You.

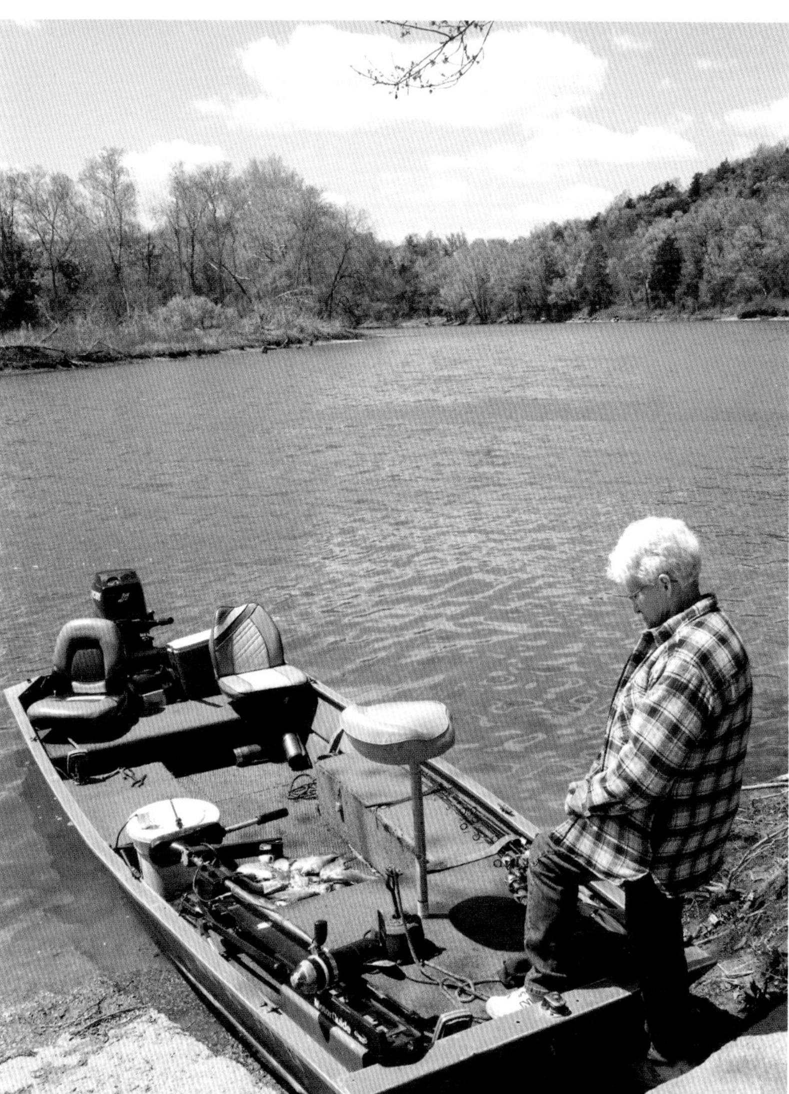

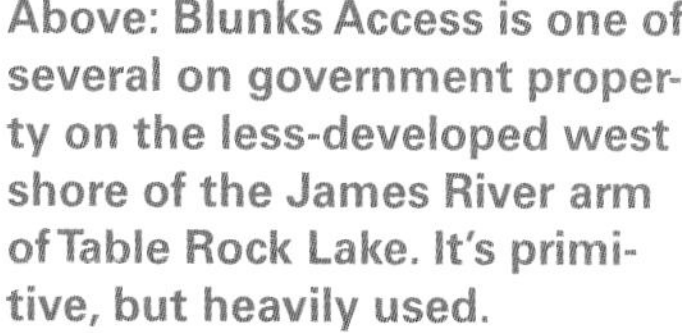

Above: Blunks Access is one of several on government property on the less-developed west shore of the James River arm of Table Rock Lake. It's primitive, but heavily used.

Opposite top: White bass, like paddlefish, make a spawning run up the James River in March and April. They are savage strikers and delicious.

Opposite bottom: An old and almost impassibly rutted road runs along the river.

Traveling west on State Route 248 from Galena in the spring, pickups towing boats are encountered turning south on Blunks Road. Should you follow one you will, in less than two miles, dead end at water. You are at Blunks Access, property of the Army Corps of Engineers. Depending on the level of Table Rock Lake, the crude boat ramp leads to flat water or flowing – sometimes it is hard to tell. Blunks is the last takeout for floaters or the first put in on the James River arm of Table Rock Lake.

It's a happening place for fishermen who don't throw back their catch. Paddlefish and white bass are the quarry of these anglers who are not catch-and-release tournament sportsmen. Their catch will end up in the skillet. The lady by the aluminum johnboat (above) and her husband had several dozen white bass that would be fare at a church fish fry. A paddlefish snagger was casting and jerking when the ramp wasn't being used (opposite top).

FAREWELL BEAUTIFUL JAMES RIVER

I am just an old broke down river rat,
Have a story I want to tell,
How they're fixin' to ruin our beautiful stream
I tell you folks, it's h--l!
Now, you can take old Mother Nature,
She has done her work with care,
Then take Man's beautiful pictures,
You see, it's nothing to compare.
I know this old river like a book,
Almost to every rock and tree,
But I have been floating it for forty odd years, you see.
Many and many a night I have camped on her nice clean gravel bars,
Sleeping out in the wide open spaces beneath the bright shining stars,
So come all you good fishers, and float while you may,
I hope to see you at Camp Rock Haven, at the Fisherman's Hat Cafe!

Written for Camp Rock Haven—By River Rat George Foster
(Rock Haven Guide)

Mail Address Route No. 3
Galena, Missouri

Above: "River Rat George Foster" guided for Camp Rock Haven, located on the west bank of the James River a few miles below Cape Fair. Lyle and Alma Chamberlain and their son Scotty built the camp in 1930 on the site of an earlier resort, the Aurora Fishing Club House. As well as providing guides, shuttles, and cabins, they operated the Fishermen's Hat Café.

When Table Rock Lake took their businesses, the Chamberlains moved some of their cabins to their nearby farm. They would live in one for forty-three years.

October 1954 marked the beginning of the end of guided floats on the James and White Rivers. Construction began on a 252-foot tall, 6,423-foot long dam just above Branson. Like the Jim Owen Fishing Service, Camp Rock House mailed invitations to their customers to come "float while you may."

Foster was one of those old-time river men like Tom Yocum and Charley Barnes. Larry Dablemont said in his book *Rivers to Run*, "About these men, who were a part of the stream in the purest sense, not enough was ever written. And the shame of it is, Owen was only the organizer. His guides were the real thing, men who knew the river and how to find the fish and help mediocre fishermen catch them."

A shadow hung over the entire fifty-year life of the White River float business. Dams were announced that were never built. Virgin Bluff Dam on the James was a flawed scheme but it had been taken seriously. Some tentative work was done in 1913 before its financing evaporated and federal permit lapsed. Young George Foster was a water boy for ten cents an hour, supplying the laborers with buckets of spring water and a ladle.

Empire District Electric provided mule-pulled wagons to portage little Powersite Dam. The Army Corps of Engineers would not offer this service. Johnboats would need to paddle across many, many miles of still waters to reach sections of ice-cold releases devoid of bass and goggle-eye. Before Table Rock closed in 1958, Bull Shoals had already eliminated the popular float to Cotter, Arkansas.

Robert Page Lincoln raged against these river-destroying government constructions in his "Floating Down the River" article in 1948. He blasted Bull Shoals Dam for ruining "this scenic part of the stream." He continued, "Table Rock Dam near Branson, Mo., will wipe out the last vestiges of this beautiful stream and will succeed in doing no more than add another disgusting mud hole."

Elegies for the soon-to-disappear James and White Rivers were published in the *Missouri Conservationist.* Harry Bruton's "Swan Song of the White River" in the May 1948 issue expresses regret for the loss of float streams and the destruction of the remnants of pioneer lifestyle in the White River hills. Bruton wrote,

> There are those who believe that the permanent flooding of the most productive bottomland of the entire region is economically destructive, and that the loss of natural beauty, aesthetic and intangible values, is an even greater sacrifice. And there are some who favor the dams as an economic opportunity for the recreational field. From the viewpoint of economics alone, it is hard to say who is right in the matter of dams. But one fact is incontestable. When the development is completed and the plans are off the blueprints and have become reality float fishing on a mountain stream will be a thing of the past as far as the White river and lower James are concerned.
>
> So let this be the swan song, the death chant, of a great stream that will become a series of man-made lakes. For when it is gone, it will have taken with it into oblivion something traditionally Ozarkian, something very dear to those of us who have known the White and James rivers.

Right: Bill Rogers' 1950s once neon-lit sign. When Table Rock Lake took his float service near the Kimberling Bridge, he relocated to Galena. Most of the float camps and their guides went out of business or retired.

Above: "About the Author" in a 1968 edition of *Missouri Ozark Waterways*: "Dr. Oscar "Oz" Hawksley, Professor of Zoology at Central Missouri State in Warrensburg, Missouri, has spent many years exploring streams in the Ozarks and in the Western states. In the course of some twelve years Dr. Hawksley covered over 3,500 miles by canoe in gathering data for this guide."

Top: Cover of the book seminal to the modern era of floating Ozark rivers.

Guided fishing trips in handmade wooden boats were already entering a twilight era when Table Rock Dam blocked the Galena-to-Branson float. Technology, the courts, environmentalism, expansion of Conservation Department services, and changing patterns of leisure conspired to relegate that Ozark tradition to memory. At the end of World War II, Grumman Aircraft Corporation discovered they could bend aluminum into boats as well as fighter plane wings. A Grumman canoe didn't require four sinewy country lads to unload. These canoes would float in very shallow water and, unlike the older wood frame and canvas models, were almost impervious to rocky shoals. This opened the headwaters of streams and encouraged self-guided expeditions on major rivers.

On May 13, 1952, parole officer George N. Elder took a day off, and he and his wife put their canoe (very likely a Grumman) in from a low water bridge across the upper Meramec River. They paddled downstream until they encountered a wire water-gap fence. Farmer J. M. Delcour advised fly fisherman Elder, as he pressed down on the wire to get his craft through, that he was trespassing and would be prosecuted if he continued. Elder asserted his rights to fish the stream. Apparently amiably, the two agreed to make a test case of Missouri riparian law concerning the rights of floaters.

Elder V. Delcour eventually ended up before the Missouri Supreme Court where, June 14, 1954, the case was decided in favor of the canoeing fly-fisherman. The Missouri Department of Conservation stood with the fishermen when the case went before the high court. Some department personnel had regretted not opposing the building of Table Rock Dam. The loss of the great James River float was lamented in articles and editorials. Since that 1954 legal precedent, the Conservation Department has been very supportive of floating. Several years after the high court clarified floaters' rights, the Department began facilitating a new era of river recreation. Beginning with the Ross Access on the Big Piney, the MDC has acquired property and built accesses. To date they maintain 217 accesses that provide (usually) a concrete boat ramp, a parking lot, and often a sealed-vault privy. The current MDC map of the James River charts 61.7 miles of floatable water. There are eight Conservation Department accesses beginning with Joe Crighton at mile 6.8. Ralph Cox Memorial Access is the last at Galena, just before the Y Bridge.

In 1965, the Department published *Missouri Ozark Waterways*, a mapped guide to thirty-seven rivers by Dr. Oscar (Oz) Hawksley. It became an accessory second only to a canoe paddle for this new class of urban and suburban floaters. It sold for a dollar. Hawks-

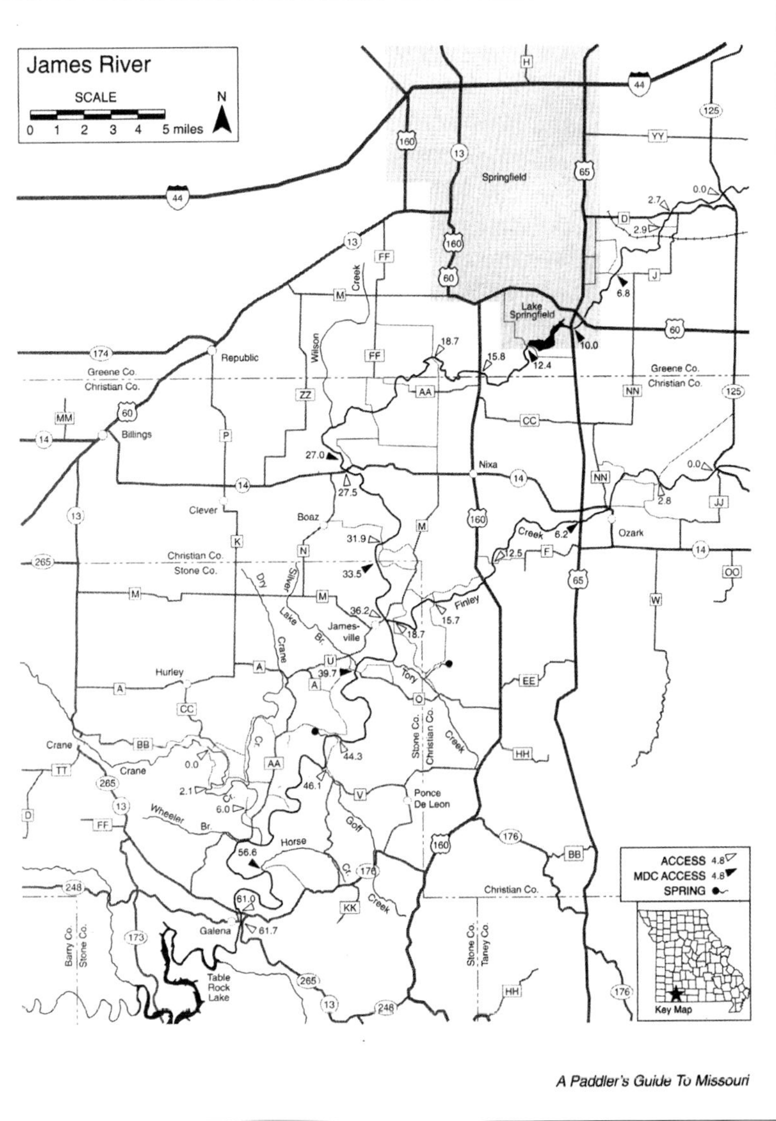

Above: The last MDC access on the James at Galena.

Top: Cover of the 2013 edition of *Paddler's Guide,* "based on and expanded from *Missouri Ozark Waterways* by Oz Hawksley."

ley's book has been enlarged to fifty-eight streams (with some in north Missouri) and renamed *A Paddler's Guide to Missouri*. It is now priced $8. Interestingly, the original description of the James has been retained, confirming the great float's legendary status:

> Float trips, for which the Ozarks are famous among smallmouth bass fishermen, reputedly originated at Galena on the James. John boats 18-24 feet long and 4 feet wide were used long before canoes and kayaks became popular and are amazingly maneuverable craft for their size. Some anglers still prefer the stability they provide for casting while standing, and the comfort of folding arm chairs which they can carry. Before the days of Table Rock Dam, a five-day float of about 125 miles was available from Galena to Branson, but now little, if any, of the river is floatable below Galena. However, one of the fine fishing floats always has been the 22-mile section from "Hooten Town" to Galena and this may still be floated even with john boats. In high or medium water, paddlers can run another 40 miles above this as well as some of the larger tributaries. Most of this water provides fine fishing.

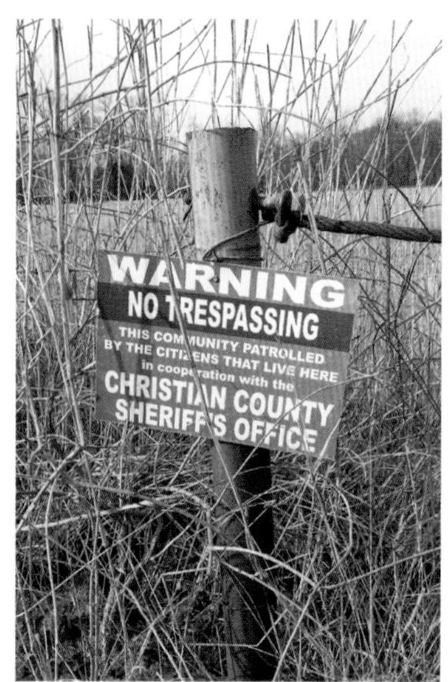
WARNING
NO TRESPASSING
THIS COMMUNITY PATROLLED
BY THE CITIZENS THAT LIVE HERE
in cooperation with the
CHRISTIAN COUNTY
SHERIFF'S OFFICE

Above: With or without evoking the support of the local sheriff, "No Trespassing" signs are common near streams. Beyond the trees of this one is the James River. Enmity between farmers and city hunters and fishermen began when railroads penetrated the Ozarks. Conservation agencies and hunting and fishing organizations have labored to minimize friction between urban sportsmen and rural landowners.

Johnboat fishermen rarely antagonized farmers. When canoes began floating smaller streams, there were occasional standoffs. The Elder v. Delcour court ruling seemed to settle most such confrontations.

Drifting by in an aluminum canoe may irk owners of adjacent land, but environmentalists' attempt to pass laws that would manage some of their property to enhance its natural appearance brought universal resentment. Powerful farm organizations and politicians branded these petition drives to regulate riparian zones and control boat activity as an attack on freedom and private property.

After Elder v. Delcour, the idea that Ozark rivers were public waterways was grudgingly accepted. Canoers with ever-expanding access became convinced Ozark streams were endangered by development, even dams. A complex regulatory law called the Natural Streams Act was drafted and signatures were collected to get it on the November 6, 1990, ballot as Proposition A. Perception that this law would give government bureaucrats control of property bordering streams ignited a war between urban environmentalists and rural landowners, or so the media characterized the dispute.

"Float down Finley River brings relaxation, sadness" was the provocative headline of a feature by Charlie Farmer in the August 12,1990, *Springfield News-Leader*. A few small sunfish were caught but largely the piece relates the disappointing changes he observed on a family float. Algae-covered rocks, shallow water, timber cutting, and a new house "on a once-magnificent bluff" were transformations that caused Farmer to reverse his opposition to the Natural Streams Act: "My hope and efforts were placed in voluntary programs like Stream Team and Stream For the Future." These, he wrote, "have made some progress but it boils down to clout. Right now there is none." Three weeks before the vote Farmer affirmed his support for the Act in an October 14, 1990, article. The passionate freelance outdoor writer puzzled at the schism between ecology-minded advocates of the measure and old-line conservation organizations and bureaucracies who didn't back the measure:

> Those opposing the Natural Streams Act are primarily the same forces that have fought other conservation initiatives in the past. Big business and development versus the Environment. ... The Natural assumption would be that the Missouri Department of Conservation (MDC) and the Conservation Federation of Missouri (CFM) would and should support the Natural Streams campaign in the face of wholesale stream abuse and pollution. When in fact the MDC opposes Proposition A and the CFM has taken a neutral stand.

Twenty years earlier there had been another petition drive to protect streams. Unlike the 1990 effort, which would have been administered by the Department of Natural Resources, the 1970 attempt would have put the Conservation Department in charge. Frustrat-

PLEASE VOTE YES
on Proposition A November 6
Save Our Streams
ADVERTISING SUPPLEMENT TO: Kansas City Star, St. Louis Post-Dispatch, Columbia Tribune, Columbia Missourian, Springfield News-Leader, Jefferson City News Tribune

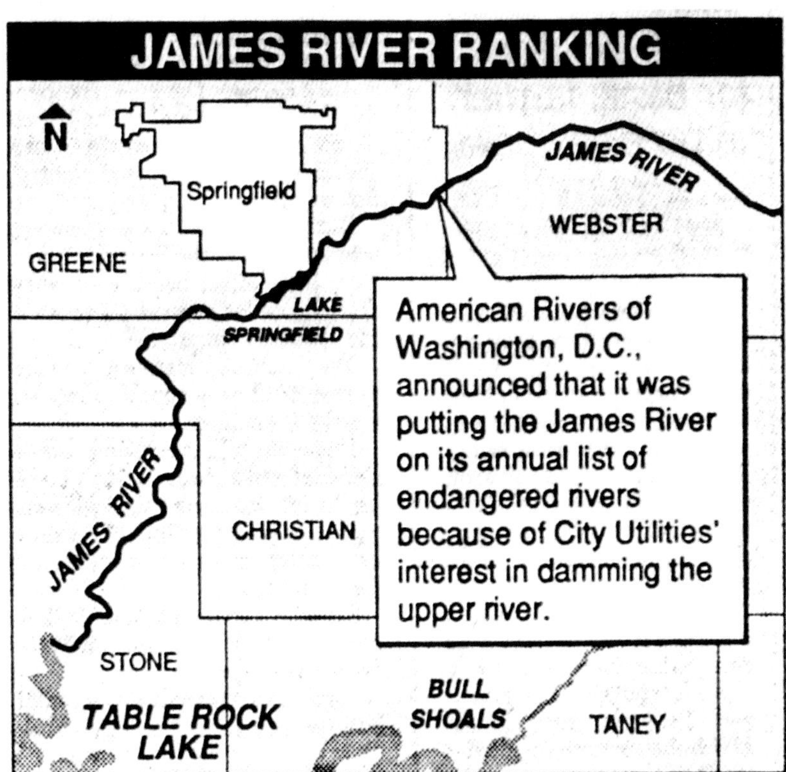
JAMES RIVER RANKING
N
Springfield
JAMES RIVER
WEBSTER
GREENE
LAKE
SPRINGFIELD
American Rivers of Washington, D.C., announced that it was putting the James River on its annual list of endangered rivers because of City Utilities' interest in damming the upper river.
JAMES RIVER
CHRISTIAN
STONE
BULL SHOALS
TABLE ROCK LAKE
TANEY

Right: Map from March 22, 1990, *News-Leader* article, "James River makes list of endangered." A representative of the American Rivers organization told reporter Mike Penprase putting the James on the endangered list was due to "information provided by proponents of the Natural Streams Act." A coordinator of the petition drive said he was unaware of their involvement. Questioned further the president of American Rivers admitted, "County Line Dam was the real reason ... the James may not be as spectacular as some other Ozark rivers, but it is worth saving from a dam."

Members of the Citizens to Preserve the Upper James River Valley were reluctant to embrace the environmentalists, although they opposed the proposed Corps dam in Webster County, which had died and come back to life several times. "Beware of groups with ulterior motives, officials cautioned," read the headline of another article concerning river preservation in that issue. Missouri Landowners' Association Secretary Bill Barham admitted that while opposition to a dam on the James coincided with farm interests, river-saving issues were in general an "urban-rural fight."

ed with trying to get a river protection bill through the state legislature, members of the Ozark Wilderness Club, the Meramec Canoe Club, and the Sierra Club organized a Scenic River Affiliation and launched a drive for signatures. A June 25, 1970, article in the *St. Louis Post-Dispatch* quoted Chairman Roger W. Taylor: "The idea is to freeze these rivers in their primitive state. ... The concept is preservation of the natural beauty for the canoeist-sightseers as opposed to creating mass recreation facilities." A three-hundred foot strip on each side of twenty Ozark streams would be zoned to prohibit development. The James River was included.

In a February 27, 1970, letter in the *Post-Dispatch*, Roy P. Pollman, owner of a mile of Big Piney riverfront, wrote, "What a horrible law to contemplate. If an owner has to get permission from the Conservation Commission as to what crops, what use his land can be put to, then we have Communism in the making."

On April 27, 1970, about 11:30 p.m, Roger Taylor, his wife, and

If it's Tourist Season...
Why can't we shoot them?

Right: Tension between rural Ozarkers and city floaters has lessened, but bumper stickers like this can still be seen occasionally on natives' pickups.

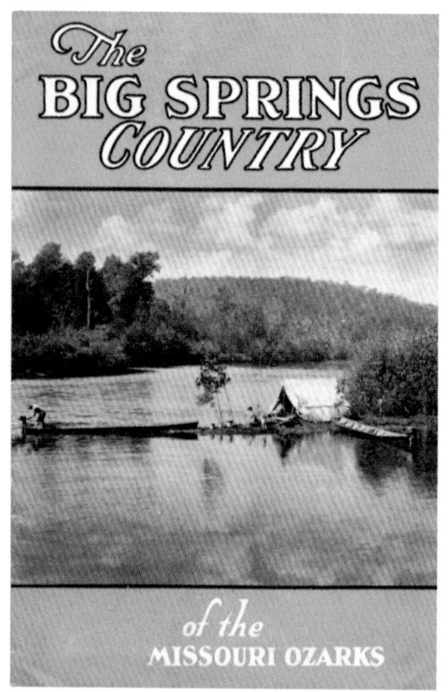

The
BIG SPRINGS
COUNTRY
of the
MISSOURI OZARKS

Above: Booklet published by the MO-Ozark Chamber of Commerce (1920s) promoting travel and economic opportunities in the eastern Ozarks. Compared to the quantity of tourist literature on the Shepherd of the Hills Country and Branson, printed efforts to attract vacationers to this large, rugged region are scant and restrained.

All Ozark rivers are clear and run over chert gravel, but there are geographic differences and corresponding cultural distinctions. The Current River has a larger spring flow than the James, and its watershed is more isolated and forested.

This semi-wilderness ambience was valued by early St. Louis sportsmen and later revered by ecology-conscious canoers. Tourism was cultivated along the lower James River and White River hills. Mass tourism was an obscenity to elite St. Louis environmentalists like Leo Drey, the driving force behind the Natural Rivers Act.

two sons were startled by an explosion. His 1968 Chevy had been dynamited in the carport outside his St. Charles home. Throughout the campaign there had been insinuations of violence. After the car bombing, they became more specific. "You're next" messages were left on the answering machines of Affiliation leaders. Nine days later, the initiative petition was officially withdrawn. The Show-Me State Heritage Association, a landowners' group that fought the bill, denied involvement and offered a $500 reward for the arrest and conviction of those responsible.

Nineteen years later, Loring Bullard, director of the Watershed Committee of the Ozarks, attended the kickoff campaign for the Natural Streams Act in Columbia: "Bitter feelings remain after the Scenic River fights – which put large portions of the Current, Jacks Fork, and Eleven Point rivers under federal protection in the mid 1970s," Bullard remarked in an April 1, 1989, *News-Leader* article. A summary of the act by Mike Penprase revealed the twelve-page document would place fifty-two rivers under the administration of the Missouri Department of Natural Resources – though local committees would be allowed to develop a management plan for each stream. The seven thousand-word lawyered act would require floaters to purchase a license, imposed a decibel level on outboard motors, and banned dams. Fines would be imposed on transgressors: "Along with encouraging certain uses, DNR could limit land subdivision; establish building and subdivision controls; prohibit or control septic tanks, landfills, dumping and littering; and limit the number of rafts, tubes, canoes, boats or other watercraft according to stream segment or time period."

A guest editorial appeared in the April 21 *News-Leader* by Rep. Don Koller of Summerville confirming Bullard's suspicions. He called the Natural Streams Act a "property rights take-away." Koller zeroed in on Leo Drey, who was bankrolling the campaign: "Drey tries to avoid paying his fair share of taxes for our schools, while at the same time he wants to impose stringent zoning and land use control on other landowners in our region. ... In my opinion, if Drey wishes to run the state of Missouri, I would suggest to him to concentrate his efforts on a campaign entitled 'Drey for Governor.'

Leo Drey's 160,000-acre Pioneer Forest, a heroic attempt to prove cut-over Ozark forest could become productive again without clear cutting, was the largest private holding in Missouri. Contrary to accusations, Drey was not in favor of any land confiscation; he preferred zoning. The wealthy St. Louis conservationist had not wanted his, or anyone else's, property along the Current River acquired by the Park Service for the Ozark National Scenic Riverways. Leo

Environmentalists were disappointed by the public's rejection of the Natural Streams Act, but believed good came from raising awareness of threats to rivers, contributing to the later success of the Department of Conservation's alternate volunteer solutions. The head of the department, Jerry Presley, denied this, pointing out the successful Stream Team approach was an outgrowth of conferences held with the Missouri Conservation Federation years earlier. Those meetings to discuss river protection were attended by environmentalists who initiated the petition campaign out of frustration with the department's lack of action.

The conservation and ecology movements have philosophical differences, but their current partnership in Stream Teams indicate they have many shared values.

Right: River Rescue, a volunteer cleanup at Lake Springfield, 2016, organized by the James River Partnership.

would donate $412,700 to publicize the Natural Streams Act, and some of the stipulations did reflect his elitist fear of "a degrading influx of visitors" to Ozark rivers.

No one's car was blown up this time. Both sides claimed that misrepresentations were being made. Proposition A easily got enough signatures to get on the ballot, but it crashed in the November 6, 1990, election – 315,663 yes votes to 938,427 no votes. It failed to carry a single county. Greene County voted 43,398 no to 9,922 yes. Even St. Louis County rejected it. "City slicker insults seen" was the headline of a November 8, 1990 *News-Leader* story that quoted John Ball of the University of Missouri Extension: "These folks have messed up the urban areas and now they want to tell the rural people how to manage."

The Missouri Natural Streams Act (1990): How an Environmental Campaign Was Waged and Lost by Karen A. Bradley examines the complicated social implications of this effort to preserve Ozark rivers. She doesn't evaluate the hydrological or ecological merits of the law, but examines the differences in outlook between the old-line conservation establishment and crusading environmentalists, whose perceived attitude of moral superiority and assertions of scientific justification many Missourians found off-putting. Even the most vocal opponents agreed that the clear Ozark rivers were perhaps Missouri's most beautiful natural feature. Voters may have feared the law would create a rigid "command and control" bureaucracy over which they would have little control.

Leaders of the campaign forgave the Conservation Department's slight, and many became active in Stream Teams. Soon, Leo Drey again became "Santa Claus" for special projects of the MDC. In 2005, Drey donated his vast forest to the L.A.D. Foundation, a gift valued at $180 million. It's open for hiking, camping, and hunting.

TABLE ROCK LAKE

Above: Virgin Bluff, three miles south of Cape Fair on Table Rock Lake. Like hundreds of other cliffs, it has a "lover's leap" fable attached.

Moon Song, the lovely daughter of an Indian chief, threw herself off this cliff when her father threatened to kill a handsome, gold-seeking Spanish soldier she loved. The chief ordered the medicine man to place a curse on the tragic place. Moon Song's anguished cries can yet be heard on dark nights, some say. Before the lake, the shoals below claimed the lives of several floaters.

Legends claim that photographing Virgin Bluff is nearly impossible. Crystal's clear image lit by a late winter's sunrise seems to have defied the chief's curse.

In 1958 modern technology irrevocably transformed the primitive lower James Fork of the White River. Table Rock Dam, built by the Army Corps of Engineers, backed up the White River almost fifty miles into the James, obliterating the famed Galena-to-Branson float. A tumultuous half-century of schemes to convert these free-flowing streams to flat water preceded the closing of that 252-foot high plug.

Governments today have a virtual monopoly on building large dams. Even farm ponds can be regulated. Corporate ownership of significant natural resources was once not only allowed, it was encouraged. The era when central government began to restrict private control of such sources of wealth coincided with early attempts to dam the White River and its tributaries.

An all-but-forgotten effort to dam the James River exemplified the passion progressives had to clamp down on capitalistic exploitation of hydropower. President Theodore Roosevelt vetoed this project, although its novel engineering and unqualified promoters doomed it. Virgin Bluff Dam was an enterprise of exquisite weirdness. The trust Teddy busted was a group of small-town merchants from southwest Missouri led by General William H. Standish.

VIRGIN BLUFF & THE RAPIDS
ON THE JAMES RIVER. STONE CO. MO.
GALENA MO. TO BRANSON FLOAT.
792 HALL PHOTO CO.

Above: Real photo postcard by George Hall circa 1915. Virgin Bluff was a landmark on the Galena to Branson float. While tame compared to the shoals of the upper reaches of some Ozark rivers, the rapids just before the big bluff were sporty for the James.

Stone County farmers likely never heard the phrase "riparian zone," but they left a line of trees along the river bank.

Virgin Bluff was a well-known scenic landmark on the James. In August 1895, a fishing party put in at the junction of the Finley and floated to Forsyth. They took a camera and reported to the *Springfield Republican* "a very fine picture of Virgin's bluff was obtained."

General William Henry Standish, a native of rural New York, had been a sergeant for four and a half months in the 153rd Volunteer Infantry at the end of the Civil War. Afterward, Standish practiced law in Ohio, Illinois, and Minnesota before landing in North Dakota. There he served two years (1893-1894) as state attorney general before decamping to Aurora, Missouri, where he launched his quest to extract electricity from the James River. This task was more commensurate with the leadership qualities of a general than of a sergeant, so he did not object to the attachment of that rank to his name. He was, a North Dakota biography stated, a direct descendant of Miles Standish of Mayflower fame.

The courtship of William Standish of investors was reported in the July 16,1908 *Springfield Republican*:

> Capitalists Confer With Standish. W. H. Standish, the promoter, met a number of capitalists at the Springfield Club last night and endeavored to interest them in his scheme to harness (the) White river and compel that stream to furnish electric power for Springfield. ... It is quite likely that a stock company will be organized soon to furnish the electrical power of the city at a great savings. Mr. Standish would make no statement as how definite he has arranged his plans.

Either the Springfield newspaper reporter wasn't taking notes at the pitch or Standish moved his dam's location, because only six months later a bill giving federal permission to build a tunnel dam on the James River passed Congress and landed on Theodore Roosevelt's desk, where he promptly vetoed it.

Given the president's reputation as an outdoorsman, one might conjecture he had fished the James and wished to preserve it as a premier smallmouth stream. But there is no indication he ever floated any Ozark river. His objections to Standish's dam were not

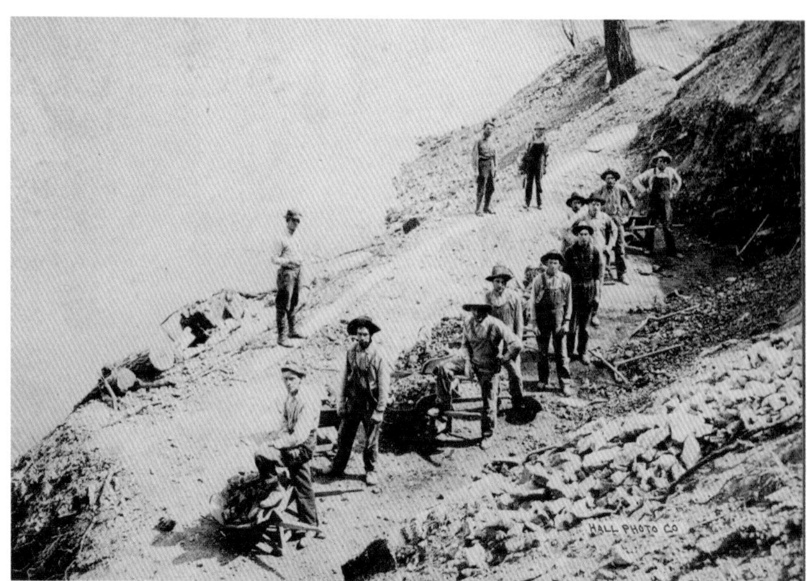

Above and right: Cabinet photograph by George Hall of site preparation at Virgin Bluff dam, circa 1913.

A consequence of Roosevelt's veto of the original Standish bill was that Congress began requiring work on authorized projects to begin within one year of approval and be completed within three years. These photographs may have been commissioned to prove compliance.

Possibly the photos on these two pages were used as well to show potential new investors that work was underway. A few roads were scratched out before his money ran out.

environmental, or based on feasibility. On January 16, 1909, *The New York Times* summarized them in an article:

> Roosevelt Sends In Veto: James River Dam Bill Would Be Monopolistic Grant, He Says:
>
> Washington, Jan. 15 – President Roosevelt sent a special message to the House to-day with his veto of the bill providing for the construction of a dam across James River, Stone County, Missouri, the purpose of the dam being to get water to create electric power.
>
> He declared that the movement to secure control of the water power of the country is still in its infancy, but that "unless it is controlled the history of the oil industry will be repeated in the hydro-electric power industry with results more oppressive and disastrous for the people." "It is true," he added, "that the great bulk of our potential water power is as yet undeveloped, but the sites, which are now controlled by com-

HALL PHOTO CO.

HALL PHOTO CO.

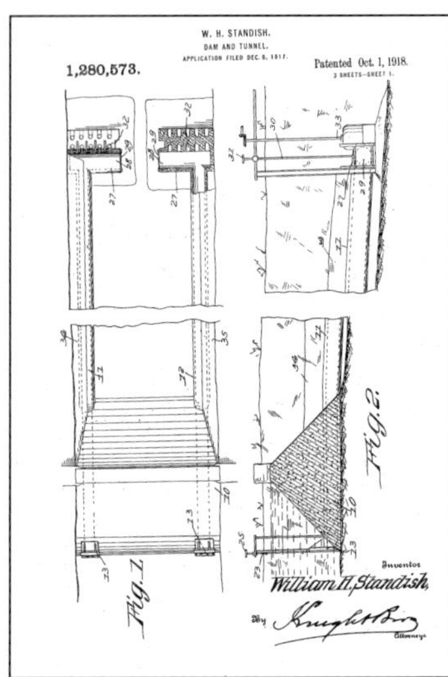

Above: Application for W. H. Standish's "useful improvements in dams and tunnels," filed Dec. 8, 1911, patented Oct. 1, 1918.

We cannot evaluate the engineering worthiness of Standish's patent; nor do we know if his ideas were ever employed. Hydraulic installations that cut through river bends are uncommon, although a similar scheme was attempted in the Arkansas Ozarks, also abandoned.

Tunnel Dam on the Niangua River, completed in 1930, uses an 800-foot-long tunnel to achieve a forty-foot head, cutting off about seven miles of river. It still produces a modest amount of electricity for its current owner, Sho-Me Electric Cooperative.

> binations are those which offer the greatest advantages, and therefore hold a strategic position."
>
> He says that "the bill gives to the grantee a valuable privilege, which by its very nature is monopolistic, and does not contain the conditions essential to protect the public interest."
>
> "I consider myself bound." He continues, "As far as exercise of my executive power will allow, to do for the people, in prevention of monopoly of their resources, what I believe they would do for themselves if they were in a position to act."
>
> The message was received at the close of the day and was received indifferently. After its reading it was referred to the Committee on Inter-State and Foreign Commerce.

Roosevelt was out of office only months after killing the Standish dam bill. William Howard Taft, the new president, was a progressive but not as aggressively anti-monopolistic as his one-time friend, Theodore. A new dam-on-the-James bill had been introduced to Congress and it easily passed both chambers. "Taft Signs Bill and Work Can Commence: Springfield Men and Their Associates Will Spend $150,000 On Project" (*Springfield Republican,* March 4, 1911). Even in 1911 that was a modest amount for "an immense concrete barrier across the 'Jim' and a 3,000-foot tunnel to give a fall of about forty feet." The article noted, "Gen. Standish is now conferring with his co-workers to ascertain their views before employing an engineer to begin survey work."

Astoundingly, the General sent yet another bill to Congress seeking authority to more than double the length of the tunnel. It passed and was signed as well. In "Utilizing the Power Sites of the Ozarks" (*Western Contractor,* February 28, 1912), Standish's overly ambitious plan is laid out against the context of the developing bonanza of Ozark hydropower:

> Providing for the cutting of a tunnel 7,000 feet long to change the course of a part of the James River, the proposition of Captain W. H. Standish of Aurora, Mo., to construct a dam for hydroelectric power in Stone county, has been made possible in the passage of an amended bill by Congress and the financing of the project by promoters. Early development of the tunnel project and the dam proposition will be undertaken by Captain Standish. The original Standish Water Power bill granted the right to dam James River at a point in township 23, range 24, in Stone county near the Virgin Bluff, and divert the waters of James River by tunnel through the mountain across to a loop in the river channel thus giving some 40 feet of head. The new bill grants the right to extend the tunnel to a point 5,000 feet further, entirely across the neck of a great clover-shaped bend 35 miles long, obtaining a head equal to a dam 85 feet high.
>
> While the flow of the James river is estimated at not-to-exceed 400 cubic feet per second, the great head obtained by the construction of a dam and tunnel will develop no less than 3,500 horsepower. It is now

practically certain that this project will go through. Just what will be done with the output of the Standish power plant has not been determined, but the close proximity of Monett and Aurora offers a waiting market. Monett is thirty miles and Aurora is about twenty-two miles by direct line from the Standish power site. These two towns probably would not consume 3,500 horsepower at present, but should a transmission line reach them, their manufacturing interests would be expected to develop quickly. But the scheduled completion of the Ozark power and water project, eight miles east of Hollister in Taney county and the assurance that the Standish project is financed, a tremendous stride toward the utilization of water power in the Ozarks has been made. The possibilities of water power in Stone and Taney counties are so vast that these two projects are regarded merely as the beginning. At least half-a-dozen power sites are available on the lower James and White rivers which combined will someday develop a hundred thousand horsepower, sufficient to manufacture all the cotton raised in Arkansas and Oklahoma.

Above: Grave of William H. Standish.

A large dam would indeed be built near Hollister, but it would be built two World Wars later. General Standish would not be involved. The once-attorney general of North Dakota and failed James River dam builder lived off his Civil War pension on a small farm near Reeds Spring.

After his death at age 79 he was buried in nearby Yocum Pond Cemetery. His headstone reads "William H Standish, Ohio, 1St Sgt 153 Regt. Ohio Inf Civil War, March 15 1843 Feb 20 1923."

"Stone County Dam Project Is Financed: Amended Bill of Captain Standish Approved by Congress and Work Will Start Soon," announced the *Springfield Republican* (February 18, 1912). The *James River Republican* (March 6, 1913) stated that Standish "has a force of men now at work on the foundation and as soon as he gets his connection with the electric power at Aurora he will have 60 teams on the road daily." In spite of the headlines, no dam ever diverted the flow of the James River at Virgin Bluff. News of it evaporated from the papers.

A short notice in a June 19, 1913, Ste. Genevieve paper is the only mention we found of this bizarre undertaking's collapse:

> "Ozark Dam Site Changed." Springfield. – The Virgin Bluff Project involving the erection of a dam across James river and the digging of a tunnel which would shorten the course of the river nearly 30 miles has been temporarily abandoned, pending the possible obtaining of legislative authority to construct a dam near Hollister, the proportions of which would treble those of the one at Powersite.

A November 23, 1958, *Springfield News-Leader* feature, "The Indian Curse That Killed Dam Project," by Gerald H. Pipes, is a rare remembrance of Standish's plan. Pipes did acknowledge the adverse financial climate of the times, but speculated the abandonment of Virgin Bluff dam might have been due to workplace accidents related to the Indian legend:

> Today the lonely "cries" of Moon Song may still be heard along the bluffs, but the dangerous shoals will soon be gone, for they will become a part of mammoth Table Rock Lake. The waters will climb over and hide the Indian maiden's grave and the scars left by the dam-builders. But will they erase the curse placed on the bluff by Moon-Song's chieftain father? Only time will tell.

November 1931

OZARK LIFE OUTDOORS

15c copy

OUTDOOR SPORTS OF THE OZARKS—BOATING, HUNTING, FISHING, CAMPING, TRAPPING, CONSERVATION, TOURING

What's Wrong With Missouri's Fish and Game Department?

A Series of Articles of Vital Interest to Missouri's Sportsmen Commencing With This Issue---By George Pascal Meek.

Above: ***Ozark Life Outdoors*** **was a short-lived magazine covering boating, hunting, fishing, camping, trapping, conversation, and touring. The one-page float-fishing article in the November 1931 issue did not mention either the effort to cut a tunnel through Big Bend of the James or the legend of Moon Song. The rapids below "six hundred foot high" Virgin Bluff was described as "glorious," not life-threatening. Charles Finger described the cliff as towering one thousand feet above the river – it's actually less than three hundred feet high.**

Until the mid-1950s the James continued to provide memorable float trips, accounts of which frequently appeared in print.

OZARK LIFE

Around the Big Bend

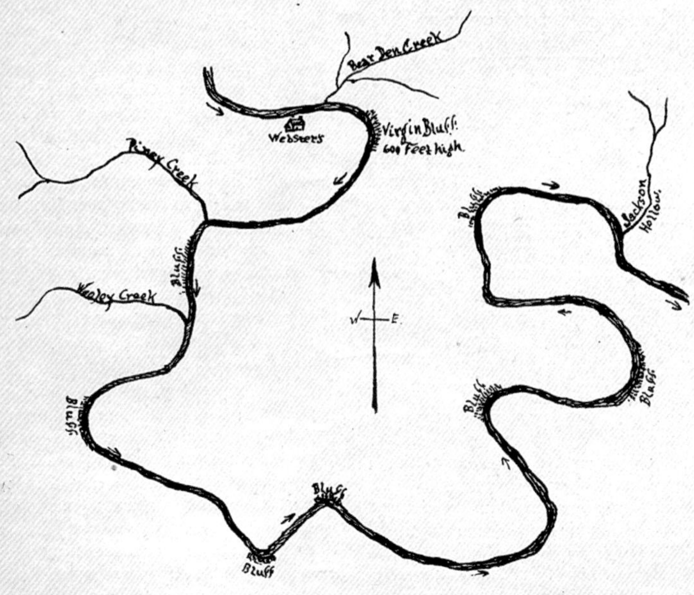

By A. M. HASWELL

In the southern part of Stone county the James river enters on a succession of irregular curves, sweeping to every point of the compass for twenty miles or more, but returning at last to within a mile and a half of its starting point. These curves of the stream form the "Big Bend" of the James. Close to the upper "heel" of the bend lived William Webster, and his farm house was our headquarters for many an outing.

One summer morning several of us boarded our old flat bottomed skiff for a float around the bend. Webster steered and we needed no oars, for the stream took us along in its swift current.. Almost at once we were in a glorious rapid, with Virgin bluff towering six hundred feet high on our left. Two of us stood casting our spoon hooks right and left, and before we reached calmer water below that first rapid, we had each taken a fine black bass.

Down stream we swept—in and out around abrupt curves, each showing a more thrilling view than the last; towering cedar-clad bluffs, decked out with millions of the scarlet and gold bells of the columbines; rapids that rushed us along at breathless speed; shaded pools where pond lilies bloomed; and fish!—smallmouth bass in the swift water, and large mouth "side-liners" in the quiet pools, until we wound up our lines, simply ashamed to take another one.

Noon found us camped in the shade of a bluff, and beside a rippling spring, eating a lunch with an appetite found nowhere except in such an environment. Then on again, through a continuous panorama of matchless scenery as the Ozarks, and the Ozarks only, can show. Then as the sun began to touch the tops of the western hills, Webster steered the skiff to the bank at the mouth of the Jackson Hollow, where we found young Webster with a farm wagon. Into that we loaded our skiff and ourselves, for a jolly ride over the hills to the upper heel of the bend, just a mile and a half from Jackson Hollow, and moored our boat to the same tree from which we had taken her in the morning. Ready for another trip the next day.

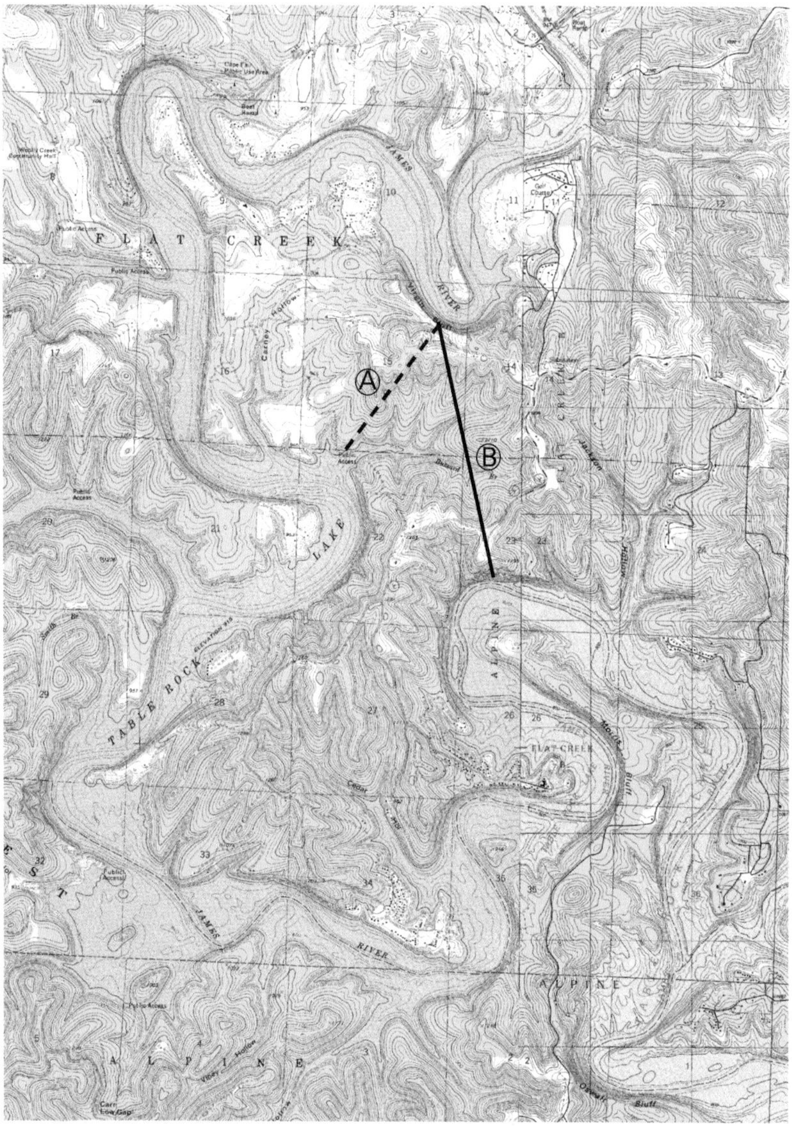

Right: General Standish's original plan to dam the James was to bore a hole through 3,000 feet of solid rock (A), and install hydroelectric turbines driven by 40 feet of head. As if that weren't challenging enough, he then proposed cutting a 7,000-foot tunnel to provide 85 foot of head (B). This would dry up 35 miles of river and eliminate the then-popular Galena-to-Branson float.

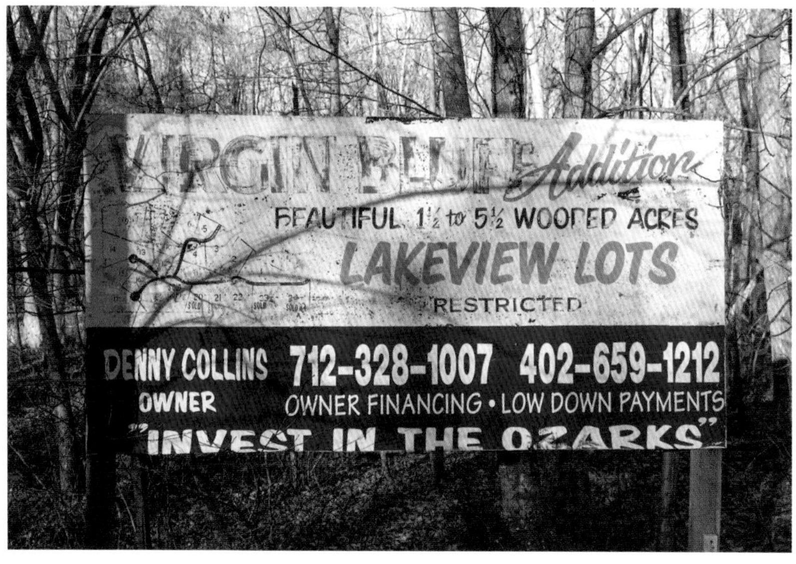

Right: Sign advertising lots for sale on Virgin Bluff. Among the homes built here, many of which have a view of Table Rock Lake, is a small winery. Lewsi Winery produces on site nine varieties from local grapes, including Moon Song Blush, Virgin Bluff Red, and Virgin Bluff White.

No steamboat ever chugged up the James, so there had been no cries to Congress to "improve" it. Before the War Between the States, businessmen, like Springfield's founder John P. Campbell, had sought government help in modifying the White River. After building three locks and dams near Batesville in the early 1900s, Army Engineers realized the White River Railroad would successfully compete with river transportation. The Corps gave up trying to deepen the swift, shallow, chert-floored Ozark rivers. The engineers would return half a century later with a bolder plan to convert the defiant White River into a servant of man.

Before that massive intervention of the central government, private enterprise attempted to exploit Ozark river power. At the same time General Standish's Virgin Bluff plan was coming apart, a hydroelectric dam was being built near Forsyth. It was a small affair, but it opened the gates to vaster development schemes, most of which would suffer the fate of Standish's projects although they were advanced by large corporations.

Like Bagnell Dam, Powersite Dam was started by men who soon encountered financial difficulties and sold out to bigger concerns. The St. Louis investors who organized the Ozark Power and Water Company engaged the Ambursen Hydraulic Construction Company of Boston to build it. Nils Ambursen, a Norwegian immigrant engineer, had designed a hollow cement slab and buttress structure used successfully elsewhere. Replacing the original backers was Wall Street accumulator of energy companies, Henry Latham Doherty. Doherty had already acquired a handful of small utility companies in southwest Missouri that were branded Empire District Electric Company. The White River operation kept its original name until being folded into the Empire group in 1927.

William Standish was not alone in his obsession with being part of the electrical revolution. Everything about it excited those who believed in the promise of technology. Enthusiastic as Doherty and his corporation were about progress, their core business was marketing power to towns and cities. Unlike the railroads, which were trying to transport tourists or sell land, they made no effort to influence the public's perception of the Ozarks.

Powersite Dam was not architecturally blatantly industrial. The narrow, twenty mile-long lake it created became regarded as part of nature, indistinguishable from the free-flowing river it replaced. A March 12, 1913 article in the *Springfield Republican,* "Lake Taneycomo Is Name Bestowed By Branson Club," compared the lake to the more famous Lake Como in the Alps. The new lake

Right: Cutline for this 1933 press photo reads "Col. and Mrs. Doherty watched happily a Christmas party which the Dohertys gave at Coral Gable's FLA."

The next year Doherty organized the National Committee for Birthday Balls which sponsored dances across the country to raise money for Franklin Roosevelt's Warm Springs Foundation to treat victims of polio. The president had been paralyzed from the waist down himself with the disease since 1921.

Henry L. Doherty built his holding company Cities Service into a gigantic combination of all three sources of energy – gas, oil, and electricity. His charm and friendship with FDR kept him from many of the problems capitalists had during the New Deal.

Right: Powersite Dam was hardly a visual embodiment of modernism like the high dams out West. It resembled a big milldam. Its forebay was little more than a pool in the White River. As it was a run-of-the-river dam, Lake Taneycomo's shoreline fluctuated very little. Until Table Rock's discharge of frigid water turned it into a trout environment, Taneycomo was popular with swimmers and bass fishermen.

Above: Turbines of Powersite Dam.

Some local promoters got it in their heads that the price of electricity near the plants would be so low that factories would automatically spring up. A headline in the *Springfield Republican* (November 18, 1911) proclaimed "Cotton Mills Will Come to White River: Dam Proposition Is to Furnish Power for Big Industries From New England." None of this happened. Electric rates were not less close to the dam. Cotton production did not swell.

Opposite: Made in Germany souvenir plate. The first hydroelectric dam on the White River, only fifty feet tall, was not regarded as intrusive. It presents as a waterfall, not the blank face of later high dams.

"nestled among the bluffs of the beautiful Ozarks" was part of the White River, "which no more picturesque stream can be found." The Branson Club created the name from Taney County Missouri.

A rugged geography had isolated the White River hills from forces that were changing agrarian America into an industrial nation. Floaters and folklorists preferred the primitive landscape and relic pioneer culture, though natives were adapting rapidly after the railroads connected them. Though the White River Line facilitated change, it embraced a primitivist vision in its promotion. City folks of that era desired to spend their vacations in a natural setting. Railroad brochures promised they could find an earlier version of America in the Shepherd of the Hills Country. Missouri Pacific advertising wasn't shy about mentioning Harold Bell Wright's earnest, bucolic novel of that name.

When the first hydroelectric dam was built on the White River below Forsyth just before World War I, one might think that the prevailing image of an Edenic Ozarks would be challenged. Modernism and Arcadianism instead formed an unorthodox union for the sake of tourism.

Not everyone entertained this back-to-nature vision of the Ozarks. Except for Branson's tomato canning plant and a pencil factory (neither of which used a lot of electricity), Powersite Dam had not created an industrial complex. This would have been a disappointment to advocates of progress like journalist William E. Draper. In "The Ozarks Go Native" (*Outlook and Independent*, Nov. 10, 1930), he celebrates the beneficial effect dams will have on this backward region. Draper blames the natives, whose primitive traditions intrigued the Arcadians, for standing in the way. "The Ozarkians, if such a tribe could be called, have lived lazy, kin marrying, morally clean, but none too God-loving lives." But, he wrote, "their shoulders are on the mat":

> Progress is lifting the Ozark hill billy by the seat of his overalls from the rocky hillside farm and providing him a more profitable job feeding cotton spindles. ... The machine age will soon overcome the slow-going people who live in the mountain area of Missouri and Arkansas. Noisy factory whistles will drown the soft music of clear swift water running over the gravel bars. But not until these people put on the gloves and fought to the finish.
>
> The Ozarks are going in for big water power development. ... Thousands of miles of twisting, spring-fed streams are now being harnessed and put to work, creating the driving energy for silk mills, cotton spindles, shoe, shirt and overall plants; all of which will dot a landscape in a country where the sound of the noonday whistle will be a nasty noise to the original settler who would much rather hear the tinkle of the big cowbell calling the boys into their dinner.

POWER DAM, LAKE TANEYCOMO, MO.

WHITE RIVER DAM
BRANSON, MO.

"YOU WILL GO A LONG WAYS
BEFORE YOU FIND A HEALTHIER
PLACE THAN THIS TO LIVE."
Harold Bell Wright.

The White River Country *in the* Missouri Ozarks

THE WHITE RIVER IN THE VICINITY OF BRANSON

Gypsy Journeys in the Ozarks

By Alice Mary Kimball

HOW shall I tell you of the country that I love? Where shall I find word-fragrance to make you feel its gypsy witchery, its wildwood charms?

One cannot analyze the perfume of a wild rose, nor may one explain wholly the lure of the White River country—the noblest pleasure ground of the Missouri Ozarks. After you have fished its streams, floated in a canoe through the blue magic of its moonlight, cantered over its trails in the freshness of early morning, and slept, night after night, beneath its stars, you will understand—a little. When, after many visits, you have come to know the land in the misty tenderness of springtime, the full-blossomed beauty of summer, and the amazing gold-and-purple pageantry of flaming autumn; when you have made friends with the cosmopolitan fraternity of nature-lovers who are settling its villages and farms; when, by primitive firesides of quaint Ozark natives, you have listened to thrilling tales of the strangely romantic history of the region—then you will find that the charm of Ozarkland has stolen into your heart, holding you a delighted, healthy, happy, red-blooded prisoner.

Year after year they come—the friends of the White River country. Niagara may beckon, the Northern Lakes may call, the seaside resorts of the East may flaunt their attractions, outgoing steamers may hint the fascinating secrets of foreign lands, but their spell is vain for those who have twined their heartstrings around the summer playground of the White River country.

Your adventurer on the White River trails knows where he may find mountains as untamed as the Adirondacks, as wild and craggy as the highlands of the West. He can show you bluffs as romantic as those which rise above the castled Rhine and mountain glens which might have made a rendezvous for Rhoderic Dhu and his kilted clansmen. Mounted on a sure-footed pony you may follow him along the edge of canons and ravines. He will take you in his canoe under the shadow of high precipices emerging into riffles which seethe and foam like the rapids of the St. Lawrence. He will guide you through subterranean caverns, vast and mysterious, which remind you of the weird hiding places of the robber Doones. He will sail with you down forest-broidered rivers which pour their blue waters into a lake of unsurpassed loveliness.

Lake Taneycomo

Nestled in the green bosom of the White River country, surrounded by mile upon mile of emerald beauty, lies Lake Taneycomo—with a single exception, the largest body of fresh water between the South Missouri boundary and the Great Lakes. Mighty bluffs, rivaling in grandeur the palisades of the Hudson,

BUFFALO SHOALS ON WHITE RIVER AND A BEAUTIFUL RANGE OF ARKANSAS HILLS

Above: Missouri Pacific pamphlet, circa 1920.

Opposite: Souvenir plate with a Harold Bell Wright quote on the back.

Near the end of the *Shepherd of the Hills,* the Old Shepherd gazes off into a valley and laments:

> Before many years a railroad will find its way yonder. Then many will come and the beautiful hills that have been my strength and peace will become the haunt of careless idlers, and a place of revelry. I am glad that I shall not be here. ...

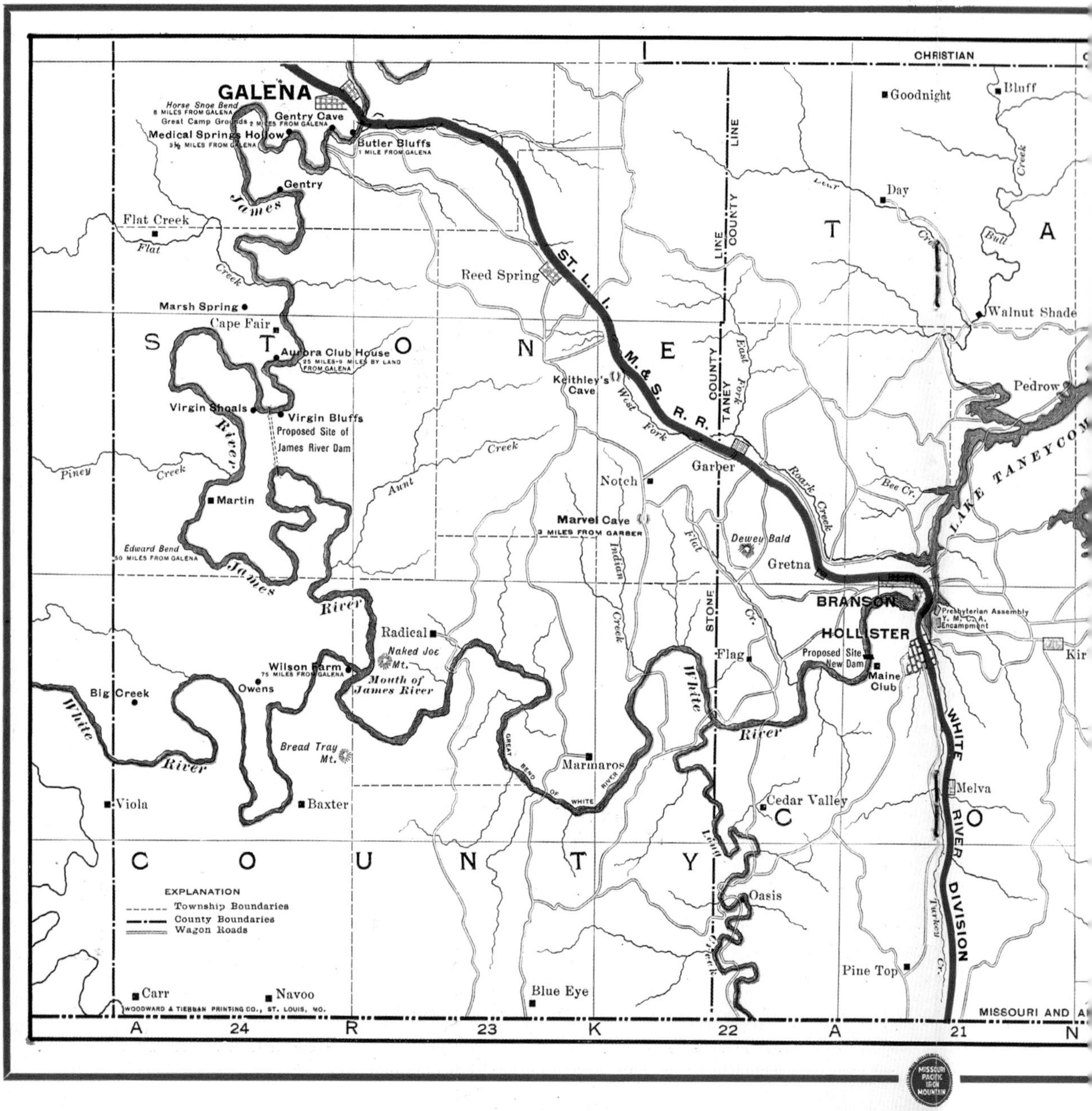

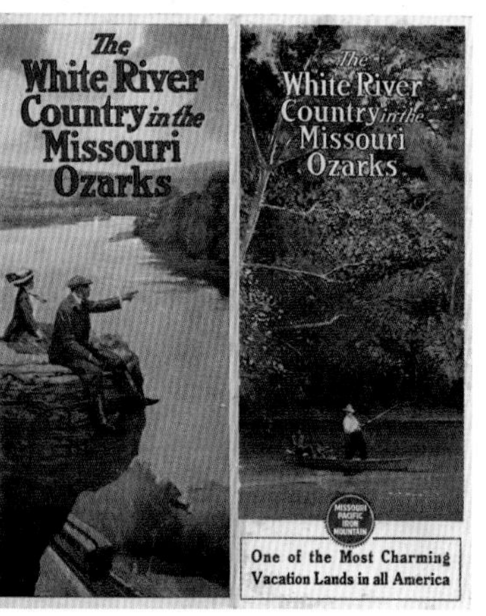

Nevertheless "careless idlers" came to the "beautiful hills" by the trainload (and soon after by the carload), many clutching dog-eared copies of Harold Bell Wright's bucolic novel. Missouri Pacific-Iron-Mountain Railway promotions fairly dripped with purple prose that, if anything, bested Wright's romanticism. The frontier had lingered in the Ozarks; similarly, Arcadian tourism persisted through the urbane and unsentimental 1920s.

Lake Taneycomo became part of that idyllic landscape. A resort on the artificial lake and a tour boat were named after characters from *Shepherd of the Hills*. There were indications that hydrologic trans-

formations might still arrive. The location of the defunct Virgin Bluff dam, which would have radically altered the James River, was still on the 1920s railroad map (opposite). On a 1929 railroad promotion (below), an even more transformative lake was inked in. The proposed Table Rock Lake dwarfed Lake Taneycomo.

"Ozark Power And Water Company Announces Tentative Plans for Developing Additional Projects," stated a February 19, 1922, *Springfield Republican*. Even before Taneycomo had filled, its builder had been purchasing additional dam sites on the White River:

For many years Henry L. Doherty (said to be the greatest promoter in America, head of the Cities Service company a $200,000,000

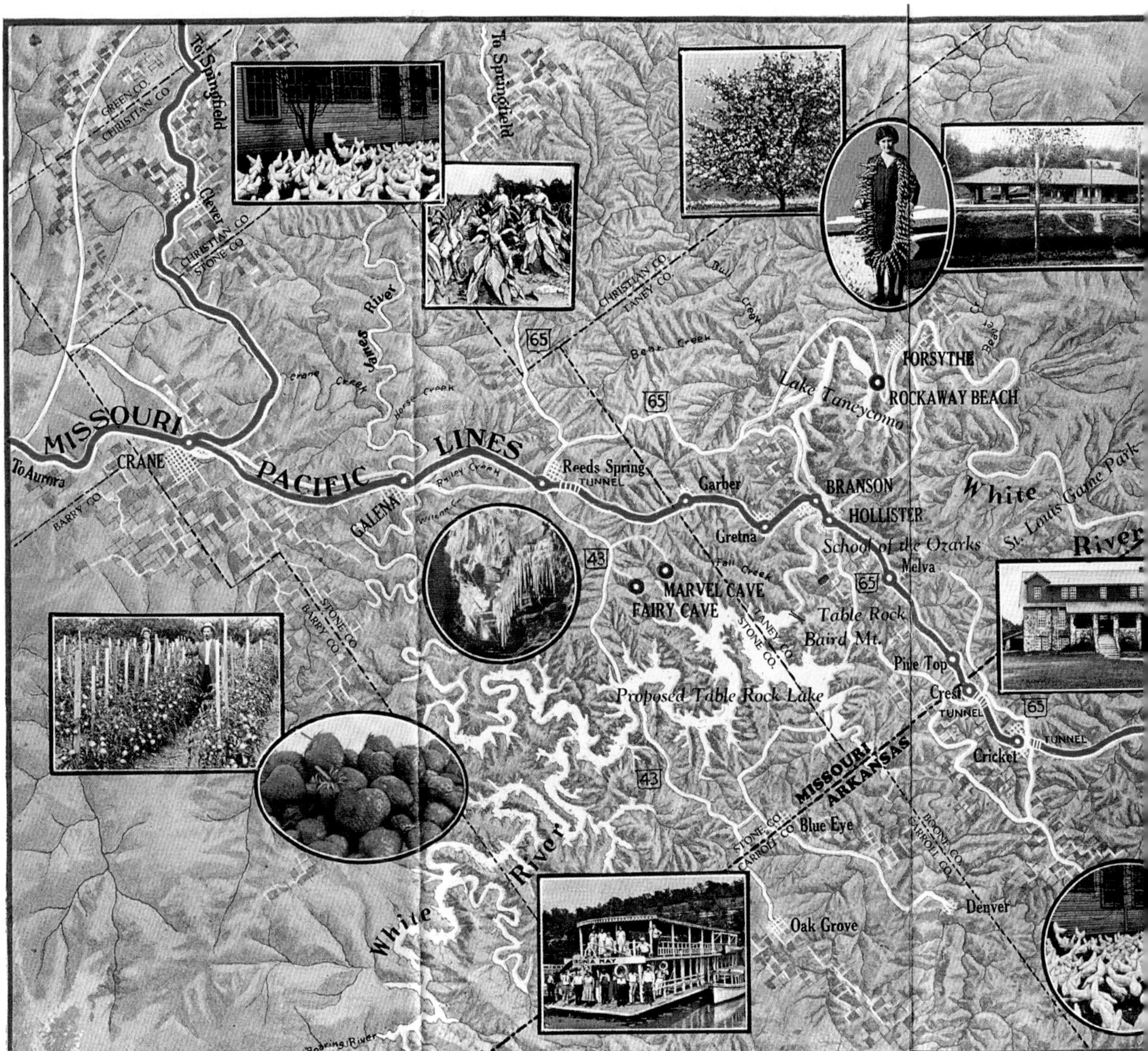

Blake Photo

ROCKAWAY BEACH ON LAKE TANEYCOMO

BRANSON LANDING

OUTDOOR LIFE
Is Pleasant in
The White River Country of the Ozarks
Easily Reached via
The Missouri Pacific Lines

Above: Photo montage from a 1929 Missouri Pacific brochure. At the lip of the Great Depression this portrait of gentlemen floaters and sunbathing girls is idyllic.

Opposite top: Real photo postcard, circa 1930. Sturdy johnboats were the craft of choice on swift Ozark rivers. Canoes and motorboats plied placid Lake Taneycomo.

Opposite bottom: Real photo postcard, 1925. Motorized tour boats accommodated auto-delivered tourists who came to sightsee, not fish, float or commune with nature. Lake Taneycomo was compatible with Arcadianism, but it opened the door to mass tourism. Branson Landing is today a big shopping center.

corporation), has had dreams of a wonderful hydro-electric and navigation development in the Ozarks. For more than 10 years, it is said, he has had a map showing a chain of power plants and connecting lakes, hanging on the wall of his private office, which will be, when completed, as he says in his letter of February 15, quoted above, "equal to any similar project within the United States."

The newspaper article continues – Table Rock, "probably the most scenic spot in Taney County," would permit the erection of a 200-foot-high dam, which "would create a lake 100 miles in length and extend up the James to Galena." Other mega White River dam projects by other companies had also been waiting for congressional authorization, the article stated. A few locations, like Powersite, managed to obtain approval, but until the creation of the Federal Power Commission in 1920, the government had been reluctant to allow private companies to exploit the hydroelectric potential of navigable streams. The Army Corps of Engineers was in charge of America's inland waterways and didn't much care for dams at this point. They routinely gave adverse reports on the feasibility of hydropower projects, especially if located in remote regions like the Ozarks.

Capitalists like Henry Doherty were cognizant as well of the problems of building profitable dams at a distance from markets for their electricity. Transmission lines were expensive and they lost a lot of current. Bond markets were fickle. Coal-fired plants were becoming more efficient, diminishing the nation's reliance on hydropower. This has been a long-term trend. In 1920, hydro-electricity supplied 40 percent of our needs. It has shrunk today to about 6

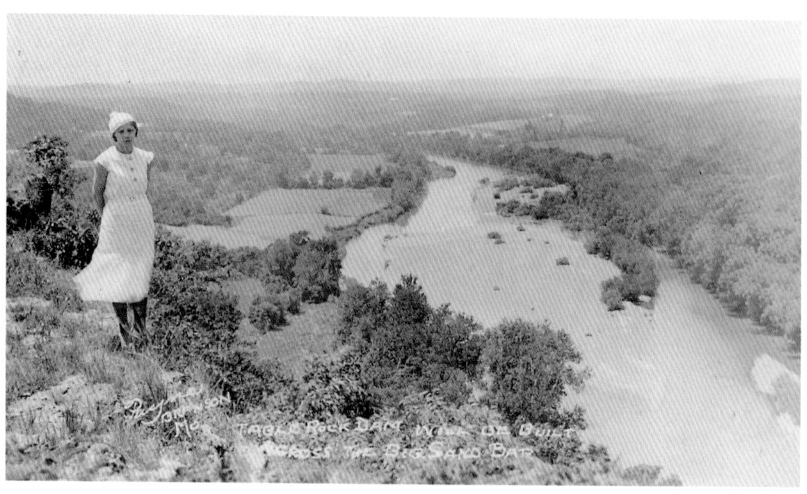

Above: Real photo postcard, 1920s, by Payne Johnson, Branson, Missouri."Table Rock Dam will be built across the big sand bar."

Most bluffs along Ozark rivers are named. Table Rock Bluff had a relatively flat top and was accessible by road. A visit to this overlook was on many vacationers' itinerary. For decades locals anticipated seeing machinery below building a huge dam. That this never occurred frustrated dam supporters and led them to question if the utility really intended to proceed.

percent, most of that produced in the northwest.

Powersite, in 1922, supplied only 661 customers so Empire District Electric applied for and received a preliminary permit to build a large dam at Table Rock, five miles southwest of Hollister. World War I had concluded satisfactorily, and Americans were optimistic about the prospects of better living through technology.

It would be thirty-six more years before the lower James River became the James River arm of Table Rock Lake. During that time utility companies constructed three hydroelectric dams within the Osage River system after Powersite Dam (1911-1913). None of the much-publicized private projects in the White River basin would go forward. The once dam-averse Army Corps of Engineers ultimately changed the free-flowing White River into a series of huge reservoirs.

A lot happened in America between 1922 and 1958 when Table Rock Dam was finally completed. These societal changes impacted Ozark dam projects but often in an obtuse, even hidden, way. In *Damming the Osage* we discovered a buried history of Lake of the Ozarks. Union Electric's account doesn't mention that two of the three men most responsible for Bagnell Dam did time in a federal penitentiary. But no felons were connected with Table Rock Dam. Oddly though, the 192-page official history of Empire District Electric Company, *Celebrating a Century of Service* (2009), does not mention Table Rock Dam. Yet that firm's plan to build a huge dam at that location was frequently mentioned in local newspapers in the 1920s.

Headlines of an October 8, 1926, *Springfield Leader* piece were encouraging. "War Department In Favor Of Building Dam At Table

Rock." The small print was less positive. Empire District Electric "has not been pressing their application" because improvements in their Branson, Missouri, and Riverton, Kansas, plants have produced "more electricity than will be consumed for sometime. Building Table Rock Dam will not begin until there is increased demand for electricity. This may be two years and it may be ten years."

News releases in the *Springfield Leader* alternately raised then dashed the hopes of Table Rock Lake supporters.

October 9, 1927. "Resort To Grow As Dam Goes Up – Local Men To Build Cottages Where White River Is Impounded"; November 16, 1927. "Ozark Water Era Is Near – Vast Development To Follow Big Dams Is Predicted"; January 22, 1928. "Name Being Sought For New Ozark Lake"; April 10, 1928. "Bridge Stumbling Block In Way Of $5,000,000 Payroll – Veritable Resort Paradise Which Would Attract Tourists From All Over Nation Is Offered In Table Rock Project Held Up By Court"; February 16, 1929. "Table Rock Dam Controversy Ended – Last Great Obstacle To Erecting $35,000,000 Dam Apparently Removed."

May 20, 1930. "Delay On Dam Due To Market Short Asserts – Table Rock Power Project Will Be Built As Soon As Power Can Be Sold, Congressman Tells Members Of Rotary Club." Recently elected member of the U. S. House of Representatives Dewey Short assured the Rotarians,

> I feel sure the dam will go through. It is only a question of time if we can get factories established here that will contract for the power. It

Right: Photo from Table Rock Bluff, 1940s. Still no dam. The federal government ultimately took dam building away from private companies in the late 1930s. World War II and then Korea delayed construction of many projects. Again, local dam advocates became nervous that the feds would repeat the stalling tactics of Empire District Electric.

will not be long but H. L. Doherty has too much sense to spend 30 to 35 million dollars unless he has contracts in advance.

During the Roaring Twenties neither Doherty's company nor any other major energy producer could quite convince themselves that investing tens of millions of dollars in a hydroelectric installation in the deep Ozarks would pay off. Many toyed with the idea, but couldn't find a market for the power.

After October 29, 1929, when Wall Street's collapse changed the trajectory of capitalism, the notion factories were going to spring up in remote Stone and Taney Counties and use enough electricity to cause Cities Service to build Table Rock Dam was beyond ridiculous. American stocks wouldn't reach their 1920s high until November 1954. Heavy manufacturing in the Ozarks couldn't recover; there had never been any.

Grim economic realities didn't extinguish the hopes of Table Rock Dam promoters. If they couldn't get a big free lake from Henry Doherty, they turned to a dam builder with even deeper pockets – Uncle Sam.

Hard as the Great Depression was on major corporate construction projects, it turned out to be a golden age for dam building, just not privately financed ones. Government wasn't a business. If expenditure furthered social or political goals, what did it matter if it didn't make a profit? Congress imposed regulations that required water resource projects to return costs plus interest but the re-educated,

Right: Hollister flood, 1943. Springfield lawyer and land speculator William H. Johnson started building a Tudor style complex by the train station in 1909 to accommodate tourists. As the faux half-timbered buildings were in the floodplain they were periodically immersed when Lake Taneycomo overflowed.

Table Rock Dam has kept the historic district, as it is now called, dry. Still some Hollister and Branson properties have suffered flooding, necessitating government buyouts. Believing the dam would afford complete protection, some people built even closer to the river, ignoring the Corps' warning.

Right: Press photo of Forsythe in the 1927 flood taken from Shadow Rock. Rising in the Boston Mountains and flowing through a narrow valley, the White River would rise quickly and put buildings on low ground underwater. The Corps of Engineers' solution protected most of Branson and Hollister from flooding but permanently submerged most of the agricultural land along the upper White River. Valuable farmland hundreds of miles downstream was protected from normal rises.

As these government dams were premised on flood control (power generation was an option), local advocates like the White River Boosters Association cried out to Congress for relief from floods, supporting the Corps of Engineers' claims.

Felicity to the new patron of dams required a revised chant from the Missouri business community. When Empire District Electric was considering building Table Rock Dam factory creation was the mantra. Local supporters really didn't care who built the dam, or why. They just wanted a nice lake, a bigger Taneycomo, at no cost to them.

dam-friendly Corps of Engineers became renowned for their creative cost-benefit calculations.

Increasingly, government had been taking on the responsibility for preventing water damage to the public since the Progressive era. Failure of the levees-only policy, which became apparent during the epic 1927 Mississippi flood, led to adoption of the equally hydrologically questionable idea that overflows of rivers could be completely controlled by a series of storage dams. That concept got a boost when features like hydroelectric generation, improved navigation by supplementing low water flow, irrigation, water supply, and later recreation were added. A multipurpose dam all but defies a negative cost-benefit analysis.

President Franklin Roosevelt signed into law the Flood Control Act of 1936. Requirement for cost sharing by beneficiaries of flood control was dropped. Eventually 375 large multipurpose reservoirs would be built, 100 percent paid for by the federal government. In follow-up legislation in 1941, six dams on the White River were authorized. Table Rock was one of these.

Doubtlessly that good news was celebrated by the passionate and long-suffering advocates of Table Rock Dam. In *A History of the Little Rock District, U.S. Army Corps of Engineers,* the author discusses the construction of Table Rock Dam and Beaver Dam. "As with other Corps projects, these dams had a long history of proposals, refusals, counter-proposals, delays, despair, investigations, and political involvements." Authorization and funding are two

Opposite: "Location Of All Reservoirs And Damsites Studied." Map from the 1932 308 Report on the White River Missouri and Arkansas.

In the Corps of Engineers' survey of the White River were six existing structures, and thirty-four possible dam sites were identified. Ultimately, dams and reservoirs were built on or near six of the locations listed in the report. The blue dots locate these dams.

Clearwater, 1940-1948; Norfork, 1941-1944; Bull Shoals, 1947-1951; Table Rock, 1954-1958; Greer's Ferry, 1959-1964; Beaver, 1960-1966.

Of the remaining twenty-eight possible dam sites, some were not pursued for engineering reasons, or lacked a sponsoring politician. Army engineers favored some good sites that had once been considered by private energy companies but encountered fierce local opposition. Missouri sportsmen railed against damming the Current and Eleven Point Rivers. Governor Forrest Smith, it has been reported, threatened to call out the National Guard if the Corps proceeded. A similar bitter conflict arose over Arkansas' Buffalo River. All three streams are now protected by federal acts. New environmental laws and the evidence that reservoirs do not offer protection against great floods make future large dams unlikely. Hydropower dams with a moderate head do not produce a significant amount of power at a competitive cost.

different things. It would be another agonizing fifteen years until heavy equipment began pushing dirt on the Stone-Taney county line. Two wars and a Republican administration unkind to pork barrel projects stood in the way.

The blueprint for the vast water resource project that was embarked upon during the Great Depression had a curious origin. For half a century the federal government struggled over decisions allowing private hydroelectric dams on navigable rivers. Theodore Roosevelt denied Virgin Bluff Dam's permit. Empire District Electric went back and forth with the Federal Power Commission over their permit for Table Rock Dam. In an effort to understand what the hydropower potential of the US was and how dams would interact with navigation and flood control, the Secretary of War, who was chairman of the FPC, asked the Corps of Engineers what a complete survey of American rivers would cost.

In April 1926, the Army Engineers concluded they could survey 180 rivers for $7.3 million. Congress agreed. House Document 308 of the 69th Congress defined what these studies – which came to be called 308 reports – would contain.

Even those averse to Corps' projects cannot doubt its engineers are well trained. Between 1929 and 1948, 176 reports were submitted to Congress. Not only did Army personnel boat and wade streams; they also consulted with private power companies, academics, and other agencies. The Roosevelt administration, looking for infrastructure improvements with a conservation overtone, requiring a lot of manpower, latched onto the 308 reports, even though on most sites no federal action was recommended. Before long the government began a campaign of blocking rivers. Ultimately more than $20 billion was spent, making this second only to the highway program in cost.

White River Missouri and Arkansas 308 report is a 462-page, paper-covered book issued in 1932. It finds that the upper White River system indeed has dam sites that could be developed for hydropower. However, "It is not evident at the present time that there is a market to absorb this power," the report concluded. Flood control by ten reservoirs would have reduced the stage of the Mississippi during the 1927 Great Flood about 2.56 feet at a cost of $31,258,000 per foot. "Not recommended."

New Deal arithmetic replaced the old math once used to calculate the feasibility of water resource development – it didn't factor in job creation and local stimulus. Flood control and creating electricity

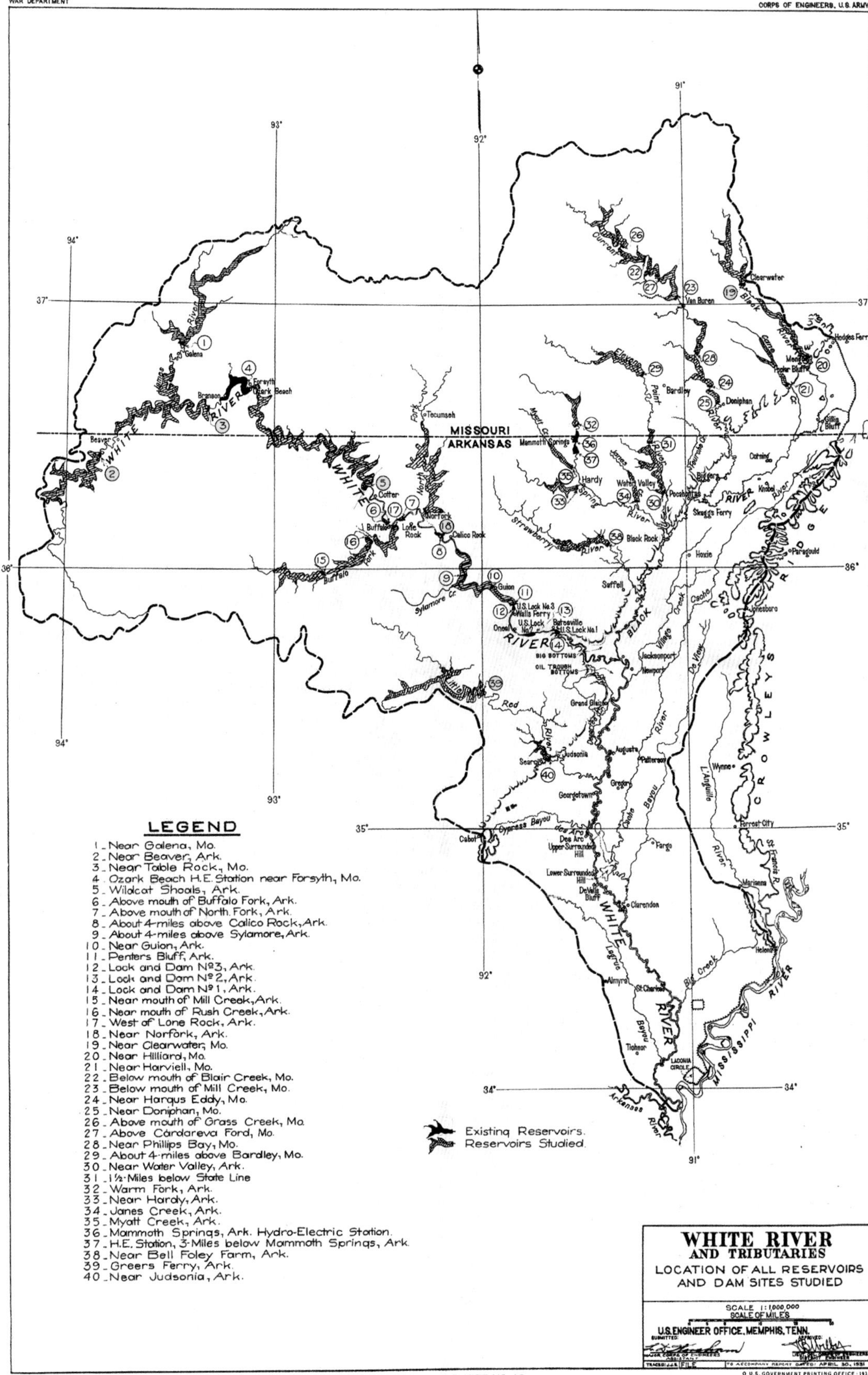

O U.S. GOVERNMENT PRINTING OFFICE : 1934

The Ozarks
MOUNTAINEER

Table Rock Victim of Present Anti-Public Policies

Table Rock dam at this writing seems doomed. It joins Southwestern Power Administration in Washington's discard of public power projects here and throughout the nation.

Primary responsibility for the failure of the present Congress and national administration to provide further funds for the construction of Table Rock, rests, of course on the Congressman in whose district the project lies and whose own constituents are affected. His own party has control of the government. It was his job to get that party to take favorable action.

That the Congressman himself has been derelict in the performance of this duty is evidenced by the fact that other members of Congress, particularly those of opposite political faith in the Senate, have had to wage the Table Rock battle. That his party and the present administration must share the responsibility for its defeat is proved by the fact that at no time, either in the Budget or otherwise, has the President and his immediate advisers sought to secure Table Rock or to intervene in Congress in its behalf.

That the President and his administration are opposed to public power projects wherever located is shown by their record during their fourteen months of office. They have stopped further construction of government dams. They have surrendered public power projects to the private power monopolies. They are strangling TVA. They are breaking up integrated power pool systems, such SPA; they are starving rural electric coops,—all for the purpose of forcing those enterprises out of business and into the laps of the private companies. Every move, every key appointment to important cabinet or agency posts have had that one purpose in mind.

Congressman Short occupies an anomalous position. He for years has favored the administration's policy of wrecking public power projects and of turning over the public power resources to private monopoly. He for this reason joined his party brethren in killing SPA, thus benefitting his principal local supporter, Empire District Electric Company (that has opposed Table Rock unless given a monopoly of its power). His efforts for the dam, whether weak or strong, were doomed to failure because they ran counter to his own convictions about public power and to those of his own party colleagues in Washington.

Table Rock is far more than a victim of a Congressman's ineptitude and lack of influence. Its death knell was sounded, just as was that of SPA and just as are all projects for the development of public resources in the public interest, when the policies of the present administration and the majority members of Congress became known and were put into effect. There was in the nature of things no reason for Table Rock to survive when other projects of like character throughout the nation were killed.

Private power monopoly now is in the saddle back in Washington and will win every battle so long as this administration is in power. This statement is made reluctantly but the record of the past 14 months permits of no such conclusion.

Right: Cartoon criticizing Dewey Short's advocacy of private over government power. *Ozark Mountaineer,* March 1954.

Short did oppose Southwest Power Administration becoming the marketer of the electricity generated by Table Rock Dam, preferring that Empire District Electric market it, but he didn't let that issue stand in the way of funding, as the editorial suggests.

For a magazine premised on the superiority of old-timeyness, the *Mountaineer* was curiously enamored of dams and reservoirs. Few aspects of modern technology have been so disruptive of traditional rural societies.

Two of the publication's most prominent writers, May Kennedy McCord and Mary Scott Hair, resigned over the smear of Dewey Short. McCord wrote to Roscoe Stewart, the publisher: "The last straw always breaks the camel's back. This is to tell you that I will not be writing any more for the *Mountaineer,* and please remove my name from the heading as a member of the staff. I have tried hard not to do this, and for your sake, but I cannot reconcile the disgraceful, stupid looking thing on the front page of this last issue (thanks to my good friend Steve Miller!) with a publication that I should in any way be connected with."

In *Dewey Short: Orator of the Ozarks,* Robert S. Wiley gives examples of Dewey's "revivalist" but compelling speeches. The New Deal, Short called the "Raw Deal." Newspapers across the country picked up his 1935 denunciation of the House of Representatives: "I deeply and sincerely regret that this body has degenerated into a supine, subservient, soporific, superfluous, supercilious, pusillanimous body of nitwits, the greatest ever gathered beneath the dome of our National Capitol. ..."

He didn't hesitate to compare President Roosevelt to Hitler: "It has been my privilege since the War (World War I) to have seen and heard Mussolini, Stalin, Hitler, and Horthy, but not a single dictator in all Europe has the power with the money back of him that the present occupant of the White House has."

In spite of these salvoes, Adolph J. Sabath, a prominent Illinois Democrat, found Short's oratory irresistible, if wrong-headed: "I have frequently heard him designated as the sage of the Ozarks. In dealing with any question he is a master, a recognized savant, always having at hand a fund of devastating information that disarms and paralyzes an opponent before the opponent fairly starts. No great question is finally settled before he speaks."

were real goals, but political appearances were important, too. Control of society and nature were obsessions of the New Deal. These utopian concepts had their genesis during the Progressive era, but Theodore Roosevelt did not have the onerous task of providing jobs for the masses like his cousin Franklin. Conservation, defined as the rational use of natural resources for humanity's benefit, became an imperative of FDR's empowered central government.

Victory over Germany and Japan led to a postwar economic boom. Americans chafed under the controls war and the Depression had imposed on their lives. General Eisenhower was in and New Dealer Truman was out of the White House. Ike wasn't completely against public works projects; he just preferred building interstate highways to building dams. FDR left hundreds of authorized, but unfunded and unfinished, water resource projects.

Through much of his career Dewey Short had been the lone Republican congressman from Missouri. Moving dams on the White River forward hadn't been difficult, as the Democrats supported such projects. Embarrassingly, when the Republicans returned to power, he was forced to defend Table Rock Dam. Harry Truman, good Missouri boy that he was, had recommended $10,800,000 for Table Rock. Congress approved $3 million dollars, but President Eisenhower left nothing in the spring 1953 budget for the dam on the White that would inundate the lower James.

Days later, on May 26, 1953, Hon. Dewey Short addressed the House of Representatives of the 83rd Congress First Session. "For the first twenty years that I have been in Congress I have been working for Table Rock Dam." Most of the rest of the printed proceedings discusses how beneficial the dam would be not only to his district, but also for the nation. Though he admits to having been president for six years of the National Rivers and Harbors Congress, a lobbying group, he asserts his objectivity by stating he has voted against some water resource projects. This is true. Short was not a rubber stamp for every pork barrel dam proposal. But he could log roll with the best, trading his vote to get support for his pet projects, like Table Rock Dam.

Short discouraged the Corps of Engineers from pursuing a project that would have taken the rest of the floatable James River above Table Rock Reservoir. Site No. 1 of the Corps' 308 Report on the White River describes a 145-foot high dam with 17,790-acre reservoir above Galena that, with Table Rock Dam, would have eliminated virtually the entire main stem of the James River:

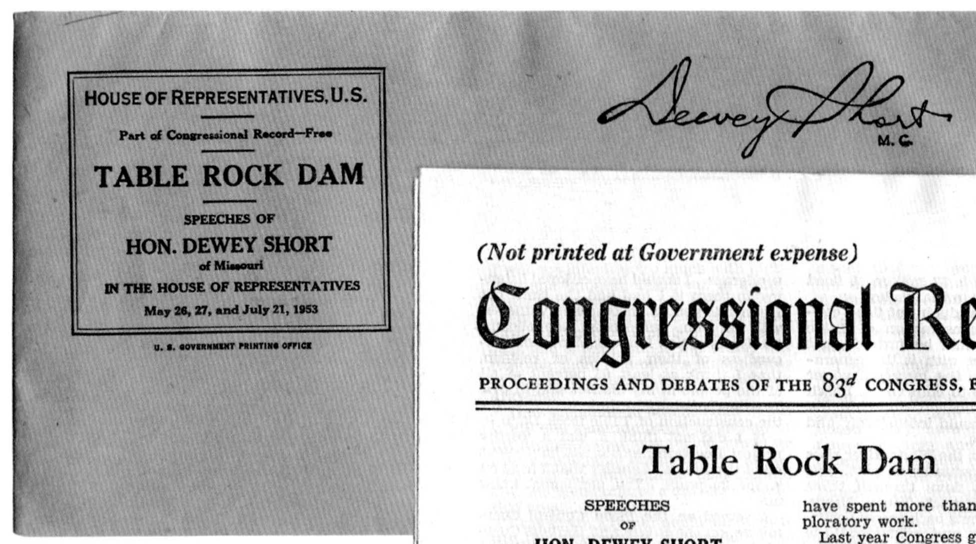

HOUSE OF REPRESENTATIVES, U.S.

Part of Congressional Record—Free

TABLE ROCK DAM

SPEECHES OF

HON. DEWEY SHORT

of Missouri

IN THE HOUSE OF REPRESENTATIVES

May 26, 27, and July 21, 1953

U. S. GOVERNMENT PRINTING OFFICE

Dewey Short M.C.

(Not printed at Government expense)

Congressional Record

PROCEEDINGS AND DEBATES OF THE 83d CONGRESS, FIRST SESSION

Table Rock Dam

SPEECHES OF HON. DEWEY SHORT OF MISSOURI IN THE HOUSE OF REPRESENTATIVES

have spent more than $800,000 in exploratory work.

Last year Congress gave us $3 million for the beginning of construction.

Both Table Rock and Bull Shoals were authorized in 1941, but because of the

Above: Mailing piece sent by Congressman Dewey Short in 1953. After Bull Shoals Dam was built, the plan was to move upriver and construct Table Rock, then Beaver. Depression-era public works projects, however, were losing their allure in the booming consumer era of the 1950s.

Short felt the need to make a speech reminding his colleagues in Congress of the need for Table Rock Dam. He then sent his constituents a copy to reassure them he was still fighting to get the dam built.

> I want you to know now that I do not want to turn my district into a lake.
>
> The engineers have a lot of projects in reserve on the shelf, which I could never support. They even want to build a dam above my little hometown of Galena. We do not want that one built. It would cover up Crane, Hurley, and Nixa, because the land up there is more of an open and level nature, but down at Table Rock on the White River above Bull Shoals and above Ozark Beach Dam the valleys are deeper or the hills are higher, put it either way you like, the canyons are narrower, and the construction of that dam will not cover up railroads or utilities or industries, and it will not interfere too much with highways and bridges. There will be a minimum of dislocation.

Congressman Short did get the appropriations for Table Rock Dam flowing again. Construction got underway in 1954, and the White River was backed up behind a $65 million, 252-foot-high dam two miles above Table Rock in 1958. Dedication ceremonies were held on June 14, 1959, when the powerhouse was completed. Dewey Short had been defeated in a close race in 1956 by Democrat Charles Brown. Dewey was appointed an Under Secretary of the Army. Both Brown and Short were on the platform along with the Chief of Engineers Major General E. C. Itschner and Senator Stuart Symington. In a press photo taken of the dignitaries, the normally smiling Dewey Short was described as having "a rather tragic expression on his face."

Those whose land was being taken by the reservoir were chided by proponents, like the Table Rock Boosters Association. In an article in *Missouri Historical Review*, "In the Shadow of Table Rock Lake," John R. Hemsley wrote, "The Association while recognizing that some people would be harmed or inconvenienced by the loss

Congressman Dewey Short and unidentified colleagues looking at the White River. On the back of this Townsend Godsey photograph is written, "Table Rock Dam site 9-14-41"

Dewey appears to be pointing out the location where the long delayed dam would be built. Only a month earlier the President had signed the Flood Control Act of 1941, which included both Table Rock and Bull Shoals. Headline of the October 11, 1952, *Kansas City Times* announced, "Start A Big Dam Barbecue And Music At Launching of 76-Million-Dollar Reservoir." Mayor Claude Binkley of Branson remarked he had 'hurried to the Ozarks twenty-six years ago' to be here for the construction start."

of their homes, churches, schools, cemeteries, roads and bridges," should look to the "common good" and consider that "the world is in flux. We are in changing times. The death rattle of a passing age mingles with the birth pangs of a new order."

Triumphant dam supporters in southwest Missouri rejoiced their letters to Congressmen had finally been rewarded. Actually, that vast effort to control the nation's rivers began long before John Woodruff and owners of Branson tourist cabins began traveling to hearings at Washington, DC, to tell sad stories about White River floods. More powerful political forces had been at work than the Table Rock Boosters Association. Omnipotent decision-makers do not always know, or care, about the specificities of individual projects or their effects on locals, be they good or bad. Such a big idea person was the 26th president of the United States of America.

Theodore Roosevelt believed it was his solemn obligation to control what he saw as the growing power of large corporations. "Trusts," as they were called, were there to be "busted," like lions were there

to be shot and mounted for public display. In spite of his encyclopedic knowledge of nature, Teddy cared little about hydrology. Rivers were there to be controlled, like Standard Oil or the Union Pacific Railroad. Having busted the largest industries in America for nine years, he leveled his sights on William Standish's technically problematic and woefully underfinanced project to blast a hole through Virgin Bluff on the James River to create a hydropower installation.

Congress rubber-stamped the federal permit for the dam below Galena, but unexpectedly the president balked. Roosevelt vetoed it, writing, "The people of the country are threatened by a monopoly far more powerful, because in far closer touch with their domestic and industrial life, than anything known to our experience. A single generation will see the exhaustion of our natural resources in oil and gas and such a rise in the price of coal as will make the prices of electrically transmitted water power a controlling factor in transportation, in manufacturing, and in household lighting and heating. "Fear of the depletion of natural resources was a standard justification of the progressives' unprecedented government controls over private enterprises.

Above: Cartoon by Victor Gillam, ***St. Louis Post Dispatch***, **May 9, 1909, titled "If he should ever come back." Upon leaving office, Roosevelt departed for Africa. The ugly hog in the cartoon is the "Water Power Trust," who trembles with fear that the great trust buster will return from safari and deal with them as he has other monopolies.**

Top: 1931 news photo of dusting the bust of Theodore Roosevelt. The "conservation president" had some preservationist instincts, but his progressive administration began a massive federal program of water resource development.

Roosevelt could not have picked a more insignificant and inappropriate example of the alleged nefarious plot of giant corporations to monopolize the nation's production of hydropower. This veto is a textbook case of the tendency of central governments to ignore actualities and act on generalities. Because he squelched the James River dam did not mean Roosevelt was anti-dam. This "conservation president" created the Bureau of Reclamation, an agency that would ultimately build more than six hundred dams, the majority of which proved to be environmentally disastrous. Nor was he against monopolies. Teddy wanted the government to own all dams, not just those built in arid regions.

Roosevelt's successor, William Howard Taft, did not veto the flawed Virgin Bluff project when Congress resubmitted it. Taft was progressive but not as anti-big business as Theodore. The good friends became foes, ultimately splitting the Republican Party and putting a Democrat in the White House.

Roosevelt's prediction that the dreaded trusts would try to lock up every possible dam site in the country was not a complete fantasy.

Above: Press photo of President Truman and Arkansas Governor McMath at the dedication of Norfolk and Bull Shoals Dams, 1952. Because the hydropower of Norfolk was considered useful for the war effort, it was built in the early 1940s. Bull Shoals behind them was recently completed and the Corps was ready to start on Table Rock Dam.

Permits to build hydropower dams were secured, but only a few like Union Electric's dam on the Osage River were ultimately completed. Most of the best places for power generation were not close to the consumers of electricity. Coal-fired plants proved to be more cost effective.

Theodore Roosevelt's belief that dam building should be the exclusive purview of the federal government appealed to his cousin Franklin. When the big-business friendly 1920s slumped into the anti-capitalist 1930s, President Franklin Delano Roosevelt dusted off Theodore's belief in federal water management and the Democrats began pouring concrete, lots and lots of it. Wars slowed down their goal to convert the free-flowing White River into a series of reservoirs, but by 1952 they had finished Norfork and Bull Shoals dams and were ready to move upstream to Table Rock and Beaver dams.

Harry S. Truman was a New Deal Democrat through and through. He shared his fallen chief's desire to develop all the waterpower of the nation à la TVA. Such complete federal domination would only in the end be achieved in Tennessee, but many systems like the White would be tamed by Army Corps of Engineers multipurpose dams.

In the July 2, 1952, press photo of the president and Arkansas Governor Seth McMath posed in front of the newly completed Bull Shoals Dam, Truman stares off into space with the vacant expression of a rest home resident, not the occupant of the White House. A few months earlier, he had announced he would not run for re-election, citing his age. Americans were back to gambling on Wall Street, buying new cars, and expanding the suburbs everywhere. The country was weary of being managed by idealistic bureaucrats. Truman's approval ratings approached historic lows.

A light rain apparently woke Harry from his reveries and he began his speech. After a few jokes, he ripped into the "private selfishness" of "private power companies" who tried "by every means – fair and foul alike – to prevent these dams from being started." They did this, he went on, "to stop farmers of this area from getting the benefits of low-cost hydroelectric power. ... The private power companies around here made a great hullabaloo about these dams being what they called socialism."

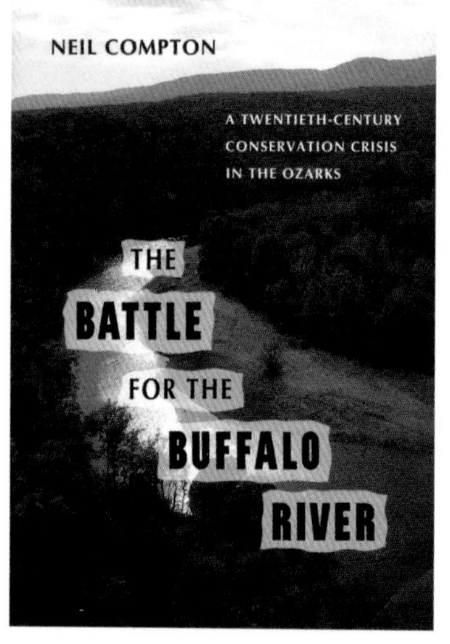

Above: Volumes have been written on the struggle between preservationists and the Corps of Engineers in Arkansas. This large fork of the White was declared a National River in 1972, ending the threat of impoundment.

Top: Chrome postcard. A 1964 act of Congress created the Ozark National Scenic Riverway, protecting the Current River from being dammed.

Truman didn't use the word "trusts," but he lambasted the "special interest lobbies" who "have fought against flood control and power development." He continued, "My friends, I say to you that the progressive policies of the last twenty years have been the salvation of the country." Both presidents Roosevelt would have been pleased.

President Truman assured the crowd these two dams were but the beginning: "Right here in this area, we need at least a half a dozen more dams like Bull Shoals and Norfork before we will begin to have the rivers harnessed for the welfare of the people. I have just asked the Congress to appropriate money for Table Rock Dam on this same river up in Missouri." With the cooperation of Congressman Short, funds were appropriated and Table Rock Dam was started. Only one more dam was built, though. The grandiose water resource development plan of the New Deal was not fulfilled largely due to economics, but partly because of the opposition of sportsmen and later environmentalists.

"Conservation Federation is Alarmed by Flood Control Dams," read the headline of an article in the November 19, 1939, *Sedalia Democrat*: "The Board of Directors of the Conservation Federation of Missouri, an organization composed of 10,000 members ... views with great alarm the proposed building in Missouri of thirty large flood control dams using Federal funds, and calls on the people of Missouri to give serious consideration to the threatened destruction of natural resources and the resulting loss of many economic and recreational values."

Later, the Missouri Department of Conservation took basically the same position on dams. They especially opposed damming the Current, Eleven Point, and Meramec Rivers. The Conservation Department waivered on the Corps' plans to impound the upper White River. Most of those projects were in Arkansas to start with. "The Damnable Current River Dam and Other Topics: A Conversation with Dan Saults, 1982," published in *Ozarks Watch* Winter, 1992, gives an insider's insight into that controversial decision not to fight Table Rock Dam:

> The Commission automatically opposed it, because by then they were used to opposing dams. But here was a situation where there was [already on the White River] a Taneycomo Dam in Missouri and Bull Shoals in Arkansas. Maybe we should go ahead and not oppose this dam on White River. Let Table Rock go. ... White River was ruined as a river anyway. Beaver Dam would have been built anyway so there was no point trying to block Table Rock. ... One of my problems is that it turned into such a beautiful lake. It's just so lovely that I'm almost glad that I finally went along with its support. Prettiest lake in the whole Corps system, I think.

Saults acknowledges opposition to Table Rock Dam and anger at the Commission's position: "Some farmers opposed the dam very strongly, with good cause, and they raised hell with the Commission, which they had every right to do. ... On the whole, we reached the conclusion that most people on the Upper White favored it because they figured they would make money out of it. Those who opposed it were committed to a [certain subsistence] way of life.

"However, the powers that existed at that time, such as Jim Owen, were very strongly in favor of it," Saults said. Apparently, the "King of the White River" had been lamenting the destruction of his float trip business while secretly investing in lake shore real estate.

Soon after the creation of Lake Taneycomo in 1913, plans were announced to create further impoundments in the White River hills. "Table Rock Lake Awaited by Galena," read a headline in the September 18, 1929, *Joplin Globe*. While noting the thriving float trip business based there, the town nevertheless was excited by the proposed Empire District Electric dam at Table Rock: "Galena is preparing to come into a new and glamorous heritage. The magic word is Table Rock. ... Already, land values are soaring as rumors of a new lake resort area creep abroad – and that predicates prosperity for Galena, nearest community of any size of the new lake."

Speculators, investors, and businessmen had been waiting to cash in on a bigger Taneycomo for nearly fifty years. Thirty years after the 1929 newspaper article the magic word was still Table Rock. Even opponents had to admit the lake was transformative.

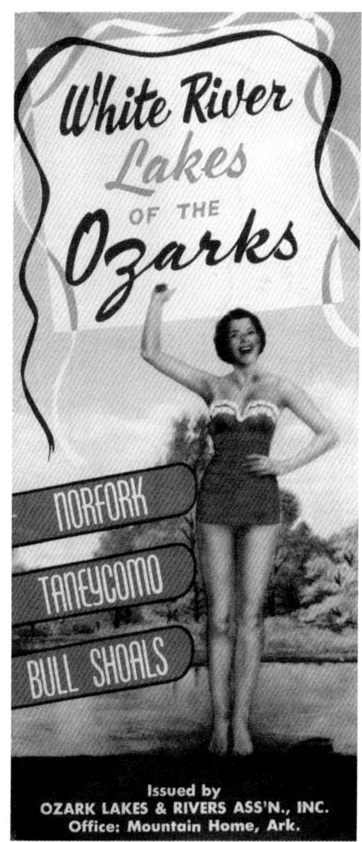

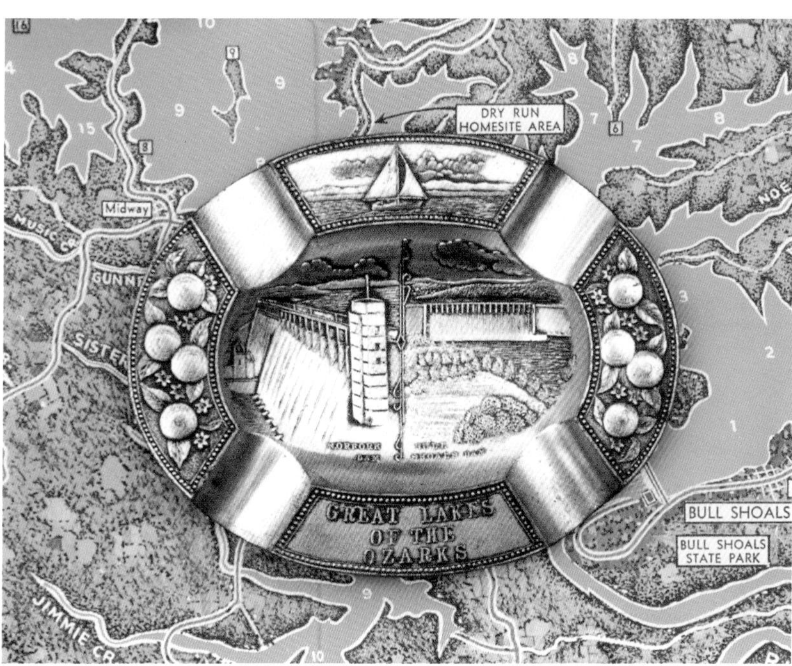

Above: An early promotion of the new Corps reservoirs. This map said this "man-made paradise" was a "refuge from the stress and strain of today's urban life." Arcadian sentiments in advertising have since lessened, but not disappeared.

Right: Made in Occupied Japan, antimony ashtray picturing Norfolk and Bull Shoals dams. Before the big Corps of Engineers reservoirs which initiated mass tourism, Ozarks souvenirs were mostly locally made crafts.

Next two pages: Artist's rendition of a bird's-eye view of Table Rock Lake on the Missouri-Arkansas border, early 1960s.

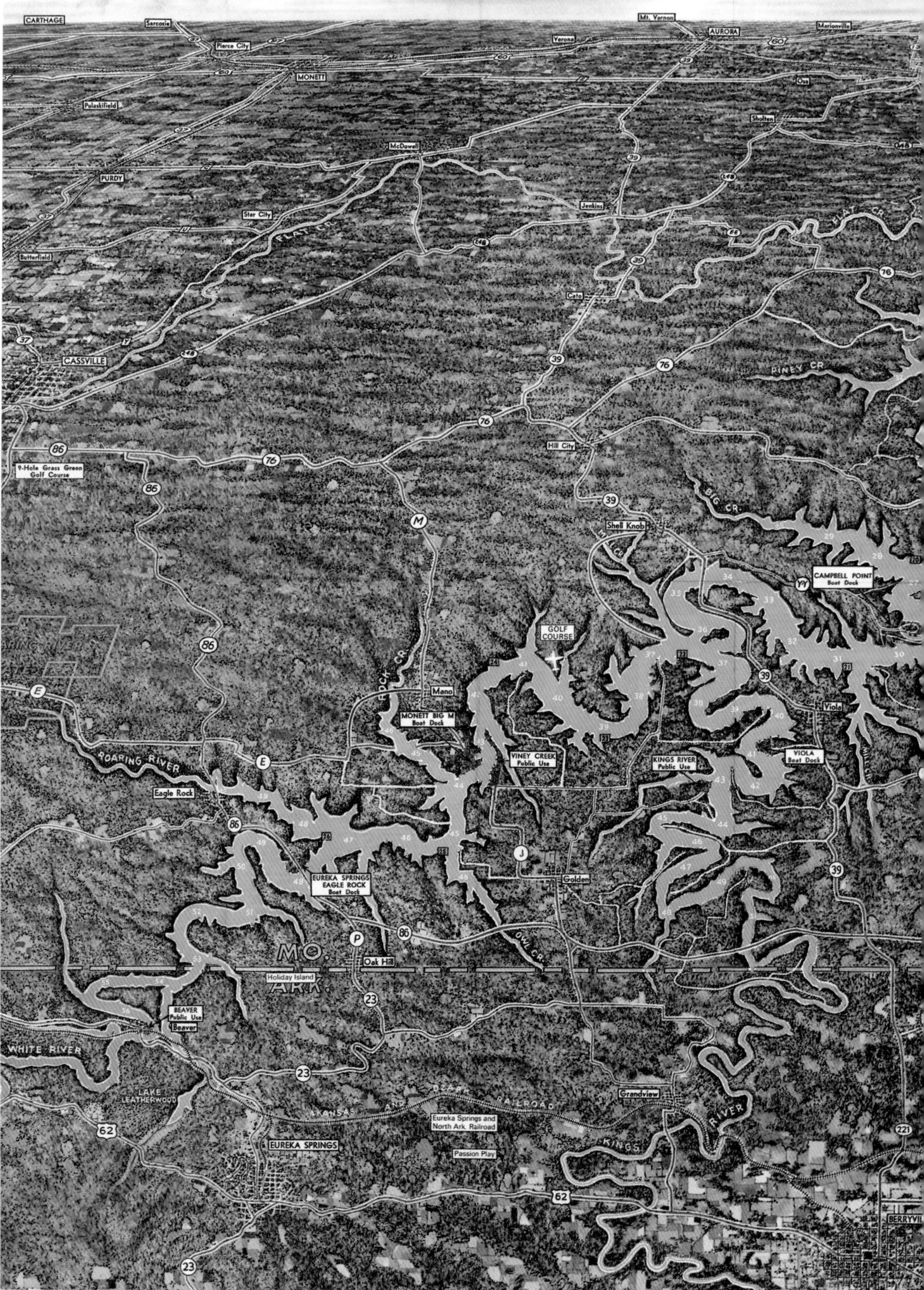
CARTHAGE
Sarcoxie
Pierce City
MONETT
Verona
Mt. Vernon
AURORA
Marionville
Pulaskifield
McDowell
Sholten
PURDY
Star City
Jenkins
Butterfield
FLAT CR.
Cato
CASSVILLE
PINEY CR.
Hill City
9-Hole Grass Green
Golf Course
Shell Knob
BIG CR.
CAMPBELL POINT
Boat Dock
GOLF COURSE
ROCK CR.
Mano
MONETT BIG M
Boat Dock
VINEY CREEK
Public Use
KINGS RIVER
Public Use
Viola
VIOLA
Boat Dock
ROARING RIVER
Eagle Rock
EUREKA SPRINGS
EAGLE ROCK
Boat Dock
Golden
OWL CR.
MO.
ARK.
Oak Hill
Holiday Island
BEAVER
Public Use
Beaver
WHITE RIVER
LAKE LEATHERWOOD
ARKANSAS AND OZARK RAILROAD
Eureka Springs and
North Ark. Railroad
Grandview
KINGS RIVER
EUREKA SPRINGS
Passion Play

SPRINGFIELD
Clever
OZARK
SPARTA
Oldfield
Dogwood
Highlandville
Chadwick
Spokane
Abesville
JAMES RIVER
GALENA
Garrison
Tauria
RAILEY CR.
BULL CR.
Swan
Reeds Spring Junction
PEACH ORCHARD CR.
Reeds Spring
Irma
Walnut Shade
BEARDEN CR.
LAKEVIEW
LAKE TANEYCOMO
AUNTS CR.
SHEPHERD OF THE HILLS COUNTRY
UNCLE IKE'S POST OFFICE & HOMESTEAD
TALKING ROCKS CAVERNS
NORTH INDIAN CR.
AUNTS CREEK Public Use
MARVEL CAVE PARK Silver Dollar City
Gretna
INDIAN POINT Boat Dock
BRANSON
9-Hole Grass Green Golf Course
Hwy. 13 Kimberling Park & Boat Dock
KIMBERLING CITY
JESSE JAMES MUSEUM
WHITE RIVER
HOLLISTER
School of the Ozarks
JOE BALD Public Use
TABLE ROCK DAM
MILL CREEK Public Use
TABLE ROCK STATE PARK
BAXTER Recreational Area Boat Dock
COOMBS FERRY Public Use
Baxter
Thomason
Lampe
COW CREEK Public Use
OLD HIGHWAY 86 Public Use
LONG CREEK Boat Dock
DOGWOOD CANYON
BRUSHY CR.
COLE SPRING HOLLOW
MISSOURI
ARKANSAS
Nauvoo
Blue Eye
MILLS BR.
BLAIR CR.
CRICKET CREEK Boat Dock
Oak Grove
COSMIC CAVERNS
Maple
YOCUM CR.
Yocum
LONG CR.
Denver
Farewell
GREEN FOREST
TABLE ROCK LAKE
Copyrighted by
MWM DEXTER, INC.
AURORA, MISSOURI
This map may not be copied without the written consent of MWM Dexter, Inc.
White lake numbers show miles to dam.

Table Rock Lake is deep. The Corps of Engineers' 6,423-foot-long dam is 252 feet high. In front of the dam the water is 220 feet deep. Seventeen miles up the lake where the James River arm comes in, the water is still 150 feet deep in the old river channel.

Given the topography of the upper White River, Table Rock Dam could have been even higher but that would have flooded some parts of the governmental center of Stone County. Linn Creek, Camden County's seat, was submerged by Lake of the Ozarks, but Union Electric got their dam-building money from Wall Street, not Congress. Representative Dewey Short wouldn't have stood for flooding Galena, his hometown.

Opposite: Beginning of the James River arm of Table Rock Lake seen from Joe Bald Park.

Right: Printed postcard of the recently completed MO-13 bridge and the old bridge that is now at the bottom of the lake.

Next two pages: Rearing pools below Table Rock Dam. Enclosures are necessary to keep birds from eating the trout. Dams and reservoirs so modify the natural environment that extraordinary and expensive interventions are necessary to replace wildlife resources that formerly were self-replicating. Artificial reproduction of rainbow trout over time produces a genetically unfit semi-domesticated species.

Drowned towns have frequently been the setting for novels. "Reservoir noir," as such books have been called, have in fact been written about old Linn Creek. In the non-fiction work, *Buried by Table Rock Lake,* (2006), Tom Koob relates many heartbreaking stories of flooded out small farmers along the James who were paid a pittance for their lost land, but he found "only one settlement of any significant size destroyed." Oasis, a hamlet on Long Creek, had a mill and a store but fewer than two dozen residents.

Because the water for power generation is drawn so deep, it is very cold. Forty-eight degree discharges meant Taneycomo was no longer habitat for native game fish. By law the Corps had to compensate the state of Missouri for the loss. Mitigation money allowed the Department of Conservation to build the Shepherd of the Hills Hatchery for trout below Table Rock Dam. Equipment from Sequiota Park's hatchery was moved to the new facility, and the park grounds were transferred to the city of Springfield.

Table Rock Lake—Kimberling Bridge (The Old and the New)

Above: Table Rock Dam was not built at Table Rock; the geology two miles upstream was better. The name followed the dam. The original location is still a much-visited overlook. A projected smaller dam here was never constructed.

Opposite, below: Table Rock Dam seen by dawn's early light.

For a little more than one hundred years, the curious have stood on this natural, flat dolomite formation at the top of a bluff and stared down at the rushing White River below. For several decades following Powersite Dam, they wondered, "When will Mr. Doherty start building his bigger dam here?" Later the question became, "When will the Army engineers start building their great dam?"

The Corps moved the site upstream, but planned a lower dam at Table Rock to generate electricity twice. An article in the February 24, 1942, *Neosho Daily News* stated John T. Woodruff, "who has kept in closer touch with developments on the dam than perhaps any other person in the area," confirmed that plan. Local Chambers of Commerce and the White River Boosters League passed a resolution that this smaller dam be named Woodruff Dam. It was never built and Woodruff died nine years before Table Rock Dam was completed. The Corps of Engineers Visitor Center is named after Congressman Dewey Short.

YESTERDAY

a wilder[illegible]

AND NOW ! ! — — New 60-Unit HOLIDAY INN

KIMBERLING CITY

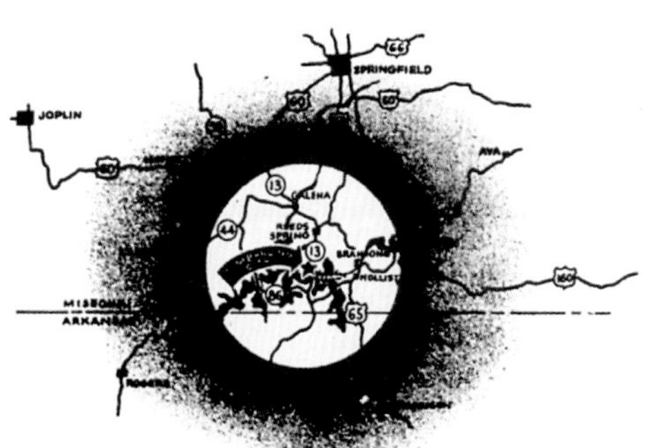

ENJOY A BUSINESS IN VACATIONLAND

There are openings for every conceivable type of business . . .

RESORT SITES—HOME SITES—LODGE SITES—NOW AVAILABLE! New businesses and existing firms are invited to KIMBERLING CITY. A 30-mile trading area and annual income of over thirty million dollars from permanent residents and over two million yearly vacationers assure a ready market for all kinds of goods and services. Additional informaton, at no obligation to you.

HARDWARE
GROCERY
SPORTING GOODS
DRY CLEANERS
RESTAURANT
DRUG STORE
VARIETY STORE
APPLIANCES
CLOTHING
GIFT ITEMS
LAUNDRY
BARBER AND BEAUTY SHOP
SERVICE STATION
MEDICAL, DENTAL AND OTHER PROFESSIONAL SERVICES
BOWLING

Call, Wire or Write

KIMBERLING DEVELOPMENT CORPORATION
John Q. Hammons Building 1535 South Glenstone Springfield, Missouri

John Q. Hammons, President TUxedo 1-7701
Lloyd E. Kipp, Gen. Manager TUxedo 1-0484

Above: Bronze statue of James Quentille Hammonds. John Q, as he called himself, grew up on a struggling dairy farm in southwest Missouri but had extraordinary success as a builder of upscale hotels. His Kimberling City Holiday Inn venture was his introduction to the hospitality industry.

Opposite: 1960s promotion of Kimberling City.

Right: R. Layne Morrill's father named the family business Shepherd of the Hills Realtors. Layne's grandfather was Levi Morrill, "Uncle Ike," the only character drawn from life in Harold Bell Wright's novel that sparked tourism to the White River hills. In spite of the Morrills' use of a covered wagon logo for their real estate firm, Uncle Ike was not an Ozark pioneer. He was a Yankee born in Maine, who worked as a newspaperman for Horace Greeley in New York before winding up as Postmaster of Notch, Missouri, in 1893. Morrill arrived in the region only a few years before the writer discovered the fictive potential of those he erroneously believed to be early Ozark settlers.

"Yesterday a wilderness – And now!! (a) New 60-Unit Holiday Inn." John Q. Hammonds' 1960s ad invited "new businesses and existing firms" to "enjoy a business in vacationland." The developer's vacationland was a privately created new community designed to serve the anticipated tourism boom that publicly funded Table Rock Lake would stimulate. "This was absolute mountaintop. He cut the mountain top off and started the new city of Kimberling City," Layne Morrill, a partner in the venture, told KY3 News in 2013.

An earlier Springfield hotelier, John T. Woodruff, invented the town of Camdenton when Lake of the Ozarks flooded Linn Creek. Kimberling City didn't replace Galena, but it would soon become the largest town in Stone County. Hammonds named it after William Kimberling's ferry across the White River. A small community on the north side there was called Mayberry, then later Radical.

Kimberling City's Holiday Inn franchise was the beginning of Hammonds' rent-a-room empire, which grew to seventy-five hotels scattered around the country. Bold as Kimberling City was, he built a grander development on a hilltop just north of Table Rock Dam. "I snagged the best spot on Table Rock Lake and held onto it for years until the time was right to build a masterpiece that mirrored the enchantment of a European castle or chateau." Indeed, Chateau on the Lake, a 301-room luxury resort, spa, and convention center, owes no inspiration to anything remotely Ozarkian. Thirty years earlier Hammonds' promotion of Kimberling City at least acknowledged the place before Table Rock Lake had a frontier heritage – "Yesterday a wilderness."

Chateau on the Lake serves Branson vacationers. That tourist destination's atmosphere is now more corporate-eclectic than old-time

Above: Townhouse overlooking the James River arm of Table Rock Lake. A coral-painted, split-log facade may not be derived from the frontier heritage – but it isn't a nod to modernism, either.

Top: Hillbilly Lanes was one of Kimberling City's first businesses. Jim and Vicki Barrett who ran the bowling alley and restaurant recall John Q as astute and personable: "He never forgot little people, and I was a little people," remembered Barrett. The hillbilly icon does have a tenuous claim to pioneer ancestry.

country. The Kimberling City website differentiates the James River arm of Table Rock Lake from those lake areas closer to the famous live entertainment and shopping complex: "But there are no glaring huge neon signs, no overbearing glitz and glamour, for this is still the quiet part of the lake."

Only the western fringe of Kimberling City is actually part of the James River watershed, but the town, which consists of strip malls and highway-accessed businesses, is a trade center for the considerable post-Table Rock growth. John Q's town has about 2,400 residents. Scattered through the wooded hills between it and Branson West are eight thousand more aficionados of country living.

It's a low-density recent settlement without a shared past, and almost no architectural relics. Barns, houses, and structures relating to previous agriculture and tourism were largely along the river. These sites are now under water. While "City" was added to Kimberling, Hammonds' spec development and the lakeshore community it serves is hardly an urban enclave. Natural is a byword. Stone or log-sided exteriors are an advertisable feature in real estate listings. Barbecue grills and bird feeders are fixtures on native tree-shaded lawns. Many of these ranch houses have campers and boats in the driveway. Interiors are replete with mounted fish and deer heads. Hooked rugs lie on the floor and on the walls are prints of old barns or Labrador Retrievers.

Au naturel as it may seem, this lifestyle owes little to the Arcadian era. These "lake life" immigrants do not have an anti-urban prejudice. Copies of *Walden Pond* or even *The Shepherd of the Hills* are not read in the evening. They, like their relatives back in Des Moines or Chicago, watch television. It is a rusticated version of suburbia.

"Lure of Outdoors Is Pushing Suburbia Deep Into Ozarks" is a May 8, 1969, article written for the Associated Press by Jack Harshaw, reporter for *The Carthage Press*. He traces the "new demand for real estate once relegated to the acorn and the razorback" then taking place around government impoundments of Ozark rivers to the phenomena of retirement homes that sprang up around the reservoirs of the southwest. Theodore Roosevelt's Bureau of Reclamation irrigation projects were the locations where this unanticipated utilization began. Hershaw acknowledges, "There are some old-timers who decry the demise of the Ozark river float trips and the solitude of fishing on a riverbank. The lakes ended much of that in affected areas but there is no denying the impact on the economy." He closes,

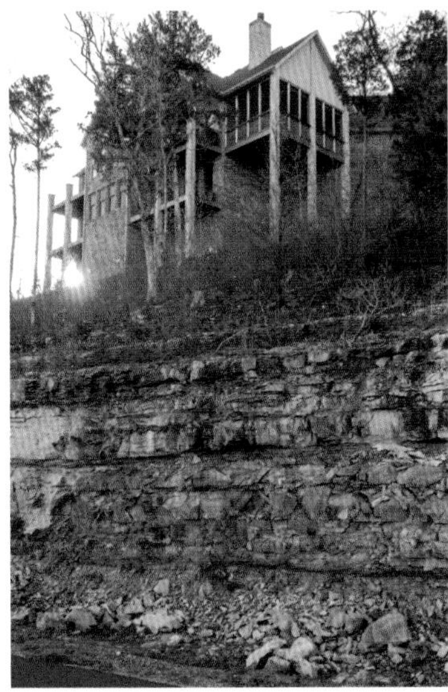

> Tourism is still a major industry in the Ozarks but with the advent of the permanent resident with an eye for a retirement home, the Ozark landowner today is not fretting about some of his "skimpy-producing farmland" being inundated by lake water. Instead, he's either subdividing what's left or building a boat dock or bait shop on it.

Sadly, only a few of the original chased-out landowners had the prerequisite skills and resources of John Q. Hammonds to "subdivide what's left" after the "skimpy-producing farmland" was inundated.

Unlike Lake of the Ozarks, which was a private project, Corps of Engineers impoundments do not permit shoreline housing development. Hilltops with a view become high value real estate.

Above: Aunts Creek, a tributary of the James River, was named for old Aunt China Bowman. She was a Yocum and said to be part Indian, tribe unknown. In the 1876 census, the Bowman's assets were "5 horses, 12 cattle, 10 sheep, 17 hogs, 36 bushels of wheat, 300 bushels of corn, 20? tobacco, and 16 cds of wood." The little stream is now the largest finger of the largest arm of Table Rock Lake.

At its entrance the water is 120 feet deep – three times the depth of Truman Lake in front of its dam.

Aunts Creek Campground is a "multiple-use park" made possible by a multiple-use dam. It is maintained by the Army Corps of Engineers on a backed-up creek just off the James River arm of Table Rock Lake. There are fifty-five reservable campsites, a swimming beach, and a boat ramp. Amenities include hot showers, a dump station, and electric hookups. It's clean and safe, and fees are reasonable. Come summer, it's busy, but not crowded – activities are distributed over a fair expanse of woods and water. Recreation.gov describes the setting: "The campground is primarily wooded with most sites offering a sweeping view of the water and surrounding foothills of the Ozark mountains."

Providing thrifty family vacations was never the goal of the US Army Corps of Engineers when they first sought Congressional approval to dam the upper White River. Empire District Electric's Table Rock Dam plans were solely for hydropower. The Corps' ostensible reason for spending several hundred million dollars to control this river system was flood control. Power generation was an afterthought. Back in the late 1930s and early 1940s, camping out along the cove of a reservoir was hardly a national priority.

As reservoirs will accommodate many more boats and have a much longer and more accessible shoreline than rivers, dam advocates often invoke "the greatest good for the greatest number" utilitarian justification.

Compared to rivers, artificial lakes have left a small imprint on art, literature, and legend. Most of those who recreate on Table Rock Lake, however, think it is natural and beautiful. As yet this constituency has not recorded their appreciation in art, literature, or legend. In time they may.

It might be argued that drying out hardwood swamps and keeping water out of cotton fields may not be considered of the utmost importance in the Depression or the shadow of a World War, but Franklin Roosevelt embraced big dams as symbols of a powerful, active central government.

John T. Woodruff and a phalanx of Springfield and Branson boosters desperately wanted a bigger lake than Taneycomo to develop, but they didn't have tens of millions of dollars, engineering expertise, or the legal authority to block the White River. Republican Congressman Dewey Short preferred Empire District Electric to develop Table Rock. When Empire demurred, like the area's Chambers of Commerce he got behind the Corps, motivated by the prospect of a free lake that would enhance tourism.

As things turned out, the promised flood control benefits are debatable, and the small amount of electricity supplied by these installations has come at a high price. Recreational development of Table Rock Lake, however, exceeded everyone's projections.

That Table Rock attracts a lot of visitors and generates a considerable amount of economic activity is asserted in a study undertaken in 2004 by the US Army Engineer Research and Development Center, titled "Characterization of Park Visitors, Visitation Levels, and Associated Economic Impacts of Recreation at Bull Shoals, Norfork, and Table Rock Lakes." Beaver Lake wasn't studied. Norfork and Bull Shoals dramatically underperformed Table Rock: "Table Rock Lake had the largest economic significance of the three lakes, accounting for a total economic effect of 3,645 jobs, $88 million in labor income, and $142 million in value added."

This was explained by its better accessibility and already established tourist complex: "The higher incidence of new and infrequent visitors to Table Rock Lake may reflect the closer proximity of Table Rock to major highway arteries, its greater availability of sightseeing opportunities and close proximity to the tourist destination of Branson, Missouri."

Corps officers routinely toss off astronomical monetary figures of prevented flood damages, but this investigation uses verifiable data. Table Rock Lake has without doubt enhanced tourism.

An article in the June 7, 2009, *Springfield News-Leader* begins with an acknowledgement that the dam ended the legendary James and White River floats. In "Table Rock Dam gives back much to the Ozarks," journalist Kathleen O'Dell quotes Jim Owen: "My float

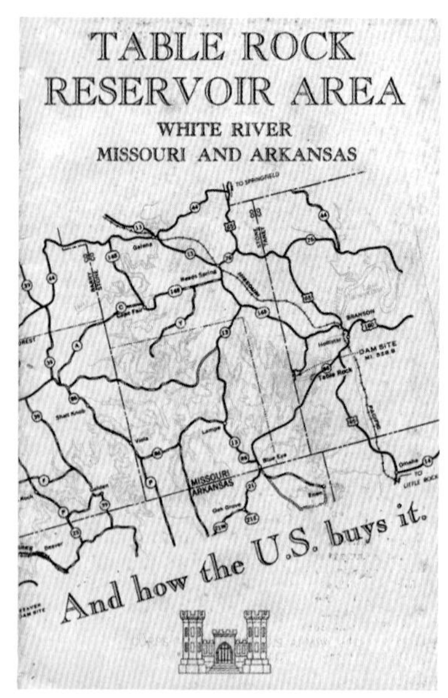

Below: Insensitive photographs in a Corps booklet given to those being displaced from the banks of a world famous float stream.

business, which is the biggest in the world, will suffer, but even so Table Rock will mean far more to us all than any one form of fishing or any one individual idea or enterprise."

After quoting a Branson Chamber of Commerce official who said the project brought "incalculable benefits to the region," O'Dell nevertheless gives some economic snapshots: "Tourism sustained nearly 14,000 jobs in Stone, Taney and Barry counties in fiscal year 2008. ... Taney County saw more than $461 million in expenditure in seventeen tourist-related sectors in fiscal year 2008. Stone saw $143.5 million that year."

She quotes Pete Herschend, co-owner of Silver Dollar City, on the three-way partnership that explains Branson's phenomenal growth: "Now you have taken advantage of both what God put here and the Corps of Engineers built, and what the private sector did."

The same day, the *News-Leader* article was published attorney Harry Styron posted on his blog *Ozark Law and Economy*, "Table Rock Lake and the Cost of Economic Activity." He does not dis-

FLOODED FARM HOME, WHITE RIVER VALLEY

The information contained in this booklet is intended to explain as briefly and as clearly as possible the methods and procedures employed by the Corps of Engineers in acquiring land for the Table Rock Reservoir project.

In the development of the nation's natural resources, it often becomes necessary to purchase private property for public use. The rights of private citizens are protected by the Federal constitution which requires that privately owned land cannot be taken except by payment of just compensation. Rules, regulations, and procedures governing land acquisition have been developed over the years through numerous court decisions. However, these long-established procedures are not well understood by many in the proposed reservoir area where land must be obtained in order to provide storage to impound and control flood waters and put them to use for the public's good and for other uses which are to the public's benefit.

1

RESERVOIRS PROVIDE RECREATION

18

Above: Headstones were modest, and many burials were only marked with rocks to indicate a grave. A new marker was made for Granny Gore, a Cherokee medicine woman and wife of pioneer Tipton Gore.

Above right: There were many small family cemeteries in the basin of Table Rock Reservoir. Headstones and remains of twenty graveyards, such as they were, were dug up and relocated in the new Joseph Philibert Cemetery just north of Kimberling City.

pute the largesse Table Rock Lake provided for some like Silver Dollar City, Shepherd of the Hills Homestead, and the music industry: "Where would Bass Pro Shops be without Table Rock Lake? A massive public works project benefits most those who have the capital, industry, ingenuity and proximity to benefit from it."

Styron concedes the population of Taney and Stone Counties has increased 400 percent. Rarely factored in to the celebration of such growth is the sobering fact the expanded infrastructure necessary to accommodate new residents is costly considering their dispersed locations and the rugged karst terrain. Employment in the tourist industry is low paying and seasonal. According to census data, "Per capita income in Southwest Missouri lagged for those counties with higher numbers of employees in the tourism sector."

Styron recognizes the tradeoffs: "Millions of people have had great times on Table Rock Lake. An ecologist would shudder at the habitat destruction caused by the lake. But an economist would look at the investment and the returns and ask several questions that are not raised or addressed in the *News-Leader* article."

A few hillfolk, though lacking sophisticated business backgrounds or access to capital, did benefit from the public works project that transformed the White River. Artie Ayres was born in 1926 in a log cabin half a mile from where Table Rock Dam would be built. He calls himself a hillbilly, which he says "denotes strength of character, thriftiness and the ability to thrive under adverse conditions."

The Stone County native was a paratrooper in World War II, and used the GI Bill to get a degree in agricultural education from the University of Missouri. Returning to the hills of home he found government employment helping farmers adapt to changing markets. He grew up tending free-range cattle so, with his schoolteacher mother's help, he bought a two-hundred-acre farm. Fortuitously, it was at the junction of Highways 76 and 13. As Branson grew and then boomed in part due to Table Rock Lake, so too did the crossroad community called Lakeview. Artie found selling parcels of his farm more profitable than raising cattle. He became mayor and changed the name to Branson West. In ten years the population grew from thirty-seven to more than four hundred.

Above: Book published by Artie Ayres on the Yocum silver dollar, 1982.

Top: Roadside sign for Lost Silver Mine theater, 1980s.

Down in a deep hollow, across the highway from the town's Walmart Supercenter, which was once Ayres' pasture, are the ruins of an amphitheater that featured a drama written by the hillbilly-made-good. The Lost Silver Mine Theater opened in 1983, a year after he wrote and published *Traces of Silver*, a book on the legend of the Yocum dollar that obsessed both him and his father.

In the 1850s, Ayres' great-great-grandfather, Robert, ran a trading post on Bear Creek. Guerrilla warfare during the Civil War induced him to relocate to Butler, Missouri. Artie's father Ben returned to the region when the railroads came through in the early 1900s. Recalling tales his grandfather told him of receiving Yocum silver dollars at his store, he spent years digging, and exploring caves trying to find the source of the valuable metal. In time, Artie took up the quest, buying heavy machinery to dig for the lost silver mine. One rumored location was at the junction of the James and White Rivers, now under a hundred fifty feet of water. A Yocum descendant showed up with a map that conveniently located the mine on Ayres' property. Extensive excavation uncovered no silver.

Not only has the mine remained lost; no authentic example of the mythic coins exists. It's a fabulous saga and by many accounts the play staged at the hillside outdoor theater was well received. Artie Ayres is familiar with all the theories of the mysterious Yocum dollars. He admits the most likely explanation is they were recast US coins created to disguise the Yocums' illegal sale of liquor to the Delaware Indians. Other less probable but more dramatic versions of the tale should not be forgotten, however, Ayres seems to believe.

Above: Tourists stream through Branson West, and its businesses supply residents of the James River arm of Table Rock Lake.

Right and below: Ruins of the Lost Silver Mine Theater.

Above: Woodwalker Lure invented by Charlie Campbell.

Forsyth coach Charlie Campbell's boys basketball team won a state championship in 1973. That year he resigned to become a guide and pro bass fisherman. In 1974, he won a Bassmaster Federation National Championship at Table Rock Lake. Bass Pro began sponsoring Campbell and hired him to help perfect Tracker Boats.

Known for his skill with top water lures, he designed the Woodwalker to tease bass out of flooded timber.

The Rape of the Ozarks was the title of a 1941booklet the Missouri Conservation Federation published. Rivers were the victims of this assault, and the perpetrator was the Army Corps of Engineers. Ted Butler, the Federation's executive secretary, stated a few of their objections to dams in a June 5, 1941, "Huntin' and Fishin' " column in the *Neosho Daily News*: "The Table Rock Dam, if put in, would back the water up to Eagle Rock in the winter when it was full, and then only to the mouth of James River in the summer when our tourist crop is coming in. ... In between those two points we would have some wonderful, scenic, mud flats to show our tourists. The fluctuation on all of these proposed dams will run from twenty-five to eighty-six feet. How could fish live in that kind of place?"

Those huge drawdowns for flood storage, which were originally planned, have been moderated due to pressure from the public. Fish very definitely now "live in that kind of place" and an industry has been created devoted to catching them. One species drives sport fishing on Table Rock Lake, and hundreds of other government reservoirs – the largemouth black bass. They are superbly adapted to artificial lakes and they hit artificial lures with wild abandon. Back in float trip days, the slower White River contained a higher percentage of largemouth than the clearer, faster James River, noted for its smallmouth. Today, the James River arm is arguably the most productive largemouth habitat on the lake due in part to nutrients released by Springfield. Excessive enrichment of course can also cause fish kills.

Early dam opponents conceded fishing was good in newly filled reservoirs. Decaying vegetation and flooded timber provided fertility and cover. But, wrote the champion of float fishing, Robert Page Lincoln, "Yet I have it on the word of J. N. Darling that the average

Right: Table Rock bass, 1962.

Above: Table Rock B.A.S.S. Tournament patch, 1999.

As well as the Bassmaster Tournament Trail, Walmart sponsors the F.L.W. Tour. There are college and high school competitions, and thousands of locally produced amateur bass fishing events.

Table Rock Lake has played a significant role in the growth of this phenomenon. It has been a laboratory for the improvement of tackle, fishing techniques, and craft. More than ten thousand boats competed in 250 tournaments on Table Rock in 1986.

fishing life of an artificial reservoir lake of this type is not more than ten years. Ted Butler says seven years. Thus, between seven and ten years are needed to silt in a lake to the point where fishing starts downhill."

As expected, Table Rock was excellent fishing soon after the dam was completed. The 1962 photograph of Virgil Ward and guide Dick Hovick with a two-day catch of Table Rock big mouth was in an ad for Ward's "Bass-Buster" Lures. This syndicated fishing show was often filmed there. Fifty years later, bass growth has slowed, but "The Rock," as Table Rock Lake is called, hosts hundreds of bass tournaments.

Since the lake filled, Missouri Department of Conservation biologists have kept track of fish populations. The Department's "Annual Prospects Report" stated, "Fishing for black bass should be good in 2016. Electrofishing surveys conducted in the spring of 2015 revealed a very high number of largemouth bass in 14-16 inch range present as a result of high water levels in 2011. These fish should exceed the legal size limit of 15 inches in 2016. A quality population of spotted bass in the 13-15 inch range exists as well with numerous spotted bass larger than 15 inches present."

Bass fishing as a modern, media-savvy competitive sport began on Beaver Lake, the last of the Corps' White River dam projects. Just above Table Rock, the slightly smaller reservoir was where Ray Wilson Scott, a Montgomery, Alabama, insurance salesman staged the All American Invitational Bass Tournament on June 5-6-7, 1967. Five thousand dollars was divvied up among the top ten contestants. The winner got two thousand dollars and an Acapulco fishing trip. Scott quit his job and founded the Bass Angler Sportsmen's Society (B.A.S.S.), which publishes *Bassmasters*. Unlike other sporting magazines it is devoted to one species. He required tournament participants to wear life vests, not cheat, and return their catch to the water alive after being weighed. Scott sold his operation in 1986 reportedly for $15 million. ESPN (Disney) later acquired the organization, and tournament bass fishing became a staple of cable television.

One of the contestants in a 1970 Ray Scott tournament held on Table Rock Lake would launch a chain of nearly a hundred sporting goods stores that took in more than $4 billion in 2014. The firm's leaping largemouth bass logo can be seen on boats and ball caps

Above: Hanging over the shoreline of Table Rock Lake near the center of the photograph is a $33,175 Nitro 218 boat, the overall prize for the biggest bass in a 2016 Big Bass Tour event. Another $42,350 was paid for the biggest hourly fish caught. Bass Pro has become the title sponsor of this nine-state amateur event.

Said John O'Costa, director of marketing at Bass Pro shops of the Big Bass Tour: "The format and activation strategy provides Bass Pro Shops with a terrific platform to showcase our destination stores, promote the great brands we carry and get more people out on the water fishing!"

around the world. Bass Pro's founder, Johnny Morris, was interviewed by Robert H. Boyle in his biography of Ray Scott called *Bass Boss*: "Because I was competing as a regular on the early B.A.S.S. tournament circuit I had a good insight into which products were really hot. Everybody who read Ray's magazine would want this or that. Ray was creating a frenzy for tackle, and he was also creating heroes in the sport. There was a tremendous demand, and fishermen simply couldn't find the stuff elsewhere. That's what gave birth to my business."

In *The History of Fishing Table Rock Lake* (2003), Tom Koob links Bass Pro's early success with Springfield and the new Corps of Engineers' lake: "Bass Pro Shop became a destination for anglers headed to Table Rock from all over the country. In 1974, Bass Pro premiered their catalog. This helped make available to large numbers of fishermen, the growing assortment of fishing tackle, particularly equipment suitable for bassin' on Table Rock."

Ted Butler's pronouncement that in seven to ten years silt would send fishing downhill obviously didn't happen. Table Rock's feeder streams are not that turbid. Storage loss is significant in Lake Taneycomo as he believed, but it will be a long time until those deep Corps reservoirs fill in. Dam opponents, like dam advocates, often had little grasp of hydrological and ecological realities.

Such matters were scientifically knowable in 1941. But no one could have predicted the transformation sport fishing in these waters would experience. From ten-mile-a-day johnboats to 80 mph bass boats, the change is dramatic. Might the fact that a significant part of the evolution of pro bass fishing took place here indicate some continuity of the float fishing tradition? Johnny Morris feels a kinship with generations of anglers though his sport is a high-tech game played in an industrially constructed impoundment. But float fishing down the James and White Rivers was, after all, facilitated by a railroad.

Above and right: Smallmouth, largemouth, and spotted bass were all weighed in at the Table Rock Big Bass event on April 2-3, 2016 at Long Creek Dock.

The various large sunfish species, *Micropterus*, known as black bass, have replaced trout as the most celebrated American game fish. They are ideal for catch-and-release tournaments. Bass will survive more handling than trout. They thrive in reservoirs, and the amazing amount of technology devoted to catching them drives a billion dollar enterprise.

Trout fishing may inspire poems and paintings, but bass fishing tournaments have sufficient action and theater to make compelling, if somewhat repetitive, videos for cable television. Such programming educates fishermen and provides makers and sellers of equipment with a receptive audience.

Above: In the green waters of the James River arm next to the restaurant carp, bluegill, turtles, and ducks accumulate to be fed pellets obtainable from coin operated glass globes.

Just off the large Corps of Engineers Cape Fair Campgrounds is a privately run marina. At this complex are private slips, fishing boats, jet skis, and kayaks for rent, marine gas, a store selling tackle and Table Rock T-shirts, and Koppies, a grill.

Is a little girl subverting natural selection when she begs a quarter from her dad and gets a handful of pellets from a coin-op machine to toss in Table Rock Lake? As it hits the water, carp, turtles, bluegill, and mallards converge to gobble the free lunch. Will this welfare for wildlife start them on the road to becoming feral, then finally domesticated? Unlikely, but the increasing interaction between humans and nature can alter behavior, which over time could have evolutionary implications. Studies show certain bass are naturally harder to catch than others. When the smart ones and the easy-to-catch ones are separated and reproduce, their offspring show the parents' degree of susceptibility to being hooked. If this trait is genetic, will repeatedly being hauled out of the water during tournaments somehow create a lure-resistant race of bass?

In a post on Bass Resource, Debra Dean stated fisheries biologists have found that "long-term catch-and-release fishing can impact a fisheries in a negative manner. Smaller, more aggressive fish deplete the food resource of a lake faster and more efficiently than larger fish." Big bass are the goal of fisheries management so apparently sometimes keeping smaller fish might be desirable. The evolutionary implications of bass fishing may be speculative, but of a higher order of probability than little girls throwing fish food off the Cape Fair Marina. Other examples of human influence are not speculative. The impact of dams is anything but subtle. Dams change the environment, not just behavior.

All of the high Corps' dams on the White River release frigid water from deep below the surface. Riverine stretches below these dams became inhospitable to native game fish. Introducing trout proved to be an acceptable mitigation, and was subsidized by the Corps

Above: Contestants in a small local bass tournament had to wait to weigh in while an elderly couple cleaned their crappie at the Cape Fair marina's sink. Catch-and-eat fishermen find the James River arm productive as do catch-and-release bass fishermen.

Top and right: Turtles sun in front of a floating restaurant. Occasionally one would plop down in the water and swim over to compete for fish food.

of Engineers. Natural reproduction in the tail waters is limited to brown trout. Rainbows and a few cutthroat and brook trout are raised in hatcheries to be released for fishermen.

In the warmer waters above Table Rock Dam, another species was stocked, a much larger creature with a tragic story. Paddlefish are native to the White River, but were not common in the clean, fast-flowing upper reaches. They found the rich zooplankton-laden waters of the James River arm to their liking, and have grown to extraordinary size. A six-foot long, 140-pound, Missouri record paddlefish was snagged near Cape Fair in March 2015.

Neither the river fish that were impacted by Table Rock Dam nor the imported trout are in danger of extinction. Paddlefish are not endangered nationally, but their future is cloudy. How they came to be part of Table Rock Lake's ecosystem is due to the building of another giant Corps of Engineers dam on the Osage, the next river system north of the James. Department of Conservation writer Joel M. Vance explained the dilemma in the *St. Clair Chronicle*, "Paddlefish in a new home," September 12, 1973:

> Because of the continued pollution of the James River, the James River arm of Table Rock Lake is fertile, and produces large quantities of zooplankton, a prime food of paddlefish. Paddlefish spawning grounds in the Osage River watershed, largest in the free world, are endangered by Truman Dam. Fisheries biologists feel that the flooding of the Osage River spawning beds eventually will result in the deterioration of the snagging fishery, which annually attracts from 15,000-20,000 anglers to the Warsaw area unless some alternatives are found.

The destruction of the most important known spawning ground of the paddlefish was a major issue in a lawsuit brought by the Environmental Defense Fund challenging Truman Dam. Much of our

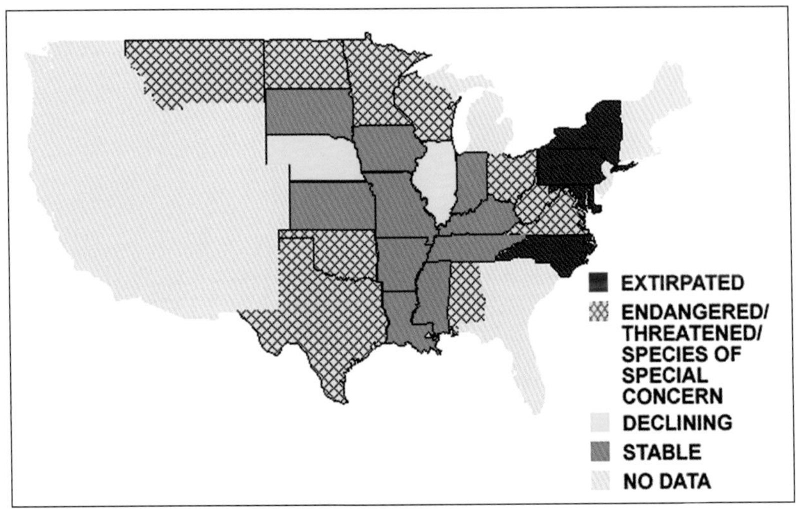

Above: Map from USGS paddlefish study showing the diminishing range of the paddlefish:

"Paddlefish (*Polyodon spathula*) were a common component of fish communities in the large rivers of the Mississippi River drainage before 1900. Overharvest and human alteration of rivers have resulted in significant declines in paddlefish populations. Construction of dams on rivers has especially affected paddlefish by altering traditional river habitats and disrupting spawning migrations and other movements.

"Paddlefish have been lost from four states and Canada, and eleven of twenty two states within the remaining species range now list the paddlefish as endangered, threatened, or a species of special concern. Restoration of paddlefish populations is a shared goal of many state and federal agencies."

previous book, *Damming the Osage* (2012), deals with this contentious legal action. The Corps of Engineers won and the paddlefish lost. The Corps never said they were sorry, but they did pay the Conservation Department to try and find a solution.

Led by department biologists Tom Russell and Kim Graham, spawning was documented for the first time. Hatchery personnel mastered artificially spawning paddlefish and raising the young. While this species can prosper in several reservoirs, only Table Rock had a feeder stream that, it was believed, might permit spawning. Paddlefish did well in this new lake habitat, and they will ascend the James River in the early spring, but hopes that the James would replace the Osage as a spawning ground have been dashed. Current Missouri Department of Conservation expert Trish Yasger answered our inquiry about this disappointment:

> Table Rock paddlefish make spawning runs up the James River Arm and can make it all the way up to Lake Springfield. To date we have not documented any successful natural reproduction in Table Rock Lake. I looked back through some old information and found out that in 1983, we did find paddlefish spawning in the James River. Eggs were laid, however receding water levels prevented the eggs from hatching. We've not documented any survival of naturally reproduced paddlefish and have not found eggs since then. Just because fish spawn doesn't mean that there is successful reproduction.

Put-and-take fisheries, like Missouri's paddlefish and White River trout, may be necessary, but they have flaws. Genetic problems can arise from generations of hatchery-raised fish resulting in unfitness. Unlike kids feeding carp, hatchery propagation is a step down the path of creating a domesticated species. These programs are expensive. Should budgetary constraints eliminate raising paddlefish in Missouri, populations would plummet to the occasional wandering example in the Mississippi River, origin unknown. Truman

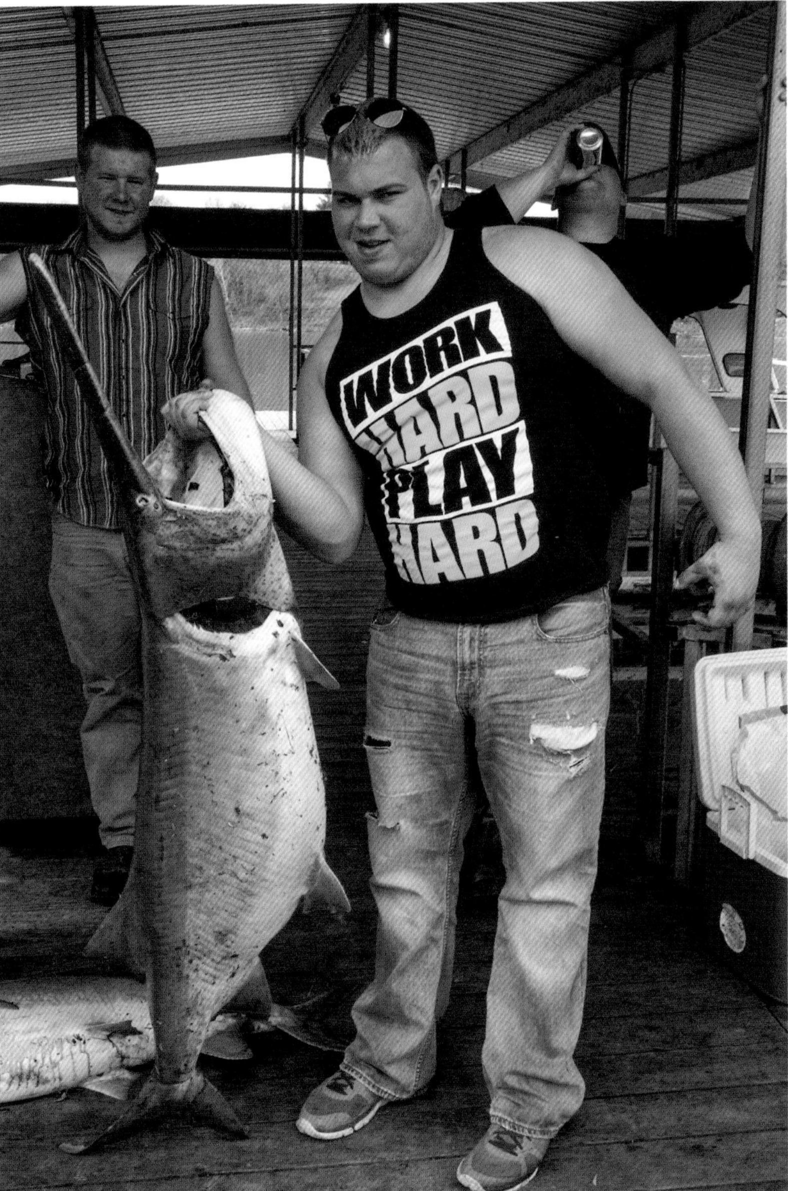

Right: Paddlefish legally snagged on the James River arm of Table Rock Lake near Cape Fair. The flesh of this fish is quite good, but the eggs can be big trouble. Sturgeon, the traditional source of roe, which is processed into caviar, are endangered worldwide. Paddlefish eggs are a decent substitute, but most states like Missouri prohibit the sale of wild fish roe.

On February 2, 2009, US District Judge Ortrie D. Smith sentenced Thomas Jerry Nix, Jr., formerly of Shell Knob, to one year and one day in federal prison. Nix sold 387 pounds of paddlefish caviar for $35,820 from fish gill-netted on the James River arm of Table Rock Lake. He was also fined $30,002 and his boat and motor, were confiscated.

In 2013 more than one hundred people were arrested and charged with trafficking paddlefish roe in Missouri. An adult female can contain twenty pounds of eggs salable for $4,000. Members of Russian organized crime are often involved in this black market.

Dam has downgraded Missouri from a paddlefish sanctuary to a place where intense intervention is necessary for survival.

Joel Vance has retired from the Conservation Department, but he still eloquently and truthfully writes about wildlife issues. Forty years later he hasn't forgotten the ecological disaster that is Truman Dam. In 2013, Vance blogged, "In addition to fish kills, the river below the dams has suffered erosion and flooding from heavy releases, and (in) the stretch that now is Truman Lake once was hosted the only known spawning areas for paddlefish. Subsequently, the Conservation Department developed a method of artificially spawning paddlefish and that has helped mitigate the loss of natural spawning, but it still is no substitute for the real thing."

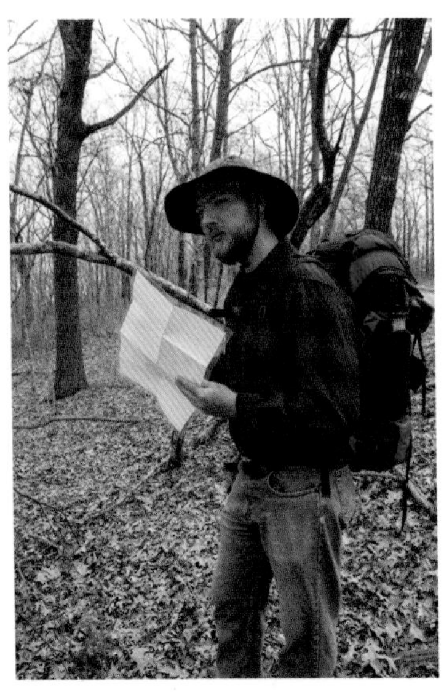

Above: Piney Creek Wilderness has both mapped and confusing unofficial trails.

As the James Fork of the White was never, even in high water, ascended by steamboats, it was not the subject of pleadings to Congress for funds to "improve" it, like the White and Osage Rivers. Land along the James, though, has been subject to intense improvement efforts aimed at producing revenue. Some improvements became productive, some were not worth the effort, and many, like timbering and farming steep slopes, produced short-lived benefits. Early travelers and settlers remarked often on the beauty of the original forests of the James River watershed. No remnant of that pristine landscape exists. Along the breaks of the James are extensive second- or third-growth forests often of different composition and old fields overgrown with cedar trees.

The Piney Creek Wilderness is an 8,178-acre, especially rocky, dissected patch of cut-over land. Piney Creek drains through it into the James arm of Table Rock Lake below Cape Fair. It was designated a wilderness by Congress in 1980 and is managed by the US Forest Service. They realistically admit its hardscrabble developmental history. Caleb Knowlton (left) still considered hiking it a worthwhile reason to drive down from Overland Park, Kansas. Another hiker, Steve Schibler, posted his Piney Creek Wilderness experience online: "It's a land like its pioneer stock – no love handles, muscle, gristle and bone. The hills don't scrape the sky but

Above: A very old concrete basin collects the water of Siloam Spring.

with only 400 feet of physical relief no land should be so steep – a maze of knife-edge ridges that drop off abruptly toward the hollows below. ... Nowadays, a mixed hardwood second-growth forest has taken over the area." No motorized vehicles are allowed. Horses are, but some riders prefer more sure-footed mules.

By strict standards the Piney Creek tract is not "untrammeled," a word rescued from oblivion by the language of the 1964 Wilderness Act. That the forest isn't virgin and traces remain of the futile effort to produce something more valuable than deer, squirrels, and copperheads doesn't bother hikers and trail riders. No chainsaws have echoed through the deep stony draws of Piney Creek for three decades. The forest is definitely growing back.

One can get lost in the Piney Creek Wilderness. One can get lost here contemplating the transformations the Ozarks has undergone. If exploited at times recklessly, the James River country has a long tradition of its nature being appreciated, and at last in places protected.

As Table Rock Lake took the good bottomland farms along the lower James, there is no architectural evidence they existed. There are some relics of the subsistence farms in the hills that bordered the river. Along Wooley Creek, just north of Piney Creek, is a sandstone-faced schoolhouse built around 1900 to educate the children of these rural families. Originally it was a frame structure that was "rocked" in the 1930s. Consolidation came in 1952, and the one-room school sat empty until 2005.

Retired Reeds Spring teacher Glenda Chamberlin and others formed a committee to restore the abandoned school. To help pay for the work a series of bluegrass festivals were held. Chamberlin interviewed Vada (Stone) Wilson, who attended Wooley Creek School for eight years before going to high school in Crane. Her account and several others are posted on rootsweb.com:

> Vada Stone started first grade at Wooley Creek School when she was five years old along with her twin sister, Vera. They rode on horseback from their house about a mile and a half with their older brother Clarence and had to cross Wooley Creek to get to the school. When the girls

Above right: Stage on the grounds of the Wooley Creek School. Bluegrass bands played here to support fund-raising festivals for restoration expenses. Ozark.net helped publicize these events.

Opposite: "Giraffe stone" buildings are derived from Arts & Crafts era styles introduced to the region when the White River Railroad came through. The Wooley Creek School near Cape Fair is one of the best examples extant.

> were little all three rode the same horse but when they got bigger the girls had a horse of their own. ... So each morning the children had to carry their books, lunch pails and a bag of feed for the horse when they came to school. ... She said, "We always got out of school early in the spring because everyone's family picked strawberries. Walter Calhoun and Wayne Wilson had big strawberry patches and hired adults and children to pick. Berries were always ripe for picking by the fifteenth of May. Mama and us kids rode our horses from home to the berry patch several miles away."
>
> She will tell you that as children they felt very fortunate because they always had everything they needed. She remembers having dolls when the girls were little and always getting to buy a sack of candy when they went to town. But they were never allowed to take the candy to school unless they had enough to share with the other children.

Earl Jones also went eight years to Wooley Creek School. He graduated in 1933:

> Directly in front of the black chalkboard at the front of the school room there was a teacher's desk sitting on a raised platform or stage as it was called. It was probably referred to as such because that is where the children would perform little programs and plays at various times throughout the year. These programs were most generally presented when a pie supper was held at the school. ... There was no money for the school to buy supplies. Those who had crayons shared with those who didn't have ones of their own. ... He also recalls "kangaroo courts" held at the school just for fun and entertainment. Some person would be "accused of a petty crime" like stealing a chicken or some silly thing like having dirty feet. Someone would be appointed as the "judge" and there would also be a "jury." A "lawyer" would plead the case and then the "punishment" would be decided. Of course it was all a big joke and everyone had a good time taking part.
>
> Wooley Creek School would also be used as a Sunday School from time to time throughout the years. ... Times were hard and money was scarce. Consequently the school was an important place for community gatherings and a way for neighbors to get together and visit.

IDEAL PLAYGROUNDS
MISSOURI PACIFIC LINES
"A Service Institution"

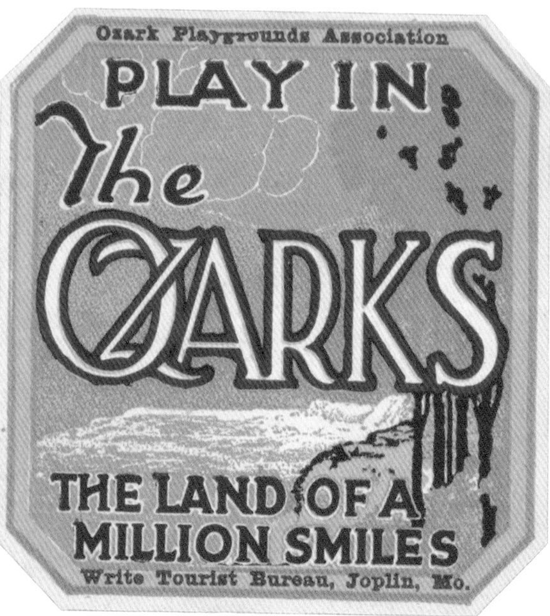
Ozark Playgrounds Association
PLAY IN
The
OZARKS
THE LAND OF A
MILLION SMILES
Write Tourist Bureau, Joplin, Mo.

THE ORIGINAL
Shepherd of the Hills farm
OLD MATT'S CABIN
MEMORIAL LODGE
DR. AND MRS. BRUCE TRIMBLE ...
Branson, Missouri
Old Matt's Cabin

Branson · GUIDE · Hollister
to
Your Vacation
fun land
by
STEVE
MILLER

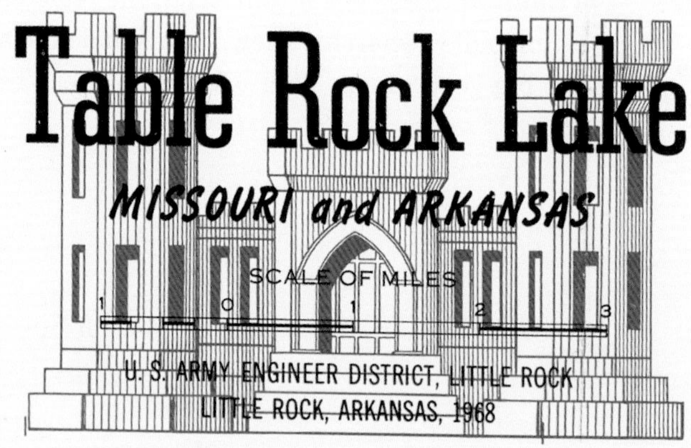
Table Rock Lake
MISSOURI and ARKANSAS
SCALE OF MILES
1 0 1 2 3
U. S. ARMY ENGINEER DISTRICT, LITTLE ROCK
LITTLE ROCK, ARKANSAS, 1968

THE OZARK SMILE GIRL

Above: During the Depression, cartooned rustics began replacing cute flappers in Ozark tourist promotions.

Opposite: Logos of corporations, companies, and tourist organizations incorporate motifs borrowed from successive forms of regional literature. If not always literal, this branding created a distinct identity for a region deficient in valuable resources and having few material advantages. Corps of Engineers symbols are not, however, region specific.

Railroads were essential to the modernization of America. They delivered food and raw materials to cities, and returned manufactured goods to the hinterlands. The Missouri Pacific recognized that the rugged terrain of the lower James and White Rivers had assets other than oak ties and lead. They promoted the isolated, sparsely settled region as a natural paradise with abundant recreational and investment opportunities. Fishing the James and farming the adjacent country were very different land uses, but the railroad had both tickets and real estate to sell. Their Arts & Crafts style brochures extolled nature. Advertisements commissioned by an industrial corporation had a curiously anti-modern flavor. New settlers were encouraged to build log cabins on small, forested tracts bought on time. Former factory workers would clear the slopes for tomatoes and strawberries, which were shipped by rail back to the cities they had fled.

Urban sportsmen detrained at Galena and rested in twiggy Adirondacks-style cabins before leisurely floating down the James to Branson. Around a campfire the local guide would spin interminable, but fascinating, tales of outlawry, revenge, and catfish bigger than a float boat. Freelance writers and journalists found an audience for accounts of this vernacular culture. The Missouri Pacific Railroad, however, promoted genteel rusticity, not primitivism. Before the publication of this folk literature, the railroad's publicity department found a book that did describe natives they approved of. The *Shepherd of the Hills* was a novel with characters loosely based on recently arrived diligent, God-fearing agriculturalists that the Missouri Pacific Corporation preferred to the colorful, scofflaw descendants of the original pioneers. Harold Bell Wright's portrait of (mostly) moralistic bucolics inhabiting a land in which scenery compensated for a lack of fertility fit the railroad's corporate vision.

Trains delivered fewer tourists to the region as roads improved and automobile ownership grew. Branson floats lasted until 1957, when the big government dam backed up the White and James Rivers. Ozark Empire Electric Company built Powersite Dam in 1913 and planned another at Table Rock. Unlike the Missouri Pacific Railroad, the power company exerted no influence on the place's image. Businesses on Lake Taneycomo, which was created by Empire Electric's low hydroelectric structure, relied on the Ozark Playgrounds Association to get the word out that "A Surprisingly Economic Vacation Now Awaits You In This Region of Romance."

Organized in 1919 at "a convention attended by 237 delegates and boosters from thirteen counties in southwest Missouri and northwest Arkansas," the collective became a model of regional promotion. Resort, town, and county members paid a "quota" of $100 to $5,000 to be included in an illustrated yearly guidebook. Roadmaps were distributed and newspaper display ads ran in Midwestern city papers. Geared to the needs of the auto tourist, the association lobbied relentlessly for better roads and bridges. Wooded hills, clear streams, and an inviting climate were celebrated, promising an escape from the stress of urban life. This was a resource the region had in abundance – much of the Ozarks was relatively undeveloped. In 1923, Herbert Barnes, manager of the Galena Boating Company, reported the condition of the James River twice weekly to the association's headquarters, a log cabin in bustling downtown Joplin. In 1926 Gurney Lowe, Playgrounds field secretary, visited member units in a new motorcar covered with paintings "done in natural colors" of "cliffs, cabins, tumbling streams, mountains, and woodlands." Storm O. Whaley, treasurer of the Ozark Playgrounds Association, coined a slogan in 1926 that branded the region with an implication of safety and civility, an important consideration to travelers. "The Land of a Million Smiles" was not only stamped on the copious printed material put out by the association; other tourism organizations borrowed it, even the Missouri Pacific. A contest was held every year to choose the "Ozark Smile Girl."

Opposite, top: Dewey Short Visitor Center. Exhibits in the modern building promote the benefits of Table Rock Dam, but make little mention of the society that lived in the White River valley for more than a hundred years. With a keen awareness of brand management, Corps of Engineers logos embellish the displays, buildings, handouts, and the massive concrete powerhouse.

Opposite, bottom: Weigh-in stage at Big Bass Tour, April 2-3, 2016, Table Rock Lake. Sponsored fishing tournaments are opportunities to photograph and video successful anglers in front of corporate logos. From these events social media content and cable TV programming can be created. They are a branding bonanza. Bass Pro, the primary sponsor, promotes outdoor sports that are more competitive and outcome-driven than the float-fishing era.

Nevertheless, these affairs are reminiscent of that combination of conservation, kinship, and commerce promoted by the Missouri Pacific White River rail line a century earlier.

Then the mighty engine of 1920s prosperity sputtered and ran out of gas, stranding the middle class. Beware lovely Smile Girl; a shabby, gun-toting, moonshine-swigging primitive is leering at you from the shadows of economic collapse. The indifference of self-absorbed, funny-paper mountaineers for economic betterment captivated a disillusioned public. Li'l Abner and Snuffy Smith scoffed at the American dream and were a thorn in the side of missionaries of progress. The belief our pioneer forebearers were heroic and pious is turned upside down by hillbilly antics.

As the Ozarks, like the Appalachians, were considered to be the natural habitat of such primitives, this symbol of self-sufficiency became attached to the touristic image. Here the transition from folk to joke was brief and complete. Not everyone was enchanted by this personification of rebellious rurality, but during the Depression and through the 1960s, the hillbilly ruled the region's iconography, dethroning the Smile Girl. The Land of A Million Smiles became the Land of A Million Rube Wisecracks.

In the mid-1950s as heavy equipment began the monumental transformation of the free-flowing upper White River and its James Fork, hillbilly-ness reigned. Jim Owen's buddy, artist Steve Miller, penned a small pamphlet for the Branson Chamber of Commerce,

DEWEY SHORT
VISITOR CENTER

Bass Pro Shops
TOYOTA
HUMMINBIRD
POWER PRO

written in the tortured folky dialect the float trip impresario insisted his guides speak: "This here shows the way fer you'ens ter see Big Dam Number 1 Table Rock. You'ens will shorely want tew see Table Rock Dam under construction. Cost is $78,000,000.00. Watch 8 tons of concrete pored frum giant buckets."

Such rustic hijinks cannot be found today in the sanitized capital of live entertainment just to the east of Stone County. Table Rock Lake became the catalyst that transformed White River hills' tourism from rustic to pop eclectic. This multipurpose dam facilitated the growth of a multicultural entertainment complex. Branson has misremembered its past. Backwoods misfits continued to be an acceptable part of American frontier mythos for several decades after World War II. Silver Dollar City invited *The Beverly Hillbillies* TV show to film half a dozen episodes in 1969. The Presleys and the Baldknobbers – the original hillbilly shows – have deleted the word from their advertising, but the humor is still corny.

Opposite, top left: Springfield's management of surface streams is historically utilitarian.

Opposite, top right: Co-author standing on a blue epoxy terrazzo rendition of the James River Arm of Table Rock Lake, Springfield-Branson National Airport.

Opposite, bottom left: Terrazzo floor map of James River Arm of Table Rock Lake, Dewey Short Visitor Center, Branson.

Opposite, bottom right: Table Rock Lake from the observation deck of the Dewey Short Visitor Center. The two figures interrupting the building's shadow are the authors.

Rivers have a historical and aesthetic record that impoundments lack. No matter how rational engineering solutions for the management of streams seem when they are imposed, they do not always prove useful over time. When a dam is closed, a clock starts. Rivers, unlike reservoirs, have no expiration date.

With the rise of image-conscious corporations and a circumspect government, rude players from pop culture have exited stage left. Companies and government agencies have become the stars themselves. On T-shirts, ball caps, and numerous building and signage applications, their logos announce their brand. Fortunately, local historical societies and The Ralph Foster Museum at College of the Ozarks have preserved a semblance of the overlooked past. National chains, attracted by eight million visitors, pay little homage to area history. An exception is Bass Pro, which displays float trip relics and enlarged vintage photographs from the Arcadian era.

Contemporary bureaucracies and businesses avoid historical context. Both strive for consistency, uniformity, and assured outcomes. Control over consumer spending is pursued by statistical analysis of many streams of data. Similarly, controlling rivers is attempted by a quantified study of watersheds and climate. Companies are uninterested in their customers' culture and beliefs and the Corps of Engineers is indifferent to what exists in the basins they will flood. Begrudgingly, they obey archeological salvage laws.

Governments and corporations find human behavior so unpredictable they attempt to shape desires and control taste. Rivers proved more complex and unpredictable than the Corps imagined. Reservoirs may fulfill some of their promises, but they are another industrial development in a landscape of sameness that requires constant maintenance. Artificial lakes lack the individual character and capacity of renewal of the rivers they replace.

SHALL WE GATHER AT THE RIVER?

Above: Cooling off in the Finley during River Jam.

An amalgam of hydrology, economics, politics, and fate has kept the upper James Fork of the White free from high dams. That middling dam built to cool the James River Power Plant has a fraction of the transformational effect Table Rock Dam had on the lower James. The three fractured milldams on Finley Creek have had even less effect. Were these relics of frontier technology blocking salmon spawning runs, there would be a movement to tear them down. Milldams are not exactly good news for warm-water streams, but their ecological impact is not as profound as megadams.

Water mills are enshrined in popular song and memory. They were largely obsolete by 1910 (except in the Ozarks), when millions of copies of "Down by the Old Mill Stream" were sold: "My darling I am dreaming of the days gone by, / When you and I were sweethearts beneath the summer sky;/ ... The old mill wheel is silent and has fallen down, / The old oak tree has withered and lies there on the ground;/ ... It was there I knew that you loved me true, / You were sixteen, my village queen, by the old mill stream."

The town of Ozark has a rare survival of an old milldam, the mill itself, and an antique iron bridge. Its forebay backs up along the Finley River Park. Here, in June of 2016, the James River Basin Part-

Above: Ads for Dam Jam and River Jam. Shortly after their River Rescue cleanup, the James River Basin Partnership hosts a celebration. First held at the milldam at Ozark, Dam Jam moved to the Springfield Square, then to the Finley River Park. It's now called River Jam.

Right: Milldam at Ozark, an iconic iron bridge.

nership held its annual River Jam. Dam Jam was the first name of the event which twenty years ago was held below the Ozark milldam. Current Executive Director Tiffany Frey said the continuing purpose of the festival is to "focus on connecting local people to their local rivers." For a few years it was held on the Springfield Square, but the park along the Finley has more room for vendors, exhibitors and its growing audience. As usual, boiled crawfish and beer are on the menu and local bands provide entertainment. Well-behaved kids and dogs, kayakers, canoers, fishermen, and nature lovers stroll, swim, or take boat rides provided by Bass Pro.

Since the failed effort to protect Ozarks streams through laws passed by petition drives, river recreation has become ever more democratic. The amalgam of private and governmental organizations that today advance river conservation acknowledge that shift. Even the bands that entertain River Jam are populist eclectic. SpringFed String Band "performs original tunes and covers from rock, country, Celtic, blues, old-timey, and folk-fusion influences."

Though altered by development, there is a strong attachment between the citizens attending River Jam and the streams of the James River watershed. Early technologies have not been as transformative as the giant federal efforts to control floods and generate electricity. Rivers are not only places to wade or float; they are life-giving symbols. Robert Lowry's hymn of 1864, a favorite of moviemakers, is familiar to secularists and churchgoers alike. "Yes, we'll gather at the river, / The beautiful, beautiful river; / Gather with the saints at the river / That flows by the throne of God."

Lowry derived the lyrics from Revelation 22: 1-2. The King James Bible version is English we still comprehend: "And he shewed mee

OZARKS
WATER
WATCH
www.OzarksWaterWatch.org

Bass Pro Shops
WE SALUTE OUR
CONSERVATION PARTNERS!
PRESENTS
KING OF BUCKS

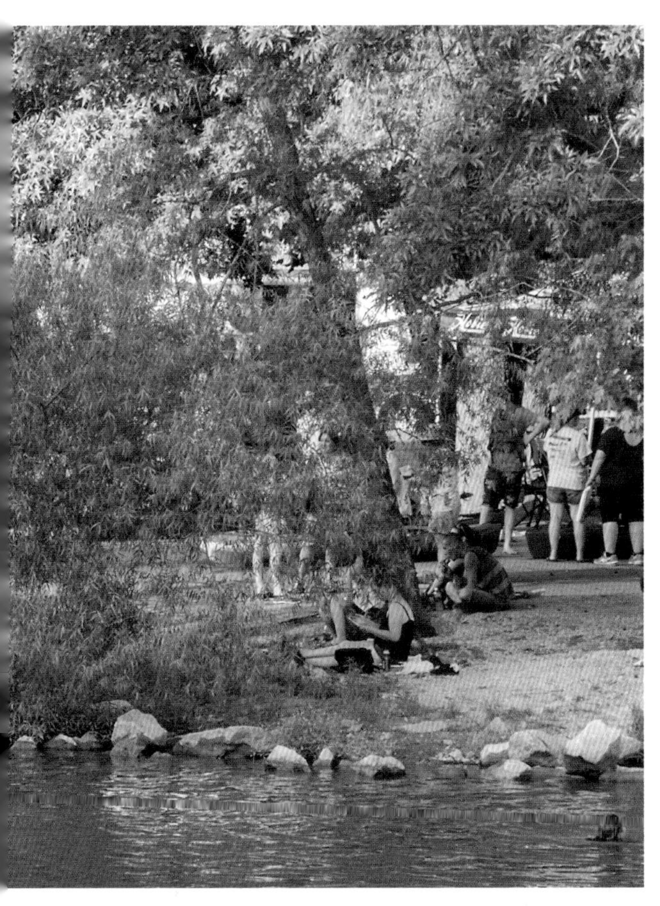

a pure riuer of water of life, cleere as chrystall, proceeding out of the throne of God, and of the Lambe. In the middest of the street of it, and of either side of the riuer, was there the tree of life, which bare twelue manner of fruits, and yeelded her fruit euery moneth: and the leaues of the tree were for the healing of the nations."

Will there someday be comparable scripture verse or music about modern dams? "Down by the old Corps of Engineers Multipurpose Project" or "Shall we gather by the tail waters below the four 50,000 watt generation units"? Possibly not. There are many who recreate on reservoirs, but there is little art, religion, or expression about these functional stream-blocking structures that create vast static bodies of water. Rivers have movement and they move us.

Those who "gather at the river, the beautiful, beautiful river" at River Jam on the Finley confirm that ancient connection.

GUARDIANS OF WATER QUALITY

"Real solutions are needed, state Department of Natural Resources director says, but funds are tight." So reads the subtitle of a *Springfield News-Leader* article headlined "Guardians of water quality meet" (November 26, 2002): "The briefing at Bass Pro Shops Outdoor World included members of the Upper White River Watershed Foundation, the James River Basin Partnership, the Watershed Committee of the Ozarks, Table Rock Water Quality, and more than a dozen area legislators." The article by Mike Penprase quoted not only government officials and politicians but also David Ledford, executive editor of the paper, and Pete Herschend, co-owner of Silver Dollar City. Ledford moderated the meeting and like Herschend expressed concern about pollution caused by inadequate septic tanks. Representative Roy Holand didn't disagree but cautioned about depending on state financial involvement: "It's going to be a tough year, or two, or three."

Thirty years after the passage of the 1972 Clean Water Act, progress had been made reversing the deterioration of the nation's water quality due to industrialization and indifference. Standards had been set, and the Environmental Protection Agency, through state government agencies like the DNR, tested and enforced regulations. Municipalities and corporations whose discharges violated these laws could be forced to comply. Individuals with a leaky septic tank were another matter. Agriculture was and is largely exempt.

Unlike divisive issues of water resource management like dams, everyone agrees on water quality. How to achieve clean water without oppressive regulation and burdensome taxes was the problem that led to forums like the 2002 meeting at Bass Pro. Many at this assembly were familiar with the deficiencies of regulation and lack of funding. Organizations had already formed to address these problems. Undoing the undesirable side effects of progress on our natural resources is a Herculean task, but progress had been made due in part to these "guardians of water quality." The Clean Water Act's goal to make the nation's waters "fishable and swimmable" would ultimately be realized in the James River basin to a greater degree than in many of the nation's river systems. That 1999 algae bloom on Table Rock Lake galvanized local action.

With the public's rejection of petition drives to zone Ozark rivers and subject their management to bureaucratic control, these groups presented a less coercive and confrontational approach to stream protection.

WATERSHED COMMITTEE OF THE OZARKS traces its beginnings to a memo by the Chair of the Board of Public Utilities, N. L. "Mack" McCartney, sent to Springfield Mayor Harry Strawn in 1983: "With your concurrence, I have appointed an ad hoc task force to develop a program for the protection of surface and subsurface watersheds which supply Springfield and the surrounding area with drinking water." A Watershed Management Coordinating Committee was established that in 1989 became a nonprofit renamed Watershed Committee of the Ozarks. Three sponsors, City Utilities, Greene County, and the City of Springfield, sustained the budget, but state and federal grants and private donations enable the Watershed Committee to take on large projects. In 2013, $1.1 million in federal funds with a $770,000 local match allowed twenty projects to be undertaken, most involving the control of storm water. As a priority of the organization is protecting Springfield's water supply, the Little Sac as well as the upper James are their primary focus.

Many of the Watershed Committee projects like planting trees along streams rely on volunteers. Guided tours of the Jordan Creek underground by Watershed staff are not only adventurous, but insightful into the development of a historically significant James River urban stream.

A substantial subgrant from the DNR has allowed development and implementation of a plan to control erosion and pollution on the Little Sac. At Valley Water Mill north of Springfield a $1.2 million facility for environmental education relating to watershed management has been opened. Loring Bullard was the executive director of the Watershed Committee from its beginning in 1989 until 2012 when he retired and education outreach coordinator Mike Kromrey replaced him.

Website: watershedcommittee.org

JAMES RIVER BASIN PARTNERSHIP formed in 1997 as a committee of the Southwest Missouri Resources Conservation and Development Council and the Lakes Area Chamber of Commerce. At that time the excessive nutrient levels of the James had created a tourism-killing algae bloom on Table Rock Lake. Two years later the Partnership became a nonprofit. Presiding Greene County Commissioner David Coonrod was a founder and has stayed active as a board member and sometimes president. Joe Pitts became executive director in 2010. When Pitts retired in 2015, Tiffany Frey became director. On a KSMU radio interview in 2013, Joe Pitts summarized the Partnership's mission:

> When you look at water quality in a basin the size of the James River, no agencies' or cities' or county governments are extensive enough to impact the problem. And so the James River Basin Partnership is the buffer between, or the connector between, what the regulators want done, what the cities want done, and what people say. Bottom line: If we weren't doing it, then who would?"

The group's year in review (2013) stated they had conducted riparian corridor restoration, acquired conservation easements, subsidized septic tank pump-outs, as well as holding their annual River Rescue, which cleaned up trash along a section of the Finley River. In 2013, their Dam Jam Festival was held on the Springfield Square. In 2016 the event was renamed River Jam and returned to its original location on the Finley at Ozark. Since 2006 the Basin Partnership had received twelve government grants which along with local funding totaled more than $4 million, all expended in restoring the James River and its tributaries. As the sphere of interest of the James River Basin Partnership is the entire watershed, they have a dedicated corps of volunteers to implement scientific study and remediations.

Website: jamesriverbasin.com

OZARKS WATER WATCH (2001) was like the James River Basin Partnership organized in response to the hyper-eutrophication of Table Rock Lake. Originally it was called the Upper White River Basin Partnership:

> We promote water quality in the Upper White River Basin watershed through bi-state collaboration on research, public policy, and action projects in Arkansas and Missouri. ... The watershed includes four major impoundments, three major rivers, and numerous smaller lakes and streams crisscrossing over 14,000 square miles in nineteen counties in southwest Missouri and northwest Arkansas. With your help, we will work together to make Beaver, Table Rock, Taneycomo, and Bull Shoals lakes the four cleanest man-made lakes in North America.

Initially officials and lawmakers from Arkansas were uninterested, but in time they joined the effort to protect the region's water quality. As mentioned, Peter Herschend was, along with brother Jack, a founder. Other early board members were John Morris and Martin McDonald of Bass Pro, banker Todd Parnell, Drury University President John Moore, Camp Kanakuk founder Joe White, and Tim O'Reilly. Arkansas trustees include Tim Maupin of Cargill, Charles R. Zimmerman of Walmart, and Kevin J. Igli of Tyson Foods.

Table Rock Lake Water Quality, one of the participants in the November 2002 meeting at Bass Pro, merged with Ozark Water Watch in 2014. The nonprofit had been organized by the Table Rock Lake/Kimberling City Area Chamber of Commerce in response to the algae crisis of the late 1990s. They continue to provide help in cleaning up the lake and support for individuals with inadequate septic tanks.

A Status of the Watershed report is published annually, and it reflects the changing levels of pollutants in this large region. David Casaletto is the president and executive director. He also heads the Ozark Clean Water Company, a sister organization that helped with a $2 million grant from the EPA to address failing septic systems. This cooperative is projected to manage one thousand private on-site systems by 2017.

Website: ozarkswaterwatch.org

OZARKS ENVIRONMENTAL AND WATER RESOURCES INSTITUTE at Missouri State University provides scientific data for all the organizations concerned with water quality.

> Ozarks Environmental and Water Resources Institute's mission is to advance our scientific understanding of water resource quantity, quality, and distribution in Ozarks watersheds. Centrally located in Springfield, Missouri, OEWRI provides technical expertise, analytical capability, and student training to support environmental research, watershed monitoring programs, and watershed group activities in the Ozarks. It directs and collaborates on research projects aimed at solving water quality and supply problems by working in partnership and cooperation with university researchers, environmental groups, local communities, and government agencies.

To understand OEWRI's impact on watersheds, it is necessary to study natural processes. Students and professors conduct research into how different eras of land use have impacted geomorphology and their results are published. The institute's array of laboratory equipment enables them to supply reliable water quality data. Biologists on the faculty evaluate the ecological as well as the hydrological state of streams. Other academic specialties are represented such as geography and agriculture. Robert T. Pavlovsky is the director. Dr. Pavlovsky has a special interest in the transformation of Ozark rivers due to human impact.

Website: oewri.missouristate.edu

A LANDSCAPE LIVED IN, BUT STILL LIVING

"We must, in fact, not divorce the stream from its valley in our thoughts at any time. If we do, we lose touch with reality" – H. D. N. Hynes, 1974, Edgardo Baldi Memorial Lecture, "The Stream and its Valley." In a biography of Noel Hynes on the International Society of Limnology website, this often-cited talk was described as "a lucid synthesis of ideas about the connection between rivers and their drainage basins that expanded aquatic ecology to the landscape scale."

To further expand and paraphrase Hynes' concept, "We must, in fact, not divorce the stream from *the culture of the people who occupy its valley* in our thoughts at any time. If we do, we lose touch with reality." Natural processes and human development interacting within the watershed created the present state of the James Fork of the White. Not only are the river, its valley, and its inhabitants inseparable; earlier geomorphic and human history continues to exert influences. These complexities, even if not fully understood, should be acknowledged or "We lose touch with reality."

Does drawing a line around the top of creeks and ravines that feed the James River create a distinct geographic entity? Of course not. Nor have we put up a fence to keep out wandering outside influences. But Dr. Hynes believed, "Streams differ from one another," and this is true of the James and its tributaries. Spring-fed Crane Creek is trout habitat; rain sinks into Dry Crane Creek's bed as it gathers.

Cultural distinctions exist too because of geographic differences within the watershed. No other Ozark waterway has a true city in its basin releasing copious chemical and cultural discharges. To the chagrin of civic leaders like John Woodruff, downstream rustics challenged Springfield's progressivism. Rural/urban clashes are widespread in the world, but because writers and tourism have created a folk/hillbilly mythos in the White River hills, that dichotomy has been exacerbated. Due to the heritage of the senior author we may have occasionally tilted toward the primitive. Hopefully that leaning is balanced by the junior author's superior educational and more civilized background.

The reality we have tried not to lose touch with is visual, not scientific. There are 345 contemporary photographs and 202 vintage images in this book. Unmanipulated photographs may not be art or reveal higher truths, but they can credibly document ordinary reality. Real photo postcards reveal the texture of past lives. Without seeing the work of George Hall, who produced hundreds of sharp-focus real photo postcards of Galena and the James River, it's likely we wouldn't have undertaken this project.

It's also likely we wouldn't have appreciated the documentary veracity of old postcards if we hadn't glimpsed a man striding by our booth at a Manhattan Pier antique show in 1985 carrying a tin sign in the shape of a pig. We futilely tried to buy it. That's how we met John Margolies. A June 2, 2016 obituary in *The New York Times* said he "was considered the country's foremost photographer of vernacular architecture." John's books mix postcards and tourist souvenirs with his straightforward photographs. We borrowed this technique. It worked for roads; hopefully it works with rivers. This book is dedicated to the memory of our long friendship with John.

Another influence was the writing of Carl O. Sauer. Like John Margolies, he had a taste for the vernacular, and saw meaning in landscapes others ignored. Sauer was drawn to rural environments and Margolies to manifestations of pop culture, but both sought reality, not confirmation of ideological or political truths. At the back of this celebrated Missouri-born geographer's published PhD thesis, *The Geography of the Ozark Highlands of Missouri* (1920), are fifty-two black-and-white images, a mixture of his snapshots and photographs taken by the Frisco Railroad. Twenty-one have streams. Like the text, they do not advance theory, but keep us in touch with reality, a stark reality as it sometimes is.

The valley of the James Fork of the White is a lived-in place, and in places it shows. There is a significant movement to study and rehabilitate degradations. The importance of watersheds in river restoration is locally recognized. This is in agreement with Dr. Hynes' conclusion, "In every respect the valley rules the stream."

Old postcards of floaters and fishermen show the James was cared about then. Our digital photographs of paddlers approaching Galena and the gathering at the Finley during the 2016 River Jam prove it still is. The James Fork of the White and its valley are a living cultural and ecological continuum and entanglement. Embrace this reality.

Leland and Crystal Payton
Springfield, Missouri, 2017

BIBLIOGRAPHY

BOOKS

Ayres, Artie. *Traces of Silver*. Reeds Spring, Missouri: Ozark Mountain Country Historical Preservation Society, 1982.

Beckman, H. C., and N. C. Hinchey. *The Large Springs of Missouri. Vol. XXIX*. Rolla, Missouri: Missouri Geological Survey and Water Resources, 1944.

Beveridge, Thomas R. *Geologic Wonders and Curiosities of Missouri*. 1st ed. Rolla, Missouri: Missouri Division of Geology and Land Survey, 1980.

Blevins, Brooks. *Hill Folks: A History of Arkansas Ozarkers and Their Image*. Chapel Hill, North Carolina: University of North Carolina Press, 2002.

Bright, Wanetta L. *Smallin Civil War Cave: The Center of Ozarks Culture and History*. Ozark, Missouri: Ozark Cave & Caverns, 2013.

Bullard, Loring, Kenneth C. Thomson, and James E. Vandike. *The Springs of Greene County Missouri*. 1st ed. Rolla, Missouri: Missouri Dept. of Natural Resources, Geological Survey and Resource Assessment Division, 2001.

Bullard, Loring. *Consider the Source: A History of the Springfield, Missouri Public Water Supply*. Springfield, Missouri: Watershed Press, 2005.

Bullard, Loring. *Healing Waters: Missouri's Historic Mineral Springs and Spas*. Columbia, Missouri: University of Missouri Press, 2004.

Bullard, Loring. *Jordan Creek: Story of an Urban Stream*. Springfield, Missouri: Watershed Press, 2008.

Callison, Charles. *Man and Wildlife in Missouri: A History of One State's Treatment of Its Natural Resources*. Harrisburg, Pennsylvania: Stackpole Company, 1953.

Cochran, Robert, and Michael Luster. *For Love and For Money. The Writings of Vance Randolph: An Annotated Bibliography*. Arkansas: Arkansas College Folklore Monograph Series No. 2, 1979.

Cochran, Robert. *Vance Randolph: An Ozark Life*. Urbana and Chicago, Illinois: University of Illinois Press, 1985.

Halverson, Anders. *An Entirely Synthetic Fish: How Rainbow Trout Beguiled America and Overran the World*. New Haven, Connecticut: Yale University Press, 2010.

Hawksley, Oz. *Missouri Ozark Waterways*. Jefferson City, Missouri: Missouri Conservation Commission, 1965.

Hayes, Brian. *Infrastructure: A Field Guide to the Industrial Landscape*. New York, New York: W. W. Norton & Company, 2005.

Ingenthron, Elmo. *Indians of the Ozark Plateau*. Branson, Missouri: Ozark Mountaineer, 1970.

Koob, Tom. *Buried by Table Rock Lake: Tales, Anecdotes and Facts about Everything Covered by the Lake*. Shell Knob, Missouri: White Oak Lodge Publishing, 2006.

Koob, Tom. *The History of Fishing Table Rock Lake*. Shell Knob, Missouri: White Oak Lodge Publishing, 2003.

Lave, Rebecca. *Field and Streams: Stream Restoration, Neoliberalism, and the Future of Environmental Science*. Athens & London: University of Georgia Press, 2012.

Morrow, Lynn, and Linda Myers-Phinney. *Shepherd of the Hills Country: Tourism Transforms the Ozarks, 1880s-1930s*. Fayetteville, Arkansas: University of Arkansas Press, 1999.

Morrow, Lynn, ed. *The Ozarks in Missouri History: Discoveries in an American Region*. Columbia, Missouri: University of Missouri Press, 2013.

O'Brien, Michael J. *Paradigms of the Past: The Story of Missouri Archaeology*. Columbia, Missouri: University of Missouri Press, 1996.

Paukert, Craig, and George Scholten, eds. *Paddlefish Management, Propagation, and Conservation in the 21st Century*. Bethesda, Maryland: American Fisheries Society, 2009.

Peters, Thomas A. *John T. Woodruff of Springfield, Missouri, in the Ozarks: An Encyclopedic Biography*. Springfield, Missouri: Pie Supper Press, 2016.

Rafferty, Milton D. *The Ozarks: Land and Life*. 2nd ed. Fayetteville, Arkansas: University Of Arkansas Press, 2001.

Randolph, Vance. *We Always Lie to Strangers: Tall Tales from the Ozarks*. New York, New York: Columbia University Press, 1951.

Ray, Jack H. *Ozarks Chipped-Stone Resources: A Guide to the Identification, Distribution, and Prehistoric use of Cherts and other Silceous Raw Materials*. Special Publication No. 8. Springfield, Missouri: Missouri Archaeological Society, 2007.

Sare, Ted. *Recollections of an Ozarks Float Trip Guide*. 1997.

Sauer, Carl O. *The Geography of the Ozark Highland of Missouri*. Chicago, Illinois: University of Chicago Press, 1920.

Saults, Dan. *The Rivers of Missouri*. Columbia, Missouri: Missouri Conservation Commission, 1949.

Schoolcraft, Henry Rowe. *Rude Pursuits and Rugged Peaks: Schoolcraft's Ozark Journal 1818-1819*. Edited by Milton D. Rafferty. Fayetteville, Arkansas: University Of Arkansas Press, 1996.

Turner, William. *Voices of Missouri's Rivers*. Jefferson City, Missouri: Missouri Dept. of Conservation, 2014.

Vineyard, Jerry D., and Gerald L. Feder. *Springs of Missouri*. 1st ed. Rolla, Missouri: Missouri Geologic Survey and Water Resources, 1974.

Weaver, H. Dwight. *Missouri The Cave State*. Jefferson City, Missouri: Discovery Enterprises, ND.

Weslager, C.A. *The Delaware Indians: A History*. Rutgers University, 1989.

Wiley, Robert S. *Dewey Short: Orator of the Ozarks*. 1st ed. Vol. 1. Cassville, Missouri: Litho Printers and Bindery, 1985.

Williams, Walter. *The State of Missouri: An Autobiography*. Columbia, Missouri: Press of E. W. Stephens, 1904.

Williamson, Thames. *The Woods Colt: A Novel of the Ozark Hills*. New York: Harcourt, Brace and Company, 1933.

Wohl, Ellen. *Rivers in the Landscape: Science and Management*. Oxford, UK: Wiley Blackwell, 2014.

MAGAZINES

"An Enchanted Land." *The Ozark Empire Magazine*, September 1933, 11-14.

Bradshaw, Hank. "Jim Owen, Flat Boat King of the Ozarks." *The Fisherman*, July 1958, 18, 19, 86.

Lincoln, Robert Page. "Floating Down the River." *Fur-Fish-Game*, March 1948, 8-11, 24.

Lincoln, Robert Page. "Betrayal of the Ozarks." *Field & Stream*, August 1946, 23.

McCord, May Kennedy. "Hillbilly Heartbeats." *The KWTO Dial*, July 1951, 4+.

Saults, Dan. "Gently Down the Stream." *Sports Afield*, May 1974, 78, 79, 184.

Saults, Dan. "Jim Owen's White River Floats Discontinued." *Sports Afield*, March 1957, 78+.

"The Beautiful James River." *Ozark Guide Yearbook*, 1964, 44.

Rayburn's Arcadian Life: A Journal of Folklore and Rural Idealism, Commerce, Texas. June 1935.

A Tourist's & Sportsman's Guide to the Magic of White River. Fayetteville, Arkansas: C. D. Craig, 1963.

NEWSPAPERS

Springfield Republican, 1895-1925

Springfield News-Leader, 1987-2016

The Springfield Leader, 1884-1930

The Leader Democrat, Springfield, Mo., 1895-1899

The Springfield Democrat, 1891

The Springfield Daily News, 1927

The Neosho Times, 1919-1932

The Neosho Daily News, 1920-1946

St. Louis Post Dispatch, 1880-1965

Moberly Monitor-index, 1930-1971

Rolla Herald, Rolla, Mo., 1892-1953
Washington Citizen, Washington, Mo., 1952
Joplin Globe, 1922-1953
Jefferson City Post-Tribune, 1934-1974
The News and Tribune, Jefferson City, Mo., 1971, 1976
Sedalia Democrat, 1935-1973
Macon Chronicle-Herald, Macon, Mo., 1935, 1949, 1988, 1989
The Kansas City Times, 1957-1966

PAMPHLETS, BOOKLETS, BROCHURES, AND MAPS

Among the Ozarks: The Land of "Big Red Apples" Kansas City: Hudson-Kimberly Publishing, 1891. 40 pages
Come to the Ozarks: The Land of a Million Smiles. Joplin, Mo.: Ozark Playgrounds Association, 1920s. 72 pages
James and White River Float Trips. Trifold. Galena, Mo.: Galena Boat Company, 1930s.
Float Trips in the Ozarks: Outfitting at Galena, MO. Galena, Mo.: Galena Boat Company, C. 1940.
The White River Country in the Missouri Ozarks. St. Louis, Mo.: Missouri Pacific-Iron Mountain Railroad, 1920s.
Pictorial Map White River Country of the Missouri-Arkansas Ozarks. Map. Missouri Pacific Lines, 1930s.
Roads, Rivers Recreations Around Springfield. Map. Springfield, Missouri: Chamber of Commerce, 1930s.
White River Country Missouri-Arkansas Ozarks: Ideal Playgrounds. Map. Missouri Pacific Lines, 1929.
White River Lakes of the Ozarks. Map. Mountain Home, Ark: Ozark Mountain Lakes and Rivers.
Table Rock Lake. Map. Aurora, Missouri: MWM Color Press, nd.
Play Places in the Ozarks (White River Country). Map. Missouri Pacific Lines, nd.
Float Trips in the Ozarks: Outfitting at Galena, Mo. Galena, Mo.: Galena Boat, Nd.
The Shepherd of the Hills: Now in Pictures. Folder. Harold Bell Wright Story-Picture Corporation.

JOURNALS AND GOVERNMENT PUBLICATIONS

Table Rock Reservoir Area: White River Missouri and Arkansas - and How the U.S. Buys It. Little Rock District, Arkansas: Corps of Engineers, U.S. Army, C. 1950s.
White River, Missouri and Arkansas. Washington, DC: War Dept., Office of the Chief of Engineers, 1933.
Water Treatment & Supply F. Y. 2015 Annual Report. Springfield, Missouri: City Utilities, 2015.
Historical Land-Use Changes and Potential Effects on Stream Disturbance in the Ozark Plateaus, Missouri. By Robert B. Jacobson and Alexander T. Primm. Water-Supply Paper 2484. U.S. Geological Survey, 1997.
Chapman, Carl. H. ed. *The Missouri Archaeologist* 13, no. 2. (October 1951).
Bray, Robert T., ed. *The Missouri Archaeologist* 44 (December 1983).

DISSERTATIONS AND THESES

Rafferty, Milton D. *Persistence versus Change in Land-Use and Landscape in the Springfield, Missouri, Vicinity of the Ozarks*. PhD Dissertation, University of Nebraska, 1970.
Robbins, Lori A. *"A'Lyin' To Them Tourists: Tourism in Branson, Missouri."* Master's thesis, University of Mississippi, 1999.

ONLINE RESOURCES

James River Basin Partnership: jamesriverbasin.com
Missouri State University Center for Archaeological Research: www.missouristate.edu/car
Ozarks Environmental And Water Resources Institute: oewri.missouristate.edu
Ozarks Water Watch: ozarkswaterwatch.org
Watershed Committee Of The Ozarks: watershedcommittee.org

ACKNOWLEDGEMENTS

Rollie Sparrowe, Ross Payton, Strader Payton, Karen Craigo, Martha Oresman and TWP, Loring Bullard, Robert Pavlovsky, Brooks Blevins, Thomas Peters, Jeremiah Buntin, Joe Pitts, Carrie Lamb, Mike Meinkoth, Kenny Short, Robert S. Wiley, Keith Oxby, James Burks, Alan Chilton, Johnny Edgmon, Kem R. Reed, Steve Stepp, Stuart Westmoreland, Shane Bush, Trish Yasger, Mark R. Owen, Springfield-Greene County Library, The Special Collection and Archives, Missouri State University, The State Historical Society of Missouri, Wayne Glenn, Chris Barnhart, Patricia McCord McDonald, Charles McCord, Springfield History Museum on the Square, Tony Aid, Neil Heimsoth, Kevin George, Steve Pokin, Harry Styron, Alex Primm, Jack Ray, Neal Lopinot

PICTURE CREDITS

Barry County Museum: 80 (bottom), 95 (top)

Landsat Satellite Image: 106, 163

McCord, Charles (permission): 243

Missouri Department of Natural Resources: 204 (bottom)

Missouri State University Archives, Danzero Collection: 57, 60, 61 (top), 116, 165 (middle),

Missouri State University Center for Archaeological Research: 39 (provided artifacts)

Oxby, Keith: 97 (top)

Ozark Environmental and Water Resources Institute at Missouri State University: 8, 9

Payton Collection: Front flap, 2, 10, 11, 22, 23 (bottom), 33, 40, 41, 46, 48, 56 (right), 65, 67, 72, 82, 85 (top), 87 (top two), 94 (top right), 99 (top right), 100 (right), 112 (right), 113 (top), 124, 129 (bottom), 133, 136, 138, 139, 140, 141, 157, 158 (top), 160, 161, 169, 172, 182, 183 (top), 201 (middle), 204, 205 (top), 213, 214, 215, 218, 219, 221, 224, 225, 226, 228, 229, 230, 231, 232, 233, 234, 235, 236, 237, 238, 239, 240, 241, 242, 244, 245, 246, 247 (bottom), 249 (top), 256 (top right), 262, 264, 266, 268, 272, 273, 276, 279, 280, 281, 282, 283, 284, 286, 287, 288, 289, 290, 291, 293, 294, 296, 297, 298, 299, 300 301, 302, 303, 305, 310, 316, 318 (bottom), 320, 321, 332, 333

Payton, Crystal: Back flap, 18, 19, 24, 28, 32, 42 (bottom), 44, 49 (left), 53 (right), 55 (left), 56 (bottom), 60 (bottom), 64, 66, 77 (top), 80 (top), 88 (top), 89 (bottom), 90, 91, 98 (top), 103 (top), 105, 107, 117 (right), 120 (left), 126, 147 (top left, and bottom), 165 (bottom), 168, 173 (bottom), 176 (top), 183 (bottom), 188 (bottom), 189 (bottom), 198 (bottom three), 207 (left), 210 (top), 252, 253, 260, 261 (middle), 264 (bottom), 265, 266 (bottom), 269, 270, 311 (bottom), 312 (top), 313 (top), 319 (two right), 327, 330 (bottom), 338

Payton, Leland: Front and back covers, 1, 3, 4, 5, 6, 12, 13, 14, 15, 16, 17, 20, 21, 23 (top left and right), 25, 26, 27, 29, 30, 31, 34, 35, 36, 37, 38, 39, 42, 43 (top), 45, 47, 49 (right), 50, 51, 52, 53 (left), 54, 55 (right), 56 (left), 58, 59, 61 (bottom), 62, 63, 73, 74, 75, 76, 77 (bottom), 78, 79, 81, 8 84, 85 (bottom two), 86, 87 (bottom), 95 (bottom), 96, 97 (bottom), 98 (bottom), 99, 100 (left), 101, 102, 103 (bottom), 108, 109, 110, 111, 112 (top left), 113 (bottom), 114, 115, 117 (left), 118, 120 (right), 121, 122, 123, 125, 127, 128, 129 (top), 130, 131, 132, 134, 135, 137, 144, 145 (bottom), 146, 147 (top right), 156, 158, 159, 164, 165 (top), 166, 167, 170, 171, 173 (top), 174, 175, 176 (bottom), 177, 178, 179, 180, 181, 184, 185, 186, 187, 189 (top), 190, 191, 192, 193, 194, 198 (top), 199, 200, 201, 202, 203, 206, 207 (right), 208, 209, 210 (bottom), 211, 212, 217, 222, 223, 225 (bottom), 227, 248, 249 (bottom), 250, 251, 254, 255, 256, 257, 258, 259, 261 (top and right), 275, 277, 304, 306, 307, 308, 309, 311 (top), 312 (bottom), 313 (bottom two), 314, 315, 317, 318 (top), 319 (two left), 322, 323, 324, 325, 328, 329, 330 (top), 331, 337, 339 (bottom), 340, 341

Skinners: 247 (top)

Springfield-Greene County Library: 104 (top), 201 (top, right)

Wiley, John (gift): 290

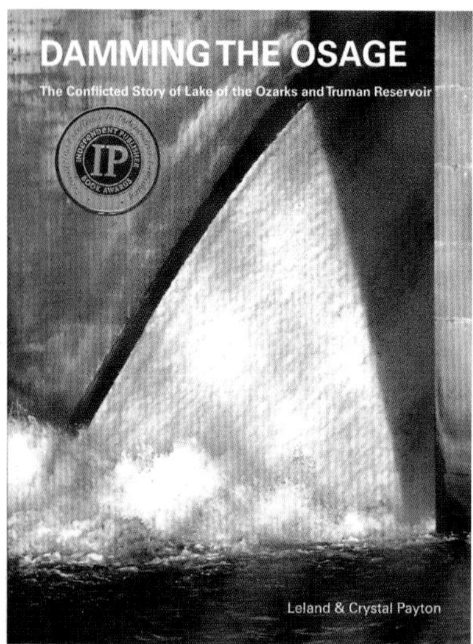

Only fragments remain of the native prairies of the upper Osage watershed. It's been two centuries since the warrior culture for which the river is named, and who maintained the buffalo grasslands by fire was pushed west by displaced Eastern tribes and land-hungry Americans. Two massive dams have turned the main stem of the river into huge reservoirs. Leland and Crystal Payton find the tale of these transformations compelling but turbulent. In researching journals of soldiers, explorers, missionaries, and in old newspaper accounts and court documents, they discovered a cast of passionate and sometimes doomed personalities. If changed by development, the authors still find the present Osage valley landscape expressive. Illustrated with hundreds of contemporary color photographs, period maps and vintage images, this book tells a dramatic story of human ambition pitted against natural limitations and forces beyond their control. *Damming The Osage* presents scientific objections to multipurpose dams. The book also protests the lack of realism in popular history, journalism, and advertising. This critique, the authors acknowledge, is derived from Mark Twain, the arch enemy of Romanticism. The region's history certainly abounds in the kind of characters and action Twain loved. The Paytons agree with Twain that American history, raw and contentious as it may be, demands truthful literary treatment.

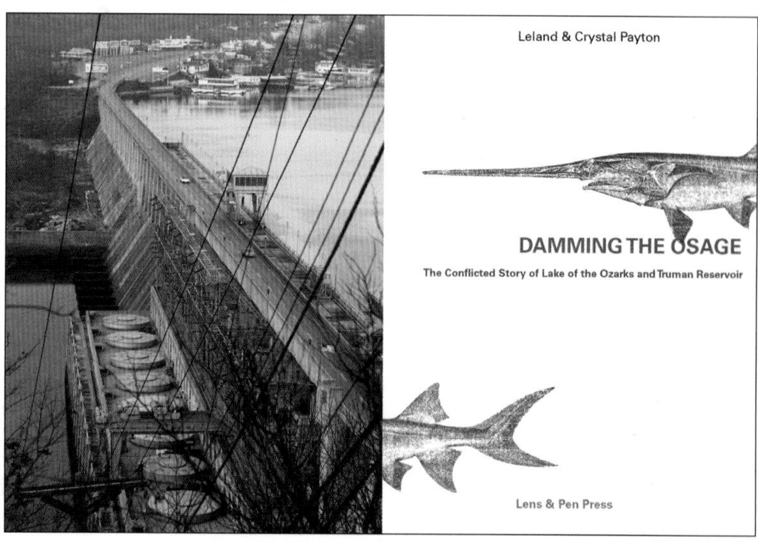

DAMMING THE OSAGE
Leland & Crystal Payton
$35 paper, 7.5x10 inches
304 pages, 435 illustrations
ISBN: 978-0-9673925-8-5

One of the highlights of Damming the Osage *is its copious illustration. Leland Payton, an accomplished photographer, includes many of his own works. But the book is illustrated even more with a marvelous assortment of historical images, some comical, some whimsical, and some heart-wrenchingly sad.*
–Steve Wiegenstein, *St. Louis Post Dispatch*

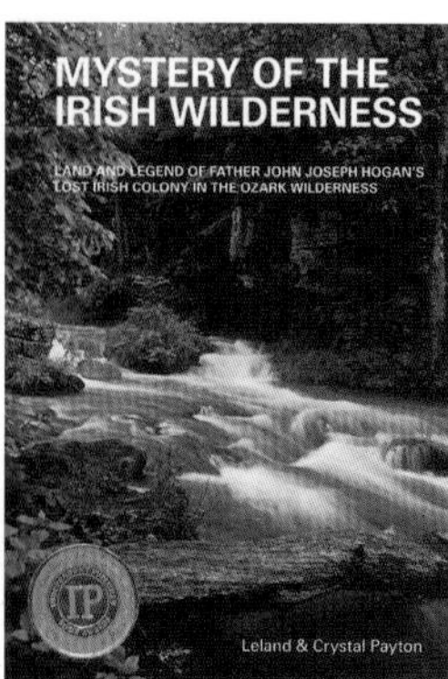

MYSTERY OF THE IRISH WILDERNESS
Leland & Crystal Payton
$18.95 paper, 7x10 inches
128 pages, 80 color plates
ISBN: 978-0-9673925-4-7

A fresh inquiry into the fate of Father John Joseph Hogan's colony of immigrant Irish that mysteriously vanished during the Civil War. Illustrated with color maps and photographs of the still-wild Ozark landscape where the legendary settlement was located. Gold Medal Winner, Best Regional Non-fiction, Independent Publisher Book Awards, 2009.

ON THE MISSION IN MISSOURI & FIFTY YEARS AGO: A MEMOIR
Bishop John Joseph Hogan
$22.50 paper, 7x10 inches, 224 pages
ISBN: 978-0-9673925-5-4

Two Irish-American classics with extensive historical commentary by Crystal Payton. John Joseph Hogan, first bishop of Kansas City, was a pioneer priest and gifted writer. *On the Mission* contains the only firsthand account of his Irish Wilderness colony. Few recollections of an Irish country childhood are as beautifully told as his memoir, *Fifty Years Ago.*

THE BEAUTIFUL AND ENDURING OZARKS
Leland Payton
$19.95 paper, 8x8 inches
80 pages, all color
ISBN: 978-0-9673925-0-0

The mystique of the Ozarks in a book of striking color photographs and insightful text. Considered a modern classic.

SEE THE OZARKS
Leland & Crystal Payton
$24.95 hardback
8x10 inches, 96 pages
ISBN: 978-0-9673925-1-9

The story of Branson, Lake of the Ozarks, Eureka Springs, and the primitive Ozarks. All color. An Independent Publisher Award Finalist.

LENS & PEN PRESS WWW.DAMMINGTHEOSAGE.COM WWW.BEAUTIFULOZARKS.COM